Transforming Justice Responses to Non-Recent Institutional Abuses

CLARENDON STUDIES IN CRIMINOLOGY

Published under the auspices of the Institute of Criminology, University of Cambridge; the Mannheim Centre, London School of Economics; and the Centre for Criminology, University of Oxford.

Recent titles in this Series:

Constructing Victimhood:
Beyond Innocence and Guilt in Transitional Justice
Lawther

Crime and Civilization:
The Birth of Criminology in the Early Nineteenth Century
Kivivuori

Palestinian Political Organizations in Israeli Prisons
Bernstein

Victims and the Labour of Justice at the International Criminal Court:
The Blame Cascade
Ullrich

Law and Personality Disorder:
Human Rights, Human Risks, and Rehabilitation
O'Loughlin

Policing Sport Mega-Events: Security, Spectacle, and Camouflage in Rio de Janeiro
Pauschinger

Character, Circumstances, and Criminal Careers:
Towards a Dynamic Developmental and Life-Course Criminology
Wikstrom, Treiber, and Roman

Children in Police Custody:
Adversity and Adversariality Behind Closed Doors
Bevan

Victims and Criminal Justice: A History
Cox, Shoemaker, and Shore

Rethinking Drug Laws:
Theory, History, Politics
Seddon

A Precarious Life:
Community and Conflict in a Deindustrialized Town
Willis

From Conflict to Modern Slavery:
The Drivers and the Deterrents
Heys

Transforming Justice Responses to Non-Recent Institutional Abuses

Anne-Marie McAlinden
Professor of Law and Criminal Justice, Queen's University Belfast
Marie Keenan
Associate Professor, School of Social Policy, Social Work and Social Justice, University College Dublin
James Gallen
Associate Professor, School of Law and Government, Dublin City University

OXFORD
UNIVERSITY PRESS

OXFORD
UNIVERSITY PRESS

Great Clarendon Street, Oxford, OX2 6DP,
United Kingdom

Oxford University Press is a department of the University of Oxford.
It furthers the University's objective of excellence in research, scholarship,
and education by publishing worldwide. Oxford is a registered trade mark of
Oxford University Press in the UK and in certain other countries

Published in the United States of America by Oxford University Press
198 Madison Avenue, New York, NY 10016, United States of America

British Library Cataloguing in Publication Data

Data available

Library of Congress Control Number: 2024951963

ISBN 9780192871060

DOI: 10.1093/9780191967399.001.0001

Printed and bound by
CPI Group (UK) Ltd, Croydon, CR0 4YY

MIX
Paper | Supporting responsible forestry
FSC® C013604

The manufacturer's authorised representative in the EU for product safety is Oxford
University Press España S.A. of El Parque Empresarial San Fernando de Henares, Avenida de
Castilla, 2 – 28830 Madrid (www.oup.es/en or product.safety@oup.com). OUP España S.A.
also acts as importer into Spain of products made by the manufacturer.

Series Editor's Preface

The *Clarendon Studies in Criminology series* aims to provide a forum for outstanding theoretical and empirical work in all aspects of criminology and criminal justice, broadly understood. The Editors welcome submissions from established scholars, as well as manuscripts based on excellent PhD dissertations. The Series was inaugurated in 1994, with Roger Hood as its first General Editor, following discussions between Oxford University Press and Oxford's then Centre for Criminological Research. It is edited under the auspices of three centres: The Centre for Criminology at the University of Oxford, the Institute of Criminology at the University of Cambridge, and the Mannheim Centre for Criminology at the London School of Economics. Each supplies members of the Editorial Board and, in turn, the Series General Editor or Editors.

Transforming Justice Responses to non-recent institutional abuses by Anne-Marie McAlinden, Marie Keenan and James Gallen offers a thoughtful and detailed analysis of the historical and cultural contexts in which non-recent institutional abuses occurred in Ireland—North and South—and the barriers to justice experienced by victims/survivors locally, nationally and internationally. Ireland is presented as a case study for thorough empirical and theoretical consideration of abuses by the church and state. The authors reflect on the challenges presented by national and international legal, policy and institutional responses to non-recent abuses, drawing on a body of literature on transitional justice, restorative justice, human rights and public law, as well as the wider criminological and victimological scholarship.

Notwithstanding considerable media attention to non-recent institutional abuses in various countries, not least Ireland, there is as yet little academic research on this matter. This book therefore fills a gap in our understanding. It argues that various factors have coalesced to problematise justice responses within Ireland and internationally that obfuscate discourses and practices on accountability and impede engagement between victims and the church or state actors. Such factors are explored in the first few chapters which situate the relationships between church and state in their historical, ideological, and legal contexts before considering inquiries, redress, reparations and other responses within criminal, civil, and institutional legal frameworks—national and international. To address these different levels of accountability, the authors develop a grounded understanding of responsibility. Responsibility here is intended to go beyond a moral and legal framing to look to its relational and ideological dimensions, to explicate the parameters of a transformative, transdisciplinary paradigm of justice. In so doing, the voices of the victims and responsible institutional actors come to the fore.

In considering these complex matters the authors draws on close reading of a wealth of material from comparative documentary and media analysis, a survey of religious institutions, and interviews with 60 'elites' – high-ranking people, including in politics, the church, the civil service and justice as well as 14 victims. While empirically focused on Ireland, comparative thematic analysis of international mechanisms for investigation and redress will resonate with audiences beyond her borders.

This is an engaging yet troubling book which asks us to think about how best to respond to non-recent institutional abuses. A focus on serious abuses by those in positions of power does not make for easy reading. That said, the authors offer some optimism in contemplating what it means to do justice in such difficult cases, while being clear that experiences of abuse and appetites for justice are inevitably personal and individualised, and that even the best approaches cannot fully address the wrongdoing. Writing this introduction at a time when abuses within the church are back in the media, this seems to be a good time to reflect on past mistakes in order to imagine a more considered response to future cases. As such, we are pleased to include this challenging and novel study in the Clarendon Studies in Criminology.

Mary Bosworth and Carolyn Hoyle
General Editors
Centre for Criminology, University of Oxford
November 2024

Acknowledgements

This book would not have been completed without the assistance and support of many people. We would like to thank our Post-doctoral Research Fellow, Dr Sophie van der Valk, for all her sterling work on the project including in particular the scheduling of the interviews, help with the NVivo coding and formatting, and proofreading the manuscript. We would also like to thank Dr Paula Shilliday and Dr Allely Albert for the research assistance and for their help, along with Sophie, in writing several of the policy outputs from the project (see https://transformingjusticeproject.org/).

Thanks to our various colleagues at QUB, UCD, and DCU for their support in organising or attending the QUB workshop (held at Queen's in September 2023) and the UCD seminar (May 2024) and final project conference (held in Dublin in September 2024). Special thanks are due to Prof Luke Moffett and Prof Cheryl Lawther for providing feedback on several draft chapters of the manuscript.

We are indebted to our funders—the Higher Education Academy North-South Research Grant (Grant Ref: TJHIA-NSRP) as well as the British Academy which funded the pilot work (Grant Ref: SRG21\210319) and the AHRC which funded Anne-Marie McAlinden for a Fellowship dedicated to the project (Grant Ref: H/W011077/1).

Special thanks are also due to our academic and professional colleagues who formed our International Advisory Group and who gave generously of their time and wisdom at project meetings, many of whom made the journey to Dublin for the final project conference: Prof Ivo Aertsen (KU Lueven), Prof Kathy Daly (Griffith University, Australia), Prof Jennifer Llewelyn (Dalhousie University, Canada), Prof Gordon Lynch (University of Kent), the Honourable Peter McClellan AM (Chairperson, Australian Royal Commission into Institutional Responses to Child Sexual Abuse), Dr Rosemary Nagy (Nipissing University, Canada), and Prof Clair Wills (University of Cambridge).

To our families and friends who gave support to us as authors in lots of small but significant ways when the book was being completed. We are immensely grateful.

Finally, above all, sincere thanks are due to our interviewees across the island of Ireland, North and South, who participated in the project including victims/survivors, legal professionals (including lawyers and judges), government officials (including politicians and state-appointed officials), civil servants, the clergy and church officials, civil society activists, journalists, and academics.

We are especially grateful to the victim/survivors who shared their experiences with us. We are genuinely humbled by your stories and hope that the words on these pages do justice to your experiences.

While we gratefully acknowledge the participation and support of all interviewees, we thank the following people who are happy to have their participation acknowledged: Rosemary Adaser, Diane Byrne, Tom Clonan, Elizabeth Coppin, Patrick Corrigan, Catriona Crowe, Bernadette Fahy, Fionna Fox, Astrid Hamilton, Mary Harney, Paul Harrison, Alan Keating, Stephan Kirwan, Marcella Leonard, Fred Logue, Samantha Long, Patricia Lundy, Wendy Lyon, Ruadhán MacAodháin, Andrew Madden, Gerry McCann, Jon McCourt, Eilis McDaniel, Patsy McGarry, Margaret McGuckin, Claire McKeegan, Niall Meehan, Breeda Murphy, Katherine O'Donnell, Turlough O'Donnell, Conall Ó Fátharta, Louise O'Keeffe, Michelle O'Neill, Maeve O'Rourke, Yvonne O'Rourke, Tressa Reeves, Fiona Ryan, Phil Scraton, Colin Smith, James Smith, Leo Varadkar, and Katherine Zappone.

October 2024

Contents

PART II. JUSTICE RESPONSES TO NON-RECENT INSTITUTIONAL ABUSES

PART III. TOWARDS TRANSFORMING JUSTICE

Tables

Table of Cases

UNITED KINGDOM

UNITED STATES

PART I

FRAMING JUSTICE RESPONSES TO NON-RECENT INSTITUTIONAL ABUSES

1
Introduction

1. Justice Responses to Non-Recent Institutional Abuses

Over the last few decades, the issue of non-recent institutional abuses against women and children in both residential and non-residential settings has resonated across the world. It is very difficult to form an accurate picture of the nature and scale as much of our 'collective knowledge' comes from official investigations into institutionalised or out-of-home care or from individual victim/survivor accounts (Wright 2017).[1] However, the breath of academic literature and policy and legal responses globally indicate the significance of the problem. The preponderance of academic and policy literature has focused on Anglophone countries such as Canada and Australia (Llewelyn 2002; Daly 2014b), England and Wales (Gilligan 2012), Scotland (Carr et al 2019), the United States (Terry 2015), and Ireland (Keenan 2012; Brennan 2015). Nonetheless, there is a growing body of scholarship on non-recent institutional abuses in non-Anglophone countries such as Belgium (Aersten 2014), Austria (Adriaenssens 2014), Germany (Dressing et al 2021), the Netherlands (Langeland et al 2015), Italy, and France (Marotta 2021) and beyond Europe including in Latin American countries such as Argentina, Chile, and Peru (Reaves and Tombs 2019; Figueroa and Tombs 2020). This includes scholarship on inquiries and broader redress processes within Scandinavian countries such as Denmark (Rytter and Rasmussen 2015), Norway (Simonsen and Pettersen 2015), and Sweden (Arvidsson 2015) and, more recently, within countries such as Switzerland (Patrizi

[1] Many of the inquiries worldwide (including eg the Australian Royal Commission (Royal Commission 2017, Summary, 6); Commission to Inquire into Child Abuse (CICA 2009, Executive Summary, 21); Canadian Truth and Reconciliation Commission (TRCC 2015, Vol 1, Part 1, 570); National Inquiry into Missing and Murdered Indigenous Women and Girls (NIMMIWG 2019, 3)) note the difficulties in establishing incidence and prevalence due to various issues such as under-reporting, the passage of time, and the lack of historical records.

Transforming Justice Responses to Non-Recent Institutional Abuses. Anne-Marie McAlinden, Marie Keenan, and James Gallen, Oxford University Press. © Oxford University Press 2025.
DOI: 10.1093/9780191967399.003.0001

2021), Germany (Andresen 2021), and Israel (Attrash-Najjar et al 2024). Indeed, residential institutions such as 'industrial schools'[2] and 'Magdalene Laundries'[3] also operated within either church or state-run settings in countries such as Germany, Belgium, France, the Netherlands, and Scandinavia (see eg Sköld 2013; Sköld and Swain 2015).

Adopting the island of Ireland, North and South,[4] as a twin case study, this book offers a broad comparative examination of the historical and cultural contexts in which non-recent institutional abuses occurred and the barriers to justice experienced by victim/survivors locally, nationally, and internationally. Moreover, while there is evidence that individual perpetrators abused women and children in both Northern Ireland (NI) and the Republic of Ireland (RoI) (see eg HIA Inquiry 2017, Vol 3, ch 10) and that victim/survivors were affected by cross-border abusive practices (see eg forced adoption in the context of the CoI MBH 2021), the broader comparative and transnational aspects of non-recent institutional abuses have not yet been examined. This book also investigates this gap in the literature.

Official state responses to non-recent institutional abuses within the island of Ireland have been dominated by formal adversarial and legalistic approaches (see eg Ring et al 2022), including inquiries or commissions of investigation (see eg McAlinden and Naylor 2016; Gleeson and Ring 2021).[5] As discussed further in Chapters 5 and 8, however, other jurisdictions have configured justice responses, and investigatory mechanisms in particular, very differently. This includes, for example, investigations by scholars or professionals in non-adversarial and non-legalistic settings and via restorative approaches focused on the welfare of survivors. Beyond official investigations, in several jurisdictions, investigatory mechanisms have

[2] 'Industrial schools' were intended to combat 'child vagrancy' by removing poor and neglected children to a boarding school in order to give them an education or teach them a trade. See Raftery and O'Sullivan (2001).

[3] 'Magdalene Laundries' were institutions run predominantly by the Catholic Church on behalf of the State for 'fallen women' and operated in Ireland from the eighteenth century to the late twentieth century: see Smith (2007).

[4] As Daly (2007, 72) notes, the term 'Ireland' is contested and denotes 'the name of an island in the North Atlantic' as well as 'the name of a state, comprising roughly three-quarters of that island, which secured independence from Britain in 1922'.

[5] See eg The Age of Inquiry website which maps public inquiries and investigatory commissions across a range of countries including Australia, Canada, Denmark, Germany, Ireland, New Zealand, Norway, Sweden, Switzerland, the UK, and the United States (Wright et al 2020): https://www.lib.latrobe.edu.au/research/ageofinquiry/projectteam.html (accessed 1 June 2024).

been accompanied by criminal prosecutions as well as reparative measures such as apologies (McAlinden 2022a; 2022b) or monetary redress schemes (Winter 2018; Daly and Davis 2019) and legal and policy reforms. Victim/survivors have also sought redress and accountability through private civil cases as has occurred, for example, extensively against the Catholic Church in the United States (Edelman 2015) and Australia (Daly and Davis 2021). In addition, within the context of responses by the Catholic Church in particular, reparative responses such as apologies, restorative programmes, and cooperation with investigatory processes take place against a backdrop of canon law which, as other research has shown, may impede broader engagement with state processes of redress, justice, or accountability (see eg Coughlin 2002; McAlinden 2022b). Notwithstanding the wide array of justice responses, a key part of the originality and focus of this book lies in the in-depth, critical analysis of the extant strengths and inherent limitations of a broad range of justice approaches used to address non-recent institutional abuses, across a range of settings from the perspective of multiple stakeholders.

Despite the recent proliferation of 'justice' responses to non-recent institutional abuses across a number of jurisdictions, it is a subject which is insufficiently understood in the relevant literature. Existing work, for example, has tended to concentrate on either (1) the historical and structural context of institutional abuses (eg Raftery and O'Sullivan 2001; Arnold 2009) or campaigns for justice (eg McGettrick et al 2021) and the interests or needs of victim/survivors more broadly (eg Balboni and Bishop 2010; Lundy and Mahoney 2018) or on (2) single aspects of justice processes such as inquiries (eg McAlinden 2013; Gleeson and Ring 2021), apologies (Sköld and Swain 2015; McAlinden 2022b), redress schemes (eg Daly 2014b), civil justice (eg Daly and Davis 2021), restorative justice (eg Gavrielides 2013; Keenan and Zinsstag 2022), human rights (eg Gallen 2019a; O'Rourke 2019), and, more recently, transitional justice (eg Hamber and Lundy 2020; Gallen 2023a). The small number of studies examining a broader spectrum of justice approaches have been carried out within the confines of a single discipline (eg law—see Ring et al 2022; or transitional justice—Gallen 2023a). Further, there is also a dearth of empirical work on non-recent institutional abuses internationally, including with victim/survivors (see exceptionally Pembroke 2019; Hamber and Lundy 2020). This book addresses these various gaps in the literature by providing a timely theoretically and empirically informed reflection on the particular challenges stemming from a broad range of national and international legal, policy, and institutional responses to non-recent institutional abuses. It draws on a range of fields including transitional justice, restorative justice, human rights, public law, criminology, and victimology. It thus represents a broader and more rounded discussion of what is both shared and diverse within the island of Ireland and internationally, contributing to a richer and more nuanced narrative on the meaning, limitations, and potential of justice related to non-recent institutional abuses.

The overall purpose of this book, therefore, is to critically examine 'justice' responses to non-recent institutional abuses by both church and state in a comparative, international, and interdisciplinary context and explore how they can be enhanced. The core argument is twofold: first, that a number of factors have coalesced to problematise justice responses within the island of Ireland, North and South, and internationally, obfuscating discourses and practices on accountability and impeding engagement between victim/survivors and church/state actors. These include (1) the historical church–state relationship within both Protestant and Catholic societies including the impact of empire and colonialism and the role of power, identity, and religion (Chapter 2); (2) the profound, complex, and evolving contexts of victimisation experiences (Chapter 3); (3) ideological, structural, and legal barriers imposed by church and state within the context of criminal, civil, international, and institutional legal frameworks (Chapter 4), as well as within 'inquiries', redress, and reparations, including apologies (Chapters 5, 6, and 7). Second, addressing these complexities and the various levels of accountability—encompassing moral, political, institutional, individual, and societal aspects—necessitates developing a multifaceted and empirically grounded understanding of responsibility, informed by a range of literatures.

Responsibility is presented throughout in much broader terms than is traditionally understood. This includes not only the moral and legal dimensions but crucially the human or relational and ideological dimensions of dealing with the legacy of non-recent institutional abuses. Reframing responsibility and accountability in more expansive terms means incorporating both the backward- and forward-looking elements of dealing with the past. Moving away from a purely legalistic focus, and its latent elements of censure and blame, and drawing on innovative justice philosophies and practices including restorative, transitional, and transformative justice, has the potential to remove some of the traditional barriers to justice. This may thereby open up engagement between victim/survivors and church/state actors and ultimately augment accountability for non-recent institutional abuses.

Our previous individual strands of critical scholarship on non-recent institutional abuses—derived in law/criminology, including truth-seeking mechanisms and apologies (McAlinden); sociology, criminology, social policy, and social work, including restorative justice, and clerical sexual abuse and the Catholic Church (Keenan); and transitional justice and human rights frameworks (Gallen)—have highlighted the need for continued critical reflection on legal and policy responses including the development of alternative justice approaches. Our collective approach has also been underpinned by existing critiques of legal and policy responses within public discourses (eg media reports and advocacy campaigns highlighting a lack of justice or healing for victim/survivors despite the resources and efforts involved) (O'Rourke et al 2018; Pembroke 2019); as well as our extensive engagement in policy, practice, and outreach work with statutory bodies and advocacy groups.[6]

Based on insights from the interdisciplinary literature (eg law, political science, history, sociology, criminology, and social policy), the diverse disciplinary backgrounds of the authors, and the empirical data, the book charts the parameters of a new 'transformative', transdisciplinary paradigm of justice drawing on some of the values and principles of restorative and transitional justice and international human rights discourses (Part III). In critically evaluating the value-added and potential limits of this 're-packaged' approach to justice, the book seeks to consider how we might (1) better frame discourses on responsibility and accountability at the level of theory and praxis in order to better address the historical complexities of non-recent institutional abuses; (2) include the lived experiences of both victim/survivors and responsible institutional actors in this space as core voices to be centred and engaged; and (3) create space for innovative justice thinking and processes to be part of a normative way of responding (eg via restorative and transitional justice as well as criminal and civil justice). The aim of these reconceptualised understandings of justice processes is to enhance mechanisms of accountability at individual and collective levels and ultimately improve justice processes, experiences, and outcomes nationally and internationally.

The empirical research is focused predominantly on the island of Ireland, comprising NI and RoI, against the comparative thematic analysis of investigatory mechanisms and of redress and apologies internationally.

[6] See staff profiles at https://transformingjusticeproject.org/ (accessed 1 June 2024).

However, the arguments and debates will have resonance for other jurisdictions and religious traditions dealing with the legacy of abuses currently and in the future. In offering new and holistic ways of thinking about non-recent institutional abuses, and by relating contemporary religious, legal, and policy responses to the historical, socio-political landscape, the book represents an original and significant theoretical and empirical contribution to international discourses on dealing with the legacy of the past that continues in the present for many.

2. Definitional and Thematic Context

A necessary starting point is to define key terms including what we mean by 'non-recent institutional abuses' and 'justice' as well as to outline some of the complexities relating to accountability and responsibility in this specific context.

'Non-recent institutional abuse'

The term 'historical institutional abuse' has tended to dominate transitional justice (eg Lundy 2020; Gallen 2023a), legal (eg McAlinden 2022a) and criminological discourses (eg Daly 2014b), as well as official investigations. Other scholars, however, have adopted various terms such as 'non-recent abuses', including within medical (Silverio et al 2021) health (Hindley and Lord 2021), or legal or criminal justice settings (Maslen and Paine 2019) or 'non-recent child sexual abuse reported by adult survivors' (Ring et al 2022) to describe retrospective disclosures of abuses by women and children committed in institutional settings in the past. Consistent with contemporary academic discourses and survivor experiences, the present analysis utilises the term 'non-recent institutional abuses'. Before offering a considered definition later, it is useful to briefly unpack each of its components.

First, 'non-recent' denotes the fact that there was a delay or temporal gap between the harms occurring and additional efforts to get those harms recognised at a national or political level. In many cases, the abuses occurred decades or generations previously. By adopting the term 'non-recent' over 'historical', this book remains mindful of the risk that such abuses could otherwise be viewed as disconnected from the often lifelong or intergenerational impact of the harms experienced by victim/survivors[7] or their families (see eg O'Rourke 2019 in the context of Magdalene survivors) or as irrelevant or unjustified as a basis for contemporary law- or policy-making. Rather, the book is keen to explore the extent to which official engagement with the history of institutions and abuses suffered by survivors shapes contemporary law, politics, and policy. As noted later, some forms of institutional abuses continue to occur, while others are the result of policies no longer operating in the present. The primary focus of the study is historical forms of abuses committed within the past.[8]

Second, although the term 'institution' is often used in broad or vague ways within social and behavioural sciences (Voss 2015), we use the term in two senses to include (1) 'total institutions' (Goffman 1961), typically located in the community, such as residential care homes, Magdalene Laundries, hospitals, and military institutions; and (2) other institutions run by or under the legal authority of church or state such as governments, schools, and public bodies which share broadly similar, often complex, rules and standards placing formal or informal constraints on human interaction and behaviour (Greif 2006). There is also a commonality in 'how institutions think' (Douglas 1986) in terms of their collective structures and values, some of which may have contributed to institutional wrongdoing and abuses.[9] The definition of non-recent institutional abuses that we adopt is informed by this social science scholarship. Broadly defined, we see an institution as an organisation founded with a particular purpose (including religious, educational, professional, medical, military, political, legal, or social) with shared norms and values comprising both material and discursive aspects.[10] While the focus of the book is predominantly on abuses within institutions run by religious orders on behalf of or with the acquiescence of the state, the analysis and findings also extend to abuses within this

[7] We use the conjoined term 'victim/survivor' throughout, in keeping with the breadth and diversity of adverse institutional experiences, the diverse self-description of those individuals who had such experiences, and the work of advocacy and representative groups. An additional term preferred by some survivors is that of 'resister' (see further Chapter 3).

[8] Note, however, that some official investigations have examined both 'historical' and contemporary forms of institutional abuses (see further Chapter 5).

[9] More generally, scholars have highlighted the 'darker side' of institutional culture, including risk-taking behaviour, 'mistakes' and 'misdeeds', and the normalisation of deviance (Vaughan 1999; see also Catino 2013).

[10] While some discourses use the terms institution or organisation interchangeably, we use the term institution/al but in a broader sense to denote abuses outside a purely physical building or space.

broader range of institutional contexts, some of which were emerging at the time of writing.

Third, what 'abuses' might encompass is arguably the most complex part of the term and lies at the heart of the legal and moral complexities of addressing such harms in the present. We adopt a dual and fuller understanding comprising two elements: (1) the range of specific abuses committed within closed institutional settings, many of which were and remain violations of criminal law—this includes, for example, forms of child abuse and neglect and violence against women; and (2) 'historical policy wrongs' as part of a spectrum of criminal justice or emergent welfare policies of institutionalisation which were legally permitted or mandated at the time providing legitimacy for the institutionalisation itself (see Chapter 2). Daly and Davis (2024) interpret 'historical policy wrongs' to include 'short-form historical injustices' targeted at particular vulnerable social groups such as 'women, girls, and mothers', 'rooted in colonialism, nation building and WWII'. This includes, *inter alia*, forced labour, coerced adoption or family separation, and non-consensual medical treatment, now recognised as violations of international human rights norms (see eg O'Rourke 2011; Gallen 2019a). Broadly speaking, the former category, (1) above, is characterised by forms of abuse which continue to be criminalised in the present; whereas the latter category, (2) above, has been re-evaluated and reconceptualised from institutional 'care' to abuse through a period of policy rupture made possible by a series of temporal social, policy, and legal changes including via the evolution of human rights law. There is also an acknowledged overlap between these core categories. For instance, many children and adults suffered further physical, sexual, or emotional abuses or neglect once brought within institutional care.

Contemporary responses to 'historical policy wrongs' are often viewed via the lens of history and the concept of historical relativity. Official discourses on non-recent institutional abuses, such as investigations or public apologies, may seek to locate abuses within the moral framework of the distant past with reference to the 'politics of time' (Arvidsson 2020) decades or generations previously. However, what emerges as being important within contemporary justice responses to non-recent institutional abuses by church and state actors is explicit recognition of the harms and suffering experienced by survivors and clear evidence of changed institutional thinking and practices within a more enlightened present.

As a synthesis of this discussion, our working definition of the term 'non-recent institutional abuses', based on extensive reading of the subject and informed and refined through original primary research, is that:

> Harms occurring in the past within institutional contexts, comprising either acts which are violations of the criminal law and/or historical policies of institutionalised care which violate contemporary international human rights norms.

Given the ongoing public and political controversy which contextualises our contemporary understanding of institutional abuses, the relevance and significance of the term within a range of institutional contexts will be examined in relation to the primary research, grounded especially in the voices and experiences of victim/survivors as well as elite-level actors.

This interpretation is illustrated by reference to a number of broad categories of abuses, including (1) the othering, categorisation, institutionalisation, and past abuses of women and children in residential care settings (Daly 2014b), such as care homes, industrial schools, workhouses, mother and baby institutions, 'Magdalene Laundries', and hospitals; (2) past abuses by members of religious institutions, including 'clerical sexual abuse' (Keenan 2012) and diocesan abuse; (3) the forced removal of children from their families where many suffered abuse and neglect whilst in and out of institutional care such as within the context of forced adoption, including that relating to child migration overseas (see eg Lynch 2020a; 2020b) and fostering or placement in 'cottage homes' or private homes in the community (see eg Nagy and Sehdev 2012 in the Canadian context and Cuthbert and Quartly 2013 in the Australian context); (4) sexual abuses in non-residential community-based settings such as state- or religious-run day schools; and (5) abuses in other closed state settings, including sexual violence and harassment of women within the armed forces.[11] Thus, in tandem with the realities and complexities of such abuses, this book counters the often siloed and case-specific approach of previous work to different forms of non-recent institutional abuses. Each of these broad categories was examined through the empirical research in the course of stakeholder interviews.[12] In addition, in

[11] In relation to abuses within the military, the interview sample only related to RoI as the campaign by the Women of Honour for an official investigation was ongoing at the time of the field research. However, it is a form of institutional abuse recognised internationally (see eg McCormick and Bennett 2023).

[12] The term also covers abuses in a range of other contexts including abuses in private settings such as The Scout Association, St John's Ambulance, and sport, not specifically examined here.

acknowledging the 'ripple effect' of trauma surrounding abuses, the primary research focus, while focusing predominantly on the experiences of victim/survivors, also encompasses their families. While there are commonalities in experiences of non-recent institutional abuses, the experiences of 'justice' among victim/survivors emerge as being complex and contextualised.

'Justice' discourses

The meaning of justice is often subjective or at least variable between individual victim/survivors who may have multiple or varying interests and needs. Studies have examined what victim/survivors of clerical sexual abuse or 'historical institutional abuse' want from justice processes (see eg Balboni and Bishop 2010; Lundy 2016). As explored further via the empirical research, victim/survivors in such contexts seek a broader range of outcomes than can be provided by conventional justice processes, including 'voice' and an opportunity to tell their story; truth and access to documents and records; acknowledgement and recognition; vindication and validation of their suffering; prosecution or punishment of perpetrators; face-to-face encounters with church authorities to hear them take responsibility for wrongdoing and abuses; remorse and accountability on the part of the perpetrator; appreciation of the impact of the abuse on the lives of victim/survivors; support by the state and the church; stopping the abuse by the individual and by the institution for current and future victim/survivors; and a broader 'package' of 'redress' including monetary redress, acknowledgement and apology, access to records, and memorialisation. The justice interests of victim/survivors lie with immediate perpetrators, church and state actors, and institutional leadership and may also extend to civil society. In this respect, for victim/survivors the plurality of justice interests at play is well represented in the notion of 'kaleidoscopic justice' (McGlynn and Westmarland 2019) which reflects not only the diverse and composite understanding of 'justice' for individual survivors but also its fluidity over time.

There is also increasing consensus in academic and policy debates that justice must be 'victim-sensitive' (Wright 2002), 'victim-centric' (Hamber and Lundy 2020), or 'epistemic' in nature (Enright and Ring 2020). This means accepting victim stories or testimonies within official discourses as well as taking explicit account of the wide spectrum of victim experiences.[13] At the level of praxis, this has particular relevance on three fronts. The first is in relation to the inclusion of victim/survivor experiences and testimonies within inquiry and investigatory commission processes and in the official reporting of such (testimonial epistemic justice) (see Chapter 5). The second and third are in relation to reparations—monetary redress schemes which are designed to be holistic and fair regarding eligibility and access (see Chapter 6) and official public apologies which are constructed and choreographed in conjunction with victimised communities, taking account of their needs and experiences (hermeneutical epistemic justice) (see Chapter 7). To date, however, aside from the small literature acknowledged above, there are very few empirical studies with victim/survivors which examine their perspectives of justice processes. This book, therefore, also addresses this deficit in the literature by examining the lived experiences of victim/survivors of a range of justice responses to non-recent institutional abuses as well as their aspirations of justice, on the island of Ireland.

While the meaning, scope, and limitations of the term 'justice' in relation to non-recent institutional abuses is one of the central tropes to be explored in the course of this book and will be informed in particular by the empirical research, for introductory purposes, 'justice' has a number of important modes. This includes 'adversarial justice' which characterises public inquiries or commissions of investigation as well as prosecutions and civil suits. As McGlynn and Westmarland argue (2019, 186), one of the key limitations of conventional criminal justice approaches to sexual violence is the focus on consequences in a narrow sense, particularly tied to the punishment of perpetrators as distinct from a more inclusive interpretation of 'justice as consequence' with a focus on accountability, recognition, dignity, voice, prevention, and connectedness in the sense of healing and belonging. The goal of conventional justice is often not a universal or objective sense of 'truth' or accountability for victim/survivors but rather adjudicating on the contested nature of 'blame' or attributing 'guilt', which inevitably results in the avoidance of responsibility for wrongdoing until a verdict is reached (see eg Farrow and Jacobs 2020; McAlinden 2022b). These arguments also underscore the need to move beyond purely legalistic modes of justice and

[13] Enright and Ring (2020) base their theory on Fricker's (2007) model of epistemic injustice which takes two forms: (1) testimonial—where testimony is ignored or disbelieved and (2) hermeneutical—where experiences are obscured from collective understanding.

traditional understandings of responsibility and accountability in order to satisfy the diverse justice interests of victim/survivors.

There is an additional complexity attached to utilising legal standards to make factual determinations for non-recent events where questions of testimony and evidence are usually at their most challenging. Within the context of investigatory commissions (see Chapter 5) or prosecutions and redress schemes (see Chapters 4 and 6), there are myriad system, evidential, and procedural barriers to seeking justice for non-recent institutional abuses. Some of the principal barriers include issues such as delay (Smith and Duff 2020; Keenan et al 2023), memory and recall of 'traumatic history' (Herman 2015), the availability of historical records, and inequality of arms between victim/survivors and the institutions of church and state. Within the civil sphere and tort law, legal rules pertaining to institutional liability (including vicarious liability of organisations such as churches for the actions of individual religious employees) (Gallen 2023b, 393; Ring et al 2022, ch 9) and statutes of limitation (stipulating specific time periods for the commencement of legal proceedings) (see Chapter 4) which operate in jurisdictions such as Ireland, England and Wales, and Australia, may effectively bar victim/survivors from bringing legal proceedings (Gallen 2018; Ring et al 2022, ch 8).

From the perspective of 'procedural justice'—which includes consideration of the procedures and decisions which ultimately shape outcomes—the experiences of victim/survivors during justice processes, including their perceived trust and legitimacy in the fairness of the process, are just as crucial as any outcomes they may produce (Tyler 1988; Lind and Tyler 1988). Daly's work (2014b, 117) identifies the benefits of procedural justice in meeting some of the core 'justice' interests of victim/survivors of institutional abuse in terms of 'participation, voice, validation, vindication, and offender accountability'. Procedural justice may also alleviate any concerns with secondary victimisation which would otherwise occur as a by-product of formal adversarial processes (Parsons and Bergin 2010) and ultimately restore the dignity of victim/survivors.[14] However, whereas previous work has highlighted the normative value of procedural justice more generally and to a lesser extent with respect to historical abuses, it has stopped short of examining the conceptual implications

[14] See Declaration of Basic Principles of Justice for Victims of Crime and Abuse of Power, GA Res 40/34, UN GAOR, 40th sess, 96th plen mtg, UN Doc A/RES/40/34 (29 November 1985), Annex art 6(b).

for justice discourses, as well as questions of praxis, as this book also seeks to do.

The broad failures of adversarial justice underline the need to seek a 'new way'. This entails examining the values and principles of other forms of justice such as restorative justice and transitional justice in addressing the twin elements of public norm violation as well as the private suffering of individual victim/survivors surrounding historical wrongdoing and abuses. In relation to 'restorative justice' (RJ), two definitions have dominated the field. On the one hand, 'process-based' definitions have been used to describe non-adversarial processes between victims, perpetrators, and communities which aim, *inter alia*, to 'restore' power to victim/survivors through engaging all stakeholders in 'facilitated encounters' that also aim to re-establish trust (for overview, see eg Walgrave et al 2021). The term is also used in a reformist sense to denote the transformative aims for structural as well as interpersonal change and offers a theory of justice that views justice via an entirely different 'lens' in comparison to formal criminal justice (see eg Zehr 1990). The values that support restorative justice include respect, responsibility/accountability-taking, relationality, empowerment, healing, and reintegration.

Although subject to sustained critique, including the need for additional safeguards with respect to sexual violence (see eg Jülich 2006; Stubbs 2007),[15] other scholars have proposed the use of RJ as applied to gendered and sexualised violence more broadly (Hudson 2002; Keenan and Zinsstag 2022) and with particular regard to institutional abuses (Gavrielides and Coker 2005; Keenan 2012) including in non-recent contexts (Keenan and Lyons 2023). Several examples of restorative-based schemes have been operationalised, including within the context of the Catholic Church, as a 'justice' response to non-recent institutional abuses (see eg Keenan et al 2016; see further Chapter 8). However, RJ has largely remained on the margins rather than within the mainstream of justice responses to non-recent institutional abuses. The book adopts a reformist interpretation of RJ, or what Walgrave (2000; 2021) terms 'a maximalist' or 'consequential' model and Keenan and Zinsstag (2022) refer to as a 'restorative criminal justice system', where restorative justice philosophy and practices permeate justice responses to non-recent institutional abuses at conceptual and grass-root levels.

[15] Critics point to concerns with power imbalances, re-traumatisation of victims, and lack of perpetrator accountability.

Transitional justice (TJ), initially conceived of as a framework within post-conflict settings (Arthur 2009; Quinn 2017), comprises a number of key elements central to dealing with the legacy of the past, including truth-seeking (via inquiries or investigatory commissions), accountability, reparation (including via apologies or monetary redress), institutional reform and the promise of non-recurrence, and reconciliation (UN Security Council 2004). More recently, the TJ framework has been extended to non-paradigmatic 'settled democracies' (Winter 2013) or 'settler colonial states' (Henry 2015) to address large-scale or systemic human rights abuses, including non-recent institutional abuses. For example, Australia (McAlinden and Naylor 2016; Gleeson and Ring 2021), Canada (Llewelyn 2002; Nagy 2013), and Ireland (McAuliffe 2017a; Gallen 2020) have used a mixture of inquiries, truth commissions, redress schemes, or apologies in response to institutional abuses.[16]

However, the specific features which characterise TJ processes within settled democracies—such as the blurred break with the past and the mixture of transitional and 'ordinary' justice (Álvarez Berastegi 2017)—place greater onus on TJ as a means of reparation and achieving 'justice' in such settings. Despite the acknowledged overlap in the utility of transitional and restorative mechanisms, chiefly in terms of their core values of accountability, reparation, and reconciliation (see eg Llewelyn 2006; Clamp and Doak 2012) and of repairing individual and societal relationships, the distinction lies in the broader emphasis within transitional frameworks on renewing a relationship between citizen and state. As discussed further in Part III, the nature of the 'transition' within justice discourses on non-recent institutional abuses envisaged here, as Gallen (2023b, 390) and others posit (see eg Arthur 2009, 363), relates to a broader 'regime' or 'system change' (McAlinden 2013, 214). This potentially incorporates (1) the prioritisation of the care of the marginalised and most vulnerable in society (McAlinden 2013; McAlinden 2022a); (2) structural, epistemic, and ideological changes (Gallen 2023b); and (3) listening to and centralising the multiplicity of victim/survivor voices (Shilliday 2022). It is in this sense that justice becomes 'transformative' (Gready and Robins 2014; McAuliffe 2017b)—shifting focus 'from the legal to the social and political'—rather than merely 'transitional' or 'restorative'.

As Gallen (2023b, 395) has previously acknowledged, addressing the complex legacy of historical injustices concerning abusive regimes, as this

[16] See also comparative studies: Daly 2014b; Ring et al 2022; Gallen 2023a.

book hopes to do, 'remains highly contested, challenging, and political'. In particular, the longevity of institutional abuses across the island of Ireland and the enmeshed political, legal, and institutional structures, some predating partition, make it difficult to attribute responsibility for institutional policies and processes and to pinpoint where the identification of problems or legitimate critiques might begin (see Chapter 2). This book aims to place victim/survivors front and centre in the envisaging of 'a new way' or new justice approach to non-recent institutional abuses. However, at the level of theory and practice, the final part of the book in particular also acknowledges and seeks to balance the multiple and often competing interests at stake—state, church, institutional, individual, societal, and victim/survivor.

'Accountability' and 'responsibility'

Accountability

A central notion in determinations of justice, and our arguments in this book, is that of accountability. As Flinders and Monaghan (2023, 3) note, accountability and its cognate concepts (eg liability, blame, responsibility) have spawned a vast interdisciplinary literature. Scholarship traverses criminology (Daly 2017), public law (Bamford and Leyland 2013; King 2013), international justice (Schabas 2013), as well as restorative (Roche 2003; O'Mahony and Doak 2017) transitional (Cohen 1995) and retributive justice (Murphy 2015). Scholars point in particular to its symbolic or moral significance (King 2013) as well as its practical utility in empowering victim/survivors and holding transgressors to account (O'Mahony and Doak 2017). There are, however, no settled meanings of accountability and responsibility across disciplinary contexts and indeed academic and policy discourses often conflate these terms.[17] Although exploring the meaning of these concepts and how they may feature within justice processes is one of the central tasks of this book, it is useful at this juncture to briefly sketch some parameters and how our framework of analysis utilises, critiques, and extends previous thinking.

Public law scholars and political scientists, writing on regulatory governance, often define accountability in narrow, retrospective terms (see eg Scott 2000; Boven 2007). Scott (2000, 40), for example, defines accountability as a 'duty to give one's account for one's actions to some other person

[17] See eg the Law Commission of Canada (LCC 2000, 87–8) and Daly's (2017, 122) analysis of the usage of these terms.

or body'. Such 'thin' interpretations, however, are correlated to what has been termed 'the dark side of accountability' (Flinders 2023) where the focus is on 'shaming' and 'blame attribution' for past actions rather than 'positive accountability' premised on future-focused approaches which facilitate 'lesson learning' (Shoesmith 2023). Purely retrospective models of accountability are therefore unhelpful in conceptualising a progressive or transformative model of justice. In this respect, Rock (2023) outlines some of the broader goals of accountability as 'transparency', 'control', 'punishment', as well as 'restoration' and 'reform'. A broader and balanced framing of accountability for non-recent institutional abuses seeks to give effect to these retrospective and prospective dimensions.

Criminologist John Braithwaite's 'responsive regulation' (2011, 510) thesis helpfully distinguishes between 'passive' and 'active' elements of accountability and responsibility—while the former is also retrospective, focusing on 'holding actors responsible for wrongs they have done in the past', the latter includes 'challenging actors to take responsibility for making things right into the future'. As discussed further in the last part of the book, it is the active element in particular—denoting not only acknowledgement for past wrongdoing and abuses but signifying a commitment to non-recurrence via changed ideologies and practices—which is integral to the meaning of true accountability within transformative justice. As such, we use the term accountability in a broader sociological sense to unpack what it means to seek accountability for past abuses and how, and in what ways, that might be achieved in the present and future.

We interpret accountability as the holding of individuals or institutions to account based on the taking of responsibility for wrongdoing and abuses. In this sense, Daly (2017, 118–21), as a criminologist writing in the context of sexual violence and drawing on the work of Duff (2011), persuasively outlines accountability as both *calling* alleged perpetrators to account and also *holding* them to account. According to Daly's (2017) view, the taking of responsibility, on the other hand, is what perpetrators actively do after they have been called to account in response, to 'make up' for the wrongdoing, or as Duff (2011, 279) puts it, 'to own the wrong'. Importantly for our purposes, however, accountability is more expansive than liability alone. In this respect, Daly (2017) notes that while criminal and civil justice are orientated towards censure and sanctions (following a finding of liability) these are part of victim vindication rather than a core part of accountability—a perpetrator, for example, may be held legally accountable without taking full or personal responsibility for their behaviour. Moreover, a similarly narrow version of accountability in a purely relational sense (eg individual representatives of offending institutions meeting with survivors) may circumvent the broader power differentials between survivors and institutions and any potential challenges to institutional thinking. Thus, as discussed in the final part of the book, a thicker and pluralist understanding of accountability also requires a maximalist version of responsibility for non-recent institutional abuses which has to be evidenced in multiple ways.

The latent problem with predominantly legal understandings of accountability based on shame and blame is that they push institutions into defensive posturing, impeding openness and engagement with victim/survivors around broader redress. In these circumstances, church or state institutions may seek to evade institutional accountability via a range of strategies including delayed compliance with disclosure or discovery requirements, victim blaming tactics in the course of interrogating victim/survivors' personal histories (Lytton 2008, 69; Gallen 2023b, 394), and purported resort to internal governance processes such as canon law (see eg Doyle 2004; Jones 2019; see Chapters 4, 5, and 6). A further distancing strategy for state and church actors is to distinguish an abusive past from a more moral present (Waldron 1992). In this respect, this book seeks to locate progressive justice responses within these broader historical, institutional, political, legal, and ideological landscapes concerning a move away from how accountability is traditionally understood.

Responsibility

Responsibility in particular is pivotal to justice discourses. As Celermajer (2014, 57) notes, 'different dimensions of responsibility ought to be encoded in measures of redress'. According to the legal or socio-legal literature, 'responsibility' can have multiple meanings (see eg McAlinden 2022b) which are pertinent for our purposes. These include 'moral', 'agentic' (Oshana 1997), or 'outcome responsibility' (Miller 2007)—which accepts responsibility for past actions in causing the abuses or failing to prevent them (Weiner 1995), as well as 'legal' or 'remedial responsibility' (Thompson 2012, 223; see also Miller 2007)—which acknowledges the violation of legal codes, including human rights frameworks, and consequently the responsibility for repair.[18] As with accountability, responsibility also has a broader meaning than censure or blame. Duff (2006), as a legal

[18] This also accords with Jaspers' (2000) classification of 'German guilt' in the aftermath of the Second World War as moral (where acts are attributed to those morally responsible), criminal (established by the violation of rights or legal norms), and political (relating to wrongdoing carried out in the name of the state).

theorist, distinguishes responsibility from liability—in that an individual may be responsible for wrongdoing (in a legal and moral sense) but avert liability by offering an exculpatory defence, excuse, or justification. Instead, Duff equates responsibility with *answerability* as part of the moral or 'relational dimensions of responsibility' (2006, 87). This involves asking: 'who is responsible, for what, to whom?' (Duff 2004).

Although on one level this framing of responsibility is helpful in directing our thinking towards the historical complexities of non-recent institutional abuses (see Chapter 2), it also presupposes a narrow, backward-looking focus. However, responsibility to serve justice to victim/survivors of non-recent institutional abuses can derive from not only past violation of their *rights* as citizens but also their justice *interests* as key stakeholders in contemporary legal or reparative processes, as well as their current and future *needs* as victim/survivors (many of them vulnerable). Indeed, what survivors want from justice processes is often not static but may evolve over time. This complex triad is explored further in the course of the analysis, informed by the empirical research (see especially Chapter 3). A fuller understanding of the 'relational' aspects of responsibility entails a broader focus on victim needs in terms of not only reparations for past wrongdoing and abuses but also more humane and transparent justice processes.

Previous scholarship has also differentiated individual and 'aggregative' responsibility' for wrongdoing (see eg Celermajer 2014). Within RoI, for example, the shared wrongdoing and complicity of the Irish State, the institutional Church, individual perpetrators, and wider society sustained 'the architecture of containment' (Smith 2007) or network of 'coercive confinement' (O'Sullivan and O'Donnell 2012; see Chapter 2). More recent historical work highlights the interdependent role of shame and silence within families and communities and an institutional regime which bureaucratised silence (Wills 2024). However, the literature also underlines the contested nature of pluralistic versions of accountability and responsibility for collective wrongdoing (see eg Isaacs and Vernon 2011). In this sense, the notion of collective responsibility is especially unhelpful in unpacking the complexities of *historical* wrongdoing and determining how we attribute responsibility for the past within the present.

Particular questions arise including whether and to what extent an organisation is morally or legally responsible for the actions of individual members and whether and to what extent individual church or state actors occupying contemporary leadership positions are responsible for historical wrongdoing. Further, cumulative terms such as 'collective responsibility' may actually displace responsibility by advancing the notion that as responsibility is shared or divided it should not be borne by any particular faction. Our analysis grapples with these and related complexities. We explore the meaning of 'responsibility' within justice discourses in terms of how, and in what ways, the state, church, and wider society were manifestly responsible for the abuses; and how, and in what ways, they may be held accountable in the present and future.

Collective understandings of 'responsibility' also encompass notions of direct and indirect responsibility in terms of those who not only perpetrated the abuse but who are responsible by way of being involved complicitly or implicitly in supporting and sustaining the processes of institutionalisation and abusive regimes. The latter accords with Rothberg's (2019) notion of 'implicated subjects'. These are individuals who 'occupy positions aligned with power and privilege, without being themselves direct agents of harm; they contribute to, inhabit, inherit, or benefit from regimes of domination but do not originate or control such regimes' (Rothberg 2019, 1). Untangling such 'modes of implication' behind historical injustices is essential to 'the pursuit of justice' (Rothberg 2019, 2) and also underlines the need to examine modes of responsibility for historical wrongdoing that sit outside traditional legal or justice frameworks.

As explored throughout the book, the rubric of responsibility is potentially problematic as traditionally understood both through the prism of existing literature as well as the voices of key stakeholders interviewed for this study. Divergent views on what it means to be accountable or take responsibility for non-recent institutional abuses may serve to undermine a common understanding of 'justice' and impede meaningful engagement of church and state actors with victimised communities. One of our core tasks, therefore, is to develop a richer understanding of what accountability and responsibility mean in this particular context. Extending the literature and derived in the primary research, we understand responsibility as a core constituent and instrument of accountability where responsibility is composite, task-orientated, and bi-directional. This reflects its multiple dimensions including not only the moral and legal dimensions but also the deeply human, relational, and emotional aspects of dealing with the legacy of non-recent institutional abuses. As a result, accountability is also presented in collective terms, advanced via extra-legal mechanisms including moral, political institutional, interpersonal, and societal aspects. Broader understandings of accountability permeate beyond justice for individuals to encompass the extant implications for state, church, and society as both conduits and barometers of material ideological and structural changes as key elements of a new approach to justice.

3. The Island of Ireland as a Comparative Case Study

The island of Ireland comprises the two jurisdictions of NI and RoI, which have a shared geographical and land border and an enmeshed cultural and political history. The complex legacy of dealing with the past—including not only colonialism post-partition but also the additional legacy of 'the conflict'[19]—has uniquely impacted on justice responses to non-recent institutional abuses within Ireland, North and South. Situated against the wider backdrop of North–South relations post-Brexit, NI is a post-conflict society where non-recent institutional abuses have occurred in a context of other widespread forms of political violence. In contrast, RoI is a relatively stable, post-colonial democracy since its inception after the partition of Ireland in 1922. The occurrence of non-recent institutional abuses in settler colonial (NI) and post-colonial (RoI) contexts adds a further layer of complexity to the analysis. Moreover, although non-recent institutional abuses have occurred in both jurisdictions at different points in time, RoI is especially significant as a case study since abuse occurred in a context where arguably the Catholic Church reinforced colonial forms of social control. This contrasts with existing studies in broader settler or post-colonial frameworks, such as Canada and Australia (see eg Daly 2014b), where abuses formed part of the colonising process. Examining justice responses across both types of society will also contribute more broadly to global debates on dealing with the legacy of the past in both transitional societies and settled democracies.

Ireland constitutes a fruitful empirical context as an island which has witnessed a proliferation of official investigations where the focus has been predominantly on the Catholic Church. In tandem with this, academic and policy focus on abuses within Protestant institutions across the island of Ireland is not well developed.[20] Although there is a lengthy history of child abuse inquiries within the island of Ireland dating back to the first half of the twentieth century (see Chapter 2), there has been a particular concentration

[19] The 'conflict' is a contested term for the civil/political unrest that occurred in NI from the late 1960s to the mid-1990s. While some use the term the 'Troubles', this is also rejected as a euphemism.

[20] Archival research has highlighted how abuses in non-Catholic institutions, including the Protestant Bethany Home in Dublin, have been a neglected dimension of both official and public discourses (see Meehan 2010a, 2010b). Similarly, Burke (2020) argues that while there were numerous Protestant asylums for women and children, abuses in Irish Protestant institutions have been 'disremembered' or continually ignored due to a prevailing sectarian divide south of the border post-partition.

of investigations related to non-recent institutional abuses within the last two decades. In RoI, this has included the Ferns Report (Murphy et al 2005), the Ryan Report (CICA 2009), the Murphy Report (CoI 2009), the Cloyne Report (CoI 2011), the McAleese Report (IDC 2013), and the final report of the Commission of Investigation into Mother and Baby Homes (2021). As discussed further, enduring controversies stemming from these investigations more broadly, as well as from the Mother and Baby Homes Commission specifically, relate to access to records for victim/survivors and their relatives, specific acknowledgement of human rights violations by the state, as well as a fuller and accurate representation of the voices of victim/survivors. At the time of writing, the Report of the Scoping Inquiry into Historical Sexual Abuse in Day and Boarding Schools Run by Religious Orders (2024) had just been published, with a number of independent investigations into other forms of non-recent institutional abuses ongoing (see Chapter 5).

In NI, where the majority religion has traditionally been Protestantism (Presbyterian, Church of Ireland, and Methodist denominations),[21] there have been much fewer inquiries to date. The implementation of the recommendations of the Hart Inquiry (HIA Inquiry 2017), including apology, were delayed for five years with the redress and memorialisation processes ongoing (see Chapters 5, 6, and 7). An independent panel was established in April 2023 to examine the experiences of victim/survivors of mother and baby institutions, Magdalene Laundries, and workhouses. Its findings will feed into a statutory public inquiry as part of 'an integrated truth investigation' model (Mahon et al 2021). As such, issues concerning 'justice' and 'redress' for victim/survivors are very much ongoing in both jurisdictions.

Within other jurisdictions, while also accompanied by official apologies and sometimes by redress schemes, official investigations also remain a front-and-centre political response to non-recent institutional abuses. As noted, existing scholarship tends to focus on investigations and redress within Anglophone countries including Australia and Canada, the UK, the United States, and Ireland (see Daly 2014b; Ring et al 2022; Gallen 2023a). The analysis presented in Part II addresses this gap in the literature by

[21] The new Northern Ireland State was made up of a Protestant majority, with a 65% Protestant and 35% Catholic population at the time of partition (see MacGinty and Darby 2002). By the latest 2021 Census, however, 45.70% of respondents identified as Catholic and 43.48% identified as Protestant: see https://www.nisra.gov.uk/publications/census-2021-main-statistics-religion-tables (accessed 1 June 2024).

drawing out some of the key themes and learning from both Anglophone and non-Anglophone countries. The recent completion or continuing nature of official investigations and redress mechanisms in Ireland and elsewhere represents a timely and appropriate juncture, therefore, at which to critically reflect on the strengths and limitations of justice responses to non-recent institutional abuses locally, nationally, and internationally, and how they might be enhanced.

Investigatory commissions elsewhere have examined the experiences of Protestant denominations and other religions within the broader context of an inquiry framework (see Chapter 5). Existing scholarship also addresses child sex abuse in Protestant congregations in the United States (Denney et al 2018; Guidepost 2022), Australia (see eg Parkinson et al 2012; Guerzoni 2021), and Germany (Spröber et al 2014). As Rashid and Barron (2019) acknowledge, however, for the most part the focus of academic and policy literature on clerical child sexual abuse internationally has been on the Catholic Church rather than other non-Catholic Christian denominations. As a counter to the available literature, the empirical research, particularly the comparative documentary analysis, also draws on broader international experiences across religions as part of the wider examination of church and state responses to non-recent institutional abuses (see later). Whilst primarily utilising the case studies of NI and RoI, the analysis contextualises the theoretical, policy, and empirical research internationally throughout the book in examining existing perspectives and experiences and the envisaging of a new way.

4. The Primary Research

The empirical research, grounded within the principal themes from the interdisciplinary literature on non-recent institutional abuses, was comprised of four strands:[22]

(1) *Comparative documentary analysis*—with the assistance of a postdoctoral research assistant (PDRA), we examined in-depth the origins, methodology, terms of reference, composition, legal powers, types of

[22] A detailed ethical protocol—comprising data protection and management, confidentiality, anonymity, and safeguarding the well-being of participants and investigators—was developed and approved by each of the authors' School Research Committees (QUB, UCD, and DCU).

hearing, time frame, and outcomes and impact on policy and practice of a sample of national and international public inquiries. This included not only NI and RoI but a wide range of Anglophone jurisdictions which have had a concentration of inquiries or investigatory commissions over the last three decades—see primarily England and Wales, Canada, and Australia. Whereas Wright et al (2020) have collated public inquiries into 'historical institutional child abuse' on the Age of Inquiry website, there is no in-depth or comparative documentary analysis of inquiry structures, reports, or outcomes to date (see Chapter 5). Our analysis also included more recent investigations in non-Anglophone countries over the last two decades, including Denmark, Sweden, Norway, Belgium, and the Netherlands. Several other countries are referred to for the purposes of illustration. These jurisdictions were chosen for the following reasons:

(i) complex multi-actor histories of abuses involving states, churches, and national societies;
(ii) shared history and experience of historical institutional abuses against marginalised groups;
(iii) use of different justice approaches to address historical abuses.

Additionally, as a counter to existing scholarship, we sought to balance:

(iv) experiences in both Anglophone and non-Anglophone countries;
(v) experiences in both predominantly Catholic and predominantly Protestant societies.

The book does not propose a comprehensive comparison of justice measures in these jurisdictions but instead adopts a focused and targeted comparison based on its theoretical and critical framework. This analysis also encompassed archival research of official apologies for non-recent institutional abuses in international settings. Again, while previous studies have conducted comparative analysis of apologies in Anglophone countries, the present study broadens the range of countries and updates these previous analyses to include more recent examples of official apologies for non-recent institutional abuses (see Chapter 7). Note, this analysis was not undertaken for redress schemes more broadly given the existing empirical research in this area (see eg Daly 2014b; Daly and Davis 2024).

(2) *Media analysis*—this component, again with the assistance of a PDRA, entailed analysis of newspaper coverage of non-recent institutional

abuses in NI and RoI over the last 25 years, including survivor voices, campaign efforts, responses to inquiries, calls for reform, or implementation. It sought to capture all-island cultural diversity within public discourses and, in addition to national papers (eg *The Irish Times*, *The Irish Independent*, *The Irish Examiner*), within NI in particular it examined local newspapers including those associated predominantly with both Catholic/nationalist (eg *The Irish News*) and Protestant/unionist communities (eg *The Belfast Telegraph*, *The Belfast Newsletter*). Beyond providing context, this data was also analysed systematically via NVivo software with themes linked to the interviews and the interdisciplinary literature.[23]

(3) *Semi-structured interviews*—following a pilot of six interviews from November 2022 to January 2023, a total of 74 in-depth semi-structured interviews were conducted across the island of Ireland (NI: $n = 17$; RoI: $n = 53$; relating to both: $n = 4$) from January 2023 to January 2024.[24] Interviews lasted at least 1–1.5 hours or longer in some cases. Utilising a purposive sampling strategy, interviewees comprised elite-level actors (high-ranking actors with decision-making capacity) including members of religious orders, societies, or dioceses, related to the Catholic Church;[25] senior politicians and government officials; senior civil servants; senior police officers and prosecutors; judges/commissioners; as well as lawyers and human rights advocates; journalists and academics; victim advocates/representatives; and victim/survivors who collectively had experienced a broad spectrum of experiences across our illustrative definition of 'non-recent institutional abuses' presented earlier.[26] The sample consisted of 38 men and 36 women including 14 victim/survivors. The overall sample size was determined by 'saturation' (Glaser and Straus 2017)—when the collection of new data did not shed any further light on the core themes of the study. Although the sample does not purport to be fully representative, it nonetheless represents a diverse spectrum of views of the multiple

[23] Our literature review, media analysis, comparative documentary analysis of inquiries and apologies, and research instruments are available open access on the project website. See n 6. The research data supporting this study cannot be made available due to the sensitive nature of the research and the fact that no interviewees consented to their data being shared.

[24] Some interview participants chose to be named. Those who wished to remain anonymous are identified only by broad sector and jurisdiction (ie NI or RI) and are differentiated numerically (see Appendix 1).

[25] Although some Protestant organisations were approached, they declined to participate.

[26] While victim/survivors interviewed for the study were also advocates, we refer to them throughout as victim/survivors in order to distinguish them from professional victim/survivor advocates.

stakeholders across the island of Ireland. The analysis draws extensively on a preponderance of views, though a small number of interview narratives are not quoted from directly but are used rather for background purposes.

A final sampling issue relates to victim/survivor diversity. While gender, and related notions of shame, is a central theme within discourses on non-recent institutional abuses particularly within Catholic cultures such as RoI (see eg Fischer 2016; Hogan 2019), our analysis recognises gender within the context of intersectionality and the regulation of multiple victim vulnerabilities. This includes consideration of marital status, religious denomination, poverty, race, disability (including mental illness), or reputed criminal or sexual transgression (see Enright and Ring 2020; see also Smith 2007). Even though multiple institutions and practices primarily affected women and children, the fieldwork sampling strategies and interview questions sought to overcome potential biases by capturing a more balanced view of gender and other diversities including the experiences of males and the institutionalisation of mixed-race women or children.

Previous empirical studies of non-recent institutional abuses have generally been conducted with victim/survivors only (see eg Pembroke 2019; Hamber and Lundy 2020). Elite-level actors at senior levels of church and state organisations are generally hard to reach and, as such, their perspectives are not often reflected in research of this nature because of access difficulties (see exceptionally Keenan 2014). However, there were very high levels of engagement by these constituencies with the research and the requests for interview, representing a unique contribution of the current study. As a result, their voices are well represented within the interview sample and played a key role, along with the voices of victim/survivors and their advocates, in informing the analysis.

The questions were focused particularly on the justice, policy, decision-making, and political aspects of non-recent institutional abuses. A broad, semi-structured interview instrument was drafted based on themes within the literature and was specifically tailored for each participant or cohort. Interviews were taped and transcribed and material analysed within the context of key themes emerging from the data using NVivo software. Transcripts were initially blind-coded and agreed by the project team and themes were reviewed periodically.

In addition, the book draws on some interviews ($n = 23$) and one focus group with victim/survivors from a previous project on apologies conducted by one of the authors, predominantly in Chapter 7. This fieldwork took place between November 2017 and June 2019.[27] A small number of interviewees ($n = 7$) were interviewed for both the previous and current project meaning that the empirical analyses presented within this book draw on a total of 90 distinct voices. However, the value of the new empirical work conducted specifically for this project lies in capturing the learning from first-hand critical accounts from key stakeholders, including elite-level actors, concerning their experiences of a range of justice processes. Consistent with most qualitative research, data analysis incorporated both inductive (where theory emerges from the data) and deductive (which explores whether the data is consistent with existing theories) approaches (see Fereday and Muir-Cochrane 2006).

(4) *Survey*—following the emergence of RJ schemes run by religious orders, societies, and dioceses as a theme within some of the interviews, the decision was made to amend the methodology and obtain further ethical approval for a survey of these institutions regarding the use of RJ broadly defined. A letter of invitation and brief survey, conducted via Google Forms, was sent to 142 of these institutions across all major Christian denominations in NI and RoI in December 2023. Data was also sought and received from the Catholic Church's Towards Healing service on the facilitation of RJ within their Facilitated Listening Programme. While the response rate to the survey was low (18%), reflections on practice from the combined data sets are included in Chapter 8.

5. Structure of the Book

The book is comprised of three parts.[28] The first part focuses on contextualising justice responses to non-recent institutional abuses across the island of Ireland and internationally. Chapter 2 examines the historical and sociocultural context of abusive regimes including the centrality of church–state relations and the differential impact and responses within Protestant and Catholic dominated societies; the historical underpinnings of institutional

[27] Anne-Marie McAlinden was senior co-investigator on an ESRC-funded study, *Apologies, Abuses and Dealing with the Past*, leading on the institutional abuses case study (Grant Ref: ES/N010825/1). See https://apologies-abuses-past.org.uk/ (accessed 1 June 2024). The interviewees from the apologies study are differentiated alphabetically.

[28] While this was an entirely collaborative project, McAlinden was lead author on Chapters 1, 5, 7, 9, and 10. Keenan was lead author on Chapter 3. Gallen was lead author on Chapters 2, 4, and 6. Keenan and Gallen were co-authors on Chapter 8.

abuses; and the broader responses of church and state to dealing with social crises. Chapter 3 examines the voices of victim/survivors, contextualising understanding of the magnitude and complexity of victim experiences of abuses and 'loss' as well as of any ensuing justice responses. This includes the complexities of what we term the 'needs–interests–rights trichotomy' pertaining to how victim/survivors' voices and participation within justice discourses might be best understood.

Part II of the book evaluates existing justice responses to non-recent institutional abuses. Chapter 4 analyses conventional justice responses including some of the key barriers to justice within criminal, civil, and international legal frameworks. The chapter also considers the role of legal culture and institutional strategies which may obfuscate or circumvent the acceptance of responsibility for historical wrongdoing and abuses, including 'remedial responsibility' in both moral and legal terms. Chapters 5, 6, and 7 critically examine three key modes of justice responses within NI and RoI and internationally—'inquiries' (and investigatory commissions), redress schemes, and apologies and the extent to which they may facilitate accountability and the official acceptance of responsibility. Common threads emerging from these chapters include inherent ideological, structural, and legal barriers to justice and the need for holistic evaluation of justice measures in terms of consistency of action by church and state and appropriate follow-through.

Drawing on the concepts and themes presented in the earlier part of the book, Part III presents the parameters of a 'new way' or transformative justice paradigm that includes all voices with an interest in non-recent institutional abuses. Chapter 8 maps the contours of a reconceptualised justice approach drawing on the principles of restorative, transitional, and transformative justice and the ways in which they may provide pathways to broader redress and more effective justice processes and outcomes. Chapter 9 synthesises the need for a new approach which addresses some of the key challenges which recur within justice discourses on non-recent institutional abuses, including the lack of engagement and trust between survivors and institutional actors as well as structural and legal barriers to justice. In so doing, it delineates a new model of responsibility and accountability—incorporating moral, legal, relational, and ideological dimensions—at a conceptual as well as a pragmatic level. Finally, Chapter 10, as the concluding chapter, offers some brief reflections on the theoretical and policy implications of our analysis across the island of Ireland and internationally.

2

Historical and Cultural Contexts of Non-Recent Institutional Abuses on the Island of Ireland

1. Introduction

This chapter evaluates the structural, institutional, and intergenerational factors that gave rise to non-recent institutional abuses, enabling subsequent chapters to assess whether and how those factors have been addressed in justice responses to date. The chapter contends that several factors, including elite decision-making, socio-economic and cultural conditions, and inherited colonial structures, impact the conditions in which non-recent institutional abuses occurred and, in turn, shape both contemporary attributions of responsibility and the nature of the engagement of state and church actors. Consideration of non-recent abuses on the island of Ireland must address their occurrence in both a single jurisdiction as part of the British Empire and two separation jurisdictions after the partition of the island in 1922, both of which retained Catholic and Protestant populations and institutions. This chapter will use 'Ireland' to refer to the pre-partition island of Ireland and the Republic of Ireland (RoI) and Northern Ireland (NI) to address the post-1922 jurisdictions (Daly 2007). The analysis will draw out the differences between NI and RoI and between Catholic and Protestant denominations, institutions, and sectors of society.

Section 2 overviews major historical and political developments affecting the island and assesses the legacies of empire, colonialism, and violence. Section 3 considers the key structural features of Christianity, such as proselytism, the Penal Laws and Emancipation, and the Great Famine, all of which impact non-recent institutional abuses. Section 4 addresses structural influences on non-recent institutional abuses, considering different denominational relationships with the state, family, law enforcement,

Transforming Justice Responses to Non-Recent Institutional Abuses. Anne-Marie McAlinden, Marie Keenan, and James Gallen, Oxford University Press.
DOI: 10.1093/9780191967399.003.0002

media, education, and healthcare. Section 5 identifies and contextualises the institutions on the island of Ireland in which non-recent institutional abuses occurred. Section 6 briefly considers the emergence of campaigns for justice responses to non-recent abuses. Section 7 concludes by synthesising the impact of historical and cultural contexts on contemporary justice discourses regarding non-recent institutional abuses, especially related to determinations of responsibility and levels of engagement of church and state actors.

2. Empire, Colonialism, and the Island of Ireland

The history of violence, religion, and empire is centuries old on the island of Ireland, which has experienced periods of both intense violence and the division of society, wealth, and land along Christian denominational lines (Connolly 2017; Howe 2017). With this long and violent context, Ireland shares the experience of several other states in the Global North and of the Christian church globally (Brock and Palmer 2008; Gallen 2023a). Within the last century, the War of Independence (1919–21) led to the deaths of 2,346 people across the island (O'Halpin and O'Corrain 2020, 10), with recent scholarship also documenting sexual violence during this period of conflict (Byrne 2021; Breathnach and O'Halpin 2022). The independence struggle led to the partition of the island. Under the Government of Ireland Act 1920, Ireland was partitioned into NI and Southern Ireland, later the Irish Free State in 1922. Partition would result in over 200,000 Protestants living in the Irish Free State (Mohr 2021, 334), with the majority living in NI. Disagreement among Irish citizens regarding the acceptability of partition and the Anglo-Irish Treaty led to an Irish Civil War between 1922 and 1923, with 1,500–4,000 fatalities estimated (Clark 2014) and recent scholarship again documenting sexual violence against women (Connolly 2021). The Irish Free State was replaced by 'Ireland' through Bunreacht na hÉireann (the Irish Constitution) in 1937 and formally became a republic under the Republic of Ireland Act 1948 (Daly 2007, 81).

In addition, between 1968 and 1998 a conflict between Republican paramilitaries, (aiming for a united Ireland), Loyalist paramilitaries, (aiming to keep NI within the UK), and British security, military, and policing forces, resulted in an estimated 3,260–600 deaths and over 40,000 injured people (O'Rourke and Swaine 2017, 1307), with limited recognition to date of conflict-related sexual violence (Swaine 2023). In April 1998, the Belfast/

Good Friday Agreement was signed by the British and Irish governments and the majority of political parties in NI, establishing new forms of devolved government for NI.

This broad history can be assessed through a range of views of Irish history in colonial terms (Kenny 2006). Some accept that Ireland was Britain's first colony and provided a 'training ground' for the use of many subsequent colonial techniques (Rolston 1993; Ohlmeyer 2016). In contrast, Howe argues that a post-colonial approach to Ireland has a questionable use of non-Irish cases and that 'its conception of colonialism itself [is] unduly homogenizing and ahistorical, its view of historians' method unduly dismissive' (Howe 2006, 245). Howe's approach in turn is criticised for placing little emphasis on the material realities and effects of colonialism (Rolston and Ni Aolain 2018, 336–7). Colonisation on the island thus remains deeply contested and its full consideration is beyond the scope of this book (see Montano 2011; Cavanagh 2013). Instead, the book focuses on Christian church and state institutions and their roles in non-recent institutional abuses, as an expression of broader, intergenerational historical–structural injustices, without asserting a definitive relationship to theories of colonialism. Nuti (2019, 45) suggests that historical–structural injustices should be understood in terms of 'unjust long-term structures that endure over time and through institutional transformations by means of changes in how they operate'. In contrast, for McKeown (2024) there are three different types of structural injustice. First, 'pure structural injustice' occurs where no perpetrator can be identified and injustice arises from multiple actors' collective conduct. Second, 'avoidable structural injustice' is where there are powerful agents with the capacity to change unjust structures but who fail to do so. Finally, 'deliberate structural injustice' arises where agents are deliberately perpetuating unjust background conditions for their own gain and they have the power to change them (McKeown 2024, 1). To address responsibility for these conceptions of structural injustice within Ireland, it is necessary to understand the nature and structure of Christianity, which have been present on the island of Ireland from the early fifth century (Charles-Edward 2000).

3. Structural Features of Irish Christianity

Several key historical features of Irish Christianity influence non-recent institutional abuses and related contemporary justice discourses, including proselytism, Penal Laws and Catholic emancipation, the Great Famine, and the Devotional Revolution. Proselytism can be defined as a policy of attempting to convert people's religious or political beliefs. Both Catholic and Protestant denominations competed for the conversion of children and the poor on the island. In 1733, Charter schools were established 'to convert the "Popish masses" of Ireland to the Protestant religion' (Barnes 1989, 27). During the Great Famine, Protestant churches and evangelical missions practised 'souperism', offering food in return for religious conversion (Byrne 2018). The end of the Penal Laws in 1829, discussed later, increased Protestant efforts to convert Catholic children (Burke 2020), leading to the development of a range of separate Protestant and Catholic charitable organisations and institutions, and precluded a coherent non-denominational welfare system on the island (Purdue 2017, 75, 78; Holme 2018, 159). Many institutions discussed later sought to either detain women and children of their own faith for fear of proselytism from the other denomination and/ or to proselytise members of the other faith. Proselytism is recognised as a cause of institutionalisation in some inquiry processes in RoI (see eg CICA 2009, Vol 1, ch 2, paras 2.16–2.25).

Penal Laws shaped the capacity of Christian denominations to influence the Irish population (Connolly 2004, 17). The Penal Laws were a series of legal statutes and regulations which operated in Ireland from 1691 to 1829 and excluded Catholics and Presbyterians from 'land, wealth, and political power' (Rolston and Ni Aolain 2018, 338), which rested in the hands of Protestant elites. By the late eighteenth century, successive English governments had passed several Catholic Relief Acts (Connolly 2004). The Catholic Relief Act 1782 allowed for the legal establishment of Catholic schools and bishops. The Catholic Relief Act 1829 permitted Roman Catholics to be eligible for the UK parliament but also prohibited the establishment and the operation of religious orders in Ireland (Costello 2021, 110). As a result of the 1829 Act, religious orders could only hold land through their members rather than directly as distinct legal entities (Costello 2021, 115). In addition to contributing to a long-term sense of Irish Catholicism as a persecuted faith, these laws shaped how the Catholic Church and its religious orders were to hold property and other assets until current times, as separate legal entities from the church and orders themselves, which has significant implications for litigation and accountability for non-recent institutional abuses (see Chapter 4).

The Great Famine significantly altered the nature and practice of Christianity in Ireland. In the 1840s, a potato blight affected potato crops across Europe and had a profound impact on Ireland which was especially dependent on potatoes as a staple food (Ó Gráda 2006, 7). Between 1845 and 1850, approximately 1 million people died from starvation or disease. A further 1 million people emigrated from Ireland, reducing the overall population by 20–5% (Ross 2002, 226). The famine rendered the Irish population smaller and more manageable from the perspective of institutional Christianity. Emmet Larkin suggests that the Catholic Church 'derived great advantage' from the Great Famine, identifying a 'devotional revolution' involving a transformation of religious structure and practice and a growing emphasis on sin among Catholics from the 1840s (Larkin 1976, 72; Larkin 1972, 195).

In the nineteenth century, the power of the Irish Catholic Church increased both institutionally and over popular practices. Archbishop Paul Cullen strengthened the internal structure and coherence of Catholicism in Ireland (Rafferty 2021, 155), evidenced in his calling of the Synod of Thurles in 1850 intended to standardise church administration, teachings, and practices and, beginning in 1829, in the surge in churches built (Barr 2018, 282). Smyth (1995a, 683) asserts that the Catholic Church sought both control of the Irish population and a strategic relationship with the British authorities, enabling a re-establishment of the English Catholic Church. In turn, the British government cooperated with the Catholic Church and its religious orders as a means of maintaining social control over the Irish population.

Additionally in the nineteenth century, several new Catholic religious congregations were created with the primary purpose of charitable work contributing to social welfare, childcare, education, and healthcare into the twentieth century (Smyth 1995a, 684). The majority of religious orders operated class-based internal hierarchies and were ostensibly under the control of a male bishop (Luddy 1995, 28, 32–5). The work of female religious organisations grew significantly by the start of the twentieth century (Luddy 1995, 23). The proliferation of religious orders played a significant role in the use of and reliance on closed institutions to address perceived social problems. Institutional Catholicism in the period concerning non-recent institutional abuses was consciously constructed and operated within a society struggling to address the impact and meaning of the profound loss and suffering of the Great Famine. It was also impacted by the competitive and proselytising relationship between Catholic and Protestant denominations and by the structural restrictions on land and legal status related to the Penal Laws. These features provide the context within which institutions emerged and persisted and non-recent institutional abuses occurred.

4. Structural Influences on Non-Recent Institutional Abuses in Partitioned Ireland

A range of factors existed on the island of Ireland during the time period concerning non-recent institutional abuses. These factors, each discussed in turn later, operated differently in RoI and NI and for Catholic and Protestant populations and institutions in each jurisdiction. The combination of these factors can function as the context in which state and church institutions operated and so appreciating the influence of these structural factors enables a contextually situated evaluation of the responsibilities of individuals, governments, churches, and society, which is explored throughout this book.

Nation and church-building

The Irish Free State began life amid widespread domestic unrest and severe economic difficulties after the Civil War in 1922. At this time, the Irish Catholic Church was a well-resourced organisation that enjoyed significant national infrastructure and personnel across the country. The Free State needed this infrastructure and the stability it represented to refute British claims that the Irish were unable to self-govern (Valiulis 2011, 574) and to demonstrate the national sovereignty of the newly formed Free State (McAlinden 2013, 204). The Catholic Church in turn sought to use laws regulating social morality, discussed later, to enable ongoing control and shaping of society aligned with its spiritual and moral teachings. However, Rafferty (2021, 156) notes that Catholicism 'developed no satisfactory intellectual framework about how the Church should relate to the state'. Instead, Rafferty (2021, 156) suggests that Catholic leadership and institutions developed a triumphalism which led it 'to insist that its existence and functions should take precedence over every other aspect of Irish life'.

In contrast, Protestant churches and institutions sought to engage differently in both the Free State and in NI, in which it retained links with the Protestant majority. After partition and the creation of NI, Ganiel (2008, 45–6) suggests that Calvinism provided Northern Protestants with a theological justification for legal and political power as 'a "chosen people," dutifully upholding God's laws and bringing order and civilization to the land'. In contrast, Catholic nationalists in NI objected to the foundation of Northern Ireland and wanted a united Ireland (McCormick 2009, 2). Catholic and Protestant institutions thus experienced radically different trajectories after the partition of the island but shared an interest in regulating poverty and morality, especially sexual morality, doubly focusing on the regulation of women and children.

Regulation of morality

Catholic and Protestant denominations in both RoI and NI were interested in the regulation of sexual morality. In RoI, Keating argues that both the Irish Free State and the Catholic Church were devoted to building a mythical Ireland as a paragon of Catholic nationhood (2004–6, 157–8). Inglis emphasises that the focus on sexual morality enabled a demonstration of moral superiority over the Protestant English and, as discussed later, also restricted inheritance for the farming class (2005, 23–4). McCarthy notes that women who transgressed public morality and gendered norms were seen as dangerous threats (2010, 162; see also Fischer 2016). A series of early official investigations in the Free State focused on social welfare and sexual morality: the Inquiry Regarding Venereal Disease (1925), the Committee on Evil Literature (1927), and the Commission on the Relief of the Sick and Destitute Poor Including the Insane Poor (1928) (Smith 2004, 208–9). Legislation that focused on sexual morality also followed the publication of these reports including the Censorship of Publications Act 1929, the Illegitimate Children (Affiliation Orders) Act 1930, the Legitimacy Act 1931, the Registration of Maternity Homes Act 1934, and the Dance Halls Act 1935 (Smith 2004, 208–9).

Significantly, in 1930 the Carrigan Committee was appointed by the Minister for Justice to examine legislative reform regarding sexual offences and sexual behaviour. Its broad terms of reference enabled it to function as 'an extended inquiry into the moral order of a new and independent state' (Finnane 2001, 519–20). Sexual offences against children, sex and 'illegitimate' children outside marriage, prostitution, and dancing in dance halls were all considered (Carrigan 1931, para C.10). The Carrigan Committee concluded that 'gross offences are rife throughout the country of a nature from which it [the Irish State] could formerly claim a degree of immunity that may perhaps have lulled it into a false state of security' (para C.18). It is notable that the Carrigan Committee report was never published or publicly debated and was suppressed by the Ministry for Justice which was concerned with its impact on the image of the Free State as morally pure (Kennedy, 2000; Finnane 2001, 519). Instead, a private committee of parliamentarians considered the report and consulted with the Catholic hierarchy. The result was the Criminal Law Amendment Act 1935, which banned the sale and importation of contraceptives, increased penalties for prostitution, and created new offences of brothel keeping and public indecency, targeting the visibility of non-procreative sex and sexuality.

In NI, McCormick (2009, 1) argues that there was 'considerable unity across the religious and political spectrum in relation to female sexuality'. McCormick (2009, 207) notes that despite its Protestant majority and links with the UK, on issues related to the regulation of female sexuality, in NI and RoI, '[b]oth governments saw their state as being morally superior to the British mainland . . . Women were seen as representing the communities, so their moral purity and good behaviour was essential to promote the image that was required.' As in RoI, the 'ideal woman' played a role in maintaining social stability and the identity of both unionist and nationalist communities in NI (McCormick 2009, 208). An emphasis on the regulation of sexual morality gave rise to restrictive access to contraception, abortion, and continued shaming and use of closed institutions for those who transgressed norms of sexual morality.

Poverty and the economy

The island of Ireland experienced sustained and intergenerational poverty and inequality within largely agrarian economies, contrasting with notable industrialisation in the majority Protestant province of Ulster. For O'Sullivan and O'Donnell (2012, 273), Raw economics rather than a concern with sexual morality ensured that many of the mothers of [illegitimate] children were incarcerated in various institutions for lengthy periods of time and their children adopted, fostered, institutionalised.' In their view, the structure of family life also impacted the rise of religious life in Ireland:

> Surplus sons and daughters largely drawn from farming communities entered religious life in their droves thereby providing a personnel resource that was cheap (vow of poverty) flexible and uncritical (vow of

> obedience) and sexually immature but morally certain (vow of chastity). As long as this source of recruitment remained plentiful the operation of a wide range of institutions could continue, at little direct cost to the state, and with the tacit support of families that saw the advantages of having a child or two enter religious life in terms that were both economic (fewer mouths to feed) and social (enhanced community standing). (O'Sullivan and O'Donnell 2012, 274)

From early in its creation, NI was subsidised by the British government, 'without which its ability to maintain similar health and welfare benefits to those in Britain would have been in doubt' (Privilege and Jones 2015, 34). Historically, NI maintained a strong basis in manufacturing and industry, with shipbuilding, textiles, and associated industries playing a large role (McCormick 2009, 2–3). However, due to industrial decline (Brownlow 2020), NI experienced lower incomes and higher unemployment than the rest of the UK for much of the twentieth century (Simpson 1983, 81). In addition, the economic impact of the conflict was enormous, with one suggestion that personal and property injuries and law and order costs amounted to £12 billion (Birnie and Hitchens 1999, 59, 150) and another study suggesting a 10% reduction in GDP (Dorsett 2013). Low standards of living and economic opportunity sustained and incentivised the continued use of closed institutions in a context of conservative fiscal policy, with particular additional impact of the conflict in NI.

Land

Land ownership had been a key site of conflict during British rule of Ireland (Ohlmeyer 2016). From 1850, after the Great Famine highlighted the risk of dividing land across families (Strassmann and Clarke 1998), family structure shifted to a 'stem family', where multiple generations lived in a single household but one family member inherited the land, with high levels of celibacy and marital fertility (Brennan 2004b, 96). Ferriter (2009, 19) identifies a range of factors that impacted land ownership around partition on the island: 'the changing rural class structure, a reluctance to subdivide larger farms, and the land war of the 1870s and 1880s which ultimately led to an almost universal shift to peasant proprietorship in the early twentieth century'. Dooley notes that in rural Ireland access to land was possibly a higher priority than political independence but one that was not addressed in the

Anglo-Irish Treaty 1921 (Dooley 2004, 177). Dooley (2004, 196) notes that the Land Commission, reconstituted after partition in the Land Act 1923, had a significant impact on Irish land ownership—moving 'over 14,500 farmers on to lands totalling over 382,000 acres'. Wills (2024, ch 4) highlights how the importance of retaining ownership of land holdings, such as farms, across generations provides a contextual understanding of why some families were reluctant to openly acknowledge 'illegitimate' children born 'out of wedlock', preferring instead to have the mother and baby institutionalised.

Class

Class on the island of Ireland has traditionally been understood as less explicit than in England and Wales (Whyte 1974, 648). British class influence on the island of Ireland, particularly in the nineteenth and early twentieth centuries, resulted in moral panic about sexual morality and a 'fetish for respectability' for the emerging middle classes on both islands (Ferriter 2009, 39). Such class trends were exacerbated in RoI after partition, with Ferriter (2009, 5) noting: 'In a state that became quite confessional, public condemnation seemed to be more pronounced than elsewhere, and sexual suspicion and class resentment made for a potent mix.'

Class dynamics played a particular role in the use of institutions, each discussed later. Industrial and reformatory schools were established to address and criminalise poverty in a context of economic recession, high fertility, and high infant mortality (CICA 2009, Vol 4, ch 3, 1). In workhouses, '[m]ost single women and children . . . would have been from very poor families, or they had fled from their families or been abandoned by them. Little is known about single women from middling/large farms or daughters of shopkeepers and other middle-class families' (CoI MBH 2021, ch 3, 7). Private orphanages tended to be subdivided on the basis of religion and social class (CoI MBH 2021, ch 3, 16). Mahood (2013) has argued that Magdalene Laundries sought to impose middle-class ideals and roles regarding sexual morality. The Mother and Baby Homes Commission noted that those institutions were operated by 'middle class women—either religious sisters or religiously minded women, who often lacked professional training in nursing, midwifery or child-care' (CoI MBH 2021, Executive Summary, 67). Unmarried mothers themselves were subject to particular class stratification. Women whose families could pay for their confinement spent less time in these institutions, leaving after the birth of their baby, whereas women whose stay was paid for by the State often remained on as 'workers' (CoI MBH 2021, Executive Summary, 3) Further, the 1927 Commission on the Relief of the Sick and Destitute Poor distinguished between 'classes' of unmarried mothers, distinguishing between first-time unmarried mothers, capable of being restored to respectability, and unmarried mothers of multiple children, who had to be especially contained (1927, para 228).

Regarding NI, McCormick notes that rescue homes were 'an important disciplinary tool for working class families, not simply a middle-class construction to impose middle-class values. Working class parents could remove troublesome daughters who generated concern or had the potential to bring disgrace to their family. The homes could not have continued to function without the support of working-class families who placed their daughters in them' (2009, 59). In such institutions in NI, as in RoI, there was also a stratification of unmarried mothers, with particular condemnation for those with more than one child (McCormick 2009, 46). In workhouses in NI, McCormick suggests that 'lower-working-class women who had no obvious occupation, who had illegitimate children, or whose appearance or companions were deemed unsuitable, were classed as prostitutes by the workhouse authorities', a majority of whom were Catholic (2009, 16, 18). Class thus structured the societies of both RoI and NI and contributed to intersectional hierarchies of victimhood and victimisation (see further Chapter 3).

Migration

Emigration has long been a dominant response to experiences of poverty, violence, and lack of opportunity across the island of Ireland, with the impact of the Great Famine particularly shaping patterns of emigration (Hatton and Williamson 1993). Emigration took particular forms for unmarried mothers and others subject to institutionalisation on the island. As noted by the Mother and Baby Home Commission:

> Emigration was a normal part of life for young women and men, so an announcement that a woman was travelling to work in Britain would not attract comment or intrusive questions. Many putative fathers also emigrated to avoid an affiliation order, pressure to marry, or the opprobrium

of the women's family and perhaps the wider community. (CoI MBH 2021, ch 7, 42)

Garrett (2000) identified a significant migration of unmarried mothers from RoI to England in post-partition RoI and an equally noteworthy process of their repatriation by Catholic charitable organisations and religious orders fearful of the proselytising effect of migration to England. The report of the Commission on the Relief of the Sick and Destitute Poor (1927, 73), noted that 'better organization . . . of the machinery for dealing with expectant unmarried mothers' would reduce 'the number impelled to cross to Great Britain'. The 1931 Carrigan Committee also considered the issue of migration of unmarried mothers to Britain, but Garrett (2000, 337) notes that 'No connection was made, however, between the migration of these expectant mothers and the punitive and semi-penal regimes they faced had they remained inside the Free State. Indeed, . . . two inspectors of boarded-out children were . . . calling for even greater powers to detain unmarried mothers in institutional settings.' Emigration was at once an economic necessity for some but also a potential escape from a shaming and restrictive social morality.

Law enforcement

Finnane emphasises that the national police, An Garda Síochána, played a significant role in shaping Irish society (2001, 520). Numerous investigations demonstrate the historical deference of the police to the Catholic Church regarding child sex abuse allegations (see eg Murphy et al 2005, 54, 223; CICA 2009, para 1.93). The McAleese inquiry regarding Magdalene Laundries found 8% of placements of women in Laundries were as part of the criminal justice system, including on the basis of remand, probation, by the courts, prison services, or Gardaí (IDC 2013, ch 9, paras 3–5, 304). In addition, women were also placed in Laundries arising from an adjourned or suspended sentence or as a step-down facility from prison or informally placed by members of An Garda Síochána for unclear reasons (IDC 2013, ch 9, 206).

In NI, the police played a distinctive role regarding institutions and abuses, owing to the largely sectarian character of the then Royal Ulster Constabulary (RUC). O'Rourke and Swain suggest that as a highly Protestant and militarised institution the RUC was ill-equipped to address sexual violence during the conflict, especially in light of its treatment of Catholic–Nationalist communities and a legitimate fear of reprisals for those who cooperated with the police force (2017, 1308). McCormick and O'Connell's (2021, 39) study on Mother and Baby Homes and Magdalene Laundries in NI confirms that 7% of entries to Good Shepherd homes were due to police intervention and suggests 'a degree of negotiation between the police and the Good Shepherd Sisters to identify the legal issues involved in individual cases'. In addition, the conflict saw an increased use of some institutions by police and other statutory agencies: 'Viewed as a place of safety by statutory and other agencies, a number of girls and women deemed to be in a crisis situation arising from the Troubles [conflict] were be sent to St Mary's Derry' (McCormick and O'Connell 2021, 258).

Historical failings of the police in NI in responding to allegations of institutional abuse are evidenced by the investigation of the Kincora Boys' Home by the Historical Institutional Abuse Inquiry, which found that the historical RUC investigation in 1974 was 'inept, inadequate and far from thorough' (HIA Inquiry 2017, ch 3, para 383). In several cases of institutional abuse allegations in NI there were delays in disclosure to law enforcement. The impact of these delays on modern criminal justice responses to non-recent abuses are explored in Chapter 4.

Media

In RoI, Keating notes that the leadership of the Catholic Church sought to ensure that any sexual immorality was hidden from the Irish public through control of the national media (2004–6, 158–9). The Censorship of Film Act 1923 and Censorship of Publications Act 1929 sought to control the media and communications landscape. Keating suggests that censorship 'was symptomatic of a lack of trust in the Irish people' on matters of morality (2004–6, 160). For example, one of the primary purposes behind the 1929 Act was to restrict information on contraception (Daly 2006, 574). According to Keating, the use of censorship showed that Church and State mobilised to protect their imagined nation of Celtic Catholic purity (2004–6, 160). The early 1960s coincided with the creation of the first Irish television channel, RTÉ, in 1961. Inglis (1998, 93) concludes that 'It was the media that broke the tradition of not criticizing the Church . . . that forced [it] into giving a public account of itself . . . and brought to an end the long nineteenth century of Irish Catholicism.'

The traditional print media in NI reflected the sectarian divisions in the region (Rolston 1991). As a result, law and order and justice issues were highly sectarian and partisan in nature (Bromley 1997). However, Greer suggests that sexual crimes offered an exception that transcended sectarian politics (2001; 2003). As explored further in Section 6, the media in both jurisdictions subsequently played a key role in publicising and legitimating victim/survivor allegations of abuse and assisted in the initiation of justice campaigns.

Family

Historically, the Irish family was the central unit of social organisation rather than the individual. Brennan notes that up to the seventeenth century, Irish marriages were subject to easy divorce and made no distinction in law between legitimate and illegitimate children (Brennan 2004b, 96). Regarding family life, O'Sullivan and O'Donnell (2012, 270) suggest that 'the Catholic Church reflected and reinforced the underlying values and beliefs of rural Ireland rather than imposing a new normative system'. However, family also played an important normative role in the newly independent RoI, symbolising 'Irish social organisation in opposition to English culture' (Nash 1993, 39). Narrow normative roles for the family were resisted throughout the twentieth century by Irish feminists and activists, particularly where the construction of the family led to the legal prohibition on divorce, contraception, abortion, and homosexuality (Clancy 1990).

Families both facilitated entry into and were forcibly separated by the network of institutions considered later. The Ryan Report noted that two of the abusive elements of the industrial and reformatory school regime were family separation and restrictions on tracing information (CICA 2009, Executive Summary, 13). The report also notes that 'Parents, relatives and others knew that children were being abused as a result of disclosures and their observation of marks and injuries' (14) but that contemporary complaints by families to the school authorities, the Gardaí, the Department of Education, health boards, priests of the parish, and others about the abuse of children were not always acted upon.

The McAleese Report identified that 10.5% of women known to enter Magdalene Laundries did so through referral by family members (IDC 2013, ch 18, para 13). The report noted a range of circumstances for family referral:

> as a means of disciplining young girls; or to provide for girls or women with physical disabilities, with mental or psychiatric illness, with intellectual disabilities and special needs or for those in advanced age. In other cases, girls or women were placed in Magdalen Laundries by their families following family disputes, as a result of abuse or neglect in the home; or after having been rejected by their families for having a child outside of marriage. (IDC 2013ch 18, para 16)

The Mother and Baby Homes Commission controversially concluded:

> Women who gave birth outside marriage were subject to particularly harsh treatment. Responsibility for that harsh treatment rests mainly with the fathers of their children and their own immediate families. It was supported by, contributed to, and condoned by, the institutions of the State and the Churches. However, it must be acknowledged that the institutions under investigation provided a refuge–a harsh refuge in some cases–when the families provided no refuge at all. (CoI MBH 2021, Executive Summary, 1)

It is in this regard that O'Sullivan and O'Donnell consider the family unit as part of the 'network of coercive confinement', discussed later. For Wills, while families may have kept secrets about institutionalisation to protect their reputation and those of their loved one, it is also true that 'the rhetoric of the Irish family was a smokescreen for the relative absence of the family as a private sphere of emotional and affective ties' (2024, 141).

McCormick and Earner-Byrne agree that despite differences between RoI and NI, both jurisdictions viewed the family as a conservative, rural, Christian, and patriarchal social unit (Earner-Byrne 2018, 659; McCormick 2009, 8). Similar to RoI, the non-martial family—the single mother—was subject to significant social stigma and exclusion in NI (Crossman 2013, 182; Purdue 2017, 89). Earner-Byrne notes that religious denomination continued to shape families in NI, with suggestions of difficulties of intermarriage even between Protestant denominations, and that by 2001 only 10% of marriages were inter-religious (2018, 656).

Families thus play a complex and contested role regarding non-recent institutional abuses in both jurisdictions on the island. In some instances, families supported or enabled the institutionalisation of women and children, unwilling or unable to meet those individuals' needs. In other instances, families were separated against their will and prevented and frustrated in reconnecting after institutionalisation or other interventions, such as foster care or adoption (see further Chapter 3). This complexity raises but does not resolve the question of the responsibility of families for non-recent institutional abuses (see further Chapter 9).

5. State, Church, and Institutions

In post-partition RoI, Catholic institutions formed a clear part of the nation-building efforts pursuing an ideal, Catholic Ireland and agreed and cooperated with the Irish State in the provision of health, social, and welfare services. In NI, McCormick and O'Connell suggest that after partition the Northern Irish government was 'content to allow religious and voluntary agencies to continue to provide services' regarding health and welfare (2021, 47). In both jurisdictions, closed institutions were operated by Protestant churches, Catholic religious orders, and both statutory and voluntary organisations and included refuges for the poor, provision for education and health, and residential institutions for women and children. In doing so, Ireland was not unique in othering and institutionalising vulnerable groups of people (Wise 2024) but perhaps distinct in combining the structural influences of State and Church, as outlined in this chapter, in the context of these institutions. In addition, comparatively, RoI in particular had a marked increase in twentieth-century institutionalisation when elsewhere in the world institutions were closing or in decline (O'Donnell and O'Sullivan 2012, 257–8). This range of institutions has been described as a 'network of coercive confinement' (O'Donnell and O'Sullivan 2012) or 'the architecture of containment' (Smith 2007) and should extend to include the provision of nascent social care in the foster and adoption systems.

The Irish Poor Laws and workhouses

The Poor Relief (Ireland) Act 1838 established 130 workhouses throughout Ireland, designed and operated in a manner to deter all but the most destitute from seeking admission and to stigmatise those who entered (Crossman 2009a, 11). Entry into a workhouse remained discretionary and dependent on a capacity of approximately 100,000. As a result, the Poor Law was incapable of dealing with the Great Famine when workhouses were filled to more than double their intended capacity (Crossman 2009a, 11). Lucey (2021,

794) notes that the poor law system had colonial functions: 'the network of workhouses and institutional relief embodied the administrative surveillance, systematic state centralization and moral regulation of the Irish poor'. By the early twentieth century, there were concerns regarding the suitability of workhouses to address the needs of the elderly, the sick, children, and those deemed insane (Geary 2018, 19–20). The Vice-Regal Commission on Poor Law Reform 1906 recommended the replacement of workhouses with appropriate accommodation for the poor who were sick. The Royal Commission on the Poor Laws and Relief of Distress 1909 concurred and recommended the abolition of workhouses and the introduction of specific institutions for different social groups.

Lucey (2021, 797) notes that reform of the Poor Law was a key element of nationalist criticisms of British colonialism. The first Dáil Éireann called for a 'native, sympathetic scheme' to replace it. It is notable that the need for a replacement for this system did not extend to other institutions, such as industrial schools or Magdalene Laundries which were operated by religious orders more aligned with the Irish nation. After independence, the Local Government (Temporary Provisions) Act 1923 abolished the Poor Law system and transferred its functions to boards of health and public assistance. In the late 1920s, workhouses were reclassified as county homes but did not change in any significant respect (O'Sullivan and O'Donnell 2012, 7). The report of the Commission on the Relief of the Sick and Destitute Poor (1927, 17) found most institutions in poor condition and were 'not a fit and proper place' to accommodate their residents. County homes were operated by a combination of religious orders and local councils.

In 1949, the RoI government established an inter-departmental committee to consider the reconstruction and replacement of county homes, which suggested little had changed since the 1927 report. The 1949 report, discussed in public in detail in a 1951 governmental white paper, noted that county homes housed ' " 'mental defectives", blind, deaf, casuals [part-time labourers] and 450 unmarried mothers and 829 children' (Department of Health 1951, 10). It recommended that specialist institutions be used instead and noted in respect of unmarried mothers that they were usually retained for a two-year period, after which the child was boarded out and they were permitted to leave (13). The scale of women and children in county homes is still only estimated, with the Mother and Baby Home Commission suggesting that 'It is likely that there were a further 25,000 unmarried mothers and a larger number of children in the county homes which were not investigated' by the Commission (CoI MBH 2021, Executive Summary, para 1).

In NI, little money was spent on poor relief in the late nineteenth and early twentieth centuries. Lucey (2021, 796) suggests that this was a result of 'a greater ethos of Protestant "self-help", often informed by sectarian tensions, and fears over fuelling inward migration from rural to urban regions'. The Poor Law system facilitated religious and social discrimination towards Catholics (Convery 2014, 259). After partition, the 1927 report of the Departmental Commission on Local Government Administration in NI recommended the abolition of workhouses and the establishment of a hospital system and homes for the relief of the able bodied. While six workhouses had become district hospitals by 1929 in Antrim (Lucey 2021, 802–4), remaining workhouses existed in NI until 1948 when the National Assistance Act 1948 and the National Insurance Act 1946 ended the Poor Laws. Lucey (2021, 801) notes that the remaining workhouses were low grade and unmodernised, leading to a high rate of deaths. Purdue (2017, 72) notes that the sectarian segregation of the poorest parts of Belfast created 'particular issues for the administration and experience of the Poor Law'. In this context of competitive and sectarian voluntary organisations, the Belfast workhouse represented 'the most easily accessible option for people seeking relief for either temporary or more permanent destitution' (Purdue 2017, 78). Although still a place of harsh and bleak conditions, the workhouse was not associated with 'rescue and reform' nor any particular religious denomination (Purdue 2017, 90). The Poor Law formed part of the colonial administration of Ireland and was adapted differently in RoI and NI after partition, reflecting the difference in demographics and welfare priorities in both jurisdictions.

Education

Prior to partition, in Ireland almost all national (primary) schools, established from 1827 onwards and publicly funded, were denominational schools controlled by the churches. From the eighteenth century, the Catholic Church had been lobbying the British government regarding the education of Catholic children in Catholic schools. The Stanley letter of 1831 established the Irish national school system with a distinctive structure for national schools: the government paid 'for the system of national education but did not manage it or administer it at the point of delivery: this function was left to the local manager, usually (invariably in the case of Roman Catholic schools) a cleric, and usually appointed by the local Bishop who was the patron of the school' (Walsh 2016, 9–11).[1] Rafferty (2021, 144) notes that 'unlike the state, the Catholic Church regarded education as supremely a religious exercise', one the Church appeared to be unwilling to share with the State. This was despite the supposed regulation by the State under the remit of the Department of Education, established by the Ministers and Secretaries Act 1924, with responsibility for primary and secondary schools as well as reformatories and industrial schools, as discussed later.

Early in the nineteenth century, a network of Catholic schools was established by newly founded religious congregations, including the Presentation Sisters (in 1791), the Sisters of Mercy (in 1828), and the Irish Christian Brothers (in 1802) (Brennan 2004a, 86). The Intermediate Education Act 1924 affirmed the existing denominational educational system for the Irish Free State and limited governmental operational control of education (Brennan 2004a, 87). However, the introduction of widespread free secondary education in 1967 in RoI diminished reliance on entry into religious life as a means of achieving higher education (Walsh 2012). Without a national and island-wide investigation, it is difficult at the time of writing to identify the extent of non-recent child sexual abuse in day schools. In 2022–3, the Irish Department of Education paid out an estimated €31m to survivors of sexual abuse in day schools, with approximately 40–50 survivors receiving payment from a government-mandated scheme, discussed further in Chapter 6.[2]

After partition, in NI the Education Act 1930 affirmed the separate denominational provision of education (Farren 1992). Protestant churches transferred their schools to State control and funding but remained represented in school management. In contrast, Catholic schools, known as voluntary schools, remained totally managed by the Church and religious orders, with costs and capital grants paid by the State (O'Callaghan and Lundy 2013). Later, State schools became 'controlled schools' and the Catholic schools became 'maintained schools'. Akenson notes that the early twentieth-century evidences a 'seemingly irresistible demand for

[1] See *O'Keeffe v Hickey* [2008] IESC 72, 10. The case concerned whether the Irish State could be held vicariously liable for the sexual assault of the plaintiff by her school principal or for the inaction of the manager of the school who failed to respond to a prior complaint in 1971.

[2] E O'Kelly, 'Dept to pay around €31m to survivors of sexual abuse in primary schools', RTE.ie, https://www.rte.ie/news/2021/1013/1253468-school-abuse/, 19 March 2024.

segregated schooling' in NI (1973, 193), deriving from both religious leaders and families and doing little to neutralise prejudice and hostility between unionist and nationalist communities (200). The Education Reform (NI) Order 1989 transferred responsibility for all Catholic-maintained schools to a statutory body, the Council for Catholic Maintained Schools (CCMS). In NI, as in RoI, the provision and governance of education involves both State and religious institutions and actors and underlines the responsibility of both church and state to address abuses in those settings. Media analysis indicates periodic allegations of sexual abuse within Northern Irish schools[3] but no province-wide investigation into the phenomenon has yet been established.

Industrial and reformatory schools

Reformatory schools were established by the Reformatory Schools (Ireland) Act 1858 for children found guilty of criminal offences. Barnes (1989, 85–6) states that these schools were intended to train children 'to be capable of supporting themselves by honest labour' and to reform the child's character away from their family's bad influence. Under the 1858 Act, Catholic provision of reformatories was 'organised and speedy', leading to similar concern from Protestants about the use of the legislation as a means of proselytism (Barnes 1989, 33).

Unlike British legislation for industrial schools, the Industrial Schools (Ireland) Act 1868 provided for denominational reformatories and industrial schools in Ireland to provide for children who had been neglected, orphaned, or abandoned. The Catholic Church had argued against the application of the British legislation to Ireland, suggesting that it could give rise to proselytism (Convery 2014, 256). Under the 1868 Act, Catholic and Protestant children had to be committed to separate schools. The majority were operated by religious orders of the Catholic Church but some Protestant schools were also in operation. The 1858 and 1868 Acts were replaced by the Children Act 1908, which provided that each school was to be independently managed, though subject to State inspection and funding and agreed rules and regulations including on the administration of

[3] See eg 'Inquiry into alleged abuse at top NI school', *The Irish Times*, 2 June 2004; C O'Neill, '"He made me strip naked and put the dress on"—New abuse allegations at leading Northern Ireland school', *Belfast Telegraph*, 6 March 2022.

discipline and punishment (CICA 2009, Vol 1, ch 2, paras 2.16–2.18; CICA 2009, Vol 1, ch 4, para 4.02) The State's financial contribution was based on a per capita grant for each child detained, a system that created incentives to fill all available places.

Industrial and reformatory schools operated in both RoI and NI. In RoI, from 1936 to 1970, 37,000 children and young persons entered Irish industrial schools (O'Sullivan 2014, 202). A 1936 governmental report into the schools expressed concern about the large number of children in care and their inadequate education, support, and stigmatisation (Commission of Inquiry into the Reformatory and Industrial School System 1936) but implementation of its recommendations was 'inconsistent and intermittent' (CICA 2009, Vol 4, ch 1, para 1.02). A 1970 report recommended the closure of the residential school system, concluding that its rules and regulations did not conform to modern standards of childcare (Kennedy 1970). It was not until the Child Care Act 1991 and Children Act 2001 that the residential school system was fully reformed in RoI. In 2009, the Ryan Report concluded that physical, sexual, and emotional abuse were features of those institutions that operated in a severe and oppressive manner. The failures of the industrial and reformatory school system were 'exacerbated by the way it was operated by the Congregations that owned and managed the schools' (CICA 2009, Executive Summary, 19). In addition, the deference of the Department of Education to the religious congregations ensured that the statutory system of inspection from the department 'was fundamentally flawed and incapable of being effective' (Executive Summary, 19). For Keating (2004–6, 156), industrial and reformatory schools ensured that 'the Irish Catholic church's ability to morally herd the Irish people, while the State sought to protect itself from social unrest and poverty and the derision of foreigners, especially the formerly colonial power Britain'.

Industrial and reformatory schools were also established in NI. In 1922 with the partition of Ireland, there were only five industrial or reformatory schools still operational (Fahy 1942). In 1925, the Ministry for Home Affairs took control of Protestant institutions (Convery 2014, 259). By 1949, there were fewer than 300 children in industrial schools in NI, compared to over 6,000 in RoI (Government of NI, 1950). The Children and Young Persons Act (NI) 1950 replaced reformatory and industrial schools with the term 'training schools' in which children could be detained for welfare and/or justice reasons for indeterminate periods (Moore and Convery 2008, 80). Under the Criminal Justice (Children) (NI) Order 1998, NI's four training schools (Lisnevin, St Joseph's, St Patrick's, and Rathgael) were renamed juvenile justice centres (JJCs). While these schools persisted until recent decades in NI, they should be understood in the context of the use of other residential institutions for children.

Other residential institutions for children

In both RoI and NI, other institutions for children operated in the nineteenth and twentieth centuries, including orphanages, residential children's homes, schools for children with physical or intellectual disabilities, and hospitals in which children were resident. Many of these were sites of alleged abuse and were the objects of state-administered redress (see Chapter 6). The shared feature across these diverse institutional contexts is that a state public body had a regulatory or inspection function for their operation. On this basis, it could be questioned whether the state in both jurisdictions knew or should have known about allegations of abuse of children.

When the conflict in NI resulted in direct rule of the region from Westminster, local government lost its role regarding social services, including education, which was transferred to the Education Board (Pinkerton 1998). In the absence of the sustained use of industrial or reformatory schools in NI, other forms of residential care for children were employed, where abuses also occurred. The 2017 Hart Inquiry investigated a range of residential children's institutions where there were allegations of abuse, including institutions operated by local authorities, juvenile justice institutions that were the successors to industrial and reformatory schools as outlined earlier, and voluntary homes operated by both secular and Christian (Catholic and Protestant) organisations. Indeed, as discussed further in Chapter 5, the Hart Inquiry documented the systemic nature of abuse (physical, sexual, emotional, and neglect) within residential childcare institutions in NI.

Magdalene Laundries

Magdalene Laundries existed across European countries and others such as the United States, Canada, and Australia (Gallen 2023a, 37–8). Magdalene Laundries operated in Ireland between 1795 and 1996 and were run largely by religious orders of Catholic nuns (IDC 2013, 17). Magdalene Laundries started in nineteenth-century England among both Catholic and Anglican orders of nuns (Kollar 2004) and were prompted by the Contagious Diseases Act 1864 in an attempt to control the spread of disease caused by women in prostitution (Mahood 2012). While in England the Magdalene Laundries sought to reintegrate women into society, Irish reformers thought that 'it was impossible to allow such a woman back into society without the expectation that she would again fall' (McCarthy 2010, 149). Luddy (2007, 93) records at least 41 Laundries established in Ireland by the beginning of the twentieth century. After 1922, four Catholic female religious congregations (the Sisters of Mercy, the Sisters of Our Lady of Charity, the Sisters of Charity, and the Good Shepherd Sisters) retained Magdalene Laundries in Ireland.

Approximately 10,012 women are known to have been detained in a Magdalene Laundry from the foundation of the Irish State in 1922 until the closure of the last Laundry in 1996, though victim/survivor groups suggest that these figures are an underestimate (McGettrick et al 2021, 115). Smith (2007, xiv) suggests '[i]n a society where even the faintest whiff of scandal threatened the respectability of the normative Irish family, the Magdalene asylum existed as a place to contain and punish the threatening embodiment of instability'. In a Magdalene Laundry, women and girls were required to work unpaid. Supervision of women by nuns, which took the form of daily prayers, penance, and physical, verbal, and emotional abuse including denial of identity, was also reported (IDC 2013, chs 19, 20). Killian notes that while the Irish State used the Laundries as one mechanism to support its new nationalist and Catholic identity, it did so:

> through a complex but unarticulated set of relationships with the institutions in which the logic of the price was consistently denied in favour *of ex gratia* payments, donations, top-ups and pocket money. Artfully unsystematic arrangements were put in place between private organisations and successive governments, and these served the state in providing distance between the daily lived experiences of some citizens and its responsibilities towards them. (2015, 29)

In NI, Laundries operated from 1867 and the last of four Magdalene Laundries closed in 1984, with 3,000 women admitted since 1922 (McCormick and O'Connell 2021, 11). Based on testimonies of women residents and the empirical research noted earlier, it can be argued that Magdalene Laundries represented a clear attempt to use the mechanisms of closed institutions to enforce a gendered sexual and religious morality on women and girls.

Mother and baby institutions

State and church in Ireland had long viewed unmarried mothers as a particular social problem (Luddy 2011, 110–11; Crossman 2009b, 40). After partition, the government in RoI and religious orders established mother and baby institutions to address a perceived moral and perhaps practical crisis involving unmarried mothers, who were framed as both sinners and damaging to the reputation of the newly independent State (Kennedy 2001, 145) and who had a need for practical support. According to the 2021 Mother and Baby Homes Commission Report, there were about 56,000 unmarried mothers and about 57,000 children in the mother and baby institutions and county homes investigated by the Commission (CoI MBH 2021, Executive Summary, 2). A total of about 9,000 (15% of all) children died in the institutions under investigation. Burke (2020, 218) notes the explicitly proselytising nature of some of the few Protestant mother and baby institutions in RoI.

In NI, four mother and baby institutions (Mater Dei, Hopedene, Marianville, and Marianvale) were established in Belfast and Newry and it is estimated that between 1922 and 1990 over 10,500 women entered mother and baby institutions in NI, with an undocumented number of single mothers entering workhouses (McCormick and O'Connell 2021, 22). In contrast to RoI, in NI 'mothers and babies rarely stayed more than a couple of months following a birth. Mothers left at the same time as their baby, whether the baby was to be adopted, fostered, placed in an institution, or if mother and baby left together' (McCormick and O'Connell 2021, 60). Mother and baby institutions on both parts of the island supported a gendered sexual and religious morality through adoption and family separation.

Healthcare

The historical provision of healthcare on the island of Ireland is intimately linked to the Poor Laws and the creation of workhouses. In response to the Great Famine, the 1851 Medical Charities Act established nationwide workhouse and dispensary systems that were funded from the poor rates and administered by the Poor Law Commission, leading to greater state involvement and centralisation (Geary 2018, 18). In turn, the Poor Law (Amendment) Act 1862 officially opened workhouse hospitals to the non-destitute sick (Geary 2018, 10). The Local Government (Ireland) Act 1898 allowed local authorities to convert workhouses into district hospitals. However, by 1919 only one conversion had taken place (Lucey 2021, 796). After partition, the development of the hospital infrastructure built on the remaining workhouse network. Geary (2018, 22–3) notes that this reform separated public medical services from the relief of the poor but retained the involvement of religious orders in healthcare (Breathnach 2022, 86) and was subject to a significant lack of investment.

Hospitals are significant in non-recent institutional abuses either as sites of direct abuses, such as child sexual abuse, coercive adoption, or symphysiotomy, or as sites of referral to other institutional contexts of abuse. Between 1922–70, five Magdalene Laundries in RoI constituted components of the public health system as 'extern institutions', meaning that although privately operated they 'were approved for maintenance of people who qualified for public assistance' (IDC 2013, ch 11, paras 36–114). Laundries also received significant referrals from the Irish health system (IDC 2013, ch 11). Mother and baby institutions additionally constituted part of the Irish healthcare system, receiving funding and inspection from the post-partition government's Hospital Commission and inspectors of the Department of Local Government and Public Health/Department of Health (CoI MBH 2021, Executive Summary, paras 25–6).

In NI, workhouse infirmaries were the largest hospital network. On partition, there were 26 workhouses with infirmaries functioning as 'mixed institutions in which the elderly, chronically ill, young and disabled poor were relieved' (Lucey 2021, 794). After partition, responsibility for health was transferred to a Ministry for Home Affairs, while daily functions were exercised by local authorities and councils (Privilege and Jones 2015, 34). In 1927, the Northern Irish Departmental Commission on Local Government Administration recommended that all workhouse infirmaries be replaced by district hospitals, ending the link between the Poor Law and medical care. However, this would not take place until the 1940s (Lucey 2021, 795). The Health Services Act 1948 introduced the National Health Service, a nationalised, universal, and free health service funded from general taxation. McCormick and O'Connell (2021, 39, 190) note that existing records show acute medical hospitals and psychiatric hospitals as locations where some women and children were placed after a period in a Magdalene Laundry or mother and baby institution or as the location from which women were referred to those institutions (67, 209). Private maternity homes in NI may have been used by women from RoI who, as non-residents in NI, would have been unable to access NHS hospitals (McCormick and O'Connell 2021, 88). This is also indicative of the largely under-explored cross-border aspects of institutionalisation and abuses.

Psychiatric hospitals

Brennan demonstrates that the Irish public asylum system, established in 1817 and operating until the close of the twentieth century, was a significant physical and social feature of Irish communities. He concludes that the rate of asylum incarceration in Ireland was the highest of all international comparators (2015, 1). There was little involvement of religious organisations in the establishment or operation of the Irish asylum system due to the establishment of the asylum system in 1817 predating Catholic emancipation in Ireland in 1829 (2015, 64).

There were two entry ways to the psychiatric hospital system. First, family members of an individual could apply directly for their admission. Second, the Dangerous Lunatics Act 1838 provided for emergency admissions but became the primary way in which individuals were incarcerated (Walsh 2022, 119). A large number of those held in psychiatric hospitals were admitted through the use of judicial warrants and classed as 'dangerous lunatics'[4] (O'Sullivan and O'Donnell 2012, 11). Finnane (1996) has argued that this administrative mechanism allowed the families of committed individuals to avoid any direct financial liability for their care, who instead became the responsibility of the county. The Act offered broad powers to non-professionals to accuse others of insanity, with non-expert Justices of Peace empowered to make the determination of sanity (Walsh 2022, 120).

The Lunacy Act 1845 provided for a system of basic requirements for asylums and regulated a system of inspections and reports. The Commission of Inquiry into Mental Illness (1966) concluded that a large number of asylums were unsuitable in design and lacked the facilities necessary for the proper treatment of patients. For Brennan (2015, 91), asylum admission

[4] Lunacy (Ireland) Act 1867, s 10.

may have had 'little or nothing to do with the mental state of the individual admitted. Insanity was a vague, changing and all encapsulating concept which could be applied to most social difficulties so as to facilitate and rationalise the admission of a family member to an asylum.'

In NI, at partition the government inherited six asylums confining over 4,000 people, administered by local councils (Prior 1993, 324). Even in 1921, these institutions were overcrowded and needed modernisation. In the absence of political will for greater expenditure, the ethos in NI remained one of confinement. In 1948, the Health Services Act (NI) established a Ministry of Health and Local Government, which was obliged to promote services to improve physical and mental health. The Act integrated the asylums into the general hospital system under the control of Northern Ireland Hospitals Authority (NIHA). In addition, the Mental Health Act (NI) 1948 abolished judicial involvement in hospital admissions (Prior 1993, 327), distinguishing NI from RoI in this period and resulting in greater expenditure in the modernisation of mental healthcare provision. There has been no sustained investigation of non-recent abuse allegations in psychiatric institutions in either jurisdiction.

Foster care and 'boarding out'

The Irish Poor Law (Amendment) Act 1862 gave powers to 'board out' children up to five years of age. The Infant Life Protection Act 1897 created and obliged inspectors to monitor the care of boarded-out children. The 1862 Act empowered boards of guardians to place orphans and deserted children 'out to nurse', which after legislative amendments in 1898 was extendable until the child was 15 years old, based on the view that workhouses were unsuitable places to raise children (Crossman 2009b, 60). The Children Act 1908 created regulations for the inspection of boarded-out children. Local authorities were required to inspect homes where children were located via the appointment of infant protection officers.

The boarding-out system was affirmed in the Irish Free State under the County Boards of Health (Assistance) Order 1924 and in the Public Assistance Act 1939 with the powers of placing children transferred to the Department of Local Government and Public Health and requiring ministerial consent to have children boarded out in towns or villages unless the child was an orphan or deserted. As a result, the children of unmarried mothers could only be boarded out with ministerial consent (CoI

MBH 2021, ch 11, para 11.20). The system was continued in the Health Act 1953 and in the Boarding Out of Children Regulations 1954, which also prohibited the placement of a child with someone not of the same religion. The Mother and Baby Homes Commission identified mixed experiences of those fostered. Some were cared for, others were 'grossly neglected; some were required to carry out work or caring duties that were inappropriate to their age, and some experienced appalling living and sleeping arrangements' (CoI MBH 2021, ch 11, para 11.2). The report notes that the evidence regarding foster care is 'scant' (paras 11.141–11.142).

In NI, the Children Act 1908 remained in force until 1950 and was the shared basis for addressing the foster or boarding-out system in that period (McColgan 1989, 79). In 1950, the Children and Young Persons Act (NI) provided that residential care was to be provided for children only when 'it is not practicable or desirable for the time being to make arrangements for boarding out'.[5] The 1950 Act was supported by statutory rules and orders establishing procedures for welfare authority oversight of the boarding-out system (McColgan 1989, 80). McColgan (1989, 80) notes that voluntary homes rarely arranged for boarding out, suggesting that this was due to the boarding-out scheme's requirement for fostering the child 'within easily travelling distance so that the mother could maintain contact and keep direct responsibility for the child's upbringing'. In turn, the Children and Young Persons Act (NI) 1968 affirmed the need for the approval of households for boarding out, primarily that the child would be placed with a family of the same religious background. The Children (Northern Ireland) Order 1995 modernised the foster-care system, moving from a criminal justice to childcare and protection paradigm (Kelly and Coulter 1997). There has been no sustained and in-depth investigation of abuses within the foster/boarding-out system in either jurisdiction.

Adoption

In Ireland, adoption functioned as a key site of nation- and religion-building, shaping 'ideal' families and enabling both Catholic and Protestant denominations to proselytise and to resist the efforts of proselytism of the other denomination. Prior to partition, illegal birth registrations were

[5] The Children and Young Persons (Boarding Out) Regulations (Northern Ireland) 1950, s 4.

criminalised under the Births and Deaths Registration Act 1874, where a birth certificate is falsified to register a child as having been born to his or her adoptive parents.

After partition, adoption was unregulated in RoI until the Adoption Act 1952, which criminalised the provision of false information to the Adoption Board. Even after the 1952 Act, illegal adoptions persisted. The Commission into Mother and Baby Homes documents evidence of illegal birth registration and adoption practices from the 1950s and 1960s (CoI MBH 2021, ch 32, paras 32.393–32.395). In 2018, the Child and Family Agency (Tusla) advised the Department of Children and Youth Affairs that at least 126 children adopted through St Patrick's Guild Adoption Society had been subject to an illegal birth registration (O'Mahony 2021, 2). A 2019 independent review commissioned by the Minister for Children reviewed a sample of records held by Tusla and the Adoption Authority of Ireland and concluded that from this sample up to 20,000 adoption records could potentially relate to cases of illegal birth registration. The Independent Reviewer report also noted that up to 50,000 adoption records remain in private ownership and that it was 'possible that there might be a higher level of irregularity occurring within the private sector' (Reynolds 2019, 53).

In 1929, the Adoption of Children Act (NI) mirrored the English and Welsh Adoption Act 1926 by providing for legal adoption. The Adoption of Children Act (NI) was amended in 1950 to provide a basic state adoption service and the Adoption (Northern Ireland) Order 1987 built on reforms in England and Wales in the Adoption Act 1976 and the Report of the Children and Young Persons Review Group on the Adoption of Children in Northern Ireland (1982). A 2018 BBC documentary evidenced a practice of illegal adoptions from Northern Irish mother and baby institutions operated by the Good Shepherd Sisters across the border to RoI and abroad. The extent of illegal adoptions in this context and non-institutional illegal adoptions in NI and across the border have not been investigated to date. In addition, the deportation of children of the poor, orphans, and those children who had been criminalised to British colonies continued until 1967 (Humphreys 2011). The Hart Inquiry report stated that many of those affected by these processes were critical of the institutions sending them to Australia and of government for permitting and facilitating this (HIA Inquiry 2017, Vol 1, para 35). Survivors of child migration alleged serious forms of physical and sexual abuse in Australian institutions and noted the profound effects of forced family separation on their lives and complained of a lack of cooperation from state and church authorities when engaging in family search and tracing (HIA Inquiry 2017, Vol 1, para 35).

Clerical sexual abuse

The rape and sexual assault of children have long been criminal offences on the island of Ireland, including through the Criminal Law Amendment Act 1885 which applied to Ireland until the Criminal Law (Amendment) Act 1935 and to NI until the Criminal Law Amendment Act (NI) 1923. Criminal offences are explored further in Chapter 4. Keating (2004–6, 161–2) notes that, based on existing court records, between the period of 1922 and 1932 the State was aware of significant sexual violence against children. Child sexual abuse occurred in a range of contexts, including industrial and reformatory schools but also within diocesan non-residential contexts and in day schools (see Keenan 2012). Only three dioceses have been subject to a state inquiry. In 2005, the Ferns Inquiry identified over 100 allegations of child sexual abuse by 21 priests in their diocese since 1962 (Murphy et al 2005). The 2009 Murphy Report regarding the Catholic Archdiocese of Dublin concluded that it was abundantly clear 'that child sexual abuse by clerics was widespread throughout the period under review' (CoI 2009, para 1.7). The report identified that 320 people had complained of sexual abuse between 1975 and 2004 and that 130 complaints had been made since May 2004. The report concluded there was 'no doubt that clerical child sexual abuse was covered up' from January 1975 to May 2004 (CoI 2009, paras 1.35, 1.133). In 2011, the Cloyne Report found that two-thirds of abuse allegations made in 1996–2009 were not passed on to the Gardai as required by the Church's own 1996 guidelines (CoI 2011, para 1.22). In relation to NI, existing media reports of criminal convictions evidence convictions in the Catholic dioceses of Armagh, Derry, Dromore and Down, and Connor.[6] There has been no specific state investigation of clerical sexual abuse in non-residential settings in NI, including regarding Protestant churches.

This range of abuses across the island of Ireland reflects harms in diverse institutional contexts, across decades, and the involvement of different

[6] See eg 'Girl's nightmare ordeal at hands of a monster', *Belfast Telegraph*, 23 November 2003; M Donnelly, '"Evil" priest who sexually abused brother and sister jailed for 12 years', *The Irish Independent*, 13 November 2004; 'Paedophile priest who abused boy 20 years ago won't apologise to victim', *Belfast Telegraph*, 7 September 2018.

state, church, and private actors. When viewed holistically, it is possible to characterise non-recent abuses in Ireland as sustained, widespread, and systemic. The pattern of abuses, and the conscious creation of institutional systems and legislative frameworks where abuse occurs, precludes an attribution of McKeown's framework of 'pure structural injustice' alone, where no single actor bears responsibility. Instead, this book intends to explore how responsibility is and should be attributed, in law and other contexts, individually, institutionally, and systemically, for the range of abuses considered as either 'avoidable' or 'deliberate' structural injustices.

6. Breaking the Silence and Shame: the Emergence of Justice Movements

The latter decades of the twentieth century saw significant changes in RoI and NI. Both jurisdictions joined the European Union (then the European Economic Community (EEC)) in 1973, which raised social-welfare protections, particularly for single mothers, lessening reliance on church-run charity (Grimes 2023). In RoI, there was significant social contestation around profound moral issues, such as the divorce referenda 1985 and 1995 and the abortion referendum in 1992 (McCafferty 2004). Irish society nonetheless struggled to publicly address its treatment of Irish women. A 1984 Garda investigation in County Kerry (the Kerry babies' case) into the killing of one newborn baby and alleged killing of another led to the arrest of Joanne Hayes who was charged with murder of a child erroneously thought to be hers. In 1988, the charges against Hayes were dismissed and a tribunal of inquiry was established, which was highly critical of the Garda investigation. In 2020, the Irish State apologised to Hayes after 36 years of wrongfully accusing her of murder and for the 'appalling hurt and distress caused' (Molloy and O'Donnell 2022). In addition, in 1984, a 15-year-old girl, Ann Lovett, died after giving birth to a stillborn child at a Marian shrine in County Longford (Maguire 2001). These cases reflect the profound secrecy, shame, and oppression of women in Irish society (Smyth 1995b, 35).

Several scholars have highlighted how a 'politics of shame' (Fischer 2016) or a 'shame industrial complex' (Hogan 2019) was integral to the moral governance of society and directed towards women and children. There was an acute gendered stigma and shame attached to unmarried mothers who were seen as a 'moral contagion' and thus removed from Irish society via institutionalisation (Earner-Byrne 2003; Garrett 2016). However, as noted in Chapter 1, our analysis recognises the importance of shame within the context of intersectionality and the regulation of multiple victim vulnerabilities including poverty, race, and disability (see Enright and Ring 2020; see also Smith 2007; O'Sullivan and O'Donnell 2012, see also Chapter 3). Shame was also a key feature of institutional regimes and of punishment practices within the institutions (see eg CICA 2009, Vol 1, chs 7, 8). In NI, scholars have noted a continued, highly conservative and shaming morality around sex and sexuality (see eg Ellison 2017). Moreover, 'shame' is often intergenerational and continues to impact the lives of many survivors and their families. Wills (2024, 45–6) notes the link between shame and secrecy: '[t]he very act of keeping something secret engenders shame'. As discussed further, addressing the legacy of shame surrounding abuses at individual, institutional, and societal levels is integral to more effective justice responses.

More broadly, ongoing discrimination and harms to women reflect a reality that Irish society knew, but did not acknowledge, the role of closed institutions as sites of potential harm. O'Sullivan and O'Donnell (2012, 278) caution that '[t]he institutions of confinement that pockmarked the Irish landscape from the mid nineteenth century until their demise in the second half of the twentieth century were not part of a hidden Ireland that was only exposed in the 1990s and beyond. Their roles and functions were widely known and they were extensively utilised'. Wills (2024, 19) suggests 'the past has not been forgotten so much as disremembered, indeed dismembered. There is an active element to the refusal, or inability, to remember or to know'. The role of media, church control of health and education, clericalism and deference, and the engagement of families with the institutions, combined to inhibit public and systemic examination of these institutions, disabling and disbelieving victim/survivors and privileging the protection of state and church reputations. The difference between knowledge and acknowledgement of wrongdoing, familiar to transitional justice contexts (Arthur 2009), is evident with respect to non-recent abuses on both parts of the island of Ireland where, prior to state-led investigations, both State and Church authorities adopted postures of denial of knowledge or responsibility, postures that continue to some extent within communities and society more broadly (Scally 2021). These postures represent a failure of official acknowledgement of what was, if imperfectly, socially known.

It is only since the 1990s that efforts began to address the impact of non-recent institutional abuses. In 1994, media focus on the case of Fr Brendan Smyth brought clerical sexual abuse to high-profile public attention. In NI, the RUC had requested the extradition of Fr Smyth from RoI in 1993. It later emerged that the request lay dormant in the offices of the Irish Director of Public Prosecutions (DPP) for seven months. Smyth (1995b, 28) notes that the case offered a 'direct insight into the real operation of power [that] broke the undemocratic habits of a state's lifetime of so-called "confidentiality" and secrecy'. In subsequent years, television documentaries played a significant role in Ireland in increasing public attention and scrutiny regarding historical institutional abuses, such as *Dear Daughter* (1996), *Sex in a Cold Climate* (1998), and *States of Fear* (1999), which prompted a State apology and investigation into industrial and reformatory schools. Literature and memoirs served as a further source of information, bringing survivor experiences to public attention (see eg Flynn 1983; Fahy 1999; Doyle 1989; Madden 2004). Colm O'Gorman was centrally involved in the 2002 BBC documentary *Suing the Pope*, which detailed allegations of clerical sexual abuse in the Catholic diocese of Ferns and led to a State inquiry (O'Gorman 2010).

In the case of the Magdalene Laundries, the removal from unmarked graves and reburial of women who died while in the laundry in High Park, Dublin at the Convent of Our Lady of Refuge in 1993 sparked public interest in the case (McCormick and O'Connell 2021, 45). The Irish government's original position was that the State had no responsibility for nor played any role in the Magdalene Laundries.[7] Instead, it was necessary to invoke international human rights mechanisms, discussed in Chapter 4, to pressure the State into more effectively addressing a legacy of historical abuse (McGettrick et al 2021), which led to the establishment of an interdepartmental committee, discussed in Chapter 5. Individual research by Catherine Corless, supported by investigative journalism, helped pressure the government from 2014 to establish an investigation into mother and baby institutions in the face of government denials and some sceptical historical accounts (Corless 2021). The growing publicity given to survivor and family member advocacy around mother and baby institutions increased political pressure on the Irish government to act (see eg O'Reilly 2018; Redmond 2018).

In NI, with the notable exception of the Kincora scandal discussed earlier, the conflict has dominated the public and political space regarding the potential for official investigations into past wrongdoing, limiting the

[7] 'O'Keeffe criticised for referring to Magdalene women as "employees"', *The Irish Times*, 19 September 2009.

political capacity to address other non-recent abuses, especially sexual violence (McWilliams 1997). However, the publication of the Ryan Report in RoI (CICA 2009) provided an impetus for victim/survivor mobilisation in NI and associated political acknowledgement of the need to investigate the issue. Victims of abuse in NI presented a petition at the Northern Irish Executive in Stormont calling for an inquiry in the North similar to the Ryan Report.[8] However, the Hart Inquiry report was published just prior to the collapse of the NI Assembly in January 2017 which delayed the implementation of the report's recommendations (see Chapter 5) and the establishment of subsequent mechanisms to address Magdalene Laundries and mother and baby institutions in NI. Similarly, the long-awaited apology was tainted for some victims/survivors by the resignation of the First Minister and further collapse of the Executive (see Chapter 7). This also illustrates that justice mechanisms for survivors of non-recent abuse in NI are inextricably bound up with broader social–political factors.

While justice and advocacy campaigns in both parts of the island continue in relation to mother and baby institutions and the Magdalene Laundries, at the time of writing justice campaigns are also underway in related contexts, addressing allegations of abuse in day schools, sporting institutions, the Irish Defence Forces, and organisations for young people such as Scouting Ireland and the Order of Malta (in RoI) and clerical sexual abuse (in NI). The continued political and legal examination of allegations of non-recent abuses suggests that a piecemeal approach to addressing the past may have delayed if not denied the demands of victim/survivors and justice campaigns.

7. Conclusion

The non-recent institutional abuses considered in this book occur in a context of significant violence, social change, and division on the island of Ireland. Religious proselytism and discrimination, the Great Famine, the independence struggle and partition of the island, the civil war, and the conflict combine to provide a deeply challenging context within which state and religious institutions operated to structure the creation and operation of institutions and non-recent abuses. Institutions such as industrial and

[8] 'Assembly to investigate extent of child abuse in North', *The Irish Times*, 3 November 2009.

reformatory schools, Magdalene Laundries, and maternity homes were created as part of moral and social reform efforts in the nineteenth century, many of them enshrined in law, in both Catholic and Protestant settings. After partition, these institutions continued in both jurisdictions as part of explicit nation-building efforts in RoI and with acquiescence and path dependence in NI. These specialist institutions combined with the growth of provision of generalised institutions such as hospitals, including psychiatric hospitals, and primary and secondary schools.

Physical, sexual, and emotional abuse and neglect took place in industrial and reformatory schools. Women were detained and made to work against their will in Magdalene Laundries, if not always under the force of law then as a result of significant social, religious, and institutional control and pressure. A disproportionately high number of children died in mother and baby institutions. A large but unknown number of children were subjected to illegal birth registrations and there is reason to suspect that a broader number were subjected to other forms of coercive or illegal adoptions. Furthermore, child sexual abuse was committed by members of the Catholic clergy in dioceses, schools, and religious orders across the island.

The chapter has highlighted the intricacies of church–state–societal roles in institutional abuses. Existing inquiry reports demonstrate that the bishops of dioceses across the island of Ireland retained authority and control over both diocesan priests and members of religious orders where they knew or should have known about allegations of abuse (see Chapter 5). Several of the same religious orders were involved in the operation of multiple forms of institution where non-recent abuses took place. Both the Irish and Northern Irish states retained regulatory and inspection functions of these institutions and knew or should have known about the abuses that took place. Families retain an ambivalent relationship to non-recent abuses, in some instances acting as units of resistance to separation and sites of victimhood and in other instances cooperating with or facilitating the institutionalisation of family members. The role of communities and civil society in these abuses along 'the continuum of knowing' (Keenan 2013, 101) have yet to be fully understood. Rather than operate with exclusively clear modes of cooperation and collaboration, the history of institutions and abuses on the island of Ireland reflects both instances of knowledge, notice, wilful blindness, or negligence by state and church leadership and on the part of successive individuals, families, and societies on the island regarding abuses.

The historical complexities and the enmeshed structural, legal, and institutional frameworks that gave rise to such abuses makes particular determinations of responsibility and accountability enormously complex. Killian suggests the 'importance of carefully building an architecture of accountability in the widest and most inclusive sense into all state relationships, particularly where services are delegated or outsourced, and doubly so when the services are targeted at groups who lack a clear voice' (2015, 31–2). This book addresses the responsibility of the state, church, families, and society for harms that were so pervasive as to become widespread, systemic, and potentially normalised in historical contexts. It is in this context of structural patterns of abuses that this book evaluates the justice responses to non-recent institutional abuses on the island of Ireland. The structural factors contributing to institutionalisation and abuses considered in this chapter complicate and deepen the challenges in attributing and distributing responsibility and accountability legally, morally, and relationally at institutional, political, and societal levels and ultimately in finding routes to justice and healing for all impacted by these legacies.

3

Victim/Survivors of Non-Recent Institutional Abuses

1. Introduction

As noted in Chapter 1, this book aims to contribute to transforming justice responses to non-recent institutional abuses by engaging with representatives of all interested parties to ensure their voices and perspectives are heard. In acknowledgement of their suffering and experience of marginalisation and rejection and given their centrality to justice discourses, this chapter focuses on victim/survivors. The purpose of the chapter is to explore the complexities and diversity of victimhood and the impacts resulting from non-recent institutional abuses; to examine the diversity in victim/survivors' understanding of responsibility and accountability and how these diversities pose challenge to popular discourses on responsibility and accountability; and to examine victim/survivors' needs/expectations of justice and their broad experiences of justice responses.

The chapter proceeds as follows: Sections 2 and 3 provide a brief contextual overview of the academic literature, focusing on the concept of victimhood, and justice discourses from rights–needs–interests perspectives. Drawing on documentary analysis and interview data with 14 direct victims from varying institutional contexts in the Republic of Ireland (RoI) and Northern Ireland (NI), Section 4 examines the impacts of institutional abuses on victim/survivors. Within the overall rubric of seeking to transform justice responses, Sections 5 and 6 address two further issues: victim/survivors' understanding and experiences of responsibility and accountability and victim/survivors' expectations and experiences of justice. The concluding section draws out the implications for discourses on responsibility, accountability, and justice that are taken up and developed as part of transforming justice responses in Parts II and III of the book.

Transforming Justice Responses to Non-Recent Institutional Abuses. Anne-Marie McAlinden, Marie Keenan, and James Gallen, Oxford University Press. © Oxford University Press 2025.
DOI: 10.1093/9780191967399.003.0003

2. The Concept of Victimhood

Victimisation can be understood as the way in which individuals or groups suffer harm, a violation of rights, or significant disruption of their well-being because of crime, abuse, or wrongdoing (see Wemmers and de Brouwer 2011). The impacts can be categorised as relating to direct or indirect victims, or to primary, secondary, or tertiary victims; categorisations which appreciate that crime and abuses affect the individual, family, community, or groups in different but interrelated ways (Spalek 2005; Erez and Meroz-Ahoroni 2011). In the context of institutional abuses, direct victims are those who have suffered the direct impacts (Huyse 2003). Indirect victims are caught up in its ripple effects and include family members and close friends of victim/survivors and perpetrators (see Goode et al 2003; Keenan 2014). It could also be argued that indirect victims include families and colleagues of those accused of failing to prevent or respond to abuse disclosures, who face significant disapprobation in public discourse (see Claffey et al 2013). Tertiary victims include individuals in the broader community and often the community itself which may be impacted in various ways, such as a sense of betrayal and loss of trust because of the abuses or wrongs (see Govier 2006; Jankowitz 2018).

Intergenerational or transgenerational effects of large-scale abuses refer to 'the unconscious transference of emotional, physical, or social pain from one person to their descendants' (Lawther 2021a, 3, 15; Luhmann 2009). In the context of non-recent institutional abuses, victims of transgenerational trauma experience a second-hand memory post the event (Schwab 2010). Post-memories are said to be transferred through the stories told by parents or guardians and through 'unexplained silences and the expression of grief, rage and despair' (Lawther 2021a, 15; Hirsch 2008). While some research has considered intergenerational impacts of abuse in societies transitioning from conflict to post-conflict (Lawther 2021a; Surenthiraraj 2022), there is a smaller literature on intergenerational impacts in the non-recent institutional abuses space (see eg Huefner et al 2007; Aguiar and Halseth 2015). Our full interview sample included primary/direct and secondary/indirect victim/survivors. While focused predominantly on these core categories, our analysis is also concerned, albeit to a lesser extent, with the impact of justice responses at the broader tertiary level (see especially Part III of book). This chapter focuses primarily on direct victim/survivors.

Christie's (1986, 18) concept of an 'ideal victim' adds further nuance to academic understandings of victimhood. This is defined as 'the person or category of individuals . . . most readily given the complete and legitimate status of being a victim' (Christie 1986, 18). The ideal victim is seen as 'respectable, blameless, relatively powerless, and a stranger to their offender' (Stanley 2015, 1149), 'passive, innocent and vulnerable' (Stanley 2015, 1153; see also McShane and Williams 1992). This concept has relevance for the broad social/organisational responses to institutional abuses in its determination of who is seen as a victim and who is not. In reality, the ideal victim is rare and in many instances the suffering of victims is not socially recognised, particularly in situations where victims are regarded as blameworthy (Walklate 2011).[1] In addition, as Ring (2018, 141) suggests, victim/survivor activists may also be low priority on the hierarchy of victimhood because the power of their activism may be seen as threatening social hierarchies in church and state. In this landscape, circumstances of contested victimhood can lead to the domination of certain voices and the silencing of others (Lawther 2021b, 890).

Furthering understanding of victimhood is the concept of 'intersectionality' (Crenshaw 1991). It offers a theoretical framework for understanding how features of an individual's physical, social, and political identity (such as gender, race, age, (dis)ability, economic status, sexual orientation, religion, ethnic background, immigration status, etc) can coalesce to create and compound unique forms of discrimination and inequality (Crenshaw 1991, 1241; Didi et al 2016, 160). Maher et al (2018, 14) suggest that when people are located at multiple intersections of disadvantage or discrimination, access to justice may be even more complex and fraught than is otherwise the case. While the unique aspects of intersectionality in relation to non-recent institutional abuses are taken up in academic debate (Fischer 2016; Gallen 2019a), the intersectional underpinnings of institutional abuses and how these impact the lives and experiences of victim/survivors have not been fully recognised in justice responses to date. This gap also emerged within the empirical research for this book.

3. Understanding Justice in Context: Rights–Needs–Interests

Daly (2018) argues that merging different groups of victim/survivors with different experiences of abuse ignores the historical specificities of abuse

[1] R Ingle, 'Turns out Blackrock College was a world away from us Pill Hill girls', *The Irish Times*, 16 November 2022.

and reduces the possibility of equitable redress for them. This speaks to the need for a highly contextualised theoretical, research, and policy agenda for studying institutional abuses (Daly 2015). Other studies highlight the need to properly understand the specific characteristics of various contexts of institutional abuse and their multifarious impacts to protect as far as possible against further harm (Colton et al 2002). Colton et al (2002, 584) see a need for institutions and bodies implicated in the abuse 'to be reflexive, self-critical and prepared to confront questions' about the extent of their responsibility. In this analysis, historical and cultural context must be considered, without a descent into historical or cultural relativism. We undertake to tread this board of complexity carefully in this book rather than ignore it.

Holder (2018) examined the most useful way to conceptualise the justice expectations and wishes of people impacted by violent crime and considered whether conceptualising victims' justice expectations as 'rights', 'needs', or 'interests' offers most promise (see also Daly 2017, 114). Drawing on human rights frameworks, he prefers justice 'rights' and 'interests' over justice 'needs', the former placing victim/survivors 'in a political relation to state institutions; as rights bearers in a relation with duty holders' (6). He suggests that criminal justice processes are 'citizenship activities founded on peoples' justice interests rather than an articulation of their justice needs' (3). From this perspective, the justice responses that victimised individuals seek are those to which they are due as citizens. Conceptualising victim/survivor expectations of justice as 'need' could lead to consumerist approaches to justice, such as 'if you tell us what you need, we will respond'. A further danger of such a perspective is of putting pressure on victim/survivors to demonstrate 'need' based on 'damage'. According to Gallen (2019b), by focusing on need there is a risk that victim/survivors will be treated paternalistically as vulnerable objects who are granted benevolent remedies by more powerful non-vulnerable subjects but only insofar as it suits the powerful and not as a matter of legal right. Daly (2015) believes it is important to identify in advance through research a set of reasonable expectations that victims as citizens have in seeking justice and to tailor the justice mechanism most appropriate for responding to those interests. She places the well-being/healing 'needs' of victims as well as their justice outcomes (eg reparation, retribution, apology, etc) outside her justice interests framework (Daly 2017). She argues that merging victims' justice interests with their healing needs results in a confused blend of justice requests and she suggests that justice interests and well-being should be assessed as separate dimensions of what victim/survivors require (115).

In contrast, Herman (2023, 2–3) prefers the broad framework of 're-covery' to consider the justice and other needs of victim/survivors and has recently added 'justice' as the fourth and final stage to her previous three-stage recovery framework, which included (1) establishing safety in the present, (2) grieving and making meaning of the past, and (3) refocusing on the present and the future (see Herman 2015; 2023). Based on interviews with 30 victim/survivors, she classified their specific justice needs (stage four of her framework) in three categories. The strongest justice needs include acknowledgement of facts, acknowledgement of harm, and vindication by the community. The justice needs in the second category (important but less dominant) are apology, fair restitution, prevention of future harm, and exposure and containment of the offender. The justice needs in the third category (that were less clear and more ambivalent) include punishment, revenge, and forgiveness. Herman's conceptualisation of justice as part of recovery has resonance with the victim/survivors in the current study (discussed later) who do not see their justice and well-being/healing needs as entirely separate but rather as inextricably interlinked. The interaction between law, justice, and healing are themes we take up later in the book.

Holder (2018, 7) argues that justice is not a single event. Rather, victim/survivors often have a complex realisation of justice over time and in interaction with different entities as their thinking 'unfolds'. His research brings to light victim/survivors' reflections on justice that are 'partial, ambiguous and yet at times both firm as well as contradictory' (7). He observed that there is nothing simple or single in victims' reflections on justice. Rather, '[t]heir thinking was refracted through the spectrum of ideas, principles, rules and criteria' that acted as heuristics in each particular case (7). This suggests the need for engagement with the idea of justice as subjective, from different perspectives even for the same individual, over time.

4. The Impacts of Institutional Abuse: Trauma, Loss, Shame, and Resistance

The suffering of traumatised people is a matter not only of individual and social psychology but of social justice and human rights. That is the approach taken in this chapter. Noting that power abuses and oppression are at the core of institutional abuses, care is taken to avoid pathologising individuals who have suffered the abuses by solely adopting an individualised psychological approach to understanding their suffering. In many cases, victim/survivor responses can be seen as a natural response to a wholly unjust situational experience that is compounded by the societal silencing and shame often experienced. Thus, a critical stance is taken towards empirical work that focuses solely on the psychology of the victim/survivor, preferring instead an analysis that locates the strategies of institutional abuse and its traumatic impacts within the context of structural power relations, oppression, and resistance. The focus of this section is on trauma, loss, shame, and resistance.

Trauma

Consistent with child sexual abuse in other contexts, Blakemore et al (2017) found that trauma is common in the lives of many former residents of childcare institutions, with some victim/survivors suffering psychologically, physically, socially, educationally, and economically (see also Flanagan-Howard et al 2009; Fitzpatrick et al 2010). Impacts on the spiritual well-being of victim/survivors of abuse that occur in religious settings, such as loss of faith or loss of trust in organised religion, are also evidenced in research (Claffey et al 2013; McPhillips 2018). Research also notes how the trauma of institutional abuses can be exacerbated by the dynamics in institutional settings, which can reduce or impede disclosure, belief, and protection from future harm (Sheridan and Carr 2020, 2). Pembroke (2017; 2020) found lack of preparation for life beyond institutionalisation, lack of training and education, perceptions of inferiority, and negative societal perceptions were some of the issues faced by victims of childhood institutional abuse after they left the institutions (see also Golding 2018 (Australia) and McGuckin 2023 (Northern Ireland) on the challenges of finding a voice after leaving care for victim/survivors of childhood sexual abuse in residential facilities for children). The ongoing impacts experienced by former residents of mother and baby institutions, Magdalene Laundries, and workhouses in RoI and NI (including mental illness, destitution, educational deficiency, and stigmatisation) continue to emerge in academic research (see O'Mahoney et al 2019; McGettrick et al 2021).

Victim/survivors of institutional abuse report common impacts of the abuse on them, as evidenced in the literature above, and these features also emerged in the current study. Some victim/survivors described the impacts as 'life-long', including self-hatred, self-blame, PTSD, difficulties in sustaining long-term intimate relationships, loneliness, isolation, depression, and a legacy of fear of authority and institutions. Some victim/survivors felt they were to blame for what happened to them as children or young adults; that they had done something wrong. This thinking took a long time to shift for many survivors. It resulted in fear of any interaction with the state and an unwillingness to engage with the state even in pursuit of their rights. Educational deficits compounded this problem. In addition, the unique features of specific institutional contexts provide for more diverse and distinct experiences and impacts which require nuanced understanding.[2] Without wishing to detract from the diversity and complexity of victim/survivor experiences, the following analysis focuses on some of the more generalised profound losses that victim/survivors experienced, their experiences of shame, and how they fought back with resistance, which will add to existing studies on these aspects of institutional abuse (see eg Zolkos 2016).

Loss

Interviewees who were reared in children's homes in NI or industrial and reformatory schools in RoI presented the varying circumstances in which they were taken into care. Some were born in mother and baby institutions, often to a young mother from whom they were separated in infancy and who were later boarded out or adopted. Others ended up in residential homes for children on foot of child welfare concerns emanating from family breakdown, sometimes related to loss of the mother or to post-partum depression. Some children were moved around from one residential facility to another. Sibling groups were separated along gender and age lines leading to catastrophic losses and deep wells of buried grief for the loss of parents and siblings. Mothers and fathers lost their children; babies lost their parents. Some girls moved to Magdalene Laundries or mother and baby institutions from residential facilities for children. In Magdalene Laundries, many of the women lived 'lives unlived' (Interview 65), sometimes till death, resulting in profound sadness and sometimes shame for their loved ones and descendants (see Wills 2024). Girls worked in boys'

[2] The effects on secondary victims, including families of victims and members of religious organisations, such as shame, regret, and sense of betrayal, are reported in other studies (Goode et al 2003; Keenan 2014).

homes as domestic workers when they were of an age deemed suitable. Some boys were 'just fit for the army, fit for the navy, fit for the services . . . [because] . . . they'd already been institutionalized . . . [and] . . . it was where [sic] all of this 10, 12, 15 years of a children's home had trained you for' (Interview 9). Several quotes reflect the profound loss and enduring grief experienced by many victim/survivors in both NI and RoI:

> So, I hardly seen my sister or my brothers then . . . My father tried to get up and there were lots of time they wouldn't even let him in. . . . But my father used to go over that wee wall or stand up and leave wee oranges and stuff. I always have oranges in my house [now]. Always, always. (Interview 2)

> I think what we've lost in all of this . . . the ultimate harm is the separation of family. And we've lost that. They're looking at how long were you in there, you know, how much did you get to eat or did you have to scrub floors. No. [I]t's the separation from your family, of your family . . . that harm continues today . . . The separation of family is the biggest human rights violation, to make us disappear. (Interview 20)

Interviewees reported the sense of loneliness and the search for reunification that often lasted throughout their adult lives. Children in a family of seven could lose the love and support of each other for many years, sometimes forever. Siblings only got to meet each other when an adult was allowed to take them out for a day or weekend. Returning to the children's home was always painful. These fractures had a long-term impact. One mother who gave birth to twins had them with her for seven weeks. One evening when she went to feed her babies, they were gone. They were in an orphanage in the same institution for nine months from where they were later adopted. As recounted by her daughter:

> In terms of the women who were in the mother and baby homes . . . many just survived and then they're surviving without their babies, which you just never fill that void. So, it's a lifelong thing and then, sometimes it's a dirty secret as well because you were sent away. You were, you know, banished from your family. I think they just lost so much. (Interview 65)

Victim/survivors of mother and baby institutions (both the mothers and the children) pointed out that they never regain what they lost. 'The loss never heals, it just doesn't all come back' (Interview 65). It is 'unrectifiable' loss, to borrow from Zolkos (2016, 321).

A particular cruelty of residential care was the lack of information given to residents in most institutions about their history and family (also discussed in Chapters 4, 5, and 9). Misleading information given to children about birth parents or heritage and no support given to find lost parents on leaving care were particularly difficult. The lack of information afforded to children who were illegally adopted about their heritage and identity was also particularly traumatic and cruel. '[W]hen he [her son] was told that he was adopted, he had no counselling whatsoever . . . he was 50 odd, 52 or something, he nearly dropped dead. He was so shocked, and he went into . . . depression . . . he went into hospital for a bit' (Interview 52). One victim/survivor reported being told at 11-and-a-half years old that her birth mother was dead. At 16 years old, she discovered that her mother was still alive, 'a real, living person' (Interview 20). Children searched for birth mothers, mothers searched for their children, and siblings searched for each other. Sometimes they found each other and navigated these reunifications and relationships with all their complexities, alone, without support. Life events, including the birth of one's own children, whilst joyous, often propelled feelings of sadness regarding one's lost birth mother.

One interviewee found out about her mother's death in a Magdalene Laundry via the media. Adopted early in life but reunited with her mother with whom she had intermittent contact, she was not informed by the Magdalene Laundries that her mother had died. She found out four months later when listening to a radio programme. The fact that she and her sister did not get to attend their mother's funeral is still a source of upset:

> [W]hen [her mother] first died, it was the subject of a [radio] programme on RTE Radio 1 . . . [Mother's] friend, who had grown up with her in the institution, phoned . . . to say that she'd found out that her friend had died and that she was buried in a communal grave . . . When [the radio host] asked the lady what her friend's name was, she named our mother, and that's how we found that she had died . . . [M]y sister joined the conversation . . . and she was absolutely seething with anger and upset that the nuns didn't find it in their hearts to tell us that [mother] was dead. (Interview 65)

In contrast, the kindness of some of the nuns and clergy towards the women in Magdalene Laundries was particularly noted, especially when compared to the county homes and industrial and reformatory schools. This kindness was also noted in brief references in some inquiry and commission reports (see eg IDC 2013, ch 19, para 37; CICA 2009, Vol 4, ch 5, para 5.50 and ch 6, para 6.07). Despite the kindness, it cannot be forgotten that the freedom of residents was still curtailed.

The loss of heritage was noted by interviewees who were not of the dominant culture. One interviewee noted how black children felt particularly excluded as they had no means of connecting with their heritage and this had a detrimental impact on them both during their time in the institutions and beyond, particularly in RoI:

> I think the dominant stream through which I experienced abuse was because of my race. There's no other way to put it . . . there's a hierarchy within every institution, and within the industrial schools, mother and baby homes, I was definitely at the lower, well I was at the bottom tier along with travellers. (Interview 22)

This respondent went on to wonder why black children were separated and dispersed around the country. 'Why separate us, why put us into these inherently hostile environments where the only image they had of black and brown people was of starving Biafrans. That was the image, and that's what Irish people had' (Interview 22). She questioned whether it would not have been wiser to keep these children together for support and acknowledgement of their heritage.

Victim/survivors of the Irish Defence Forces described loss of careers resulting from the multiple forms of discrimination and abuse experienced within their working environment, including abuse of a sexual nature, discrimination, and harassment. For them, the 'patriarchal dividend' (Connell 1995, 79–80) outweighed rank on all occasions when abuse and harassment were involved; females at officer rank were not spared abuse and discrimination from male colleagues even of a lower rank. Victim/survivors of the Defence Forces described dealing with the trauma of the sexual violence or harassment on an individual basis for many years because of fear and knowledge that there would be a significant price to pay for bringing their abuse into the open. Those victim/survivors interviewed for this research who did so suffered because of their public reporting. Some lost their job and their career. Others lost reputations by being medically retired, whilst at the same time some of the accused were pensioned off:

> I was told if you take your discrimination case against the Defence Forces, you'll win the battle but you'll lose the war. Completely true.

> I won my case but I ended up leaving the Defence Forces. I didn't want to leave... but I had no other option... [T]he medical doctors said to me... 'it's a toxic environment for you'. They said 'they're actually medically retiring people who speak out'... So we all had to leave medically, which is deplorable. (Interview 66)

Interviewees in the Defence Forces in RoI were also aware of other victim/survivors who did not report their abuses and who continue to suffer and struggle in life in other ways.

The difficulties for children abused in the context of day schools in RoI had additional features of loss including a sense of exclusion/rejection. The lack of official acknowledgement of their abuses until recent times and their exclusion from inquiries into the abuse of children in residential facilities left them feeling silenced and forgotten, 'with no place to go' (Interview 31). With the success of a case at the European Court of Human Rights on behalf of one victim/survivor and the implications of that judgment for others (see further Chapter 4), as well as recent disclosures of abuse in elite boys' day schools in RoI[3] (Scoping Inquiry 2024), the Report of the Scoping Inquiry into abuse in boys' schools run by the religious orders in RoI means that there is at last some acknowledgement of the abuse of children in day schools, albeit in those run by religious orders and not by the State (see Chapters 5 and 8 for critique of the Report of the Scoping Inquiry 2024). The lack of commitment of the Irish State to thoroughly investigate abuse of children in day schools for all children and not just those educated by the religious orders leaves many victim/survivors of that context continuing to feel unheard and excluded.[4]

Some interviewees abused as children in day schools only realised the full impact of the abuse on them during criminal trials involving an identified and later convicted perpetrator when they listened to the avalanche of testimonies from other victim/survivors with whom they identified. 'I've always described it as being like a room full of balls, absolutely packed floor to ceiling and you open the double doors and the balls come hurdling at you . . . it was like she was telling my story, my life, and it was then it hit me' (Interview 31). This speaks not only to the need for understanding of

[3] J Casey, 'Cork abuse survivor: Any inquiry into abuse in schools must probe State's own accountability', *Irish Examiner*, 21 November 2022.

[4] J Horgan-Jones, 'Wider school abuse redress scheme would involve "potentially enormous costs", official documents stated', *The Irish Times*, 20 March 2023.

the trauma underlying delayed disclosures but to the exclusion/marginalisation of victim/survivors of day schools and the impacts of official justice responses which compartmentalise abuses in silos and circumvent victim experiences.

Shame

Academic scholarship highlights 'the centrality of shame to the legacy of HIA in Ireland' (McAlinden 2022a, 140) at individual, organisational, and societal levels (Fischer 2017, 751; Hogan 2019; see also Chapter 2). Personal shame is said to involve the belief that one is inherently 'bad' (Candea 2018). In an important study on body shame, Dolezal (2015, 24–9) argues that while 'acute' body shame is necessary to socialisation (what Norbert Elias called 'the civilising process'), 'chronic' body shame is undermining of the person. Body shame, she suggests, only finds its full articulation in the presence (actual or imagined) of others within a rule- and norm-governed milieu. As such, it embeds personal, individual, and embodied shame within a social, cultural, and political context (Dolezal 2015, 20–9); an observation that has relevance for institutional abuse of women and children in NI and RoI. The persistent consequences of shame, related to poverty, and the perceived breach of sexual, religious, and social norms of respectability are evidenced in numerous reports by former residents of children's homes and residential institutions for women and girls on the island of Ireland (see eg CoI MBH 2021, paras 17.4 and 24.156; HIA Inquiry 2017; CICA 2009, ch 5, para 5.25). Personal and academic scholarship point to the ostracisation of pregnant daughters by families based on perceived family shame which led to the breakdown of relationships, some of which never healed (Palmer 2016; Willis 2024).

Addressing shame requires genuine acceptance of responsibility on the part of key responsible actors in a layered, granular manner which removes blame from victim/survivors. As discussed in Chapter 7 (on apologies) and Chapter 8 (on restorative and transitional justice), it is possible to address shame by means of restorative and transitional justice mechanisms, including restorative apologies (see eg Strang and Sherman 2003). Processes aimed at hearing the epistemic 'truth' of victim/survivors and involving truth-telling by all stakeholders through respectful engagement can enable victim/survivors to gain acknowledgement and validation and the possibility of unlocking their often-persistent sense of blame, shame, and stigma.

Resistance

While studies have found that the overall rate of post-traumatic stress and psychological problems among victim/survivors of institutional abuses greatly exceed those normatively experienced more generally, the possibility of positive psychological change or 'posttraumatic growth' in the aftermath of institutional abuse has also been noted (Sheridan and Carr 2020). Studies further caution about limitations imposed on individuals who have experienced abuse when their identities are totalised as victims or even as victim/survivors (see Keenan 2012, xxiii; see also White 2004). These labels do not do justice to the complexities and richness of the lives, skills, and knowledge to which victim/survivors who experienced institutional abuse attest. Sometimes the language of 'victim/survivor' neglects or omits to capture such vital skills, wisdom, and resistance (see Wade 1997). Further, choice for victim/survivors in how they wish to take back power and access justice is emphasised time and again in scholarly literature (see Zinsstag and Keenan 2017; Moore et al 2021).

Reclaiming lives and identity and working for justice and healing can be seen as acts and sites of personal as well as social resistance for victim/survivors (see Chapter 2 for discussion on the emergence of victim advocacy movements). The empirical data shows the lengths to which victim/survivors go to resist the abuse and its after-effects not only at social/macro levels but also in individualised and personalised ways. Whilst collective activism is part of resistance for some, accessing the care and support they need to heal and recover to the extent possible are small acts of personal resistance for many. With the help of victim support groups, victim/survivor interviewees reported they learned coping skills to manage their losses, rejection, and distress. Two victim/survivors described leaving RoI (or being forced out) and going to England where they believe they and others in similar situations fared better economically, mentally, and socially than others who had remained in Ireland. Some emphasised the importance of spirituality. A victim/survivor in NI emphasised a belief in prayer and in God and learning forgiveness. As a strong universal theme, victim/survivors in both RoI and NI described the importance of education in their recovery.

Reclaiming the wounded child was also significant in the recovery process of resistance for victim/survivors of childcare institutions. For some, in both RoI and NI, recovering the wounded child involves a lifelong process. Some interviewees recognise a wounded child in themselves that can at times make them act in child-like ways, being sensitive and hurt and taking offence, even when none is intended. Some wonder if the wounds will ever disappear. For others, separating the abuse from the child was important in their journey of healing and resistance:

> I was carrying the abuse and so, I always saw the world through that lens, until long into the journey of recovery, put it that way, I learned to separate myself a bit from it . . . and to see it as separate from me in some way, exorcised it, if you like, from my psyche and my body so I could actually see myself . . . as an individual in the world with that experience but also a whole new world. (Interview 6)

This same victim/survivor reported that she made the decision as a child that someday she would do something about the abuses she experienced and witnessed. And she did. Overall, some victim/survivors prefer to be seen as resisters rather than victims or survivors. 'We are resisters, we resisted the regime, as it were, in our own way . . . people can call it survivors. Just for me personally, I much prefer to be the resister-in-chief' (Interview 20). Victim/survivors would not be beaten—or at least did their best not to be beaten—by the abuses and injustices they had experienced.

The voices of survivors interviewed for this study collectively spoke to complex histories of trauma, loss, rejection, and suffering which, for some, continue to impact their lives. For most, reclaiming their lives and identity became a marker of personal and social resistance, despite the lack of official acknowledgement of their abuse experiences or exclusion from justice measures (such as official investigations, apologies, or redress schemes). Given the magnitude of losses and suffering, there is a broader question to be pondered as to whether justice processes and official responses by church and state can ever hope to adequately address the depth and extent of abuses and wrongs that were committed against victim/survivors. Nonetheless, as shown below, victim/survivors have suggested ways in which meeting their justice needs, interests, and rights can go some way towards healing their profound trauma, losses, rejection, and silencing.

5. Responsibility and Accountability

For many victim/survivors, responsibility and accountability on the part of church and state is a core justice aspiration, with many highlighting the significant barriers they faced in this regard. Victim/survivors were keen to point to a granular kind of responsibility and accountability that is both individual and systemic, moral and ethical, legal, political, and relational (see Chapter 9 for fuller discussion on responsibility and accountability). In this granular understanding of responsibility and accountability, all identified parties and agencies are recognised for their part in the abuses and harms, or for their lack of response, as are the social and political policy and normative contexts in which those abuses took place.

Victim/survivors in both RoI and NI identified the state as ultimately responsible for much of their suffering and saw the state as accountable for its failure to regulate church and state institutions appropriately. Whilst they also saw the church as bearing responsibility, and therefore accountable, the higher order player in terms of responsibility and accountability from their perspective was the state. Victim/survivor interviewees on both parts of the island believe the state failed in its responsibility to adequately monitor institutions for children: 'the fact that if you . . . sub-contract the care out to an institution, that doesn't absolve you of the responsibility because the institution is looking after the orphans or whoever it might be, on behalf of the state' (Interview 65). One survivor in NI pointed out that:

> Ultimately the State who allowed these institutions to open up, who funded these institutions, who put children [in there] . . . sat on the reports in '56 and '62 where the Minister of Home Affairs was part of that meeting with the order, the bishop, the police, knowing there were paedophiles in that home who were continuing to be able to stay there . . . So, the State knew, as well as the religious orders, as well as the diocese knew that there were perpetrators there and . . . they did nothing. They knew there were orphans coming into that home [who] were going to be exposed. (Interview 15)

Victim/survivors also want the state to take responsibility for the institutionalisation per se of women and children. As one interviewee in RoI emphasised: 'I just wanted them to face up to how they were treating us really . . . I couldn't say I was looking for justice. I didn't know what justice was, but I knew it was wrong' (Interview 29). Apart from actual government departments (such as Education, Justice, Health, Children and Youth Affairs, Defence), a range of other State agencies were also seen as responsible and therefore accountable for the wrongs and harms suffered by children and women in these homes and facilities, most notably in RoI. These included school inspectors, medical professionals (linked to residential facilities), the Irish Society for the Prevention of Cruelty to Children, the Adoption Authority, the police, the civil service, the courts, the judges, and social workers.

In seeking responsibility and accountability from the state, victim/survivors in both jurisdictions reported that they not only met defensiveness but sometimes downright denial, refusal, and intimidation:

> Like Pinocchio. They just say, 'No, no, it wasn't us, we didn't do it, we didn't do it'. . . . [H]ow do you deal with people like that? You give them proof. The lawyers give them proof, and this is solid proof . . . but they counter it, and the judge then has to make his decision or her decision. So it's a complicated thing. (Interview 52)

Sometimes the defensiveness of state actors was covered with what survivors experienced as 'a pretence of care':

> [They] were down at that court and nearly fighting against us and it broke [name's] heart because they were letting on to like 'wee [name], wee [name]' . . . But you're fighting against me and you're pretending that you care, and you sat throughout that judicial review taking notes and 'shhuushh' to us. (Interview 2)

Victim/survivors also experienced intimidation in their interactions with the state. As observed by one interviewee in RoI:

> After I had lost in the High Court, they were very quick to write out to people who had cases pending that I had lost my case, and that therefore you should drop the case . . . that this would now be taken as basis of seeking all their costs against them if they continue their case . . . frightening people. (Interview 31)

Victim/survivors, especially in RoI, experienced different State departments as 'fighting over which of them was responsible' for particular cohorts of victims (Interview 6) or being passed around from department to department as though 'if a letter lands on their desk, they don't want to deal with it, so they move it on. They put it into somebody else's in-tray' (Interview 31). Other victim/survivors in RoI experienced further harm in how they were treated once they had disclosed abuse in State institutions, for example the

Defence Forces. 'You just can't get over the initial incident because of what they do to you afterwards' (Interview 59). Victim/survivors observed that the state's failure to take responsibility and be accountable dated back a long way in both jurisdictions on the island. Referring to RoI, one interviewee observed: 'I think an awful lot of it goes back to the Carrigan Report in 1931. They don't want to deal with it and they don't want to publish it. They don't want it known. They want to shut us up' (Interview 31).

In relation to the Catholic Church in RoI and NI, victim/survivors experienced the Church as evading responsibility and accountability, especially for mother and baby institutions and Magdalene Laundries, and as evading financial liability for the harms of those institutions. Church strategies of evasion included passing responsibility from one church body as an autonomous entity to another, with bishops saying to some victim/survivors that 'it's not us, the religious orders are meant to deal with that themselves, we've nothing to do with it' (Interview 2). In other scenarios, Church leaders argued that responsibility belonged to their predecessors because they were not in post at the time the abuses occurred.

Other common patterns of evading responsibility and accountability experienced by victim/survivors with regard to church and state included distancing, suppressing facts, minimising, wanting to move on as soon as possible, justifying, operating delays, and using pay-offs as a means of making the problem go away. Sometimes state officials moved around from one post or state department to another, particularly in RoI, and victim/survivors would have to start all over again negotiating and engaging with new officials, causing delay and allowing responses to drag on. In all, victim/survivors felt they were being underestimated and disrespected by these systems and actors.

Victim/survivors in both RoI and NI believe now that everyone knew about children in residential homes and schools. Even if they were not fully aware of the extent of the cruelty, they knew about family separations and accepted this without question or concern, being complicit in the culture of containment of women and children. Victim/survivors of Magdalene Laundries and mother and baby institutions believe the public knew about them and turned a blind eye to them too, an argument also evidenced in recent work by Coen et al (2023). As one survivor explained:

> Everybody knew about us. People worked there, people worked in these institutions. The Magdalene Laundries . . . did all the laundry for all these big businesses . . . These industrial schools and mother and

> baby institutions were the economic engine for a lot of small villages, especially in a time when there was high unemployment in Ireland . . . and I don't get a sense that Irish society has kind of gone, 'Well that's the Church, that was then. Aren't they awful people', without acknowledging and accepting that they couldn't have done what they'd done without the rest of civil society. (Interview 22)

Part of the social context of institutionalisation for women and girls was the Catholic context of sin, evidenced also in other literature on this topic (see Brangan 2024). As Chapter 2 has shown, these norms and values were to forcefully impact women who were pregnant outside marriage and their babies. The Catholic context of sin was seen as 'a great big spider's web . . . with all these different institutions and little . . . ordinary people, as well as parish priests and big institutions like the whole of the Catholic Church' (Interview 52). With this as the context, some victim/survivors feel it is not just particular individuals or institutions who are responsible for what they suffered. Rather, responsibility extends to the whole of society as well as to specific individuals and to church and state in layered and interconnected ways. From the perspective of some victim/survivors, citizens tend to blame institutions, as they see it, to protect themselves from reflecting on their part in supporting the context and culture of the time (see Wills 2024). For many victim/survivors, the wrongs of the institutionalisation of women and children and the harms of what was being done to them by such regimes was 'the most open secret in Ireland' (Interview 9), North and South of the island. Indeed, societal denial was at its height for much of the twentieth century.

A minority of victim/survivors, especially in NI, lament the fact that the person who abused them was never charged and brought to justice before the criminal courts. This is similar to findings by Lundy (2020) and to some participants in McGlynn et al's research (2017, 188). Other studies (eg Herman 2023) found that punishment and revenge was a less clear and ambivalent interest of victim/survivors. Victim/survivors in both RoI and NI who achieved successful prosecutions were grateful for the vindication (see Chapter 4). Others, especially in RoI, were interested in the prosecution of institutional actors and third parties for breach of regulations but the legal mechanisms for such prosecutions did not exist.

The connection between testimonies given to inquiries and the subsequent lack of criminal proceedings in RoI and NI and the interoperability of different forms of justice, while a complex matter regarding evidence and due process, was of concern to victim/survivors. Some wondered whether they had been believed during inquiries in both RoI and NI (see Chapter 5), particularly when no criminal proceedings followed.

In further reflections on responsibility and accountability, victim/survivors felt that they got law, bureaucracy, 'band aids', and settlements but not justice in terms of responsibility and accountability. Monetary settlements appeared to be on the minds of state and church officials long before it was on the minds of victim/survivors, as evidenced in the following quotes:

> I didn't know what they were talking about, money. I said, 'I don't want any money'. They thought, well you know, 'All you want really is to get the money', and I said, 'What money, what are you talking about'. I didn't know what the hell they were talking about. (Interview 52)

> So, initially and to this day, although monetary compensation is in the frame now for people, that was never, ever anything that me or my sister were looking for at all, and we wanted recognition and truth and justice for her [their mother's] name, even though she couldn't get any justice from beyond the grave. (Interview 65)

Some victim/survivors felt that money was being used to pay them off as one of the strategies to protect institutional reputations and avoid real responsibility and accountability:

> Their solution was give her money and she'll shut up . . . I came home with that offer of €100,000 on the table. My husband was like over the moon. You've won. My parents were, 'Now you've won'. Everyone had said to me, 'Take that money, you have won. That's them admitting liability' and I was like, 'That is not them admitting liability. That's them throwing money at me'. (Interview 66)

Victim/survivors were on a steep learning curve in their activism work and began to feel that the only way to achieve responsibility and accountability was when it involved a monetary cost for the institutions.

> We'd be nearly offended if somebody had mentioned, are you doing this for money? . . . [W]e soon learned that the only way we were going to get anything done was if it cost people money, it was the only language they understood . . . Government you see were ahead of us, they knew it really

> was about money. We didn't. This is true, this is really true. So, they saw the implications of it much more seriously and took it much more seriously than we did. And we were learning this is how they operate . . . [Y]ou might laugh at this, but the naivety of it at the time was I remember at the very beginning . . . [Name] and I said things like talking in her house and saying things like, they could just apologise. (Interview 6)

It is interesting to note the additional perspectives of state and church officials and legal professionals on the issue of monetary reparation (as noted in Chapter 4 (on conventional justice) and Chapters 6 and 7 (on reparation and apologies)). Some church and state actors believe the landscape became highly adversarial particularly when civil litigation and lawyers for victim/survivors entered the frame. Lawyers point to the inequality of arms that worked in the interest of church and state prior to their representation of victim/survivors. The role of lawyers and legal culture is not a simple one in this space (something we discuss further in Chapters 4, 6, and 9).

Motivation of elite-level actors

Victim/survivors had several views on the motivation of elite-level actors in church and state, particularly regarding accountability and the taking of responsibility. Limiting financial liability was a top priority in their view. As noted by one interviewee in NI:

> Sir Anthony Hart stepped outside his remit in terms of his terms of reference because he shaped the redress process. And the quote I will quote . . . 'Be mindful of the public purse' and then he put a cap on the redress. So, right away we were boxed in to the max of £80,000 for sexual abuse, physical abuse. (Interview 15)

Interviewees believe fear of legal and financial liability means that church, state, and responsible institutions exercise caution in issuing public and especially private apologies (see Chapter 7). Other strategies to limit financial liability include adopting a siloed approach to investigating various institutions, such as limiting the scope of inquiries into day schools in RoI; allowing delays to occur in issuing redress to victim/survivors; designing inequitable redress schemes, such as excluding infants who had spent less than six months in a mother and baby institution from the redress scheme in RoI; and mounting defensive legal strategies to fight victim/survivors in court, despite the profound inequality of arms between victim/survivors and church and state institutions. Victim/survivors argue that instead of defending cases in litigation, these funds could be more adequately used to develop fair redress schemes, *ex gratia* or otherwise. As one survivor in RoI put it:

> I honestly believe that for all the effort, time and money that they have spent defending the case, that if that effort, time and money was actually put into doing the *ex gratia* scheme correctly, it's not as if the floodgates would open and there would be an extraordinary demand for money because, well certainly to me . . . [T[here's no money in the world can take away what happened to me. (Interview 31)

Victim/survivors see institutional reputational protection as another strong motivation of elite-level actors. As one interviewee in RoI pointed out in relation to a State institution: 'It's what can we do that will "plámás"[5] you to get you to go away while we don't have to expose all the truth' (Interview 59). Another noted in relation to the Church that 'the institution would do all that it could to preserve itself' (Interview 9). Interviewees also saw staff of Defence Forces and other institutions being crushed by their own systems:

> I think there were good people who did try to make good change, who did try to make changes and the system itself crushed them and some of them . . . actually became worse than the people that they replaced . . . And for me, that's the tragedy of it. This was about an institution protecting itself and doing everything it could to protect itself and protect its reputation. (Interview 59)

Some victim/survivors believed that wanting to move on quickly and limit the spread of the problem politically drove the motivation of some elite actors. Victim/survivors felt they were left to do all the campaigning and advocating for any improvements and change. Little was proactively coming from church or state. 'It was all left to survivors to do all the running, all the heavy lifting—always is'. (Interview 13)

[5] This is an Irish word loosely meaning disingenuous flattery.

Some survivors in RoI and NI experienced some church and state actors as being motivated by a desire to do the right thing. Individual politicians took up the cause of victim/survivors and took action as best as they could in RoI: 'my trust built up again with my interactions with [politician] and [politician] (Interview 65) and in NI 'both of them actually said that, "Don't worry, we won't let you down"' (Interview 9). The same applied to Church personnel. 'I had a very frank meeting with them and like they did understand the journeys that we had, and they did show empathy and he apologised, you know, we're trying to right the wrongs' (Interview 15). Other men and women in positions of influence stood in solidarity with victim/survivors and that made a difference for them.

In summary, accountability by church and state actors is as important, if not more important, than individual perpetrator accountability for many victim/survivors, although perpetrator accountability is important too. As Downes (2017, 35) notes in relation to sexual violence, it is the silencing strategies following disclosure that can be as (or more) harmful than the violence initially experienced. From this perspective, the silencing of victim/survivors permits unequal power relations to remain unchanged and removes the opportunity for structural injustices to be critically examined and reformed. Victim/survivors also see the social/community dimension of responsibility and accountability as hugely important but to date as lacking sufficient attention in public and social discourse (for exception, see Scally 2021; Wills 2024). Herman (2023, 12–13) calls this 'justice as public recognition' and suggests the need for public affirmation of victim/survivors by means of community truth-telling and other community events. She argues that public and community recognition of hidden wrongs helps heal the broken relationships within and between communities.

6. Justice

The broader literature outlined in Chapter 1 demonstrates that victims of non-recent institutional abuses have varying and diverse expectations of justice, for example in the United States (Balboni and Bishop 2010); Australia (Daly 2014a; Golding 2018; Holder 2018); New Zealand (Jülich and Landon 2017); RoI (Keenan 2014; Pembroke 2019); NI (Lundy 2020; Mahon et al 2021; McGuckin 2023); the UK (McGlynn et al 2017), and in a comparative context (Daly 2014b; Ring et al 2022). Our study data affirms and refines these existing studies while also adding further nuance to knowledge and understanding of what justice means for victim/survivors and, more specifically, their experiences of justice. As highlighted by Holder (2018), justice is not a single event but more an unfolding process, with justice needs and interests changing over time. While victim/survivors of institutional abuses are not a homogeneous group, and their justice interests reflect this, some themes can be determined.

Acknowledgement, recognition, and truth

Acknowledgement emerged as a leading justice desire for victim/survivors in both RoI and NI, in line with other literature on this topic (see eg Balboni and Bishop 2010; Herman 2023). However, victim/survivors were specific about the type of acknowledgement they wanted. This included (1) not only acknowledgement by church and state of their personal and collective abuses but also of the harmful contexts of institutionalisation in which the abuses and neglect took place; (2) acknowledgement not only for themselves but for members of their families who were institutionalised, some of whom are now deceased; and (3) acknowledgement by broader society of its role in what occurred, no matter how obscure.

Victim/survivors had a range of experiences of acknowledgement along a continuum from downright denial to full acknowledgement by both church and state. The experience of acknowledgement was notably different for different institutional contexts. Inadequate acknowledgement by the State for victim/survivors of mother and baby institutions, the Defence Forces, and day schools in RoI tended to be at the lower end of the acknowledgement continuum, whereas acknowledgement for the abuse of children in industrial and reformatory schools, residential care homes, and in Catholic dioceses, as well as the treatment of women in Magdalene Laundries in RoI, was somewhat further along the acknowledgement continuum. Time may be a factor here as the latter issues have been discussed and examined in public life for a longer period than the former. The depth of the acknowledgement changed over time for some institutional contexts, for example for the industrial and reformatory schools in RoI.

In NI, where there are fewer official investigations into non-recent institutional abuses than in RoI, the acknowledgement continuum looks a little different. Children abused in residential care in NI are now acknowledged somewhat; however, for other cohorts (eg clerical child sexual abuse or sexual abuse in other non-religious settings) the State is slow to acknowledge the wrongdoing and abuses. In both jurisdictions, victim/survivors reported that they meet ongoing delays and obstacles in receiving acknowledgement and in receiving redress. This causes upset as some victim/survivors are elderly and some in fact have died while waiting.

Problems with acknowledgement are procedural as well as substantive. Victim/survivors describe being ignored, disrespected, and generally shown lack of courtesy at individual and political levels, on both sides of the border, but more particularly in RoI. Letters and emails received no response, not even an acknowledgement, including when sent multiple times with reminders. This lack of courtesy was experienced not only from politicians but also from civil servants, the latter especially in RoI:

> I feel very sad about how the Irish State turn their noses up at their own citizens, and I think that they should take, walk a mile in our shoes before they, and not just the government, the ones behind the scenes as well . . . and see how we feel as human beings when they're constantly ignoring us. (Interview 29)

> I still feel that the State let me down . . . I mean, I had over 50 emails I sent to him, and I asked him . . . 'Look, can I speak with you? This is happening under your watch' . . . and I got very upset on the day . . . I slammed them, all the emails, I previously sent him, down in front of him, because he was saying to us, 'Oh I'm really sorry, I didn't realise it was as bad as it was', and I said, 'I have been writing to you since, you know, forever . . . I looked to meet with you so many times and you wouldn't meet with me'. . . . [I]t was only after the [name] documentary then that they all said they would meet with us. (Interview 66)

Some victim/survivors accepted invitations to speak at public events being addressed by politicians purposefully to gain access to them when previous correspondence had been ignored:

> I just started talking, just didn't give her secretary a chance and I just said, 'I was very disappointed in the fact that the emails I had sent didn't get a reply, didn't even get an acknowledgement of receipt . . . I was disappointed that they couldn't do that much', and so, of course, you know, photographers were there to get a scoop . . . when he saw me coming . . . she [the politician] had given the opening speech in the morning; by 12 o'clock, I had gotten an email back. But it took that. (Interview 31)

Victim/survivors were met with a 'lack of humanity within the whole system' (Interview 31) during proceedings and actions taken against the state. Rather than being met with compassion and with the provision of additional support services, state lawyers defended heavily. The significant inequality of arms in these situations emerged as a strong finding, as other researchers have found (Smith and Duff 2020). Further, when victim/survivors took on the state in litigation they felt that they were not responded to as citizens to whom the state had obligations but rather as opponents of the state who were outside the category of citizen deserving protection and care (see further Chapter 4).

Victim/survivors also experienced lack of courtesy from some Church authorities who 'fobbed you off . . . didn't respect you . . . well used to playing the game with the media and the government and ah my God, dirty filthy stuff' (Interview 6). There was a sense, however, that this kind of behaviour changed over time; initial resistance giving way to a willingness to meet survivors but with insufficient acknowledgement or responsibility-taking. Over time, legal processing became dominant. There is also now increased willingness on the part of Church authorities, religious organisations, and to some extent the State in RoI to engage restoratively with victim/survivors who desire this approach and to treat them with respect (see Chapter 8). One notable exception is how one religious order responded with a PR firm to victim/survivors' queries and requests for a meeting:[6]

> When [name, her mother,] died . . . we said that we wanted answers and that this just was not good enough in 1995, that somebody should be buried without a proper funeral and without the relatives being told . . . and their reaction to our request was to have a PR company deal with us which we thought was an appalling, appallingly cold approach to somebody who'd lived under their roof for 51 years. (Interview 65)

Variations are evident in how different Church organisations respond to institutional abuse at any one time. It is a misnomer to believe that there is one monolithic Catholic Church when it comes to responding to allegations of non-recent institutional abuse (see also Chapters 7, 8, and 9).

[6] This research team got the same response to multiple requests for an interview from the same religious order, whereas others were extremely forthcoming and spoke with candour despite their broader concerns regarding research.

As noted, some victim/survivors in both jurisdictions also commented on the kindness, respect, and compassion they received from some politicians and Church personnel. The same political and Church names were repeated many times during these interviews, including at ministerial level, as those who not only were kind and respectful but also championed the cause of victim/survivors and propelled state action. Whilst kindness was shown by some clergy, they were less impactful in propelling action at Church level. The politeness of civil servants in their correspondence with victim/survivors was often dampened by the content of the letters:

> I mean . . . nobody told the truth . . . it was like being Alice in Wonderland. You wondered, what are they talking about, that didn't happen, why are they saying that, that can't happen and it's all . . . done politely. The letters are very polite, 'Dear [name], yours sincerely, all the very best', you know . . . whoever he was, you know, and it was to shut me up, I think. (Interview 52)

Acknowledgement was made by some victim/survivors of a growing understanding at the political level at last of the need for action in responding particularly to elderly victim/survivors before their deaths.

The importance of societal acknowledgement (and, by implication, societal accountability) emerged more strongly in this research than in previous studies (see also Scally 2021; Wills 2024) and suggests that the time has come to broaden the net of responsibility and accountability for the incarceration of women and children. Such a development could ultimately lead to greater societal as well as individual healing and recovery. As expressed by one interviewee who spent time in institutions for women and children on both sides of the border: 'For me, it feels like . . . I just want to feel like there's an acknowledgement that something happened—that, you know, shouldn't have happened. And that my life was changed dramatically, and my mother's life, and my siblings. And that the country did something like really bizarre' (Interview 8).

Being cognisant of the complexities of truth and that multiple perspectives exist on even a single event, victim/survivors want truth in terms of individual, political, and institutional honesty (similar to findings of other studies or reports, eg Hamber and Lundy 2020; Mahon et al 2021). They want the terms of reference of inquiries to allow for the whole complex truth to be told, and they want answers to questions:

> Really [I want] a conversation about how this happened, why it happened and how we could stop it from happening again . . . [T]he Commission [of Investigation] . . . was just one tiny sliver of the situation. It wasn't looking at the issues involved, and why people were in institutions, you know. I think that's the story that needs to be told. It didn't look at why was Temple Hill in existence, with all those babies. (Interview 8)

What emerges in this research is that when it comes to justice as acknowledgement and truth, the experience of victim/survivors is largely one of denial, minimisation, and defensiveness but this has changed over time for some cohorts of survivors. Nonetheless, many still experience church and state defensive legal strategies. The need to examine the specific details of organisational culture as part of the problem of institutional wrongdoing in multiple contexts rather than as an excuse of being of times past is a justice aspiration yet to be realised.

Voice and meaningful participation

Victim/survivors wish to have an opportunity to speak their truth in their own words and have their lived experience regarded as part of the evidence, even thematically, coded to feed into official records. This desire is also emphasised in other literature (Daly 2017; Gallen 2023a). Victim/survivors do not want their truth disregarded as 'merely' a 'personal story'. The exercising of voice must be facilitated in a way that is 'all about mutual respect' (Interview 6) and sensitively done, unlike the experience of some victim/survivors who participated in inquiries in both RoI and NI. Co-design of inquiries, and not simply participation or consultation, was emphasised time and again (see also Hamber and Lundy 2020). However, there are latent complexities that will require careful examination as to how this can be achieved within the legal parameters of the independence of inquiry mechanisms. Nonetheless, in a strongly expressed desire, victim/survivors wish to be involved with other stakeholders from church and state in the design of inquiry models, redress processes, apologies, and memorialisation/rituals of remembering. For victim/survivors, such co-design would mean that 'lessons can be learned' (Interview 15). This interviewee recounted his experience of participation in the Hart Inquiry in NI as evidence for how not to do further inquiries without victim/survivor input: 'Sir Anthony was actually taking evidence from survivors, albeit you're steered. And

I remember leaving that witness box, Jesus Christ. I couldn't open-up because I wasn't allowed to open-up . . . rather than letting me finish what I was saying (Interview 15). Some victim/survivors described being 'nearly broken' (Interview 6) by inquiry processes and redress mechanisms.

Victim/survivors feel the exercise of their voice is often constrained by the terms of reference of inquiries. Despite state logic for the approaches taken to setting the terms of reference, including expediency, managing the parameters of the inquiry, and limiting liability, many victim/survivors found that the terms of reference of some inquiries worked against the interest of getting to the whole and complex truth. Not engaging with victim/survivors in the design of mechanisms of justice is seen by them as 'lost opportunities' to get things right (Interviews 8, 15, 20, and 22).

The Collaborative Forum in RoI brought together victim/survivors, State officials, and academics to enable victim/survivors of mother and baby institutions to identify, discuss, and prioritise the issues of concern and actively participate in developing solutions. The Forum was initially seen by some as a move in the right direction but was undermined by the RoI government's failure to publish its first report for several years, citing the right of reply of the parties named in the report (see Chapter 8).[7] In RoI, victim/survivors continue to advocate for people with the necessary interdisciplinary skills and expertise to form panels of commissioners for inquiries, to be involved in designing the terms of reference, and, in some specific cases, for tribunals to be established when other inquiry mechanisms seem to have failed (such as the IRG 2023 into the Irish Defence Forces). Victim/survivors in NI (or with an interest in both jurisdictions) point to the Truth Recovery Design Panel into Mother and Baby Homes in NI as a good example of a process designed to enable victim/survivors to co-design justice processes, exercise their voices, and for testimonies given to independent panels to feed into the full statutory inquiry (see Mahon et al 2021) (see also Chapters 5 and 9). In both jurisdictions, it has been suggested that the societal focus on abuse in institutions run by the Catholic Church allows for abuse in Protestant institutions to remain largely unexamined (see Chapters 1 and 10).

It has been important for some victim/survivors to have opportunities to exercise their voice in multiple other ways, such as by facing Church actors in restorative meetings, by training and informing clergy on issues related

[7] Mother and Baby Home Collaborative Forum, https://www.gov.ie/en/publication/0b0200-mother-and-baby-home-collaborative-forum/ (accessed 20 June 2024).

to abuse, and by influencing Church policy responses. Victim/survivors have also been involved in training and educating state actors, such as social workers and legal professionals, developing social services for victim/survivors in collaboration with state actors, and in developing services with Church personnel to address the spiritual needs of victim/survivors. The importance of these collaborative efforts to enable victim/survivors to exercise their voices based on lived experience and influence policy and practice developments cannot be overemphasised.

Vindication

Vindication at an individual, church, state, institutional, and increasingly at societal level is a theme that drove some victim/survivors in their search for justice, also noted in other literature (see Daly 2014b; Herman, 2005):

> What drove me forward was, I think, the need for vindication. Vindication was a huge aspect for me because I was a chartered engineer and I had worked very, very hard in the organisation to do my job to the best of my ability, and . . . it felt like I was being told I was no good at my job and they were doing everything in their power to nearly break me, to show the world that I was no good at my job. So, in the initial stages, it was a sense of vindication I was looking for to say, 'No, you're wrong. I can do my job and you don't have the right to do what you did to me'. (Interview 59)

Victim/survivors had mixed experiences of vindication. Vindication of child sexual abuse by Catholic clergy in the Archdiocese of Dublin was achieved in the Commission of Investigation into the Archdiocese of Dublin and the related Murphy Report (2009), which collectively highlighted failures in the handling of abuse complaints by Church and State authorities. Vindication for victim/survivors was also achieved in criminal cases where there was a conviction and in successful civil action. Successful judgments from the Workplace Relations Commission were also seen as vindication for victim/survivors who won their cases there. However, there was lack of vindication and significant disappointment for survivors in the findings of some inquiries into State institutions and reports of commissions of investigation. These include the Final Report of the Commission of Investigation into Mother and Baby Homes (2021) and the McAleese Report into Magdalene Laundries (IDC 2013) in RoI. From the perspective of victim/survivors involved in these latter processes, important details of their experiences were often ignored, reported incorrectly, or minimised.

Victim/survivors also experienced a lack of vindication in the criminal justice process when their complaints did not progress to trial or when legislation did not provide for prosecution of institutional actors for 'breach of regulations' (Interview 52) (see Chapter 4). In civil proceedings, victim/survivors sometimes had difficulty remembering dates and names of people related to their time in institutions without the benefit of their records. Similarly, they had difficulty tracking down potential witnesses from many years prior who could testify in their cases. The State approach of mounting strong legal defences in these cases, including at United Nations and European levels, added to the burden of stress experienced by victim/survivors in trying to put their cases together.

Access to records

Access to information and personal records is not often mentioned in the literature as a significant stand-alone justice desire for victim/survivors of institutional abuses (see for exceptions O'Rourke et al 2018; Lundy 2020) but it emerged strongly as a core justice interest for victim/survivors in this research in both RoI and NI. Importantly, interviewees specified the kind of information they require. This includes records and information relating to their personal history, life details and personal identity, and any records held about them and their lost children, lost siblings, and loved ones in the institutions in which they were detained. Victim/survivors of the Defence Forces also want access to any other information and records held about them in State institutions in which they were employed that are now the subject of their complaints of institutional abuse.

In their attempts to access information and records, victim/survivors are often met with delays, obstacles, and insensitivities. Many victim/survivors were simply denied access to information about their lost babies and children. Until recent times, they had to undertake these searches alone without the help of the state but with obstacles presented at every turn. One interviewee whose baby was illegally adopted in RoI reflected:

> I was looking to see if I could find out whether my son was okay, whether he was alive, where he was . . . I didn't know anything about him. I wanted to know where he was and who had adopted him . . . I would have liked

> to have a relationship with the mother and that she would keep me in touch with how he was, and then when he was grown up . . . or whenever we decided was the best, then present myself . . . I went over to Ireland . . . I think it was sometime in the '70s . . . and I went to the nuns in Middle Abbey Street and I was told that I hadn't had that child, I'd imagined it . . . There was no file on him at all and I said, 'It's ridiculous, a little boy, what happened'. She said, 'boys never want to find their parents anyway, so you don't really need to do anymore looking because he won't want you' . . . and that sort of thing is banged into my head . . . But, at one time when I came back to Dublin, I went back to the nursing home that I had lived in and [name] who was the midwife, answered the door to me and she said . . . she thought my child had gone to America. She knew he hadn't but she told me that she thought he'd gone to America, and she said, I remember her words, 'There was a lot of traffic between Ireland and America in those days and there was no paperwork so you won't be able to trace him because there's always no paper trail at all', and he was down the country . . . He was an hour away. (Interview 52)

Some interviewees were told that their lost siblings or loved ones did not want to be found. While occasionally true, many found this not to be the case:

> The Salvation Army got into it and said she didn't want to be found at that time but I took up the thing myself . . . and I did find her, that took a big chip off my shoulder . . . I remember [the adoption agency saying] you don't know if she wants to be found and it can damage, you know, doing all this. (Interview 2)

Legislation in NI[8] and recent legislation in RoI[9] provide for some information to be given to adopted and boarded-out children about their parents and siblings and to mothers about their lost children. However, victim/survivors who got access to records from some institutions often reported that documents were heavily redacted to the point that they were 'almost useless' (Interview 8). Records were often missing 'vital information' (Interview 8), for example about the circumstances of their birth or their adoption. Others disputed the content or status of records, such as forms on

[8] The Adoption (Northern Ireland) Order 1987.
[9] The Birth Information and Tracing Act 2022.

Adoption Society headed paper that survivors have no memory of signing. In many cases, records are simply non-existent, incomplete, or inaccurate. It is therefore extremely difficult for victim/survivors when written records of their lives and events are privileged over their lived experience, especially in official report findings. Victim/survivors feel in these circumstances that 'the truth still in our testimonies . . . it's being whitewashed' (Interview 20). (This cross-cutting issue is raised also in Chapters 4, 5, and 6 and addressed in Chapter 9.)

Reparations and non-recurrence

Several other themes emerged within the empirical data gathered from victim/survivors. The desire for redress and apologies (as part of accountability discussed earlier) are examined in Chapters 6, 7, and 9. Non-recurrence, including the protection of children and adults in vulnerable situations and the prevention of further institutional abuses and harms, as acknowledged in other literature (see eg Keenan 2014; McGlynn et al 2017), are examined in Chapters 4 (on conventional justice), 6 (on reparation and redress), and 7 (on apologies). In a backward- and forward-looking dynamic, victim/survivors want the lessons learnt from institutional abuse inquiries to be applied to contemporary contexts and new policy directions to take account of lessons learned so that institutional abuses will not be reproduced in other 'new' contexts, such as institutions for elderly people. Victim/survivors in both jurisdictions commended Church safeguarding practices and in RoI were heartened by the fact that the Health Information and Quality Authority (HIQA)[10] inspects residential facilities for children. However, victim/survivors did not see significant structural or cultural/ideological change in church or state institutions beyond these procedural changes in safeguarding. They saw a need for the organisational cultural aspects of the institutions in which abuses occurred to be addressed to prevent recurrence (see eg Keenan 2012 for an analysis of the organisation of the Catholic Church). Without this structural-level change, victim/survivors fear the same patterns of abuses and wrongs will be repeated in these and other contexts, lessons will not be learned, and other vulnerable children and adults will suffer as they did.

[10] HIQA is an independent authority that exists to improve health and social care services for people in RoI.

7. Conclusion: Centring the Voice of Victim/Survivors

This chapter set out to address three interrelated issues: to what extent can insights from the impact of institutional abuses on victim/survivors, their experiences of institutional responsibility and accountability, and of seeking justice contribute to a new justice approach that works to transform justice responses to non-recent institutional abuses. The discussion provided understandings of the multifarious impacts of non-recent institutional abuses on the lives of victims/survivors. It indicates the critical need for justice responses to address the distinctive experiences of institutional abuses for victim/survivors and the profound impacts of these abuses, past, present, and future. Justice for victims/survivors can arguably only be achieved by genuinely and sensitively recognising the true nature and depth of their suffering. The story of trauma, profound losses, rejection, and marginalisation at multiple levels must be at the heart of all justice and healing responses. The conclusion of this chapter is that seeking justice for victim/survivors is fraught with difficulty, not least in terms of their suffering and their differing, ambiguous, and evolving expectations but also because of their lack of power at the mercy of the elites (see McGlynn et al 2017, 188; Holder 2018, 7). Nonetheless, it is crucial that the individual and deeply personal needs of victim/survivors are addressed in official justice processes and form the basis of any recommendations made.

In highlighting the complexity of victimhood and its ripple effects, it becomes evident that this complexity problematises and complicates discourses and practices regarding responsibility and accountability (explored in depth in Chapters 9 and 10). There are different types of victimhood often within the same context and this opens the question of how justice can be administered in the individual and the collective sense. It also raises the question as to whom the church and state are responsible and for what exactly in each case. The answers to these questions may be different for different victim/survivors at different points in time. While the expectations of victim/survivors in terms of justice are diverse, sometimes contradictory, and can vary over time, there are themes now well established in literature, supported by the empirical data presented in this chapter, that can give policymakers some clarity on what these justice aspirations are. They include acknowledgement and truth; voice and meaningful participation; vindication; access to records; non-recurrence and protection of children and vulnerable adults; reparation, including monetary redress and apology; accountability; healing; and belonging.

What also emerges is that justice for victim/survivors is not synonymous with conventional understandings of justice which are often framed in individualist, legalistic, adversarial, and outcome-based terms (see Chapter 1 and Part II). The analysis suggests that responsibility and accountability also have a broader meaning for victim/survivors than conventional understandings suggest and includes social/community dimensions as well as individual and institutional obligations. While very important for victim/survivors, 'social' responsibility and accountability are difficult to capture at the level of praxis within actual justice mechanisms. New ways must be sought to address these interests. Practices and values from innovative justice mechanisms, such as restorative and transitional justice, have something to offer in this regard (see Chapter 8 on restorative and transitional justice). At the level of praxis, there is a need for more public information regarding additional justice options and opportunities.

In line with the aims of the book, the analysis presented in this chapter will be core to recommendations made for transforming justice responses for victim/survivors of non-recent institutional abuses, based on the commitment to engage with the perspectives of all interested parties, to explore the potential of innovative justice philosophies and practices, and to reformulate conceptions of responsibility and accountability. These and related ideas for theory and praxis are developed fully in the final part of the book.

PART II

JUSTICE RESPONSES TO NON-RECENT INSTITUTIONAL ABUSES

4
Conventional Justice Responses

1. Introduction

Part II of the book critically evaluates existing justice responses to non-recent institutional abuses broadly considered under conventional justice mechanisms (Chapter 4), inquiries (Chapter 5), reparations (Chapter 6), and apologies (Chapter 7). Conventional justice responses considered in this chapter include criminal law, civil litigation, international human rights law (IHRL), and canon law. These justice mechanisms contribute to a distorted approach to justice and result in perspectives on responsibility and accountability that are misaligned to the challenges of addressing non-recent institutional abuses. Barriers to justice of an ideological, structural, and legal nature permeate these justice mechanisms. Criminal law truncates potential accountability for non-recent institutional abuses and is incapable of addressing the continuities of harm. While civil litigation may establish the liability and responsibility of state and church institutions, it is limited by the available forms of liability, the temporal limitation of litigation, the availability of suitable defendants and witnesses, and by the inequality of arms in its structure and practice. Human rights law may offer the basis for empowerment for survivors and affected communities but can equally be limited in its potential and will also be likely resisted in its implementation by governments.

Section 2 examines conventional justice responses and their underlying focus and purpose. Section 3 provides an international context for the use of conventional justice mechanisms to address non-recent institutional abuses. Informed by interview data, Sections 4 and 5 evaluate the capacity of conventional justice in the Republic of Ireland (RoI) and Northern Ireland (NI) to provide justice, responsibility, and accountability for non-recent institutional abuses. Section 6 briefly considers the role of canon law on the island of Ireland in responding to allegations of abuse. Drawing further on interview data, Section 7 discerns the value and

Transforming Justice Responses to Non-Recent Institutional Abuses. Anne-Marie McAlinden, Marie Keenan, and James Gallen, Oxford University Press.
DOI: 10.1093/9780191967399.003.0004

limitations of conventional justice responses from the perspective of key stakeholders, including victim/survivors, state, and church representatives. The concluding section considers the transformative potential and challenges of conventional justice frameworks for justice, responsibility, and accountability.

2. Conventional Justice: Form and Function

Conventional justice mechanisms have strengths and limitations. Criminal justice is intended to afford validation and vindication for victim/survivors in the event of successful prosecutions, to provide mechanisms of accountability, vengeance, deterrence, rehabilitation for perpetrators, and social norm conveyance (Aukerman 2002). For isolated or recent offences, empirical evidence for achieving these goals is questionable (Mears 2010; Hamilton 2023), especially for sexual violence, neglecting broader goals for victim/survivors including recognition, voice, and healing (see Keenan 2014; McGlynn and Westmarland 2019).

Concerns about the value of criminal justice are even more exacerbated when it comes to widespread or systemic crimes where large numbers of alleged perpetrators will likely remain unprosecuted due to non-reporting, limits in legal and organisational capacity, and political will (Cavallaro and O'Connell 2020). In addition, accessing criminal justice for non-recent offences can be limited by the pre-existing criminal legal standards at the time of the commission of the offences and by delays in disclosure, which can create evidential difficulties concerning memory and recall of 'traumatic history' (Herman 2015) and witness availability (Keenan et al 2023).

Several criminal offences concern non-recent institutional abuses, with particular legislative focus on sexual violence (Ring et al 2022, 71–98). The large-scale nature of child sex abuse in Catholic dioceses and residential institutions globally has prompted survivor demands that institutional leadership be investigated and held accountable for their responses to allegations of criminal abuse (Pilgrim 2011). While allegations of sexual violence in institutional contexts may be subject to criminal investigation, the act of institutionalisation itself was authorised by legislation and/or acquiesced to by the legal system, as discussed in Chapter 2. As a result, the criminal justice system has no role in addressing accountability for institutionalisation as a policy wrong and distinct harm (Shuman and McCall Smith 2000).

Therefore, criminal justice responses alone narrow and constrict the legal expression of responsibility for widespread or systemic non-recent harms and abuses and are unable to provide broader justice outcomes that survivors may want (see Chapter 3).

Civil liability is designed to hold individuals, institutions, and states accountable for breaches of appropriate duties and standards of care (Lytton 2008, 136). The principal remedy in civil liability is compensation through damages for harm and the vindication by the judge or legitimate authority of the harm done. Several grounds of civil liability have been employed to address non-recent abuses (O'Reilly and Chalmers 2014, 32). Some, such as negligence, involve an assessment of fault of the individuals or institutions involved. Others, such as vicarious liability or non-delegable duties, are non-fault-based forms of liability, typically attaching to institutions found responsible for the harms conducted by an employee or member of the institution.[1] In recent years, vicarious liability has been imposed where wrongful conduct had a 'close connection' or constituted an 'enterprise risk' to the defendant employer.[2] While there are several conceptions of responsibility in civil justice (Goldberg and Zipursky 2014, 17–18), distinctive justifications can be found for the responsibility of state or church institutional defendants, who may be seen as 'juridically unequal' parties involved in the provision of 'public functions' (Cane 2014), compared to an individual plaintiff seeking to sue those defendants.

The use of IHRL can occur through national litigation or international individual complaint mechanisms and treaty-based monitoring mechanisms. The impact of IHRL will depend on whether a state has a bill of rights and the number of ratified international human rights treaties and is based on the subsidiary nature of international human rights mechanisms and the degree of national political will (Simmons 2009). Such IHRL treaties may be limited temporally to their date of ratification, which may preclude them addressing non-recent abuses (Gallen 2019a). Nonetheless, IHRL provides an additional framework to assess a state's responsibility to address allegations of prior wrongdoing based on whether a state has respected, protected, and fulfilled the human rights of individuals within its jurisdiction. The area of IHRL is also subject to considerable critique (Marks 2011). As a result, it is necessary to adopt a 'critical politics of rights' (Golder 2015, 80) to interrogate whether and how IHRL can channel claims

[1] *Canadian Pacific Railway Co v Lockhart* [1942] 8 WLUK 4.
[2] *Bazley v Curry* [1999] 2 SCR 534, 544; *Lister v Hesley Hall Ltd* [2002] 1 UKHL 22, [14].

regarding non-recent institutional abuses into effective legal and political demands. While several human rights are relevant to non-recent abuses (Gallen 2019a), access to personal data and records remains a particular priority for victim/survivors on the island of Ireland (O'Rourke 2022), including those interviewed for this study.

Canon law is the internal regulatory system for priests and religious of the Roman Catholic Church.[3] Although canon law has long prohibited child sexual abuse, both its legal provisions and their implementation have been criticised (Doyle 2004). Canon law sanctions are intended to 'encourage the offender's change of mind and heart'[4] rather than to apportion responsibility or to respond to the needs of victim/survivors. Canon law did not emerge as a significant justice concern within the book's empirical research.

At their best, conventional justice mechanisms could contribute to McGlynn and Westmarland's (2019) 'kaleidoscopic justice', shifting patterns of justice in a myriad of constructive ways, recognising that different victim/survivors may choose to engage with different justice mechanisms at different times. However, at the level of praxis, diverse conventional justice mechanisms can negatively impact victim/survivors' felt sense of justice, restricting their possibilities of achieving justice through law.

3. The International Dimension

Many jurisdictions have used conventional justice measures to address allegations of non-recent abuses, particularly child sexual abuse. In Australia, the criminal justice report of the Royal Commission into Institutional Responses to Child Sexual Abuse concluded that between 1950 and 2010, 1,880 alleged religious perpetrators were identified in claims of child sexual abuse (Royal Commission 2017b, 5). The Final Report concluded that children were allegedly abused in over 4,000 institutions and made 2,252 referrals to the police, leading to at least 127 prosecutions as of 2017.[5] It also criticised the criminal trial process as challenging and distressing for victims of child sexual abuse (Royal Commission 2017b, 12).

[3] Code of Canon Law 1983.

[4] Code of Canon Law 1983, canon 1341.

[5] M Davey, 'Royal commission has led to more than 100 child abuse prosecutions, says head', *The Guardian*, 15 May 2017.

In England and Wales, police Operation Hydrant was established in 2014 to coordinate all investigations concerning persons of public prominence and 'non-recent' institutional sexual abuses. Figures in early 2020 indicate that '4,024 allegations led to guilty verdicts at court after police investigations since 2014 into decades-old child sex offences'.[6] Since 2014, 7,000 suspects have been identified, with 11,346 allegations of attacks received from 9,343 victims, all concerning sexual abuse of children in institutional and non-institutional contexts.

Class action litigation has been a significant tool for validation and redress for victim/survivors from state and church organisations. In Canada, the Indian Residential Schools Settlement Agreement 2006 settled over 7,000 legal claims against the federal government and a number of churches. A second large settlement agreement in 2018 relates to the 'Sixties Scoop' of Indigenous children to foster care and adoption. Similarly, in the United States, aggregated data on the settlement of clerical sexual abuse cases against the Catholic Church reveal that 5,679 survivors received a total of approximately $2.5 billion, with an average settlement of $268,466.[7] In Australia, aggregated data gathered by the Royal Commission reveals that over 3,000 claims of child sexual abuse against religious orders were resolved between 1995 and 2015. Catholic Church authorities made total payments of $268.0 million to settle claims of child sexual abuse between 1 January 1980 and 28 February 2015 (Royal Commission 2015, 112). In England and Wales, the Independent Inquiry into Child Sexual Abuse report on accountability and reparations noted that for many victim/survivors

> the litigation process was emotionally challenging and that it compounded the trauma they had already suffered as children. They also felt dissatisfied with the outcome, either because their claims had failed or because they had succeeded, usually by accepting a settlement offer, but they had never received any explanation or apology for what had happened to them and did not feel that justice had been done. (IICSA 2019, 26)

[6] V Dodd, 'Police uncovering "epidemic of child abuse" in 1970s and 80s', *The Guardian*, 5 February 2020.

[7] Bishop Accountability, 'Sexual Abuse by US Catholic Clergy, Settlements and Monetary Awards in Civil Suits', https://www.bishop-accountability.org/settlements/ (accessed 1 June 2024); figures have not been validated by governmental inquiry or process.

Although class actions remain possible in some Scandinavian states (Molavi 2022), they have not been employed in the context of non-recent harms due to the application of the statute of limitations (Sköld 2023, 82).

In several jurisdictions, civil liability has also been employed to address significant policy wrongs. In both Canada and Australia, there has been considerable litigation in efforts to assert Indigenous access to and ownership of traditional lands.[8] In the United States, important changes have been pursued regarding racial injustice and Native access and ownership of traditional lands via litigation[9] but have also met with substantial resistance and retrenchment in court (Blackhawk 2019; Joshi 2021).

Several jurisdictions and international bodies affirm the limited effectiveness of canon law to address child sex abuse. In Australia, although national responses were established in the 1990s, the Royal Commission concluded that processes 'to dismiss priests and religious appear to have been rarely used during the 1990s and early 2000s' (Royal Commission 2017c, 64–5). In England and Wales, the IICSA report on safeguarding within the Roman Catholic Church concluded: 'The absence of published data about the number of priests laicised for child sexual abuse offences . . . diminishes confidence in the Church's handling of such cases' (IICSA 2020a, 27). Before the United Nations Committee against Torture, the Holy See asserted that it had confirmed 3,420 credible allegations of sexual abuse by priests between 2004 and 2013, resulting in the removal of 848 priests and the disciplining of 2,572 others (UNCAT 2014, para 10) More recent global figures are unavailable. While these approaches across several jurisdictions affirm the capacity of conventional justice responses to deliver some form of justice and individual and institutional responsibility and accountability, they have proven limited in challenging the full nature and extent of historical injustices (Gallen 2023a, 164–95).

4. Conventional Justice in the Republic of Ireland

Criminal accountability for non-recent institutional abuses in RoI has focused almost exclusively on child sexual abuse. Historically, there were low levels of prosecution of child sex abuse offences in RoI (Carrigan 1931, para

[8] *Mabo and Others v Queensland (No 2)* [1992] HCA 23; *The Wik Peoples v State of Queensland & Ors* [1996] HCA 40; *Tsilhqot'in Nation v British Columbia* 2014 SCC 44.

[9] *Brown v Board of Education of Topeka*, 347 US 483 (1954); *Harper v Virginia State Board of Elections* 383 US 663, 663 (1966); *McGirt v Oklahoma*, 140 S Ct 2452 (2020).

C.17). Children in Ireland in the mid-late twentieth century faced a hostile legal and social culture adverse to reports of sexual abuse (Ring et al 2022, 131–7). Ring (2017, 562–80) notes that adult victims gave evidence to Irish courts demonstrating that as children they had disclosed to adults but were ignored and their complaints not acted upon.

A 2002 documentary regarding clerical child sexual abuse in Dublin prompted a criminal investigation (O'Gorman 2010). The Murphy Report considered that the investigation was 'an effective, co-ordinated and comprehensive inquiry' (CoI 2009, para 5.43). One criminal justice professional concurred: 'the investigation was top class, the work was brilliant. There was plenty of money spent on it' (Interview 67). Between 1975 and 2014, there were 4,406 allegations of child sexual abuse by priests in non-residential settings reported to Church authorities and Gardaí from across the island of Ireland. This resulted in 95 criminal convictions, based on a Church compilation of figures.[10] A more recent media analysis gathered for this project shows media coverage of criminal convictions by priests and members of religious orders from 1990 to 2023 discussing a total of 137 convictions, including those related to residential settings such as industrial and reformatory schools.[11]

A recurring theme within the interview narratives was the significant structural and legal barriers to justice and accountability within criminal justice frameworks. One criminal justice professional in RoI identified some of these barriers: 'there were identification difficulties, there was also difficulties around . . . corroboration, getting school records or institutional records corroborating or proving that the victim was actually in a class of the abuser' (Interview 37). In RoI, the decision to prosecute is now informed by a Guidelines policy for the Director of Public Prosecutions (DPP) (DPP 2019). As one criminal justice professional noted: 'We have to be satisfied that there's a prima facia case which means that a jury, properly instructed, could reach a verdict, and also, that a prosecution is in the public interest' (Interview 37). The interviewee continued:

> We look at the consistency of the complaint, . . . counselling records, medical reports or whatever and put together a picture . . . of the victim

[10] See figures compiled from the annual reports from National Board for Safeguarding Children in the Catholic Church in Ireland, http://www.safeguarding.ie (accessed 1 June 2024).

[11] The raw data presented in this chapter is limited for comparative purposes in the absence of full data and robust statistical analysis comparing it as a percentage of total population of relevant individuals.

> in terms of their credibility and reliability . . . [T]here's a very strong public interest in prosecuting offences of . . . sexual abuse, be they historical or be they recent. (Interview 37)

The passage of time and the death of some alleged perpetrators by the time the complaint is made emerged as a key challenge for criminal and civil justice. In addition, criminal justice has had limited coordination with inquiries. Eleven criminal cases were forwarded to the DPP in RoI based on the Ryan Report (2009) regarding abuse in child residential institutions (UNCAT 2011, para 20). One criminal justice professional noted the challenges created by inquiries: 'a number of individuals had already given evidence to a tribunal then, and then they were interviewed by the Guards,[12] any little inconsistency then between the various accounts or whatever would be picked up on by the defence in a criminal trial' (Interview 37). There is a legislative use of immunity preventing the interoperability of inquiries with the criminal justice system in RoI.[13] Another criminal justice professional noted that it is not clear whether inquiry testimony, as currently collected, is suitable for a criminal investigation, as regarding the police: 'they're very experienced in how to gather evidence in a way that . . . increases the chances of its admissibility. So, where those processes haven't happened . . . I don't know . . . how we could weight it' (Interview 70). A further criminal justice professional noted that inquiries and criminal investigations are: 'not very compatible in terms of what they're looking to find the truth of' (Interview 44). In contrast, one interviewee noted that from the 2002 Garda investigation into non-recent child abuse in the Dublin Archdiocese: 'all of the paperwork and statements that were taken ended up being in the Ryan Report or the Murphy Report because when they were established . . . what they did was they applied for all our stuff' (Interview 67).

Beyond individual acts of child sex abuse, the Gardaí considered the offence of 'misprision of felony' where a person knew a felony had been committed and concealed it from the authorities but no prosecutions arose for that offence (CoI 2009, paras 5.35–5.36). The Murphy Report concluded that such investigations 'were carried out more for the sake of completeness than from any substantial belief that there would ever be such a prosecution' (CoI 2009, para 5.39). One criminal justice professional noted the

[12] This is a reference to a member of An Gárda Síochána, the Irish Police.

[13] The Commission to Inquire into Child Abuse Act 2000, s 21; Commissions of Investigation Act 2004, s 19.

evidential difficulties: 'There wasn't any big trials out of it in terms of going after a bishop for moving priests around because we could never really prove it. An awful lot of the priests who were the more serious offenders were dead' (Interview 67).

There are several reasons why there have been no recent criminal prosecutions related to Magdalene Laundries, mother and baby institutions, or illegal adoptions in RoI.[14] Fraudulent adoption was criminalised under the Births and Deaths Registration Act 1874 and the Adoption Act 1952. While offences under the 1952 Act were summary in nature, and subject to a six-month statute of limitations within which to bring complaints, offences under the 1874 Act were felonies, with no statute of limitations. In cases beyond false birth registration, the relevant criminal offence for coercive adoptions may have been a conspiracy to kidnap.[15] Investigation of these offences may include all parties to the alleged offence, such as the adoptive parents of the child who may or may not have been aware of the true circumstances surrounding the child's adoption. This factor may have inhibited disclosure or complaint regarding adoption-related offences.

In relation to non-adoption offences in mother and baby institutions and Magdalene Laundries, in 1931, the International Labour Organisation Forced Labour Convention, 1930 (No 29) was ratified in Irish law and created an obligation to make forced labour a penal offence. However, this did not occur until the Criminal Law (Trafficking) Act 2008. The Mother and Baby Homes Commission provided significant evidence of the death of children while resident in the institutions (CoI MBH 2021, ch 33). However, further forensic evidence is needed to assess the extent of criminal wrongdoing, if any, in these deaths. At the time of writing, a forensic excavation of the burial site at the mother and baby institution at Tuam, Co Galway is due to commence in early 2025.

This lack of prosecutions outside of sexual abuse in RoI contrasts with the recent criminal convictions in Scotland of two nuns and a care worker arising from physical and sexual abuse within institutions run by the Daughters of Charity.[16] Criminal justice in RoI has thus addressed only a

[14] M Milotte, 'Adoption controversy: only one person was ever charged over bogus Birth certificates', *The Irish Times*, 1 June 2018.

[15] The common law offence of kidnapping was abolished in RoI by the Non-Fatal Offences Against the Person Act 1997, s 28 and replaced by the offences of false imprisonment and abduction of a child by others under ss 15 and 17.

[16] 'Smyllum Park: Nuns and carer jailed for abusing orphanage children', *BBC News*, 18 January 2024, https://www.bbc.com/news/uk-scotland-glasgow-west-68020586.

subset of allegations of non-recent wrongdoing, limited by potential applicable criminal law standards, potential social considerations regarding adoptive families, and by the degradation of evidence over time. The result is that criminal justice plays a small, albeit significant, role as a justice response to non-recent abuses.

In RoI, regarding civil justice, there has been media coverage of large-scale settlements of religious organisations related to non-recent abuses, principally related to allegations of child sex abuse.[17] However, with no comprehensive audit of the settlement of litigation across all relevant religious organisations, it is not possible to fully evaluate this practice. There is limited successful jurisprudence regarding the direct negligence of state or church institutions. There are no cases where there has been a proven breach of the duty of care in the context of Magdalene Laundries or mother and baby institutions. Regarding symphysiotomy, there have been a small number of successful actions,[18] while other cases have been dismissed where symphysiotomy was deemed medically justified as the prevailing standard of the time.[19] One academic-advocate noted the lack of integration of inquiries with civil justice: 'How could a Mother and Baby Homes Commission find that vaccine trials are done without any legal authority or consent and yet there's no injury when the tort of battery or assault clearly is relevant' (Interview 4).

Early case law on vicarious liability rejected the possibility that an employer could be vicariously liable for acts of sexual harassment by employees.[20] While subsequent developments have enabled vicarious liability for sexual abuse, the courts have been cautious in their expansion of liability.[21] Non-delegable duties, discussed later regarding NI, have not been developed as significantly in Irish law as in NI.[22] However, in *Morrissey v HSE*, Clarke CJ considered the development of this approach in English law, before opening the potential for such duties in Irish law.[23] The idea of a non-delegable duty may provide a suitable basis to address harm that occurred

[17] See eg A Beasley, 'Spiritans disclose assets of €57m as abuse claims increase', *The Irish Times*, 23 November 2022; P McGarry, 'Jesuits have paid €7.4m in settlement costs to abuse survivors'. *The Irish Times*, 11 November 2022.

[18] *Kearney v McQuillan* [2012] IEHC 127.

[19] *Farrell v Ryan* [2016] IECA 281.

[20] *Health Board v BC* [1994] ELR 27; *Delahunty v South Eastern Health Board* [2003] 4 IR 361; *TM v JH JM Minister for Education Ireland and AG* [2006] IEHC 261.

[21] *O'Keeffe v Hickey* [2008] IESC 72; *Hickey v McGowan* [2017] IESC 6.

[22] *O'Keeffe v Hickey* [2008] IESC 72, 37.

[23] *Morrissey v HSE* [2020] IESC 6.

in the context of closed institutional settings where the State had an obligation to regulate and inspect those institutions. However, at present, the principal form of civil justice in RoI for non-recent offences thus remains claims of the vicarious liability of state or church institutions for the harm caused by an employee or member of the institution and remains subject to several procedural and practical limitations discussed later.

Despite the presence of a constitutional bill of rights, there has been no significant constitutional jurisprudence regarding non-recent institutional abuses in Ireland. One academic interviewee noted the challenges of new legal rights standards for victim/survivors to vindicate their experiences involving harms of a non-recent nature: 'you're almost inviting the court to do something entirely novel. There is nothing obvious in the text of the Constitution that gives you . . . a clear standard to work with' (Interview 12). One lawyer noted the significance of this gap in constitutional protection of Irish citizens, especially for children: 'How could the Constitution not have required the State to protect little children against paedophiles in the school? If it didn't then what we have here is not a Constitution, it's a suicide pact' (Interview 5). In contrast, the Constitution was seen to clearly restrict the State's ability to compel religious organisations to provide redress: 'It would be a huge State trespass on the rights of institutions and people who are part of them' (Interview 21). However, a retired judge, noting that the Irish Supreme Court had recently accepted in principle that the right to life may create investigative procedural obligations,[24] asserted that 'a more modern or recent view might place a lot more weight on the need for the system, as a whole, to deliver for people who are survivors of various types of wrongdoing' (Interview 40).

As a jurisdiction, RoI is distinctive in involving several international human rights mechanisms to address non-recent abuses. In 2011, the Justice for Magdalenes' campaign made a submission to the United Nations Committee against Torture (UNCAT) as part of Ireland's first periodic review under the treaty. The Committee criticised RoI's failure to investigate the Magdalene Laundries (UNCAT 2011) leading to the establishment of an inquiry (see Chapter 5). Similar efforts have been pursued at UN treaty bodies and special procedures mandate-holders regarding the issues of symphysiotomy, racism in institutional abuse contexts, mother and baby homes, and illegal adoptions (see eg UN CEDAW 2017). Recommendations

[24] *Fox v Minister for Justice* [2021] IESC 61.

of treaty bodies or mandate-holders are not binding on states and therefore require significant political pressure to implement but do engage international scrutiny, incur reputational costs for the state, or provide a global platform for victim/survivor concerns (Krommendijk 2015). In 2022, in *Elizabeth Coppin v Ireland*, Mrs Coppin argued that the State had not adequately investigated her individual experiences of torture or inhuman and degrading treatment under the UN Convention against Torture in a county home, industrial school, and three different Magdalene Laundries (UNCAT 2023). The Committee against Torture concluded that Ireland did not violate the Convention and was incapable of responding due to the non-recent nature of the harms alleged, including the death of alleged perpetrators and RoI's restrictive statute of limitations and jurisprudence on delay, discussed later (UNCAT 2023, Annex I, para 16). Unusually, three of ten members of the Committee dissented, highlighting that the majority opinion was not in line with the Committee's previously repeated recommendations to Ireland in the periodic reporting process (UNCAT 2011; 2017).

In addition to the UN treaty body mechanisms, the European Convention on Human Rights has also been relevant for addressing non-recent harms (Gallen 2019a). In 2014 in *O'Keeffe v Ireland*, the European Court of Human Rights (ECtHR) concluded that Ireland had failed to protect Louise O'Keeffe from sexual abuse suffered as a child in an Irish National School, violated the prohibition of inhuman and degrading treatment, and failed to provide Ms O'Keeffe with an effective remedy.[25] The Court considered that when relinquishing control of the education of children to non-state church actors, Ireland should have been aware, given its inherent obligation to protect children, of potential risks to their safety if there was no appropriate framework of protection.[26] However, its impact has been circumscribed significantly by the State's implementation of the judgment through an *ex gratia* redress scheme that interprets the judgment narrowly (see Chapter 6). Other cases at the ECtHR, involving symphysiotomy, were not successful, being declared inadmissible[27] due to a failure to exhaust domestic remedies in Irish courts and that some of the complaints were manifestly ill-founded as there had been an independent investigation and an *ex gratia* payment scheme.

[25] *O'Keeffe v Ireland* [2014] ECHR 96.
[26] ibid, para 162.
[27] *LF v Ireland, KO'S v Ireland and WM v Ireland* (Application nos 62007/17, 61836/17, and 61872/17) (2020).

Access to information has been a prominent human right highlighted in research for this book. Freedom of information (FOI) was introduced to RoI in 1997 and reformed under the Freedom of Information Act 2014, which enables access to records related to an individual, regardless of date of creation, and access to other records from 1997 onwards. In addition, individuals have a right of access to their personal information under the Data Protection Acts 1988 and 2003 and after the implementation of the General Data Protection Regulation (GDPR) in 2018. However, each of the major pieces of relevant legislation governing inquiries and redress have been amended to exclude and restrict survivor access via freedom of information and data protection legislation.[28] Some survivors see the misuse of GDPR as a basis for reducing the overall amount of personal data they have received: 'we're now getting less information today than I got in 2016. We're getting less information today because it's all under this pseudo-GDPR' (Interview 22). One state appointee noted that the GDPR 'has the potential to be used by those resistant to having their practices reviewed, the potential to be used as really a get out of jail clause' (Interview 17). One significant access to information concern in RoI has been regarding access to adoption information (McGettrick 2020). As explored in Chapter 2, legal adoption was only introduced in Ireland in 1952, with allegations of widespread illegal and irregular adoptions emerging in recent decades. As McGettrick notes: 'A comprehensive and independent investigation of the twentieth-century adoption system in Ireland would expose the underlying processes and power structures of the past' (McGettrick 2020, 200). RoI liberalised its adoption laws in 2022[29] and received over 3,800 applications for birth information in the first year of the new system, after some initial delays.[30] However, a holistic investigation of past adoption practices has not been pursued.

The use of IHRL mechanisms reframes issues of non-recent abuses as human rights violations and, in doing so, shifts the nature of the responsibility, including remedial responsibilities, onto the state. Access to information remains a key challenge in RoI as limited access to records related

[28] Commissions of Investigation Act 2004, s 39; Commission of Investigation (Mother and Baby Homes and Certain Related Matters) Records, and Another Matter Act 2020, s 3(2)(2); The Commission To Inquire Into Child Abuse Act 2000, s 33; Residential Institutions Redress Board Act 2002, s 30.

[29] Birth Information and Tracing Act 2022.

[30] Adoption Authority, 'The Birth Information and Tracing Act 2022—One Year On', https://aai.gov.ie/images/AAI_BITA_Press_Statement_Final.pdf (accessed 11 March 2024).

to institutions and restrictive state practices regarding FOI and GDPR requests continue to frustrate those affected.

5. Conventional Justice in Northern Ireland

In NI, recorded sexual crime is historically low compared to other offences (McAlinden 2015, 329). The legacy of the conflict has impacted justice responses to non-recent institutional abuses (see eg McCormick 2017; O'Rourke and Swaine 2017). A historical lack of trust of the police in some communities led to an increased role for paramilitary organisations regulating community behaviour (Haydon and McAlister 2015, 302–3). One criminal justice professional noted that some cases of sexual violence were treated as minor offences: 'you would see individuals being prosecuted for what was then indecent assault . . . or what would now be rape, oral rape or you know, sexual assault by penetration, both of which have got very significant sentences available and would undoubtedly be prosecuted on indictment if they were prosecuted now' (Interview 60). Similarly to RoI, evidence provided to the Acknowledgment Forum of the Hart Inquiry was subject to a use immunity in criminal or civil litigation[31] and the Public Prosecution Service created an undertaking not to use evidence given before the Inquiry in any criminal proceeding.[32]

The same interviewee noted 'spikes' in cases being reported and forwarded to prosecutors following public disclosure from survivors on the establishment and operation of an inquiry (Interview 60). However, as in RoI, the existence of the Hart Inquiry and engagement of victims with that process could potentially complicate the pursuit of criminal justice: 'it doesn't strengthen the evidential picture. It might weaken it if there's conflicting accounts' (Interview 60). In terms of a decision to prosecute, criminal justice professionals affirmed the same standards as RoI—assessing if there is a reasonable prospect of a conviction and whether a prosecution is in the public interest. The media analysis conducted for this book indicates at least 28 convictions related to allegations of child sex abuse from priests and religious in NI from 1993 to 2024. As in RoI, the value of the raw data is limited without further statistical analysis and context.

[31] The Inquiry into Historical Institutional Abuse Rules (Northern Ireland) 2013, s 19.
[32] See https://www.hiainquiry.org/sites/hiainquiry/files/media-files/Public%20Prosecution%20Service%20-%20Undertaking.pdf (accessed 1 June 2024).

In NI, any 'cover-up' of abuse by institutional actors could potentially be prosecuted as perverting the course of justice for withholding information, under the Criminal Law Act 1967, or potentially, for some institutional actors, under the common law offence of misconduct in public office. However, there have been no prosecutions to date for such offences related to non-recent institutional abuses. In addition, one criminal justice professional noted in the context of mother and baby homes that 'some of those would be statute barred offences in common assault' (Interview 71). The limited empirical studies of the experiences of victim/survivors of sexual abuse or violence within the criminal justice system in NI highlights high attrition rates (Bunting 2008) and longer delays in reaching trial stage in comparison to the rest of the UK (Killean et al 2021, ch 1). As in RoI, in many cases accused persons are also deceased when the disclosure/complaint is made. As a result, as one criminal justice professional noted, 'a lot of victims . . . have a very unsatisfactory experience of the criminal justice system . . . in the area of sexual offences, and including the area of non-recent sexual offences, the adversarial system doesn't serve victims terribly well' (Interview 60). While the broader context of criminal justice in NI differs significantly from RoI due to the conflict, this has not precluded successful use of criminal justice for non-recent offences, subject to similar rules regarding evidence, delay, and similar challenges for prosecutions related to non-sexual offences.

There is a dearth of academic and policy research on civil justice frameworks concerning institutional abuses in NI where most of our knowledge is doctrinal and derived in case law. Ring et al (2022, 199–200) suggest that under UK law, 'An organization may be liable in negligence in one of four ways: (1) negligence in employing or continuing to employ staff the organization knew/should have known were abusers; (2) failing to exercise reasonable supervision and direction of employees; (3) failing to investigate abuse following reports by victims and (4) failing to take reasonable steps to prevent or stop sexual abuse.'

The courts in NI have broadly aligned with the approach to negligence, including vicarious liability, taken in England and Wales.[33] The traditional English position on vicarious liability excluded liability for sexual abuse and intentional wrongdoing[34] but in more recent years the English courts

[33] *EJMcC v Department of Communities (II)* [2021] NI Com 12; *McGettigan v Short Bros* [2011] NICty 4.
[34] *Duncan v Findlater*, 6 Cl & Fin 894 (1839), para 18.

have held organisations vicariously liable for sexual assaults committed by employees against children.[35] The English approach has been understood as a 'close connection' test, in a manner that emphasised liability where situations of dependency created a significant risk of wrongdoing,[36] particularly in the context of residential institutions for children[37] or children in the care of the state via foster carers.[38] Not all recent cases involving sexual abuse in religious contexts have been successful, with the UK Supreme Court in 2023 reaffirming the need for a close connection between illegal conduct, such as sexual abuse, and the acts that an employee is permitted to do as part of their role within the defendant organisation, such as acting in a parental or guardian role towards a child.[39]

In addition, non-delegable duties are based on the relationship between the defendant and plaintiff, rather than between defendant and wrongdoer.[40] Such duties may be either created by statute or at common law and are 'not merely a duty to take care, but a duty to provide that care is taken'.[41] In the UK, English law on non-delegable duties has recently extended to cases where the claimant is a child or other vulnerable person and is in the care of the defendant when the harm takes place and the defendant exercises control over the vulnerable person, when the defendant has assumed responsibility for their care.[42] Regarding non-recent abuses, state and religious institutions assumed responsibility for the welfare of individuals in their care and, on this account, are liable for instances where harm took place against individuals in their care. Civil liability in UK law, applicable to NI, is thus more developed than in RoI in a manner that addresses more directly the nature of the responsibility assumed by state and church institutions.

In NI, the Human Rights Act 1998 offers the potential to address non-recent abuses from a human rights perspective in a domestic court (Balint 2016). As part of her remit for the NI Truth Recovery Design Process (see Chapter 9), O'Rourke published a background research report on continuing human rights violations, particularly: 'continuing disappearances,

[35] *Lister v Hesley Hall Ltd* [2001] UKHL 22.
[36] *Maga v The Trustees of the Birmingham Archdiocese of the Roman Catholic Church* [2010] EWCA Civ 256, [2010] 1 WLR 1441, paras 79–80.
[37] *Various Claimants v The Catholic Child Welfare Society* [2012] UKSC 56.
[38] *Armes v Nottinghamshire County Council* [2017] UKSC 60.
[39] *Trustees of the Barry Congregation of Jehovah's Witnesses v BXB* [2023] UKSC 15.
[40] *Woodland v Essex County Council* [2013] UKSC 66.
[41] *The Pass of Ballater* [1942] 2 All ER 79, 84.
[42] *Woodland v Essex County Council* [2013] UKSC 66, [2014] AC 537, [23]–[24].

continuing denial of the right to identity, continuing interference with freedom of expression, continuing discrimination, and a continuing lack of an effective investigation and other measures to ensure access to justice and redress for widespread, systematic and gravely harmful human rights abuses' (O'Rourke 2021b, 2). O'Rourke emphasised 'both the state's own participation in institutional and family separation abuses *and* its failure to prevent non-state organisations and individuals perpetrating these abuses are essential aspects of the state's responsibility under human rights law' (O'Rourke 2021b, 4).

In NI, the UN Committee Against Torture criticised the exclusion from the Hart Inquiry of women confined in Magdalene Laundries 'and equivalent institutions' as well as clerical abuse survivors. It recommended 'prompt, independent and thorough investigations into all cases of institutional abuse that took place in Northern Ireland between 1922 and 1995' and that 'where possible and appropriate, perpetrators are prosecuted and punished, and that all victims of abuse obtain redress and compensation, including the means for as full as possible rehabilitation' (UNCAT 2019, para 44). This led to the establishment of the independent panel and proposals for a statutory inquiry into mother and baby institutions, Magdalene laundries, and workhouses (see Chapter 9). In NI, access to information has also been a survivor priority and is governed by the UK Data Protection Act 1998, in turn replaced by the Data Protection Act 2018. As in RoI, access to institutional information remains challenging (Hamber and Lundy 2020, 759). While there have been recent reforms in adoption legislation,[43] it remains to be seen whether the reforms will positively impact access to adoption information for those affected.

6. Canon Law on the Island of Ireland

Canon law concentrates executive, legislative, and judicial power in diocesan bishops, until recently giving individual bishops discretion to respond to allegations of sexual abuse (Byrnes 2020, 9). One Church official noted that canon law is intended to achieve: 'the avoidance of scandal, respect for individuals who may have been innocent and ultimately justice' (Interview 19). The Murphy Report revealed significant confusion and a

[43] Adoption and Children Act (Northern Ireland) 2022.

lack of clarity in the application of canon law in the Irish Catholic Church from the middle of the twentieth century to the late 1990s (CoI 2009, paras 4.6, 4.87). The report stated that historically the Archdiocese of Dublin 'did not implement its own canon law rules and did its best to avoid any application of the law of the State' (para 1.15). Similarly, the 2011 Cloyne Report concluded that the Church had failed to carry out proper canonical investigations or to report all complaints to the Gardaí or health authorities (CoI 2011, paras 1.31–1.37).

There have been a series of guidelines and frameworks adopted by the Catholic Church concerning child sexual abuse since 1996 (1996 Framework; Our Children, Our Church 2005; Safeguarding Children 2008; Standards and Guidance 2016.) However, these documents did not receive official recognition from the Vatican and remained without standing in canon law (Mullaney 2022, 33). In April 2002, the Irish Bishops' Conference announced a nationwide audit of what was known about the treatment of allegations of child abuse by diocesan and religious priests and appointed Judge Gillian Hussey as chair of the Catholic Church Commission on Child Sexual Abuse (Hussey Commission). However, in December 2002, Judge Hussey ceased the work of this Commission following the announcement by the Minister for Justice of the establishment of a new form of statutory inquiry, which would become the Commission of Investigation Act 2004 and would lead to the establishment of the investigation into the Dublin Archdiocese.[44] The significant potential of this Commission should be noted, which was intended to provide a nationwide audit of the treatment of allegations of child abuse by diocesan and religious clergy, across both RoI and NI, rather than in a piecemeal manner.

Keenan (2012; 2015) argues that institutional factors in the Catholic Church, such as a culture of secrecy, ignorance around sex and sexuality, clericalism, a concentration of power, and an overly intellectualised and technical understanding of morality all contributed to the genesis of the problem of sexual abuse by the Catholic clergy and delays in responding to allegations of clerical sexual abuse. One senior Church official noted the enduring limits of integrating canon law and state legal responses:

> You have the situation where the person wants to come to the Church to make the complaint against the priest, wants the priest removed from

[44] P McGarry, 'Commission on clerical sex abuse to be disbanded', *The Irish Times*, 21 December 2022.

> ministry... but will not make a complaint to the police.... [S]ometimes, a survivor will want the Church to do what the legal system won't do. (Interview 69)

Despite significant changes in canon law guidance since the emergence of non-recent child abuse issues in the Catholic Church, our research found limited interest in canon law responses. More recent canon law frameworks are relatively more formal and effective in the removal of offenders from office (Zollner et al 2024). The historical lack of an effective canon law mechanism may represent an opportunity lost historically for the Catholic Church hierarchy to exercise responsibility in holding its members to account in canonical proceedings.

7. The Value and Limits of Conventional Justice Responses

Several key challenges of conventional justice were raised in interviews with stakeholders, including the need for victim/survivor access to records; the non-recent nature of the harms alleged; the inequality of arms between victim/survivors and state and church organisations; the re-traumatising experiences of criminal and civil justice for victim/survivors; and the limited recognition of the distinctive nature of state and church organisations as defendants in litigation.

Access to records

A key priority for victim/survivors in empirical research for this book was access to records. While access to records may include criminal and civil discovery through FOI or data protection access requests, it functions as a cross-cutting challenge to establish the extent of institutional knowledge and responsibilities for non-recent harms. For one lawyer, access to information is key for effective justice responses: 'if you don't know what's happened to you, you can't actually find out whether somebody has broken the law or whether your rights have been violated' (Interview 38). However, the non-recent nature of the harms alleged often means that records are incomplete or destroyed. One senior Church official noted that, 'In some cases, you have sparse records. In some cases, you have no records' (Interview 69).

Access to records was an issue in both RoI and NI. As one lawyer in NI noted:

> You're relying on an organisation who was involved in neglect of children which resulted in abuse having records to say that, actually, there was a report of abuse. The policies weren't adhered to and also, victims didn't report the crimes because they were afraid. So you don't really often have a very good paper trail. (Interview 33)

Another lawyer noted in RoI that:

> A lot of records were poorly kept at the start. It's not clear where they are, if they still exist, if they ever were properly made in the first place, if the difficulty in locating them is due to simple poor record-keeping, if things are actually being concealed, if there's been a deliberate attempt to hide records, if there's records have been altered. (Interview 34)

The central nature of access to records as a justice need for victim/survivors contrasts strongly with restrictive access to records held by many state and church authorities (O'Rourke 2022), some of which are incomplete or scare in the first instance, which may create the impression of a resistance to scrutiny, responsibility, and accountability.

Time and criminal justice

Several interviewees acknowledged that the passage of time and the non-recent nature of events and allegations complicated the use of conventional justice responses. Delay in proceedings can prejudice the defence of an accused person due to the death of witnesses, difficulties of memory over time, or the destruction or loss of material or documentary evidence (Ring 2009, 4; Keenan et al 2023). One criminal justice professional in RoI suggested that delay in reporting occurs for many reasons:

> The abuser might have been a family member or a member of the extended family or they may have been a person who was very well respected in the community, the victim didn't think they'd be believed or alternatively, because of the abuse, they had suffered from depression, alcoholism or whatever, drugs. (Interview 37)

In RoI, several criminal investigations resulted in cases proceeding to trial but being dismissed on the grounds that a fair trial was impossible due to the delayed complaint. From 1999 to 2006, the courts' approach to delay focused on whether the victim was suffering under the 'dominion' of the abuser, arising from the traumatic effects of sexual abuse, and was therefore unable to report sooner. If not, the case could be struck out on the grounds of delay.[45] This test was replaced in 2006 with one that focuses on whether an accused experienced actual prejudice that precluded a fair trial, arising from a delayed disclosure of the complaint.[46] The same criminal justice professional noted that the significance of this change 'was kind of seismic in that sense and we were much more successful after that in application for prohibition' (Interview 37).

In NI, as in England and Wales, while proceedings may be stayed on the grounds that they would cause unfair prejudice to the defendant,[47] cases may also proceed with a suitable judicial direction to the jury on the effects of delayed reporting.[48] Further, the trial judge must give a mandatory direction to the jury on the possible reasons for delayed victim reporting, including the impact of shame and humiliation.[49] As such, the passage of time does not, as a matter of formal legal rules, prevent the effective prosecution of cases of non-recent abuses in NI. In practice, however, from the figures available, successful prosecutions in NI and RoI are few in number. As noted, the limited recognition of reasons for delay in child sexual abuse cases suggests a narrow role for the criminal law in addressing the systemic nature of non-recent institutional abuses and constrained legal recognition of wider dimensions of responsibility.

Time and civil justice: statute of limitations

To bring civil litigation regarding non-recent harms, victim/survivors must overcome the law of limitation, which allows a plaintiff a specific amount of time from a specified date within which to bring an action against a defendant. RoI has the most restrictive limitation regime in the common law

[45] *PC v DPP* [1999] 2 IR 25, 68.
[46] *SH v DPP* [2006] IESC 55; *People DPP v CC* [2019] IESC 94.
[47] *AG's Reference (No 1 of 1990)* [1991] QB 630.
[48] *R v PS* [2013] EWCA Crim 992.
[49] *R v D* [2008] EWCA Crim 2557; *Breeze* [2009] EWCA Crim 255.

world (Gallen 2018). Limitation regimes did not emerge as a significant issue in interviews in NI.

In RoI, the Statute of Limitations Act 1957 provides for a two-year time limit for personal injury claims. The Statute of Limitations (Amendment) Act 1991 introduced a discoverability test for personal injuries claims where claims can be brought for two years from the date of knowledge of the person injured.[50] The Statute of Limitations (Amendment) Act 2000 extended this approach to sexual abuse where a person has a significant 'psychological injury' as a result of being sexually abused during childhood so 'that his or her will or his or her ability to make a reasoned decision' to institute civil proceedings in respect of such abuse is 'substantially impaired'.[51]

Even if a case passes the restrictions of limitation legislation, the courts retain a general discretion to dismiss cases for 'inordinate and inexcusable' delay.[52] Courts have frequently dismissed cases related to allegations of non-recent institutional abuses on this ground.[53] One lawyer highlighted the particular injustices of the limitation regime in actions against the state: 'the state doesn't have a memory and can't forget. So, why does the statute apply with equal force to a thing that is immortal? And which has its records' (Interview 5). However, despite these restrictions, one senior politician in RoI expressed concern about further reforms to the statute of limitations: 'insurers would just not stand over their policies if the government changed the rules after the policy was issued and they'd be within their rights to do that' (Interview 64). However, in the 2000 Act, the State did adjust the structure of conventional justice responses by extending the discoverability test to instances of child sexual abuse, as discussed earlier. Given the restrictive nature of the statute of limitations in RoI, it would be possible and beneficial to introduce a judicial discretion to allow cases to proceed in the interests of justice, as in the UK Limitation Act 1980.

In NI, the potential impact of delay in civil cases is governed by the statute of limitations which is prima facie less restrictive than in RoI. Under the Limitation Order (NI) 1989, a claimant has six years after the age of 18 for 'actions founded on tort'.[54] Additionally, in actions for personal injuries in negligence, the limitation period of three years runs from 'the date of

[50] Statute of Limitations (Amendment) Act 1991, s 3(1).
[51] Statute of Limitations (Amendment) Act 2000, s 2.
[52] *Primor v Stokes* [1996] 2 IR 459.
[53] *II v JJ* [2012] IEHC 327; *Kelly v O'Leary* [2001] IEHC 218; *Cassidy v The Provincialate* [2015] IECA 74; *McNamee v Boyce* [2016] IECA 19.
[54] See the 1989 Order, art 6.

knowledge (if later) of the person injured'.[55] Many victim/survivors, particularly regarding child sexual abuse, delay disclosure of abuses for years, often well into adulthood, with related implications for access to support services (see eg McElvaney 2015; Lanthier et al 2018) and to justice. Accordingly, civil justice is 'experienced by claimants as highly discriminatory' (Ring et al 2022, 183 in the context of England and Wales). Although the trial court has a discretion to override the six-year time limit,[56] the appellate courts have interpreted the equivalent provision in England and Wales[57] very restrictively where time from 'the date of knowledge'[58] is determined by an 'impersonal standard'[59] without reference to subjective factors relating to the individual victim such as education or self-esteem (see further Ring et al 2022, 182–3). The limited recognition of reasons for delay in reporting non-recent abuses suggests a narrow role for civil legal frameworks in addressing the systemic nature of such wrongs.

Costs and inequality of arms

The potential costs of litigation have a significant impact on access to meaningful justice for victim/survivors, especially in RoI. One lawyer noted that, 'In Ireland, the issue is rarely about accessing a lawyer as such . . . [I]ssues about access to justice are really about the cost issues' (Interview 38). In cases involving the potential liability of both state and church, the plaintiff is obliged to sue both or face a reduction of any award for excluded defendant liability. However, if unsuccessful, the plaintiff will therefore be liable for the costs of multiple defendants (Smith and Duff 2020, 110). One victim/survivor emphasised the significance of adverse cost findings: 'you get up in the morning and you owe the telephone bill and the ESB bill, and before you go to bed that night, you owe half a million . . . [I]t's sort of scary' (Interview 31). One academic noted the inequality of arms in suing state or church organisations:

> I think there's a power imbalance, I think the people who are bringing the cases on the fair procedure side are often institutions . . . they can bring that case, no bother. The person who would want to bring the case on

55 ibid, art 7.
56 ibid, art 50.
57 Limitation Act 1980, s 33.
58 ibid, s 14.
59 *A v Hoare and conjoined appeals* [2008] UKHL 6, [34].

> the other side is often the vulnerable survivor who doesn't have financial resources at their fingertips the way the institution does. (Interview 12)

One lawyer noted the challenges related to legal costs facing victim/survivors in seeking to litigate against state and church organisations or in the case of constitutional challenge to legislation:

> All the big firms will say they're conflicted on it. So they're not gonna do it. And then little firms, it's too difficult to survive. You can't take the risk. All the rules . . . say for example you want to challenge the constitutionality or something, that's a plenary case with witnesses and all that rest, that could take years and cost literally millions. And all of that is front-loaded, all those costs, you have to pay those costs. Sure how is that gonna happen? You'd have to have a lot of table quizzes and cake sales. (Interview 5)

Alternative sources of funding, such as private third-party litigation, have been excluded by the Supreme Court of Ireland,[60] leading to a reliance on pro bono legal representation or contingency arrangements where lawyers are paid only if the action is successful (Smith and Duff 2020, 109). Protective costs orders from the court, which would enable the plaintiff to avoid paying the defendant's costs if not successful, require the plaintiff to have no financial interest in the outcome of a case, effectively precluding victim/survivors who may seek compensation (Smith and Duff 2020, 109). One lawyer noted the cumulative effect of the inequality of arms: 'all these things are built up for the defence, they're not built up for the plaintiff. They're built up for the defence under the guise of fairness' (Interview 24). Addressing the inequality of arms in litigation would require systemic reform of civil procedure to enhance access to justice.

Victim/survivor perspectives on conventional justice processes: experience of legal professionals and risks of trauma in pursuit of justice

Survivors in RoI had mixed experiences with their legal representatives in conventional justice responses. Some survivors had good experiences of

[60] *Persona Digital Telephony v Minister for Public Enterprise and Others* [2017] IESC 27.

legal representatives but were upset by the strategies employed by opposing legal professionals. One survivor noted: 'the actual business of the law . . . I really liked it and I thought they were very good' (Interview 52). Others felt 'relatively [well] looked after' by their legal team (Interview 13) or saw their solicitor as 'brilliant' (Interview 29). In contrast, some victim/survivors noted that 'solicitors charged twice for the same work' (Interview 6) and the same survivor described some solicitors' firms as 'ambulance chasers'. A victim/survivor described how a 'particular solicitor had offered me £200 for every survivor I could sling his way' (Interview 22). The same survivor noted:

> Most lawyers thought of us as criminals and idiots because one of the biggest legal firms that represented survivors discovered that so many of us had wound up in prison, that all he had to do was put a notice in whatever prison it was to say, 'were any of you in an industrial school?' (Interview 22)

In NI, victim/survivors suggested that leading lawyers may have a 'self-serving' agenda in their engagement and representation of victim/survivors (Interview 8). One survivor noted that 'they keep saying we'll do a civil case but when they're doing the civil case . . . [T]hey [the survivors] still get a pittance or maybe even less than the Redress Board, but who gets paid, the solicitors, the barristers and the juniors . . . I know the game' (Interview 2). Victim/survivors on both parts of the island were often critical of legal culture as being unduly deferential to legal expertise instead of recognising the potential of meaningful collaboration between stakeholders and lawyers. One survivor suggested that 'the lawyers became the new priests—the government it seems to me were hamstrung at every juncture—the government wouldn't do a thing without consulting with the lawyers—far more often than they consulted with us' (Interview 6).

Both criminal and civil justice were seen as potentially traumatic. One professional victim/survivor advocate in RoI noted the traumatic experiences of the criminal justice system:

> Clients are terrified by the prospect of being a complainant witness in a criminal trial and even though there have been changes in the law and the procedures of court, it is still an incredibly retraumatising, dehumanising system, particularly the cross examination where, you know,

> especially in historic abuse cases... there's little or no forensic evidence, no witnesses. You know, the role of a good defence barrister is to utterly demolish the character of the witness so every aspect of their life being drawn under scrutiny. (Interview 26)

Others, including victim/survivors, highlighted the deep and lasting impact of adversarial legal culture, including efforts to discredit their character. A victim/survivor in NI described a criminal trial as follows: 'I mean my mother had died the previous year and losing my mother was nothing in comparison to that trial and what was the ordeal of that trial. I'll never forget it. It was absolutely horrific and it actually took me about 3 years to recover from it' (Interview T). A criminal justice professional in RoI affirmed: 'so many people leave the criminal justice system, disillusioned, their self-esteem gone, their confidence gone' (Interview 37).

Civil litigation can also be a potentially re-traumatising or marginalising process for victim/survivors. Smith and Duff (2020, 112) note that 'Aside from the chance that delay may resolve a defendant's problem by simple attrition, procedural chicanery—even if not ultimately successful—can wear down a plaintiff's stamina and diminish the resolve of even the most committed legal team.' Particular challenges arise in litigation against both state and church defendants. One lawyer in NI affirmed:

> I have abuse victims come down to court on the day of trial and . . . they're just sweating . . . Physically, their clothes are soaking. . . . It's that last hurdle, and all of them, they usually settle but that's the Church and the State taking them right to the door. Will he turn up? I don't know if he will or not, let's just wait and see. So they'll do anything to try and get a lesser pay out for these people but of course, the forked tongue and the media press release is very different is what I find. (Interview 33)

The adversarial nature of both criminal and civil justice systems takes a significant toll on victim/survivors and at worst is a site of re-traumatisation and represents a significant 'justice gap' and distortion of the potential kaleidoscopic justice effect of conventional mechanisms. Victim/survivor dignity and agency were also often inhibited or undermined by assertions of legal authority that crowded out survivor priorities or, worse, resulted in harm and distress.

State perspectives on conventional justice responses: the role of legal culture and the state as a distinctive litigant?

The state's engagement with conventional justice responses is often viewed as confrontational and defensive and creates the perception of a desire to evade legal responsibility. One academic described the state's approach as, 'deny, delay, defend . . . [W]e'll fight this with everything at our disposal, we will drag it out as long as we can, we'll threaten to pursue you for costs, we might actually pursue you for costs in some cases' (Interview 12). This was also reported by victim/survivors. In dealing with non-recent abuses and other widespread claims against the state in RoI, the claims are addressed via a specialist body, the State Claims Agency (SCA), tasked with ensuring 'that the liability of the State authorities is contained at the lowest achievable level'.[61] In its annual reports, the SCA has indicated that its 'approach to this category of claim is to put the plaintiff on proof of all aspects of the claim while seeking to ensure, in relation to out-of-court settlements, that these are in line with, and do not exceed, RIRB awards for similar claims' (NTMA 2005, 34). Similarly, regarding claims concerning abuse in day schools, the same report notes that, 'The SCA's approach to this category of claim has been to seek to extricate the State from the various plaintiffs' proceedings, except those cases where there has been an acknowledged failure on the part of the State—a tiny minority of cases . . .' (NTMA 2005, 33–4).

One senior politician in RoI noted the muted public engagement of the SCA: 'State Claims, for whatever reasons, doesn't defend itself. So what you'll always see is the plaintiff on the steps of the court with their lawyer, and lawyers are often advertising for business, quite frankly' (Interview 64). The same interviewee concluded: 'I think the impression of people, that the State forces people into court and settles at the last minute and sort of drags things out, isn't fully fair'. Another senior politician expressed concern about the role of lawyers in shaping how non-recent abuses are addressed:

> If the legal representation grows, and then you get all sorts of angles and arguments and you don't get a flowing, sort of less constrained discussion. You get kind of, everybody gets into trenches . . . I think they're

[61] State Claims Agency, 'About Claims Resolution', https://stateclaims.ie/services/claims-resolution/about-claims-resolution (accessed 11 March 2024).

> shaping as opposed to taking instruction. They will argue they're taking instruction but they're not . . . They know the game. The game is for them, bluntly put, is money. (Interview 68)

The same interviewee continued to criticise the role of lawyers:

> It then stymies the State's response. It limits the State's response, it conditions the State's response because the State is saying or the attorney general or the State Claims Agency, we see this coming a mile away. . . . Governments and politicians lose out. The Oireachtas is worked as well because it, invariably, legal firms will either through survivors or victims or whatever, and this could be to do with anything. (Interview 68)

State officials and senior politicians in RoI also noted the dominant influence of law and legal expertise in making policy, with one senior politician noting: 'I felt a requirement to, at the very least, parallel the legal process with . . . non-legal, non-adversarial and there was, at many times, no you cannot trespass into the legal approach which we've taken' (Interview 51). Another senior official described 'the lawyer bit' as 'a difficulty', creating an exclusive focus on legal liability where it is unclear if it is 'going to be a real meeting or is it going to be a meeting . . . where things are grabbed and used and maybe abused or maybe, you know, bringing into legal liability space' (Interview 55).

Such concerns from elite state actors about the perception of state responses in litigation and the role of lawyers in limiting state responses, while important, neglect to address the inequality between victim/survivors, advocates, and state institutions. One lawyer noted:

> There's this weird thing of oh, well the parties in litigation have to be treated equally when they're clearly not equal. I mean, Aristotelian equality is about treating things that are equal equally and things that are not equal differently, don't pretend that the State is just another litigant when it is the thing that controls us all. (Interview 5)

In June 2023, the Attorney General in RoI published 'State Litigation Principles'.[62] These 15 principles are intended to guide State conduct in litigation. The first five principles address the need for the State to deal with litigation in a financially prudent manner. The next five principles address

[62] Attorney General, 'State Litigation Principles', https://assets.gov.ie/289006/1afd8f32-89f8-484a-9194-3dbd33af21c8.pdf (accessed 28 November 2024).

the inequality of arms involved in an individual's litigation against the State; however, Principle 11 states: 'The State is entitled to rely on the same defences as any other litigant, but where consideration of different defences arises, the State shall consider where the interests of justice lie for all parties before relying on the defence.' Such an approach fails to recognise that the State occupies a unique position in the Irish legal system that should warrant a distinctive approach to its use of some defences, particularly regarding the passage of time and conditions in which litigation takes place. It is thus open to the state to prioritise and legislate for other values beyond cost minimisation in litigation, such as victim/survivor access to justice. In particular, if senior politicians and state officials feel unduly constrained by legal advice, it is within their capacity as legislators and policymakers to adjust the structure of legality in the legal system, for instance, by publishing redacted legal advice and potentially enabling a more cooperative conversation with all relevant stakeholders.

Church perspectives on conventional justice: lawyers, litigation practices, and a particular set of defendants

In several interviews with representatives of religious organisations, there was both concern about the role of lawyers and litigation but also reflection that religious organisations were capable of agency and directing legal representatives in a manner consistent with their values. This was especially evident among representatives of female religious orders compared to male religious orders. One senior official highlighted the challenges of deferral to the advice of legal representatives, where on the one hand survivors may have expected a representative of the Church body to be in the courtroom but counsel advice for the survivor, and for the Church body, suggests that such a presence may cause distress to survivors.

A senior representative of a male religious organisation highlighted that the potential and practice of litigation had the effect of foreclosing any other non-legal interaction between a victim/survivor and the allegedly responsible institution: 'So we'd meet somebody and then, we would get a letter from the lawyer for this person saying that they were taking a civil claim. So once that happened, any contact between the complainant and ourselves stopped, you know, at a human level' (Interview 23). Another representative of a male religious organisation was critical of some lawyers representing victim/survivors: 'could professional people be going around whipping it up, and not only whipping up people but whipping up their stories?' (Interview 27). However, a lawyer in NI countered, highlighting the justice deficit for survivors in this regard:

> It suits the Church if we have a wee meeting and sit down, and we're very sorry but here's, you know, something to help pay for wee Arty's university, and it doesn't compensate and that's not justice and there's no discovery handed over about who knew what and when, and all of the aggravating features, and for many individuals, that's really important. (Interview 33)

In contrast, representatives of female religious organisations noted their approach: 'We want to be compassionate, generous, fair to all the people involved and then, we talk to the lawyers about this and see in legal terms, how is that going to be possible?' (Interview 41) and 'we relied on legal advice but we didn't seek them . . . to make decisions for us. We . . . have many positions and papers developed over the years that we took based on who we were' (Interview 42). A senior representative of a female religious organisation affirmed the role of the charism of her organisation in the legal approach taken:

> Certainly there was no hint of being either pushed in any direction; rather it was the direction that we wanted, and what were the values that we wanted to abide by. Then, we needed to know what were the difficulties that we might face in relation to that and what implications would that have for us. (Interview 48)

Similarly, some Church officials noted the need for a distinctive ethical response by legal professionals when addressing non-recent abuse cases through conventional justice responses:

> I am really concerned about, if you like, the social conscience of lawyers who just go into these situations with big hard nail boots and no thought at all about the consequences of their actions, beyond 'All I need to do is defend my client'. Well actually no, you need to take some consideration for the actions that you're involved in and the impact of those actions on everyone who is involved. (Interview C)

Thus, the mixed views of religious orders about their agency within the context of broader legal or structural frameworks are indicative of law and legal culture as a potential influence on institutional engagement with survivors.

In relation to civil proceedings, a further significant barrier to holding religious institutions accountable is the peculiar nature of those institutions as a matter of law. In civil liability, vicarious liability has now expanded to impose liability in situations 'akin to employment'. such as for members of unincorporated associations including religious organisations.[63] The archdioceses and dioceses of the Irish Catholic Church were never incorporated as separate legal persons, such as corporations (CoI 2009, para 3.6). Remarkably, in 2009, the Murphy Report stated that, 'The precise legal status of the Archbishop of Dublin has yet to be determined by the Irish courts' (para 3.8). The peculiar legal status of religious organisations was the result of historical discrimination under the Penal Laws against Catholic organisations, (as discussed in Chapter 2). Instead, diocesan assets were typically held in trusts. In contrast, the Representative Church Body (RCB) of the Church of Ireland was incorporated by Charter in 1870 under the provisions of the Irish Church Act 1869. Its legal structure is that of a charitable trustee or trust corporation.

As a result, in law, Catholic dioceses and the entities of religious orders, for instance 'the Good Shepherd Sisters' or 'the Rosminians', do not exist. In RoI, the Supreme Court affirmed the current practice in suing such actors:

> The appropriate course in such a case is to write to the order or provincial threatening to sue all individual members of the order unless a defendant is nominated. If that course is not taken, then all members who can be identified can be joined as defendants.[64]

Religious organisations are not obliged to nominate a defendant, which in turn requires a plaintiff to sue all members of the organisation and may be obliged to sue the current leader to obtain a list of such members. Smith and Duff (2020, 111–12) suggest that the judgment shows that 'even the simple rules of pleading assist institutional defendants in frustrating access to justice by plaintiffs'. Reliance on this tactic by some religious organisations and their legal advisers, while lawful, seems difficult to reconcile with their stated aim of adopting an approach to litigation in line with their values. However, even within existing legal frameworks in RoI and NI, a more consistent and less legalistic response is possible across all religious organisations, such as restorative or transitional justice explored in Chapter 8.

[63] *John Doe v Bennett* [2004] 1 SCR 436; *JGE v The Trustees of the Portsmouth Roman Catholic Diocesan Trust* [2012] EWCA Civ 938; *Hickey v McGowan* [2017] IESC 6.

[64] *Hickey v McGowan* [2017] IESC 6, [52].

The challenges of legal culture

Across all stakeholders interviewed, there is a recognition of the potential benefits but also the distorting nature of legal culture in addressing non-recent abuses. Nelken (2004) defines legal culture as 'relatively stable patterns of legal oriented social behaviour and attitudes. The identifying elements of legal culture range from facts about institutions . . . to various forms of behaviour such as litigation . . . and, at the other extreme, more nebulous aspects of ideas, values, aspirations and mentalities.' To date, there has been limited examination of legal culture in RoI (eg Hamilton 2019; Rogan 2022) and, while there are studies of lawyers in NI (eg McEvoy 2011), the focus has been on their role during the conflict.

Literature on legal culture recognises the inherent power dynamics at work in and through the practice of law (Silbey 1998; Ewick 2006). Similarly, features of legal culture related to the authority and deference to lawyers and legal advice were a central feature of interviews for this book. In the present context, a small number of legal practitioners endorsed existing adversarial legal culture and practices, with one lawyer stating: 'I believe in the humanity of the Common Law and its ability to change as our knowledge changes' (Interview 21). Another lawyer affirmed but challenged existing legal culture and practices:

> There is an integrity to legal culture, it's built around a system to which there are significant structural elements underpinning that integrity. I think that lawyers can be at risk of being overly rigid in the spaces they occupy by reference to the structures. And I think that it is about encouraging lawyers on all sides to think outside the box and to go deeper perhaps with their clients in exploring what the client really is looking for in a given situation. (Interview 18)

Such positions align with traditional frameworks of legal advice as client service (Goriely 1994) where avoidance of legal liability and the use of any available legal defence or procedural safeguard is not only legitimate but the professionally responsible course of action. In contrast, Foley (2015, 180) criticised the legal strategy of defendant Catholic Church organisations in Australia that relied on their distinct legal status, as discussed earlier, to avoid liability, and suggested a possible alternative:

> Lawyers would first need to accept a responsibility to explicitly open to scrutiny moral dimensions of the legal approaches they are proposing

their clients pursue. This would mean, additionally, a second responsibility to advise clients that they may need to explore the morality of these approaches and take their counsel about how the approaches align with their avowed personal or institutional values.

The current approach appears to equate responsibility with liability and suggests no ethical or moral qualms in looking to extricate allegedly responsible actors using every available legal technique. In this context, deference to legal authority and advice may unduly restrict the choices of stakeholders. For instance, one judge noted the role of legal advice in the context of litigation against state or religious institutions:

> Just because you can adopt a strategy, doesn't mean you have to . . . if you're a religious Order or sort of an overall fairness imperative if you're the government, it doesn't mean you have to adopt every conceivable strategy that a private, corporate entity might well adopt if it were the defendant in proceedings. (Interview 40)

A further feature of legal culture may be financial in nature where firms seek to maximise their own revenue, particularly in representation of multiple clients or repeated representation of an institutional or state client in a mass claim context (comparatively see Baker and Herman 2020). Such an approach may be exploitative of survivors, particularly more vulnerable survivors, especially in the context of redress, as evidenced in our interview data, discussed earlier. One journalist noted that 'there were something like ten companies who were devoted, if you like. . .to chasing people who could get compensation' (Interview 53).

Collaborative forms of lawyering remain relatively recent innovations on the island, typically confined to family law matters (Healy 2011) and as a result deference to legal authority may remain a more traditional and widely experienced position. In addition, there may be limited recognition of the distinctive challenges of lawyering in the context of non-recent institutional abuses, including mass claims involving potentially high experiences of trauma and which are subject to significant delays in disclosure. A lawyer in RoI acknowledged that 'these groups in particular carry massive amounts of trauma, and it's just very difficult to deal with that sometimes' (Interview 25). The same interviewee noted that 'the training is completely inadequate, horrendous on how do you deal with vulnerable people, how do you deal with vulnerable cases and what is the appropriate role for an applicant or a defendant to be dealing with sensitively' (Interview 25). One senior politician noted the limitations of Irish legal culture and practice as 'not being able to hear the authenticity and the reality of the people's experience who were progressing the, or calling for the, change is, I think, it's largely the training . . . These are good people and the training within the system of patriarchal hierarchy' (Interview 51). As the interviewee suggested, in dealing with survivors of non-recent institutional abuses 'a rational approach to law and justice is not enough.'

Finally, the small nature of the jurisdictions on the island of Ireland should be noted. One academic-advocate noted the limited scope and interdependence of the legal profession in RoI:

> I practised in England and I definitely got the impression that there's more legal activism within professions, within the practising professions of solicitors and barristers within England than there is in Ireland. And I don't know if that's because you know, the pool of available work is so much smaller here that you have to remain available for instruction by the State, you know, any arm of the State. And it's just not that easy to make a living, you know, as someone who disapproves of State behaviour. (Interview 4)

However, legal practitioners also highlighted the implicitly personal nature of criticisms of conventional justice mechanisms as inadequate, which may impact judicial culture:

> Like there's no Jacobins up there, you know, there's no people who take like you know, Marxist analysis of law and the impact of class and all this kind of thing. As far as they understand it everything is just fine because sure I'm a Supreme Court Judge. That is evidence that everything is fine, that the system works! . . . [A]ny criticism of the system is indirectly a criticism of me because I'm at the top of the system. (Interview 5)

The intra-personal and relatively unchallenged legal culture may also have particularly negative impacts on public law involving litigation against state institutions. As one lawyer in RoI noted: 'public bodies don't really have this idea that they have to obey the law like or they don't think about that everything they do has to have a legal basis. We don't have like a European concept of lawfulness or legal basis or administrative, this kind of rigorous administration' (Interview 38). An effective justice response to such harms involves serious and significant reflection and reform of a legal culture which may have contributed to such harms and, based on the research for this book, risks causing new sites of distress, re-traumatisation and harm in seeking to provide a justice response. This challenge is taken up in Part III of the book.

8. Conclusion: Transforming Conventional Justice Responses

Conventional justice mechanisms can form part of a broad range of responses to non-recent institutional abuses and can aid in developing a multilayered form of responsibility in law, including not only individual criminal responsibility but also civil responsibility at institutional or state levels. However, the evidence gathered for this book demonstrates limitations of these mechanisms as currently practised. To build on McGlynn and Westmarland (2019), the combination of justice mechanisms and the experiences and incentives of victim/survivors, lawyers, and state and church representatives leads to a distorted kaleidoscope of justice, responsibility, and accountability that is misaligned with the challenges of addressing non-recent institutional abuses.

One academic-advocate notes that 'our existing justice mechanisms are good models for responding to justice at some level . . . [T]hey shouldn't be held out of the reach of people who have suffered some of the most serious injustices in Irish history' (Interview 4). In particular, the existing configuration of conventional justice mechanisms fails to account for the complexity of responsibility for non-recent abuses. One lawyer noted the limits of the current adversarial process in terms of establishing and distributing responsibilities:

> We aren't getting answers, as a society we aren't getting answers. We aren't hearing the full story. . . . So the system closes down inquiry often, ironically enough, and I think yes, I think it's time to recognise that this isn't doing everything it said it would do, and mere compensation, mere redress in the courts isn't enough. (Interview 21)

A realignment of conventional justice is therefore prompted by the concerns raised about the system's ability to respond to non-recent abuses and to establish and distribute responsibilities. The doctrinal, legal, and structural limits of conventional justice responses and the critiques and concerns raised by those who experience conventional justice all add further weight to the need to transform justice responses to non-recent abuses.

5
Inquiries

1. Introduction

This chapter critically examines official investigations into non-recent institutional abuses, within Northern Ireland (NI) and the Republic of Ireland (RoI) as well as internationally, and the extent to which they might deliver truth, justice, and accountability for victim/survivors. In keeping with the general aims and themes of the book, the chapter: (1) evaluates investigatory processes within NI and RoI and internationally and emerging discourses around accountability and responsibility for abuses; (2) examines the lived experiences of victim/survivors and elite-level actors of investigatory processes within NI and RoI; and (3) charts the parameters of transformative inquiries as a central part of more innovative justice responses to non-recent institutional abuses.

The chapter proceeds as follows: Section 2 provides a brief review of the literature focusing on the form and function of inquiries including truth-seeking. Section 3, based on extensive documentary analysis, examines investigatory mechanisms across a range of jurisdictions. Recent comparative studies have focused in-depth on justice responses, including investigations, in Anglophone countries (see eg Ring et al 2022; Gallen 2023a). Other scholars, however, have examined inquiries and truth-seeking processes in non-Anglophone countries such as Sweden and Denmark (see eg Sköld 2016; Arvidsson 2020); Finland (Malinen et al 2020); Germany (Andresen 2021), and Israel (Attrash-Najjar et al 2024) where the orientation of inquiries and the taking of survivor testimony is based on welfare concerns rather than adversarial justice. This chapter offers a more wide-ranging analysis by including some examples of investigations in both Anglophone and non-Anglophone countries and those relating not only to the Catholic Church but also Protestant churches and other religions. Sections 4 and 5 provide a critical account of investigations in RoI and NI. Sections 6 and 7, drawing on the interview data, address two primary questions: to what

Transforming Justice Responses to Non-Recent Institutional Abuses. Anne-Marie McAlinden, Marie Keenan, and James Gallen, Oxford University Press. © Oxford University Press 2025.
DOI: 10.1093/9780191967399.003.0005

extent the succession of official investigations in NI and RoI have been facilitative of truth and accountability and the acceptance of responsibility by church and state and the principal ideological, structural, and legal barriers which may inhibit truth, justice, and accountability and the capacity of investigatory mechanisms to comprehensively address non-recent institutional abuses and effect change. Finally, the concluding section draws out the learning in terms of reframing inquiries and underlying discourses on responsibility and accountability.

2. Inquiries: Form and Function

'Inquiry' is an umbrella term which encompasses a complex rubric of fact-finding bodies including tribunals of inquiry, commissions of investigation, parliamentary inquiries, departmental inquiries, and Royal Commissions as official forms of investigation. As a 'hybrid legal-and-administrative process' (Wade et al 2022, 757), 'inquiries' into non-recent institutional abuses typically occur on a statutory basis, giving them legal powers to compel witnesses and evidence with attendant legal and procedural safeguards. This includes provision for use immunity guaranteeing that testimony will not be used in subsequent legal proceedings. They may sit in public or private with the power to make recommendations, according to their terms of reference. As a feature of common law jurisdictions, they are usually initiated by the state on an ad hoc basis, following public outcry and calls for independent, judicially led, investigation of specific controversial events. For example, within the UK and the island of Ireland, inquiries have been used to investigate a broad range of institutional failings including 'conflict'-related killings,[1] deaths or serious abuses of individual children,[2] national tragedies or terrorist attacks,[3] medical negligence, and public health.[4]

[1] See eg the Bloody Sunday Inquiry (Saville et al 2010) and the Commission of Investigation into the Dublin and Monahan Bombings (McEntee 2007).

[2] See eg the Victoria Climbié Inquiry (1996) and the Kerry Babies Case Inquiry (1985).

[3] See eg Report into the London terrorist attacks (Murphy and Intelligence and Security Committee 2006), the Manchester Arena Inquiry Reports, https://www.gov.uk/government/collections/manchester-arena-inquiry-reports, and the Grenfell Tower Inquiry (2024) (accessed 10 October 2024).

[4] See eg the Mid Staffordshire NHS Inquiry (2013); and the ongoing UK Covid-19 Inquiry. See also Tribunal of Inquiry into the Infection with HIV and Hepatitis C of Persons with Haemophilia (Lindsay 2002).

Inquiries as an 'instrument of government' (Wraith and Lamb 1971) serve an important symbolic function. Lord Howe (1999, 295) suggested that a public inquiry has at least four functions: learning, discipline, catharsis, and reassurance. These broadly represent the search for truth, accountability, healing for victim/survivors, and restoring public trust. As Popkin and Roht-Arriaza (1995) note more broadly, investigatory commissions can achieve outcomes which other legal avenues of seeking justice or redress (such as civil or criminal proceedings) cannot. In relation to non-recent institutional abuses, scholars note that inquiries not only identify the nature and extent of wrongdoing but have broader societal aspects such as signalling a changing of social values, restoring public confidence in justice systems, or providing public acceptance of responsibility (McAuliffe 2017a) or influencing social understanding of abuse or intergenerational trauma (Gleeson and Ring 2021).

Indeed, while there is a broader literature on whether inquiries can ever hope to procure an authoritative, *factual or forensic truth* in dealing with the past (see eg McEvoy 2006; Lawther 2018a), there are at least three other dimensions to truth-seeking which are pertinent to investigatory processes into non-recent institutional abuses: *personal and narrative truth*—regarding the truths of individual victims and perpetrators (linking to healing and restorative truth); *social truth*—where collective public discourse leads to transparency and public accountability around institutional actions; and *healing and restorative* truth—where the framing of narratives about the past is orientated towards healing and reconciliation (if the latter is desired by victim/survivors), stemming from acknowledgement of individual experiences (see TRC 1998: Vol 1, paras 29–45; see also Little 2019). However, as discussed further, they are designed to deliver factual or forensic truth and work from a limited version of accountability that does not often mesh with victim/survivor needs.

In relation to the capacity of inquiries to deliver personal or narrative truth, as McEvoy and Mallinder (2012, 20) have argued, state-sponsored processes 'always run the risk of instrumentalizing victims or local communities' as the myriad of politically orientated aims may obfuscate truth and any real victim focus (see also Rolston and Scraton 2005). In addition, one of the intrinsic limitations of inquiry mechanisms is the fact that they have 'paradoxical aims and potentially competing functions' (McAlinden and Naylor 2016, 292). As Harlow (2013) illustrates, for example, a forward-looking focus may diminish accountability for past wrongs. Similarly, an emphasis on apportioning blame may mean that alleged organisational and individual perpetrators may not cooperate fully with truth-seeking processes for fear of legal or reputational consequences. Furthermore, a collective discourse which emphasises organisational accountability may obscure individual wrongdoing and provide little catharsis for individual victims (Hamber and Wilson 2002).

The broader societal aspects of inquiries, what Sedley (1989, 479) refers to as their 'curative properties', include public adjudication on allegations of systemic wrongdoing, victim access to other avenues of justice and redress such as prosecution or monetary redress, and a vehicle for policy and legal reforms (see McAlinden and Naylor 2016, 291–2). Moreover, as Delacorn (2011) has argued, inquiries that potentially reveal not only the commission of abuses but also the collective denials, collusions, and failures of state or quasi-state agencies also have the capacity to re-establish public trust via the promotion of institutional accountability. However, as discussed later, while investigatory processes are potentially important as vehicles for truth, justice, and accountability for individual victim/survivors and society as a whole, this is often limited by their specific ideological, structural, and legal functioning.

There are inherent structural limitations of inquiries as a response to the needs of individual victim/survivors which are essentially derived from the adversarial nature of the process and their latent incapacity to deliver real change. Inquiries may validate victim/survivors' interests and restore their dignity by providing an official account of events, although this is also contested (see eg Final Report of the CoI MBH 2021 later). They are also more limited in their potential to deliver other forms of 'procedural justice' (Lind and Tyler 1988) that victim/survivors want, such as having a 'voice' and ensuring perpetrator accountability. In essence, it is the second and third of Howe's aims (accountability and catharsis) which are of central importance in establishing victim-centred justice discourses yet which inquiry mechanisms usually struggle to deliver.

3. The International Dimension

Inquiries have featured in many parliamentary democracies such as Australia, Canada, Great Britain, the Netherlands, Norway, Sweden, Denmark, and Iceland. Recent comparative work, however, has focused on Anglophone countries including Australia and Canada, the UK, the United States, and Ireland (see principally, Daly 2014b; Ring et al 2022, ch 10; Gallen 2023a, ch 6). As part of this project, we conducted a detailed comparative overview of state investigations into non-recent institutional abuses across a range of countries (see Shilliday et al 2023). This section draws out the key learning from some examples of investigatory approaches in both Anglophone and non-Anglophone countries.

As regards Anglophone countries, Australia and England and Wales have had a lengthy history of inquiries into abuses of children in out-of-home care (see McAlinden and Naylor 2016). The Australian Royal Commission into Institutional Responses to Child Sexual Abuse ('the Royal Commission') (2013–17),[5] which comprised public hearings and private sessions with survivors, was notable and much praised for a number of core emphases: healing for victim/survivors; future-focused recommendations around child protection, in addition to dealing with the past; a centralised research component linked to Commission hearings (see Ring et al 2022, 221); and the production of modularised, interim research or investigatory reports feeding into public hearings. The Independent Inquiry into Child Sexual Abuse in England and Wales (IICSA) (2013–22)[6] which also comprised both investigatory and therapeutic functions, mirrors the Australian model in these four core respects.[7] What is noteworthy is that the research-based, thematic analysis, in addition to a separate modular focus on individual institutions or settings, offers a broader educative function in mapping the systemic learning across institutional contexts. Moreover, both bodies published transcripts of evidence and/or summaries of individual victim/survivor narratives on their websites as key elements of openness and transparency which are central to truth-telling and accountability.

Although both bodies focused on historical as well as contemporary abuses, the Royal Commission's focus on child sexual abuse only as 'the core transgression of childhood' (Golding 2018) was subject to criticism, including from victim/survivors. However, institutional settings were broadly defined. These encompassed a range of residential and community-based settings relating to the Catholic Church and other Christian religions (eg Anglican Church, Jehovah's Witnesses, Pentecostal Churches, Jewish religion, and the Salvation Army) and religious and non-religious contexts (eg those relating to out-of-home care, schools, sports and community groups, and detention) (Royal Commission 2017c, Vol 16). Although the

[5] Established under the Royal Commissions Act 1902 (Cth).
[6] Initially established as a non-statutory inquiry, it was converted to statutory format under the Inquiries Act 2005.
[7] See https://www.iicsa.org.uk/about-us/terms-reference.html (accessed 1 June 2024).

Royal Commission noted limitations of the available data, it found that the extent of child sexual abuse in institutional settings in Australia was significant and occurred across a wide range of institutions (Royal Commission 2017c, Vol 2).

The scope of IICSA was comprehensive and 'unprecedented in British parliamentary history' (Ring et al 2022, 243). In addition to residential contexts (including schools, looked-after children, and custodial settings), a range of non-institutional contexts were also examined (including child sexual exploitation, internet abuses, and child migration programmes). Foster settings, however, were notably absent from the focus of both IICSA and the Royal Commission. The scope of IICSA's investigation into 38 religious organisations and settings included not only the Catholic Church, but also Protestant churches (including Baptists, Methodists, and the Anglican Church), Jehovah's Witnesses, Islam, Judaism, Sikhism, Hinduism, and Buddhism. While also noting the lack of precise and reliable evidence about the scale of child sexual abuse within religious organisations and settings (see IICSA 2021, Part B.2), the inquiry found evidence of child sexual abuse in most major religious organisations and settings within England and Wales, some with no child protection frameworks in place, and significant barriers to reporting including the dynamics of victim-blaming and shame, and fear of reputational damage and external intervention (see IICSA 2021, especially Parts C–E). Many of these concerns were also echoed in the investigation of non-religious residential settings (IICSA 2022a; 2022b, Part I). As with the Royal Commission in Australia, this demonstrates not only the endemic nature of institutional abuses and commonality in abusive experiences but also shared barriers to just outcomes for victim/survivors across religious and secular settings.

In terms of outcomes, both the Royal Commission and IICSA made use of police referrals although the available figures are neither precise nor encouraging. As regards the Royal Commission, 2,252 referrals were made with eventual charges laid 'in a number of cases' and, of those referrals, 1,129 related to child sexual abuse in religious institutions (Royal Commission 2017c, Vol 1, 25). Of the 2,402 referrals made by IICSA to police over a two-year period (March 2015–June 2017), 78% resulted in 'no further action' due to a range of reasons including lack of evidence and perpetrators being untraceable or deceased.[8] Indeed, victim/survivors

[8] See https://www.iicsa.org.uk/reports-recommendations/publications/inquiry/interim/overview/operation-hydrant (accessed 1 June 2024).

expressed a 'disconnect' with IICSA and subsequent police investigations (Aldridge 2018). The Royal Commission has affected cultural and policy reforms essential for non-recurrence, including via the introduction of new state and institutional child protection policies throughout Australia[9] and has also introduced innovation around redress centred on repair and the taking of responsibility (see further Chapter 6). However, as Ring et al (2022, 240) note, some Catholic religious orders resisted recommendations for reform, including the removal of the confessional seal. Survivors and advocates have also been critical of the lack of follow-through on IICSA's key recommendations by the UK government, such as the introduction of mandatory reporting[10] as well as on monetary redress[11] (see also Chapter 6).

Within non-Anglophone countries, there have been fewer 'large-scale scandals' (Marotta 2021, 911) meriting systemic investigation. Moreover, inquiries are generally a feature of common law systems as distinct from civil law systems which characterise most of Europe and South America. Across the rest of the world, therefore, the use of inquiries or investigatory commissions as an official response to non-recent institutional abuses has been more fragmented. This lack of official or public attention via investigatory mechanisms has also shaped academic discourses. As Marotta (2021, 911) notes in the context of Italy and France, while existing scholarship documents regional patterns relating to abuses, cover-up, and the responses by church and civil institutions and society, it has 'thus far neglected to problematize the local peculiarities of the phenomenon'. As discussed in the next two chapters, however, other jurisdictions have conceived of 'redress' more broadly including via monetary redress schemes and official apologies.

As Arvidsson (2020) explains, 'state redress for abuse and neglect in children's homes has been debated in all Scandinavian countries since early 2000s'. Denmark, Sweden, and Norway, all predominantly Protestant societies, have utilised government commissions as part of the state response to non-recent institutional abuses where the emphasis is usually on non-legalistic and non-adversarial approaches. In particular, these usually take place in private with evidence gathered by scholars or professionals

[9] See the five Annual Progress Reports 2018–22, https://www.childsafety.gov.au/royal-commission/annual-progress-reports (accessed 10 October 2024).

[10] H Siddique. 'Survivors criticise "abhorrent" failure to act on child sexual abuse inquiry', *The Guardian*, 5 February 2024.

[11] K Harrison. 'Child Sexual Abuse Inquiry: survivors have waited long enough', *Law Society Gazette*, 20 December 2023.

via archival research and private interviews. In Sweden, for example, the Commission to Inquire into Child Abuse and Neglect in Institutions and Foster Homes (2011) led to an official apology and a subsequent monetary redress scheme (Sköld 2016). In Denmark, the Godhavn Inquiry (2011) examined abuses and medical experiments within a number of state-run children's homes during the period 1945–76 (see Rytter and Rasmussen 2015). While there were no subsequent prosecutions, there was an eventual state apology to victim/survivors some years later (see Chapter 7). Over the last two decades, Norway, in addition to a national investigation of abuse and neglect in child welfare institutions between 1945 and 1980 (NOU 2004), has also had a number of official investigations into non-recent institutional abuses at the regional level (see Ericsson 2015; Simonsen and Pettersen 2015).

In the Netherlands, there have been two notable inquiries—the Deetman Commission of Inquiry into Sexual Abuse of Minors in the Roman Catholic Church (Deetman et al 2011) between 1945 and 1985 and the Samson Committee of Investigation into the sexual abuse of children in state-run out-of-home care between 1945 and 2010 (Commissie Samson 2012). The Deetman Commission, in documenting the abuse of thousands of children by more than 800 priests and religious, found that the common response of church authorities at the time to allegations of abuse was 'Penance, transfer and possibly treatment' of the individual perpetrator and that '[t]here was no structural approach to the problem' (2012, 12–13). While there were no prosecutions due to the statute of limitations,[12] the Deetman Commission led to a financial redress scheme (see Aertsen 2024). The subsequent Samson Committee eventually led to an official apology and to changes in child protection guidelines (see Dekker and Grietens 2015). While limited perhaps in terms of the accountability of individual perpetrators, such investigations have value in terms not only of knowledge production about non-recent institutional abuses but also their capacity to shift institutional thinking and social and cultural attitudes about the past (Wright 2017).

At the time of writing, there are several recent or ongoing official investigations into non-recent institutional abuses across the globe: the Belgian Parliament agreed to establish an inquiry into sexual abuse in the Catholic Church in September 2023 and the Scottish Child Abuse Inquiry, with wide-ranging terms of reference, began in October 2015 with public hearings ongoing until at least 2025. The Royal Commission of Inquiry into

[12] M Corder, 'Dutch prosecutors probe Catholic institute deaths', *The San Diego Union-Tribune*, 16 August 2011.

Historical Abuse in State Care and in the Care of Faith-based Institutions in New Zealand, focusing on the experiences of Māori, Pacific, disabled people, and those with mental illness, reported in June 2024. It is notable for its systemic approach and fuller terms of reference centred on survivor experiences, including an examination of the immediate, long-term, and intergenerational impact of abuses as well as 'lesson learning' from previous policy reforms (Royal Commission of Inquiry 2024; see also Stanley et al 2024). Indeed, as discussed further in Part III, there are a range of alternative truth-recovery models where the focus is on victims' experiences, including via ongoing and widespread consultation and truth-telling and acknowledgement within a non-adversarial context.

4. Investigations in the Republic of Ireland

There are two main modes of investigation in RoI. The first is the tribunal of inquiry which is used to examine 'definite matter[s] . . . of urgent public importance'[13] such as policy issues or political controversies relating, for example, to allegations of corruption[14] and complaints concerning Gardaí[15] as well as health or medical issues. The two notable features of tribunals of inquiry are that they are inquisitorial in nature and held in public.[16] The second is the Commission of Investigation model where the proceedings are intended to be less expensive[17] and more expeditive and where evidence may also be given in private. This has been used to address matters of 'significant public concern'[18] including scandals relating to medical care as well as failures in child protection. The most common form of investigation into non-recent institutional abuses has been the Commission of Investigation where the focus has overwhelmingly been on Catholic-run institutions or abuses by Catholic clergy. Official investigations are governed by the

[13] Tribunals of Inquiry (Evidence) Act 1921, s 1(1) (as amended).

[14] See eg The Moriarty (1997–2011), http://www.moriarty-tribunal.ie, and Mahon Tribunals (1997–2013), https://www.planningtribunal.ie/wp-content/uploads/2019/04/sitecontent_1257.pdf (accessed 1 June 2024).

[15] See eg the Morris Tribunal (2002–8), http://www.morristribunal.ie/ (accessed 1 June 2024).

[16] Due to concerns about excessive costs, length, and bureaucracy, the Law Reform Commission recommended a new statutory framework (LRC 2005) which was unimplemented.

[17] See, however, H McGee, 'Tribunals and Commissions of Investigation have cost taxpayers over €500m', *The Irish Times*, 12 January 2011.

[18] Commissions of Investigation Act 2004, s 3(1).

Haughey principles which in part accounts for the highly adversarial nature of proceedings.[19]

The Ferns Inquiry was a non-statutory investigation into the handling of over 100 allegations of child sexual abuse against 21 priests in the Diocese of Ferns between 1966 and 2002 (Murphy et al 2005). The report exposed not only 'structural, institutional, and moral' (Crowe 2008, 73) but also legal failings in the face of complaints. It found that clerical sexual abuse was treated by the Church hierarchy as a 'moral' and 'medical' rather than a legal problem (see eg Murphy et al 2005, 48, 132, 135) where bishops failed to remove priests from ministry and report complaints to the State authorities and that there were ineffective investigations by State authorities (see also Chapter 2). With no power to issue recommendations, the Ferns Report was nonetheless significant for a number of reasons.

While previous inquiries had dealt with sexual abuse within family[20] or other institutional settings,[21] this was the first inquiry to focus on sexual abuse by religious. Further, it helped to legitimise the issue and encourage reporting by victims.[22] However, of the over 100 complaints examined, ten of those complained of were dead with the majority no longer in ministry. Only two individuals were prosecuted and convicted and a third committed suicide before trial (see Crowe 2008, 53). Indeed, the 'outcomes' were largely framed as the need to have more effective 'self-governance' in the form of standardised procedures across dioceses (Garrett 2013, 46). Other inquiries have broader mechanisms for ensuring institutional accountability, such as via recommending institutional reform and development of state and institutional policies on child safeguarding. Nonetheless, the low number of prosecutions emphasises the limited follow-up capacity of inquiries to deliver just outcomes for victim/survivors or accountability at an individual perpetrator level.

The Commission to Inquire into Child Abuse (CICA) was tasked, *inter alia*, with 'inquiring into the abuse of children in institutions' dating back

[19] *Re Haughey* [1971] IR 217 which establishes that a person whose conduct is potentially impugned by an inquiry must be afforded reasonable means of defence. The minimum protections are: (1) to be furnished with a copy of the evidence reflecting on their good name; (2) to be allowed to cross-examine, via counsel, their accuser(s); (3) to be allowed to give evidence in rebuttal; and (4) to be permitted to address, via counsel, the Committee in their own defence.

[20] See eg the Kilkenny Incest Investigation (South Eastern Health Board 1993) and the Inquiry into the West of Ireland Farmer Case (North Western Health Board 1998).

[21] See eg Inquiry into Child Sexual Abuse in Swimming (Murphy 1998).

[22] 'Ferns Report sparks surge in calls to rape helplines', *Irish Examiner*, 16 November 2005.

to 1936 and determining 'the causes, nature, circumstances and extent of such abuse'.[23] Thus, while empowered to make future-orientated recommendations, the focus was predominantly on the past. The Commission had a Confidential Committee where evidence could be given in private, uncontested and an Investigative Committee where hearings could be held in either private or public. It was beset by initial problems including lack of engagement from the Department of Education via delays in producing documents. Dominated by highly adversarial approaches, it was the subject of successful legal proceedings by the Christian Brothers who challenged the naming of offenders.[24] For victim/survivors, the use of pseudonyms for individual 'perpetrators', even those who were convicted or deceased, effectively prevented accountability of individual perpetrators (Gleeson and Ring 2021, 120; Gallen 2023a, 146).

The publication of the Commission's five-volume report under the chairmanship of Judge Séan Ryan (the 'Ryan Report') (CICA 2009), which had investigated more than 250 church-run institutions for nearly a decade, generated media coverage nationally and internationally.[25] The report was momentous in concluding that the abuse of children (physical, sexual, emotional, and neglect) and the failure of church and state authorities to adequately respond to the problem, was *systemic* in Irish childcare institutions (CICA 2009, Vol IV, paras 6.09–6.18). It also highlighted the historical reluctance of the institutional Church to take responsibility for abuses, describing a 'culture of silence' (Vol IV, para 29) where complaints were ignored, witnesses or families coerced into silence (Executive Summary, 14, see also Vol III), and where allegations 'tended to be dealt with using internal disciplinary procedures and Canon Law' (Executive Summary, 23). Rather than trying to address potential abuses or accept institutional responsibility for the actions of individual priests, '[t]he desire to protect the reputation of the Congregation and institution was paramount' (Vol IV, para 6.20).

Although the Ryan Report was a major milestone in State investigation of abuses, it provided limited truth recovery and limited accountability of

[23] Commission to Inquire into Child Abuse Act 2000, s 4.

[24] *Murray v Commission to Inquire into Child Abuse* [2004] IEHC 102. The Commission to Inquire into Child Abuse (Amendment) Act 2005 granted broad anonymity to 'perpetrators': see ss 5 and 8.

[25] See eg P Cullen and P McGarry, 'Systematic abuse in state institutions laid bare', *The Irish Times*, 21 May 2009 and J Banville, 'A Century of Looking the Other Way', *The New York Times*, 22 May 2009.

both individual perpetrators and the State. From the approximate 30,000 complaints made, only institutions which involved more than 20 complainants were examined by the investigative committee—all Catholic-run institutions—to allow the Commission to complete its work expediently.[26] Similarly, the report did not examine the role of race within institutionalisation including the experiences of Mincéirí and those of mixed-race heritage. Furthermore, in November 2019, the figure of 170,000 for the number of children in institutions contained in the Final Report (Vol 1, para 3.01) was announced on the Commission's website as being incorrect and closer to 42,000. While the Ryan Report was mammoth in scale and scope, such disparities undermine its capacity to deliver a 'definitive . . . truth' about institutional abuses for survivors and the wider public (Ring et al 2022, 229).

As discussed in Chapter 4, only 11 cases were forwarded to the Director of Public Prosecutions (DPP) and only three proceeded to prosecution (Holohan 2011, 25). The Church has also been heavily criticised among academics (Gallen 2020, 61) and state officials (Comptroller and Auditor General 2016) for making only a nominal contribution to the redress bill (see further Chapter 6). Further, the Ryan Commission did not investigate the State's responsibility for allowing the industrial school system to operate for so long despite clear historical evidence of systemic abuses (see Gleeson and Ring 2021, 119). In this respect, the Irish State has carefully fashioned a distancing narrative from non-recent institutional abuses, claiming to accept responsibility for failing to protect children on the one hand but also claiming 'ignorance and naïve trust in the religious running of these institutions' (Keating 2004, 323). As a result, the state tends to cast its legal and moral responsibility for those in its care in inchoate terms. This is usually presented in moral terms 'as a failure of intervention' (Gleeson and Ring 2021, 113) rather than as a violation of legally mandated human rights.

As is the case with child protection inquiries more broadly (see eg Buckley and O'Nolan 2013; Swain 2014), many of the Ryan Commission's 99 sets of action have not been implemented or followed through, demonstrating a lack of accountability at the collective institutional level. Despite a comprehensive implementation plan and monitoring group and reports,[27]

[26] While a small number of victim/survivors of Protestant institutions did engage with the Commission, ascertaining precise numbers is impossible as the report did not provide an institutional breakdown, see N Meehan, 'Child abuse and its concealment did occur within Protestant institutions', *The Irish News*, 7 June 2019.

[27] See https://www.gov.ie/en/publication/3c76d0-the-report-of-the-commission-to-inquire-into-child-abuse-the-ryan-re/#ryan-monitoring-group (accessed 1 June 2024).

Ireland has been criticised in this regard at the United Nations.[28] Moreover, following attempts to seal records and witness statements in the National Archives for 75 years,[29] there are lasting concerns for victim/survivors about visibility, transparency, and access to records.

The Commission of Investigation Report into the Catholic Archdiocese of Dublin (CoI 2009), chaired by Judge Yvonne Murphy (the 'Murphy Report'), investigated the handling by church and state authorities of a representative sample of allegations and suspicions of clerical sexual abuse over the period 1975 to 2004. It had no specific powers to make recommendations. The report concluded that clerical sexual abuse was 'covered-up' during this period (para 1.113) and that 'suspicions were rarely acted on' (para 1.35). Successive archbishops and bishops were named for failing to report their concerns to the Gardaí (paras 1.32–1.36) or transferring the suspected perpetrator to another parish or diocese.

The report also noted the preoccupation with 'the maintenance of secrecy, the avoidance of scandal, the protection of the reputation of the Church and the preservations of its assets' to which 'the welfare of children and justice for victims' were subordinated (para 1.15). These issues concerning motivation manifested within the Ferns and Murphy investigations which also faced difficulties in terms of delays in getting access to relevant material held within diocesan archives (Holohan 2011, 19). However, the methodology of the Commission has been questioned by commentators especially in terms of non-specificity in the methodology employed in the report and the failure to base its findings on a representative sample of cases (see eg McCarthy 2013; McDonagh 2013).

Some two years later, the Commission of Investigation Report into the Catholic Diocese of Cloyne (CoI 2011) (the 'Cloyne Report') examined the handling of a sample of complaints of child sexual abuse during the period 1 January 1996 to 1 February 2009, with no power to make recommendations. The report concluded that the response of the Church was 'inadequate and inappropriate' (para 1.71) and that it had failed, *inter alia*, to carry out proper canonical investigations, to report all complaints to the Gardaí or health authorities, and to implement an independent advisory panel which could assist Church authorities in

[28] See eg UN Committee on the Elimination of Discrimination against Women, https://undocs.org/CEDAW/C/IRL/CO/6-7 (9 March 2017) and UN Committee against Torture, https://undocs.org/CAT/C/IRL/CO/2 (31 August 2017).

[29] Retention of Records Bill 2019 which also extends to the records of the Redress Board.

taking appropriate action when an allegation of abuse was made, as had been recommended in the Church's own guidelines (see Irish Catholic Bishop's Conference 1996). Besides its statutory outcomes relating to child protection,[30] the publication of the Cloyne Report constituted a watershed moment in Church and State responses to non-recent institutional abuses in Ireland.

The time period demonstrates that the issues and failings raised, concerning the handling of abuse complaints by Church authorities, were not confined to the distant past. Rather, the remit of the investigation covered the period in which the Catholic Church in Ireland first put in place procedures regarding the handling of abuse complaints (see eg Irish Catholic Bishops' Advisory Committee 1996; Keenan 2012, 182–4). Further, it represented a cultural shift in the historically enmeshed relationship of church and state within Ireland. In the Dáil debates around the report, Enda Kenny, then Taoiseach, made a much lauded speech, proclaiming that 'this is not Rome. Nor is it industrial school or Magdalene Ireland . . .This is the Republic of Ireland in 2011. It is a republic of laws, rights and responsibilities.'[31] While framed as part of 'nation-building' and the collective societal transition from a darker past to a more enlightened present (see also Chapter 7), this narrative can also be interpreted more sceptically as a distancing from responsibility.

Up to and including the Cloyne Report, the focus of investigations into non-recent institutional abuses had been on abuses against children committed predominantly by priests or members of religious orders. This also had a knock-on effect in terms of discourses on church–state responsibilisation. As Garrett (2013, 61) explains, 'the Church has been hyper-responsibilized for failing to protect children' while at the same time 'the scapegoating of the "paedophile priest" has arguably acted as a screen discourse, exonerating the state from any responsibility'. Furthermore, this narrow motif concerning abuses and those responsible for abuses tends to obscure the lived realities of survivors where children were also abused by lay workers and their peers as part of the institutional normalisation of abuses (see eg CICA 2009, Executive Summary, p 13; see also McAlinden 2012, ch 5). Moreover, a compartmentalised focus on clerical sexual abuse

[30] See eg the Criminal Justice (Withholding of Information on Offences against Children and Vulnerable Persons) Act 2012.

[31] E Kenny, Dáil Debates, 20 July 2011. See eg RTE News, 'Taoiseach on Unprecedented Attack on Vatican', 20 July 2011.

obscures other forms of abuse some of which were to come to light in subsequent years.

In response to advocacy campaigns (Justice For Magdalenes (JFM): see eg O'Rourke 2011; McGettrick et al 2021), the UN Committee Against Torture (UN CAT Committee 2011, 6) recommended that the Irish government 'institute prompt, independent, and thorough investigations' into the Magdalene Laundries. An Inter-Departmental Committee was set up in 2011 'to establish the facts of state involvement with the Magdalen Laundries' (IDC 2013, 4), chaired by Senator Martin McAleese (the 'McAleese Report'). It covered the period 1922 to 1996 when the last laundry closed in Dublin. As a non-statutory investigation, it had a limited mandate and focus with no power to make recommendations. While the McAleese Commission was comprised of two strands—a Confidential Committee and an Investigative Committee—unlike the Ryan Commission, victim/survivors could give evidence to one or both Committees.

The McAleese Report investigated ten institutions and established that there were multiple gateways for women and girls into institutionalisation including referral by the State (from the criminal justice system (8.1%), reformatory or industrial schools (7.8%), the health and social services sector and mother and baby homes (7%)) as well as voluntary or self-referral (16.4%), referral from another congregation (11.2%) or another Magdalene Laundry (14.8%), and by families (10.5%) or the local priest (8.8%) (IDC 2013, Part II, ch 8, para 17). These statistics not only clearly convey both church and state responsibility for incarcerating women but also the interconnected nature of the 'architecture of containment' (Smith 2007) and therein the complexity of unpacking clear lines of organisational, political, and societal responsibility for institutionalisation as a policy wrong.

The report was criticised on a number of grounds. Due to its narrow remit and the fact that it was chaired by a state official, the UN Committee on the Elimination of All Forms of Discrimination against Women (UN CEDAW Committee 2017, paras 14–15) found that the State had failed to establish an 'independent, thorough and effective investigation'. Most critical of all perhaps was the minimisation of harm and the downplaying of the voices and experiences of victim/survivors. As McGettrick et al (2021, 103) outline, the report contained 'mounds of obfuscation' as some of its key findings did not tally with archival records or the women's testimonies. The report frames the testimony of victim/survivors as 'stories' rather than as testimony (IDC 2013, Part III, ch 19, 925) resulting in both testimonial and hermeneutical epistemic injustice (Fricker 2007) where testimony is ignored and lived experiences obscured from collective understanding. Further, in accordance with its mandate, the report did not issue recommendations regarding responsibility or accountability for abuses. Such were the criticisms of the report among victim/survivors that they renewed their call for a new independent statutory investigation into Magdalene Laundries.[32]

Scholars and activists have also pointed to the lack of tangible follow-through in terms of the State accepting full moral and legal responsibility for abuses against women within Magdalene Laundries (see McAlinden 2022a). In light of the report, the Taoiseach Enda Kenny issued an apology to victim/survivors and established an *ex gratia* redress scheme (see Chapters 6 and 7). However, as discussed further, despite some important design innovations in terms of responding to victim/survivors (see Chapters 6 and 8), there were also criticisms in how that redress scheme was implemented relating to the framing of 'harm' and the computation of 'responsibility' which ultimately undermined its capacity to deliver just outcomes and procedures for survivors.

Following claims that the remains of almost 800 babies and infants were located at the site of a former Bon Secour Mother and Baby Home in Tuam, Co Galway, the Commission of Investigation into Mother and Baby Homes was set up in 2015 with its Final Report issued in 2021. The Commission, chaired once more by Judge Yvonne Murphy, had wide-ranging terms of reference including establishing circumstances and arrangements for entry and exit of women and children and living conditions and care arrangements, examining mortality amongst mothers and children, and investigating post-mortem practices and procedures over the period 1922–98.[33] Fourteen institutions were investigated with an additional four selected as a representative sample of state-operated county homes. The Commission operated via an Investigation Committee conducted within a formal adversarial framework and a more informal Confidential Committee providing a forum in which victim/survivors could recount their experiences—both held in private.

From its many recommendations, those related to information and tracing were implemented via the Birth Information and Tracing Act 2022. However, victim/survivors remain frustrated at the legal and institutional

[32] P McGarry, 'Renewed calls for independent investigation into Magdalene Laundries', *The Irish Times*, 1 November 2013.

[33] Commission of Investigation (Mother and Baby Homes and certain related Matters) Order 2015 (SI No 57/2015), Sch.

barriers to accessing their records, including on a cross-border basis. The publication of the Final Report of the Mother and Baby Homes Commission was also met with controversy on the grounds that it had misrepresented or omitted victim/survivor testimonies and was subject to a series of judicial reviews by survivors who had not been given a right of reply as identifiable persons within the report.[34] Many survivors were unaware that they could provide evidence to both Committees (Corrigan and Lundy 2021, 12) and the victims who gave evidence to the Confidential Committee were not informed that testimony would have limited impact on the Commission's findings (Enright and O'Donoghue 2021, 3). Furthermore, as with the McAleese Report (IDC 2013), there was a distinct absence of a human rights lens despite the wide range of human rights abuses that had taken place including physical and sexual violence, illegal adoptions, forced labour, and arbitrary detention (see O'Rourke et al 2018; Gallen 2020).[35] As with the McAleese Report, the report is also notable for seeking to include Irish society as being partly responsible for institutionalisation (see eg CoI MBH 2021, Executive Summary, paras 69 and 260). Notwithstanding these failings, the report has become the official state narrative on its responsibility for mother and baby institutions.[36]

In March 2023, the Irish State commissioned a non-statutory Scoping Inquiry into Historical Sexual Abuse in Day and Boarding Schools Run by Religious Orders to inform the government's response to emerging allegations. The Scoping Inquiry Report, submitted to the Minister of Education in June 2024 and made public in September 2024, found 2,395 allegations of sexual abuse in respect of 308 schools recorded by 42 religious orders in respect of 884 alleged abusers in the period 1927–2023. It acknowledged, however, that given the general levels of under-reporting, the real numbers of allegations were likely to be higher. After engaging with survivors as well as religious orders, the proposed framework is comprised of three central elements: a Commission of Investigation model,[37] a financial redress scheme, and a survivor engagement programme to allow victim/survivors to recount their evidence in a confidential and non-adversarial way. Its terms of reference, much like the Ferns Inquiry and the Murphy

[34] J Bray, 'State to argue against judicial reviews taken by mother and baby home survivors', *The Irish Times*, 16 June 2021.

[35] See the CLANN project, http://clannproject.org/.

[36] C O'Fátharta, 'Narrative of report on mother and baby homes needs to be challenged', *The Irish Examiner*, 16 January 2021.

[37] See n 18 and accompanying text.

and Cloyne Commissions detailed earlier, will focus on the *handling* of allegations of sexual abuse in these specific institutional contexts. Despite endorsing some of the values of restorative justice such as accountability, respect for all parties, survivor-centredness, and repair and healing—core principles that we have also advanced throughout our analysis in this book—the Scoping Inquiry has proposed a similar framework to previous investigations, declining to recommend a large-scale restorative project as part of the government's response (see further discussion in Chapter 8).

Although the Scoping Inquiry Report surveyed international practices on inquiry design and processes, including in the reduction of victim/survivor distress, it provided limited incorporation of such lessons, or trauma-informed approaches more generally, in its recommendations to the Irish government. For example, no mention is made of the potential of the innovative Independent Panel model being developed in Northern Ireland. Instead, the inquiry recommended significant discretion to the proposed Commission of Investigation and in its recommended terms of reference merely restated the existing challenge experienced in the Irish context of balancing a survivor-centred approach with fair procedures (Scoping Inquiry 2024, Vol 4, 664–8).

The compartmentalised and ad hoc nature of investigations in RoI has impeded a holistic examination of 'the relationship between the different forms of coercive institutional confinement' including pathways between the institutions as well as the social, structural, and institutional norms which sustained them (Gallen 2020, 46). For example, despite a recommendation by the UN Human Rights Committee that there should be a survivor-centred and trauma-informed approach to investigating all allegations of abuse related to symphysiotomy,[38] there has not yet been a state investigation. There have also been calls for a non-statutory inquiry into the practice of forced and illegal adoptions (O'Mahony 2021, 36). Following the report by an Independent Review Group (IRG 2023), a judge-led tribunal of inquiry into the handling of allegations of discrimination, bullying, harassment, and sexual assault in the Defence Forces was established in January 2024, beginning hearings in June 2024. The broad experiences of victim/survivors and the perspectives of other key actors across the main investigatory mechanisms in RoI are examined later.

[38] E McAuley and L Dunphy, 'Irish symphysiotomy survivors welcome UN's all for criminal investigation', *Irish Examiner*, 22 July 2022.

5. Inquiries in Northern Ireland

Prior to 2013, there were a number of departmental inquiries into abuses of children in residential care. The most notable of these was the Hughes Inquiry which examined abuses in nine homes between 1960 and 1984 including Kincora Hostel, De La Salle Boys' Home, Rubane House, and Nazareth Lodge (Committee of Inquiry 1985).[39] While the Inquiry resulted in procedural changes relating to complaints and vetting procedures, many of these institutions were to be re-examined within the Hart Inquiry.

The Hart Inquiry was set up in 2013 under the chairmanship of the late retired judge, Sir Anthony Hart. The terms of reference for the Inquiry[40] encompassed making findings and recommendations on: (1) whether there were systemic failings by institutions or the State in their duties towards those children in their care between 1922 and 1995; (2) an apology; (3) an appropriate form of memorialisation; and (4) the desirability for redress. Similar in structure to the Ryan Commission, it comprised an Acknowledgement Forum where victim/survivors could recount their experiences in private and a separate statutory Investigation and Inquiry Panel with public hearings. It had specific statutory powers to compel the release of documents and require witnesses to give evidence.[41] The Inquiry remit was broad, examining physical, sexual, and emotional abuse and neglect as well as childcare practices.

The Inquiry investigated 22 institutions including residential care homes and juvenile justice as well as the Child Migration Programme to Australia and abuses perpetrated by Fr Brendan Smyth. The Inquiry covered not only Catholic-run but also Protestant-run institutions including local authority homes, Barnardo's, juvenile justice institutions, and a Church of Ireland children's home (Manor House). However, an additional 43 institutions falling within the Inquiry remit were not investigated as the Inquiry considered that it 'would not be justified' as it 'would not add to

[39] Many of the allegations relating to the Kincora 'cover-up' by the state persist: A Morris, 'Kincora victims to sue PSNI, Secretary of State and health trust over sex abuse', *Belfast Telegraph*, 24 September 2022.

[40] See statement made by the then First and Deputy First Ministers, 18 October 2012, amended by the Inquiry into Historical Institutional Abuse (Amendment of Terms of Reference) Order (Northern Ireland) 2015.

[41] While the Inquiries Act 2005 applies to the whole of the UK, specific legislation and rules were necessary for the Hart Inquiry given that its historical remit predated 2005. See the Historical Institutional Abuse Act (Northern Ireland) 2013 and the Inquiry into Historical Institutional Abuse Rules (Northern Ireland) 2013.

. . . understanding of the nature and extent of systemic abuse of children in homes and institutions in Northern Ireland' (HIA Inquiry 2017, Vol 1, ch 3, para 26). Selectivity in the sampling of cases creates procedural and epistemic justice concerns relating to victim/survivors' voices and representation of their experiences. It may also reinforce broader hierarchies of victimhood and of worthy and unworthy forms of abuse, obscuring the experiences of other survivors (Lawther 2021b; see Chapter 3)

The Inquiry found instances of 'systemic abuse' to be common across residential institutions as well as 'systemic failures' in institutional governance. The findings regarding Fr Brendan Smyth mirrored the findings of the Murphy and Cloyne Reports in relation to the handling of complaints by religious orders and Catholic dioceses. Information was deliberately withheld from other dioceses about Smyth's offending background and concerns were not passed to the civil authorities in either NI or RoI, enabling Smyth to continue offending (Vol 3, ch 10). It further found 'indifference' by the NI government to the welfare of children and the practice of sending child migrants to Australia (Vol 2, ch 6, paras 62 and 64). Like the Australian Royal Commission, the transcripts of witness statements and evidence per 'module' are accessible online thus aiding transparency and accountability.

The Final Report made a number of key recommendations including on apology, memorialisation, redress, support services, and the appointment of a Commissioner for Survivors of Institutional Childhood Abuse (Vol 1, ch 4). However, in common with the other investigatory processes examined earlier, the recommendations do not comprehensively address the full range of needs identified by victims which are necessary for truth, justice, and state and organisational accountability. As other writers have also noted, this primarily includes access to records, guarantees of non-repetition, institutional reform, adequate redress, as well as wider societal transformation as part of addressing the systemic historical and cultural contexts of the past (see eg Lundy and Mahoney 2018; Lundy 2020). Although victims reportedly felt vindicated following the publication of the Inquiry report,[42] as explored later, many subsequently recounted feeling 'traumatised' and even 'victimised'.

The report was delivered on 20 January 2017, just days after the collapse of the NI Executive. The absence of a functioning Executive significantly delayed the implementation of the recommendations relating to both

[42] A Morris, 'Victims say they feel vindicated as damning historical abuse report published', *The Irish News*, 21 January 2021.

apology and redress. As one State official attested, 'there were no ministers to engage with and there were no decision makers' (Interview 45) (see further Chapter 7). Plans are ongoing to install a permanent memorial to victim/survivors at Stormont. In fact, the State's fulfilment of the recommendations was due in large part to persistent lobbying by victim/survivors as well as the initiation of legal proceedings relating to redress.[43] Process delays in follow-through on the recommendations ultimately undermined just outcomes for victim/survivors.

To date, the NI experience demonstrates that it shares the same reactive, piecemeal, and compartmentalised approach to investigation of non-recent institutional abuses as has occurred in RoI rather than a fuller examination of the systemic historical and structural issues underlying broader state and organisational accountability. As a result, victim/survivors of abuses in other institutional contexts were excluded from the remit of the Hart Inquiry. Following campaigns by victim/survivors and a subsequent Department of Health-commissioned research report (McCormick et al 2021), a Truth Recovery Design Panel was established to work with victim/survivors on developing a framework for an independent investigation. As discussed further in Chapter 9, it recommended, *inter alia*, 'an integrated truth investigation' model comprising an independent panel whose findings will inform a statutory inquiry (see Mahon et al 2021). Initial planning has also been undertaken for a clerical abuse inquiry.

6. Inquiries and the Limits of Truth, Justice, and Accountability

This section examines the experiences of victim/survivors and other actors of investigatory processes. First, it explores the value and limitations of inquiries in terms of acknowledgement and apportioning responsibility within an adversarial framework. Second, it analyses the ideological, structural, and legal barriers which may inhibit truth, justice, and accountability, chiefly via conflicting aims, their capacity to close down victim/survivor voices and public scrutiny, or to control the official narrative about the past. It also underscores the importance of the terms of reference which may

[43] A Preston, 'Abuse survivor hits out at Stormont "stalling tactics" as payouts delayed again', *Belfast Telegraph*, 8 February 2019.

potentially restrict the capacity of inquiries to comprehensively address the legacy of non-recent institutional abuses.

Value and impact

Acknowledgement and the limitations on responsibility

In tandem with the literature on procedural justice (see Chapter 1), many interviewees framed the value of inquiries in terms of voice and validation of abusive experiences. Reflections on experiences of the Ryan Commission in RoI and the Hart Inquiry in NI included the following: 'I think for the survivors, the fact they were believed, the outpourings of public grief' (Interview 26); 'that is justice for them to be believed . . . Survivors were just over the moon about the fact that it was acknowledged there was abuse' (Interview 50); and 'being heard and having someone listen to them . . . is a key factor' (Interview 45). For victim/survivors themselves in the context of the Hart Inquiry and the campaign by the Women of Honour for an investigation into the Irish Defence Forces, 'it's about acknowledgement of somebody's journey as a child' (Interview 15), 'it did the job that it set out to do which was . . . to shed a light on that dark part of our history' (Interview 9), and it is about 'get[ting] their opportunity to have a voice . . . to voice their truth' (Interview 66). For many, therefore, the 'catharsis' (Howe 1999, 295) or 'healing truth' (TRC 1998, Vol 1, 29–45) provided by official investigations into non-recent institutional abuses relates to official recognition as well as broader societal acknowledgement of abuses.

However, whilst official acknowledgement of wrongdoing and abuses might equate to the broad attribution of moral responsibility to church and state, there is a latent incapacity of investigatory mechanisms to determine individual levels of responsibility. A judge in RoI, reflecting on the Ryan Commission as 'a model without specific findings' (Interview 40) explained:

> There is the possibility of some form of public acknowledgement, but I think even that divides it [in]to two parts. There is the sort of, what you might call generalised, public acknowledgement, these sort of 'bad things happened in this institution, you know, around this time' which is probably easier to do than perhaps what was the starting point of the Laffoy Commission where the survivors wanted it to be something along the lines of a specific finding that, 'I was abused by Brother X in Y institution'. (Interview 40)

In contrast, while the Murphy Report used pseudonyms for most of the individual priests, it identified the actions of individual bishops. Thus, while official investigations may attribute some form of political, moral, or institutional responsibility, they have limited capacity to make specific findings of legal liability in either a criminal or civil sense which some survivors may want. A focus on systemic issues means that there is a fundamental disconnect between broad acknowledgement of wrongdoing and the explicit spelling out of individualised responsibility for particular abuses.

Indeed, fuller systemic investigation of non-recent institutional abuses also emerges as an almost impossible undertaking given the passage of time and the lack of living or available witnesses. As one lawyer in RoI outlined in relation to the Commission to Inquire into Child Abuse, 'if it was to operate fairly in accordance with its enabling statute, it had to address all strands and it had to hear from everybody . . . [I]t would have to examine in every single case, whether in fact it was in a position to do so, having regard to the number of missing actors' (Interview 18). In the view of this same interviewee, however, the amendments to the enabling statute, relating to its terms of reference and procedures,[44] resulted in 'the fudge [which] has not served justice' and where the Commission's report 'took a very large, thick paintbrush and just drew it across all actors . . . It rendered [it] impossible to make specific determinations of specific acts in specific contexts. So, therefore you could never go granular on anything' (Interview 18). This broader, generalised approach to truth-finding also undoubtedly contributed to the low number of prosecutions following the Ryan Report (see Holohan 2011, 25) despite the desire of some victim/survivors for retributive justice (see Pembroke 2019, 53–4). As one lawyer explained in relation to the Hart Inquiry, 'it's not that responsibility is not taken but it isn't transparent and . . . that can cause problems for people who are looking for somebody to take responsibility' (Interview 43).

In addition, this lack of specificity in favour of more generalised findings was also problematic for members of religious orders, both more generally as well as those accused or named within the course of proceedings. One member of a religious organisation explained in relation to the Ryan Report that 'it meant that everybody was tarred with the same brush' (Interview 41) and:

> We had members against whom allegations were made that were never, ever withdrawn or never clarified . . . [T]hey were never declared

[44] The Commission to Inquire into Child Abuse (Amendment) Act 2005.

> innocent. . . . So they were presumed guilty . . . There were allegations and . . . they were at the end of their lives and . . . they went to their graves not knowing if they were [found] guilty or otherwise. (Interview 41)

Similarly, other religious actors or lawyers noted that the positive experiences of some victims of residential care as children within the 'broader work of institutions . . . weren't put into a social context, an educational context' (Interview 27). As a senior member of a religious organisation reflected:

> When the Ryan Report came out, we were shocked that it was so negative . . . There was some of the positive side of residential care, some of the complainants had that, but none of that appeared in the Final Report. (Interview 23)

Although the positive experiences of survivors were detailed in the report of the Confidential Committee (CICA 2009, Vol 3, ch 10), this approach may also result in the loss of voice for those with institutional responsibility and a blanket vilification as 'bad' based on their membership of a collective, such as religious congregations, which also becomes pertinent for posterity. As one lawyer in RoI outlined:

> Voices were excluded entirely. . . . [T]here is an inherent unfairness to this from the perspective of those who were caring for children during those years . . . [P]eople will assume that the carers of whom former residents spoke were culpable as described, although such carers will never had the opportunity of giving their side of the story or exploring each other's memories of the time. (Interview 18)

Therefore, this lack of specificity in findings not only demonstrates the need to safeguard the procedural and due process rights of all parties—victim/survivors, individuals named or accused, and the institutions—but also, as discussed later, the power of investigatory frameworks to shape social understanding about responsibility for the past.

Adversarial justice

As Rolston and Scraton (2005, 548) note, inquiries 'are concerned with "culpability"' and [i]n apportioning responsibility . . . [T]heir inquisitorial process is underpinned by adversarial purpose.' Existing studies have examined the impact of legalistic 'inquiry culture' (Brennan 2015, 56) on victim/survivor experiences. For example, Pembroke's primary research in RoI with victims shows how many found their experiences of the Ryan Commission and the Redress Board retraumatising, 'trigger[ing] feelings of shame and stigma' (2019, 51). In the context of the Hart Inquiry in NI, Lundy and Hamber's research with victim/survivors established that despite the purported aim that 'as far as possible the Inquiry should be inquisitorial in nature',[45] many recounted feeling 'vulnerable' or 'traumatised' by a highly legalistic process with some experiencing longer term emotional impacts even after the Acknowledgement Forum (Hamber and Lundy 2020; Lundy 2020).

Building on this literature, many interviewees stressed the dominance and impact of legalism. In the words of one State official, against the 'original vision' of the Commission of Investigation model in RoI, 'lawyers became a very prominent feature of it within ten years of its establishment' (Interview 55). A preponderance of victim/survivors and other interviewees on both sides of the border noted that investigatory mechanisms amounted to 'a very structured legalistic situation' (Interview 26) which was 'deeply distressing' (Interview 26), 'intimidating' (Interview 15), and 'very damaging to people' (Interview 1), often resulting in 'secondary trauma or retraumatisation' (Interview 14). Several interviewees attributed this to the fact that adversarial processes have the undesirable effect of 'put[ting] someone on proof' (Interview 25). In the words of an academic-advocate and a professional victim/survivor advocate respectively, cross-examination can erode the identity, dignity, and experiences of victim/survivors by 'destroy[ing] the person's evidence in their own head' (Interview 3) and 'where victims felt they were essentially being branded as liars by proxy' (Interview 35). As a result, victim/survivors in NI expressed regret in choosing to participate in the Hart Inquiry which was deemed to deliver on the fact-finding element but 'at a cost to an awful lot of victims and survivors' (Interview 9).

> The HIA is over for me. Am I sorry I went to it? Yeah. I'm sorry I went to it because it just put me in a bad place . . . it just broke me . . . [W]as the purpose to break people? I have no doubt it wasn't, but that's because of the framework and the shape of it. (Interview 15)

Thus, the legal culture and framework within which inquiries operate eschew the deeply human and emotional dimensions of truth-telling;

[45] See n 40.

elements which are integral to reframing discourses on responsibility and accountability, as discussed in the last part of the book.

Some members of religious orders or Church officials who were tasked with representing their institution during the public hearings also found the adversarial nature of investigatory processes relating to the Ryan and Murphy Commissions 'antagonistic' (Interview 32): 'I found myself there for five days answering questions . . . [O]ne of the questioners was a woman . . . [She] was really very aggressive . . . [A]ll I was trying to do was supply the information they were asking for' (Interview 19). Others had different experiences. For example, in relation to being questioned by the Murphy Commission and reflections on the Final Report of the Mother and Baby Homes Commission respectively, two female members of religious orders commented, 'I felt that they listened. They had read the material we had provided, they weren't in any way . . . trying to argue or anything like that' (Interview 58) and 'I read it, the section relating to the [religious order] and I did feel it was a very fair summary of it' (Interview 57). For victim/survivors, however, the crux of the adversarial framing of investigatory processes is that it undermines the calling to account of those representing the Catholic Church: 'because the process is so adversarial, that they're all about just denying, and plastering over . . . I feel like they don't really take responsibility' (Interview 15). In this vein, the upshot of a highly legalistic inquiry culture with an emphasis on proving and contesting culpability, as one senior politician put it, is that 'everybody gets into trenches' (Interview 68).

Victim/survivors or advocates on both sides of the border elaborated on particular features of inquiry infrastructure stemming from the 'quasi-legal environment' (Interview 4) and the court-like setting which contributed to their distress. This included cross-examination from multiple legal teams representing the religious orders, the presence of religious from the institutions in the public gallery, as well as the physical aspects of the courtroom: 'At a former courthouse, cross-examination, lawyers, public gallery, witness box. So, a whole apparatus and obviously the front bench . . . It's hard to distance yourself that you were basically in a court giving evidence' (Interview 15) and 'there were banks of desks with legal teams . . . there were nuns over there in the corner . . . there were all these strangers that you didn't know and they were going to be questioning you deeply about your intimate details of your life' (Interview 6). Furthermore, several survivors in NI relayed how particular tactics were deployed by lawyers representing institutions 'to get into people's heads' just before they were due to give their evidence to the Hart Inquiry:

> You're in the waiting room . . . and just on your way out the door somebody from the inquiry team then stops you . . . [T]hese are things that are shattering, life shattering to people . . . [T]hey're being told that there's the document, your mother actually put you in there. . . . Somebody who got themselves to this point, a lot of people just give up and they suddenly just have the rug ripped out from under them . . . [T]here was something going on there that they knew this would throw people off . . . so that more or less they could get into people's heads. (Interview 9)

The explanation for this may be logistical, as suggested by some lawyers, in that 'inquiries are handling a vast amount of material' (Interview 40) within tight time constraints. However, as outlined earlier, the legalistic approach to official investigations also stems from the adversarial imperative to defend and protect the good name of individuals or institutions.

Nonetheless, the case for more 'victim-sensitive' (Wright 2002) or 'victim-centric' (Hamber and Lundy 2020) reforms to investigatory processes in these contexts cannot be overstated. Developing less aggressive, and what one member of a religious organisation deemed more 'caring' and 'human' processes (Interview 32), might also lead to increased engagement from religious orders. There was also broad recognition on the part of State officials in RoI, for example, that 'the State needs to do far more in that space . . . [B]eing proactive about answering and supporting and giving information' (Interview 55). As discussed further in the final part of the book, for victim/survivors this also includes 'really listening' (Interview 15) to them in terms of their needs and experiences comprising co-design of investigatory processes and developing a range of specialist and practical support services.

7. Barriers to Truth, Justice, and Accountability

In addition, there are a number of further structural limitations to inquiries which may act as barriers to truth, justice, and accountability which may silence victim/survivors, impede stakeholder engagement, and reduce their capacity for system change.

Conflicting aims and managing expectations

Consistent with the literature which established that inquiries have 'potentially competing functions' (McAlinden and Naylor 2016, 292; see also Harlow 2013), academics, senior politicians, and legal practitioners pinpointed the tension between accountability on the one hand and aims of truth, justice, or healing for survivors on the other: 'It may be that accessing the truth and getting that full accountability are pulling in kind of opposite directions . . . and we need to think well, which one is the bigger priority (Interview 12); 'Is this fact finding or you know accountability, justice based, or is it . . . survivor led, allowing individual truths to come out . . . I'm just not sure you can do the two' (Interview 61). A judge in RoI elaborated:

> There are perhaps, sometimes, different aims that just can't sit well together . . . [Y]ou have to make some element of choice . . . a truth commission type approach, where there are no consequences . . . no adverse findings but there is often a healing process. . . . But what you give up by that, is the sort of the other sense of justice that people sometimes want, which is some kind of official recognition that bad things happened . . . [I]t's perhaps not black and white either—there's probably a spectrum from the very hard edged tribunal model at one end to a pure truth commission at the other. But I think, wherever you fit on that, you'll lose something of the alternative . . . You can't have it both ways. (Interview 40)

This argument also speaks to the need to carefully design inquiries and really consider their terms of reference, as discussed later, by thinking clearly about 'what is it going to do?' (Interview 40). In this sense, as this same individual put it, inquiries 'nee[d] to be reverse engineered' (Interview 40).

In the view of victim/survivors, however, as one State official framed it, 'we have this truth, the public tribunal . . . is the justice, not even that it will deliver the justice . . . but that it is, in itself, the process is the justice' (Interview 55). The potentially conflicting aims of investigatory processes, therefore, underline the need to manage the expectations of victim/survivors in terms of what such processes might reasonably deliver. As one lawyer in NI explained, 'people are different. Every single individual is different and what they're looking for from an inquiry varies' (Interview 43). In this vein, managing the expectations of survivors also means engaging with them on the range of options or models available. One academic attested that, 'There needs to be something around expanding the knowledge of people around what is possible . . . So go back . . . to what survivors think justice is . . . because quite often, people don't have that information to make an informed view' (Interview 50). As a professional victim/survivor advocate commented in relation to the Scoping Inquiry into Historical Sexual Abuse in Schools Run by Religious Orders in RoI, announced in March 2023, 'there's a questionnaire going out . . . to people who've expressed an interest to see what do people want, but I think that's going to be very difficult because people don't know what's available' (Interview 26).

Silencing of victims and impeding engagement

Contrary to the literature which attests to the capacity of inquiries to open up other avenues of justice (eg Sedley 1989), official investigations may limit victim/survivor recourse to civil or criminal justice via immunity afforded to individual perpetrators or institutions.[46] Moreover, O'Rourke (2021a) suggests that by constructing or 'manipulating' victim/survivors as a 'vulnerable' group, the state denies them access to ordinary justice measures in preference to 'specialised' investigatory measures without reference to human rights frameworks. Indeed, while previous theoretical research has noted that state legal responses to historical institutional abuse can be used to control the narrative (see eg Enright and Ring 2020), in practice official investigations can be used to both silence victims and close off public conversations about the past. In the words of victim/survivors, reflecting on their experiences within the context of the Irish Defence Forces, the Ryan Commission, and the Mother and Baby Homes Commission respectively, such investigations can be used 'to try to mitigate a problem before it [becomes] a bigger problem . . . [T]o be seen to do enough, but not have to do everything' (Interview 59), 'they wanted to get rid of us. They didn't want to know . . . and they were trying to minimise it' (Interview 31); and 'there was no mechanism other than to get it done, shut us up, get on with our lives' (Interview 22). Similarly, as one academic-advocate put it, in relation to their impact on broader public discourse, inquiries tend to 'just quieten

[46] See eg Commission to Inquire into Child Abuse Act 2000, s 21 and the Commissions of Investigation Act 2004, s 19 which provide for the inadmissibility of evidence given to commissions in certain proceedings.

down the issue' (Interview 4). A journalist explained in relation to the IDC Report into Magdalene Laundries:

> Once they start, nothing happens, so the whole thing drops off the public agenda until it publishes, which I think for public understanding of an issue is potentially damaging because I certainly felt when McAleese happened I was naïve to the fact that you should be reporting even more now . . . [O]nce this was published I found it was very difficult to get anything else back on the agenda again, because it's done. (Interview 1)

In the same vein, one former State official reflecting on the State investigation into mother and baby homes in RoI noted that 'there's far too much capacity to just, "let's leave this alone, let's not talk about it." We badly need to talk about it and we're not doing it still' (Interview 30). This theme is reflective of the broader societal and educative function of inquiries noted earlier. Gallen (2023a, 137) notes that inquiries should be understood as raising expectations that the testimony of survivors will not only be validated but used as the impetus for other justice measures. In this sense, as discussed later, official investigations should represent the beginning rather than the end of public and official discourses on dealing with the legacy of non-recent institutional abuses.

Moreover, overtly legalistic frameworks often inhibit the fuller probing of truth within official investigations and foster an 'excessively cautious' and defensive approach to engagement or reporting due to the fear of potential legal challenge. One academic in RoI attested:

> Sometimes the legal culture can be excessively cautious . . . [T]his idea of paralysis setting in . . . and not being willing to do things in case somebody might legally challenge it . . . [T]he Mother and Babies Homes one was a good illustration of that . . . [A[lot of the thinking of the Commission seemed to be 'we're not going to include certain testimony or we're not going to make certain findings in case there is an action taken challenging that part of the Report'. . . . Rather than taking a more principled stance of saying this is what we think the evidence is telling us . . . and if somebody wants to challenge that . . . have at it. (Interview 12)

As discussed further in Chapters 6 and 7, this restrained approach, and especially the fear of not only legal but particularly financial liability, has also characterised official state and church apologies for non-recent institutional abuses and redress schemes where responsibility has been couched in narrow, parsimonious, and non-legal terms.

Epistemological power and injustice

The broader literature on inquiries establishes their underlying power and political dimensions and their capacity to further 'the reproduction of hegemonic . . . discourses' (Rolston and Scraton 2005, 547). As Kenny and ó Dochartaigh (2021, 384) argue, inquiries can work to 'absolve powerful interest groups of responsibility . . . through the allocation of blame in a manner that deflects attention away from a challenge to the dominant institutions'. In line with this theme, a preponderance of interviewees, including a lawyer and a senior politician, affirmed that the state wants to 'contro[l] the historical narrative' (Interview 38) and where 'there [i]s a push to minimise' (Interview 61) and thus limit a deeper understanding of the nature and extent of its responsibility for non-recent institutional abuses. This motivation was attributed to the need to protect 'the vision of Ireland, of itself' (Interview 38) as an 'imagined community' (Anderson 1983) and was evidenced by three structural deficiencies: (1) investigatory frameworks which are de facto linked to the state and are therefore non-independent; (2) the lack of meaningful co-design with victim/survivors; and (3) survivor testimony being treated as 'stories' rather than evidence.

As regards the first factor, many interviewees pinpointed how the lack of independence from the state hampered the extent to which official modes of investigation could deliver fair or just outcomes for victim/survivors. Interviewees attributed this to the appointment of panel members or the choice of expert witnesses who are 'seen as a safe pair of hands' (Interviews 5 and 34) or as being part of 'the status quo' (Interview 3) and who thus act in the best interests of the state. One academic-advocate outlined how what they termed 'the professionalisation of inquiries' operates in practice:

> They are part of . . . a political ideological connection, political in the sense that they have dealt with state before . . . ideological in the sense that they are defenders of the status quo. And in that situation you have then a recipe for a slant that is so severely towards the best interest of the institutions . . . at every level, how it's set up, who set it up, the choice to set it up, the actual terms of setting it up . . . which are done in accordance with the, usually, government departments that set them up,

> the choice of the Chair, the Chair's choice of experts . . . [Y]ou have got a structure that is already state inclined . . . if not prejudicial. (Interview 3)

The significance of the lack of independent investigation is that it impedes accountability and, in particular, the taking of ideological responsibility and the capacity of investigations to challenge or transform institutional thinking and practices.

In relation to the second factor, victim/survivors on both sides of the border attested to their experiences of the Ryan Commission and Hart Inquiry: 'It was top/down. There was never, at any stage, any control given to survivors (Interview 22) and 'the fact that the opportunity of survivors' participation and co-design was ignored . . . while they had many meetings . . . with the various groups and particularly group leaders, they lost an opportunity' (Interview 15). Therefore, while victim input and advocacy are pivotal to the initial impetus to establish inquiries, this appears to diminish significantly in terms of the influence on their actual design and operation.

Concerning the third factor, several interviewees in RoI pinpointed the marked distinction in how the testimony of victim/survivors and those of the religious orders were treated within the context of investigations and subsequent redress schemes—as 'stories' and as 'evidence' respectively. A lawyer in RoI explained:

> They usually thought well, if it comes from the person that's just their claim and then they need evidence to back that up . . . [E]vidence comes from institutions and stories come from victims. You're a victim and you're talking, that's a story, but if you're a nun talking, that's evidence. (Interview 5)

This privileging of the testimony of religious orders also tended to not only undermine the credibility of victim/survivors but also their identity and dignity. One victim/survivor in the context of the Mother and Baby Homes Commission attested that 'the nuns testimony seemed to be given a carte blanche, [an] absolutely truthful stamp. Ours was, it's contaminated . . . to be dismissed . . . [W]e were once again relegated to the unworthy . . . [W]e were othered once again and almost made invisible' (Interview 20). In response to this problem, lawyers advised their victim/survivor clients accordingly: 'we had tipped them off that this was a problem, they had actually sworn affidavits and put them in' (Interview 5).

In this respect, the architecture of inquiries, with a two-tier system of engaging with victim/survivors (ie confidential committee/acknowledgement forum versus statutory inquiry) while on one hand may serve to impede accountability if taken as separate entities—one producing 'stories/accounts' and the other producing 'evidence'—if taken together they could in fact enhance accountability and church and state responsibility for non-recent institutional abuses in the form of an independent panel feeding into a statutory inquiry (see Chapter 9). As one lawyer explained in relation to the structure of the Mother and Baby Homes Commission:

> Every effort had been made to divert the evidence of survivors and victims into the confidential committee so that it wouldn't be treated as evidence. I mean, the Confidential Committee Report is an extraordinary document when you read it . . . because if it was in the real report you couldn't have the conclusions. You just couldn't. (Interview 5)

As discussed in the last part of the book, one of the values of independent panels is that the collective evidence/testimonies given by victim/survivors feeds into the statutory public inquiry as part of an 'accumulated truth' (Interview 3). This notion of common truth potentially extends and unifies the modes of truth outlined at the outset of the chapter by validating the personal narratives of victim/survivors thereby providing a restorative truth for them and simultaneously increasing social truth and our collective understanding about non-recent institutional abuses.

The confluence of these three deficits results in 'epistemic injustice' (Fricker 2007) and often further trauma for victim/survivors. As noted previously, there was widespread concern among survivors in the context of the Final Report of the Mother and Baby Homes Commission that their testimonies were 'whitewashed' (Interview 20). An academic-advocate and criminal justice professional reflected on their experiences in working with victim/survivors in this regard both generally and in relation to the Mother and Baby Homes Commission respectively: 'We didn't feel believed . . . We didn't see our stories in the way we told them and at the time we were diminished' (Interview 3) and there was 'the absolute disconnect between the testimonies given to that Commission and the conclusions they came to' (Interview 30). This is perhaps most powerfully reflected in the words of victim/survivors referring to the Final Report of the Mother and Baby Homes Commission: 'talk about re-traumatisation, reading that report retraumatised me for months. I just couldn't believe it. It was like, were we not there?' (Interview 20); and 'when they came out with the report . . . I just started reading it and it was just like a stab in the heart . . . so now it feels like it would have been better if they'd done nothing' (Interview 8).

Terms of reference: addressing non-recent abuses and capacity for change

Many interviewees, including both senior politicians and victim/survivors, pinpointed the terms of reference as being fundamental to shaping the process and outcomes of investigatory mechanisms. One of the Women of Honour in RoI elaborated on the need for openness and transparency in this regard, '[if] there is the perception that it's not trustworthy . . . you won't get the engagement . . . [I]t has to be designed to look at everything and to want the culture to come out' (Interview 59). In reality, however, as one State appointee in RoI admitted, 'the tendency is to . . . let's compartmentalise it and let's try and deal with it in instalments' (Interview 17).

For these and other victim/survivors, there is the perception that 'they're deliberately writing the terms of reference to navigate around the problems rather than unearth the problems' (Interview 59) and where 'exclusions are built in' (Interview 22). Indeed, some victim/survivors reflected on the terms of reference of the Ryan Commission and the Hart Inquiry respectively, which they described as 'just one tiny sliver of the situation' (Interview 8) and as being 'so tight and restrictive' (Interview 9). Without the right terms of reference, therefore, which may be limited regarding issues or focus, investigations may otherwise 'amount to processes of containment and control' (Interview 3) and thus work to limit justice for victim/survivors. More particularly, the exclusion of some victim/survivors from investigatory processes may subsequently limit access to redress schemes (see Chapter 6).

Although the obvious solution might appear to be involving victim/survivors in drafting the terms of reference and the setting up of the inquiry from the outset, care must also be taken to avoid placing the responsibility for just outcomes on the shoulders of survivors. As one survivor cautioned, in relation to their experience of the Murphy Commission, 'you have to be involved in that process, you have to turn up with a draft, this is what you're expecting to see and you have to have that battle' (Interview 13). Many interviewees, including state actors, articulated the central importance of the terms of reference and the need to keep inquiries manageable and reasonably expedient. As one State official and a lawyer put it, there is a 'need to draft terms of reference that are examinable' (Interview 55) or 'tight and focused' (Interview 43). Otherwise, in the words of one senior politician, 'If you don't get the terms of reference right, it's so wide that people go down cul de sacs, it goes on forever and then the victim is doubly traumatised' (Interview 68). This potential tension between a pragmatic and a holistic examination of the issues underscores the need for a realistic appraisal of the potential limitations of official investigations.

Furthermore, as noted earlier in relation to some of the commissions of investigation in RoI and the Hart Inquiry in NI, the terms of reference may also limit their capacity to make recommendations or, even where recommendations do exist, to implement them in a timely manner and to effect tangible and lasting change. One academic-advocate explained that 'this is not just a problem of political will . . . It's the fact that inquiries are not structured to be able to deliver real change . . . [T]he vast majority of recommendations have not been actioned' (Interview 3). This can also deeply impact victim/survivors. As one victim/survivor reflected in the context of the Mother and Baby Homes Commission, 'What's the point in unburdening to have nowhere to go' (Interview 36).

Finally, a minority of interviewees questioned whether inquiries or commissions are the most appropriate mechanism for addressing institutional abuses as a policy wrong (see Chapter 1). One lawyer reflected in relation to the Ryan Commission:

> [It] failed to create the opportunity to set out what were the norms of care . . . [P]art of the difficulty from the Commission's perspective was that the Act defined abuse in a way that essentially categorised as 'abuse', behaviours which in hindsight we realise to have been harmful. . . . But we needed to start from a much more honest ownership of the system that was considered normative and was how Ireland was caring for its children at the time. (Interview 18)

Thus, when compiled with the difficulties inherent in legalistic and adversarial frameworks (see also Chapter 7) there is a need to think more creatively about devising more innovative justice responses to non-recent institutional abuses. As one senior politician in RoI stated, reflecting on the Irish experience of investigatory frameworks enshrined in law, 'we should never again use a Commission of Investigation for something like this . . . the problem is . . . it's in the law' (Interview 51).

8. Conclusion: Towards Transformative Inquiries

The chapter has demonstrated that the legalistic culture of official investigations frustrates truth, justice, and accountability. *Personal or narrative truth* of survivors is in part facilitated by the process of giving testimony but acknowledgement is also undermined by adversarial justice which puts survivors 'on proof'. The omission of victim/survivor testimonies or their misrepresentation as 'stories' rather than 'evidence' within official narratives displaces procedural and epistemic justice by silencing their voices and experiences. While on one level *social truth* is furthered by public hearings and/or the public availability of transcripts or evidence, in many other cases this is severely inhibited by the withholding of personal records from survivors. Legalistic frameworks also eschew the deeply human and emotional dimensions of truth-telling for survivors and the relational dimensions of seeking accountability for non-recent institutional abuses. These tensions underline the need to re-evaluate investigatory mechanisms and recalibrate how legal frameworks around truth-telling are balanced with catharsis and *healing truth* for survivors.

Similarly, official investigations are ill-equipped to deliver a fuller version of accountability via the taking of responsibility for abuses that survivors may want. While states may accept moral responsibility for non-recent institutional abuses within investigatory reports by the broad acknowledgement of wrongdoing, the legal narrative around responsibility is usually much more limited and controlled. That is, investigation outcomes may acknowledge breaches of criminal codes and provide a pathway for legal reforms, yet states are usually careful to distance themselves from legal responsibility for abuses and thus deliberately do not construct their failings in terms of human rights violations. Thus, central to the way forward is to move away from a sole focus on legalistic conceptions of responsibility and the trappings of adversarial justice in order to diminish the need for defensive tactics and increase the engagement and accountability of institutional actors.

Indeed, a granular analysis of responsibility for non-recent institutional abuses is usually not possible within the remit of most official investigations. Restricted by their terms of reference, they usually have limited capacity to deliver specific findings holding individual perpetrators or institutions to account but are focused rather on the systemic level of wrongdoing. As one senior politician in RoI commented in relation to the Mother and Baby Homes Commission:

> I do think they [the Commissioners] acted in good faith . . . I do think they adopted a judicial approach. This is what people have alleged . . . because there's kind of three types of allegations. There's what's alleged and is true but can't be proven; alleged and can be proven; and what is alleged and isn't true. And I think they did their best to say what could be proven and I definitely think they were right to not blame the State and the Church for everything. (Interview 64)

In this respect, it is important to acknowledge the limitations of official investigations in making determinations of truth and individualised allocations of responsibility for abuses committed in the past and to manage expectations in this regard.

Investigations have also been characterised by a reactive and piecemeal approach, effectively impeding fuller understanding of the broader patterns of historical and structural issues which are pivotal to institutional reflection and reform. In this sense, the notion of ideological responsibility explicitly recognises the need for reformed institutional thinking and practices and learning the lessons from the past.[47] These twin retrospective–prospective dimensions of accountability—how institutional actors may take responsibility for the past through a reformed present and future—are fundamental to just outcomes for victim/survivors as well as to non-recurrence and the capacity of institutions to effect systemic change. More broadly, however, as currently formulated, investigatory mechanisms set the course for reparations where the shortcomings of legalistic frameworks are replicated and augmented.

[47] The Ryan Commission (CICA 2009, Vol 4, ch 7, para 7.03) made a similar recommendation though, as noted, there has been a lack of systematic implementation and review.

6
Reparations

1. Introduction

Reparations form part of the response of state and church institutions on the island of Ireland to allegations of non-recent institutional abuses. In existing literature and the empirical research conducted for this book, several distinct challenges arise regarding reparations for non-recent institutional abuses. First, can reparations schemes operate with clear and equitable eligibility criteria? Second, can the process of delivering reparations avoid distressing or re-traumatising victim/survivors and, more ambitiously, can it be of therapeutic or healing benefit? Third, what is the intended meaning or purpose behind the provision of reparation? Fourth, who is obliged to provide reparations and on what basis? Finally, what does the provision of reparation communicate regarding responsibility and accountability?

Section 2 addresses the conceptual frameworks around reparation in existing literature and international law. Section 3 provides a brief overview of existing monetary redress schemes internationally. Section 4 provides an account of reparations in the Republic of Ireland (RoI) while Section 5 examines reparations in Northern Ireland (NI). Section 6 considers the value and limits of reparations informed by the views of interview participants. Section 7 concludes by assessing the potential innovative and enhanced contribution of reparation to a fuller understanding of responsibility and accountability.

2. Reparations: Form and Function

In existing literature, 'redress', 'reparation', and 'reparations' are often used interchangeably (see eg Wolfe 2014). Moffett (2023a, 1) suggests reparations operate across 'justice, morality/recognition and reconciliation/

Transforming Justice Responses to Non-Recent Institutional Abuses. Anne-Marie McAlinden, Marie Keenan, and James Gallen, Oxford University Press. © Oxford University Press 2025.
DOI: 10.1093/9780191967399.003.0006

relational justifications'. In law, reparation was originally conceived as an obligation that states owed each other for war-related damages (Torpey 2003, 4). Subsequently, the use of reparations as remedies for human rights violations has proliferated, with a significant practice of reparations in the last 40 years.[1]

Reparations can be divided into material reparations and symbolic reparations. Material reparations can include monetary reparations or non-monetary services, such as healthcare, counselling, or housing. Monetary reparations, in turn, can be provided in a lump sum or as a pension to be distributed to victims or relatives throughout their lives or for a set period (Roht-Arriaza 2004, 159). In contrast, symbolic reparations 'refer to any form of reparation designed to explicitly recognise and acknowledge the harms done to victim-survivors and their status as rights-bearers. Symbolic reparations may include apologies, memorials, museums, or the renaming or removal of landmarks' (Gallen and Moffett 2022, 500). Symbolic reparations are linked to the expressive function of reparations (Walker 2013, 211) to communicate a message to victim/survivors and responsible actors that signals a taking of responsibility, which recognises that prior events were wrong and that responsible actors should be held accountable towards victims (Walker 2013, 208, 212). However, a symbolic and communicative goal is not always realised. Daly (2014b, 195) notes, in considering monetary reparations in Australia and Canada, that '[m]ost survivors did not see the payment as symbolic, as recognition for injury and solace for pain. Instead, they equated the amount received in an individualized scheme to the level of abuse and injury they had experienced and to their "worth".'

In international law, including in the Basic Principles and Guidelines on the Right to a Remedy and Reparation for Victims of Gross Violations of International Human Rights Law and Serious Violations of International Humanitarian Law[2] (UN Principles), victim/survivors are entitled to: (1) equal and effective access to justice; (2) adequate, effective, and prompt reparation for harm suffered; and (3) access to relevant information

[1] See the Reparations Database of the Reparations, Responsibility and Victimhood in Transitional Societies project, https://reparations.qub.ac.uk/reparations-database/ (accessed 8 January 2024).

[2] UN Commission on Human Rights, Resolution 2005/35 on Basic Principles and Guidelines on the Right to a Remedy and Reparation for Victims of Gross Violations of International Human Rights Law and Serious Violations of International Humanitarian Law, E/CN.4/RES/2005/35, 19 April 2005.

concerning violations and reparation mechanisms. In the UN Principles, reparations include restitution, compensation, rehabilitation, satisfaction, and guarantees of non-recurrence.

Restitution is understood as a return of the victim to the *status quo ante* by restoring rights, property, and benefits (de Greiff 2006, 453). In the case of gross violations of human rights, full restitution may be inappropriate or impossible, outside the return of property or restoration of employment rights. In contrast, compensation is intended to provide an *equivalent* good or benefit to make up for the loss (Thompson 2002, xii). In instances of physical and mental harm, it is unclear whether any monetary compensation could ever effectively equate to the damage suffered (United Nations 2008, 10). Without an alternative meaning effectively communicated to survivors, reparations as compensation alone may leave survivors feeling that 'their worth has not been understood or acknowledged by the party responsible for the abuse' (Sunga 2002, 41). In comparative experience, reparations understood as compensation alone may function as a means to silence victims, reflecting 'hush money' or 'blood money' (de Greiff 2006, 461).

Reparations literature also emphasises the goals of rehabilitation and satisfaction. While rehabilitation is often associated with changing the behaviour of offenders, rehabilitation in the reparations context refers to medical, social, and psychological assistance and suggests that 'victims are wounded, deserve rehabilitation and are capable of being healed' (Fletcher and Weinstein 2017, 245). To do so will depend on the *process* of reparations (Hamber 2000, 580). Reparations as satisfaction involve public recognition of victims' sufferings and symbolic gestures addressing victim/survivors' dignity and status as rights holders, including through apologies, memorialisation, or measures intended to locate and identify disappeared victim/survivors (UN Principles, Principles 19–23; De Greiff 2009, 57). Such a goal seeks to rebuild the civic relationship between citizens and state by publicly acknowledging victim/survivor suffering and vindicating their status as rights holders. More broadly, Thompson suggests that the primary goal of reparations is the repairing of the relationship between the victim/survivor and the responsible actor (Thompson 2002, 51), which could include non-state actors, including religious actors in the present context.

Finally, guarantees of non-recurrence comprise wider measures aimed at reforming the laws, institutions, and cultures of practice that gave rise to such violations, such as vetting of public sector personnel or care institutions governed by human rights law and promoting codes of conduct and ethics in healthcare and social services (de Greiff 2006, 453). Both the relational focus and a future-orientated emphasis reflect more nuanced and progressive accounts of responsibility and accountability for non-recent institutional abuses. Across these different dimensions of reparation, De Greiff (2006) distinguishes between reparations provided after litigation and reparations provided through administrative, non-judicial processes, which result in typically lower evidential thresholds and less legalistic procedures. As litigation is addressed in Chapter 4, this chapter focuses on non-judicial reparations, as several non-judicial schemes have operated on the island of Ireland, in addition to the settlement of litigation disputes.

3. The International Dimension

The provision of reparations on the island of Ireland for non-recent harms aligns with a broad trend in jurisdictions addressing non-recent abuses, such as Australia and Canada (Daly 2014b; Winter 2022). Across such jurisdictions, reparations are usually provided in national law or policy on an *ex gratia* and administrative basis and are not framed as human rights instruments. Gallen (2023a, Appendix 2) provided an overview of 40 reparations schemes addressing non-recent institutional abuses in comparable jurisdictions. Reparations also extend beyond the context of non-recent abuses. Moffett (2023b), for example, evaluated the significant practice of reparations in the aftermath of armed conflict that stretch back millennia and across most cultures.

In Canada and the United States, several schemes concerning non-recent abuses represent the outcomes of the settlement of litigation, ranging from individual and private settlements with exclusively financial outcomes, to broad, complex, and public settlements, facilitated by class action mechanisms, such as the Indian Residential Schools Settlement Agreement in Canada (Llewellyn 2002). Beyond this scheme, Daly (2014b, 146) notes that several Canadian redress schemes follow negotiations between victim/survivors, their legal representatives, and responsible actors, while others were the result of negotiations between legal representatives alone. In England and Wales, a single national redress scheme was announced in May 2023 following recommendations of the Independent Inquiry into Child Sexual Abuse (IICSA 2022b, Part II, paras I.5–I.7). At the time of writing, victim/survivors are still waiting for redress.[3]

In Australia, redress schemes have been mandated by state or national governments with varying levels of survivor advocacy and engagement and provided for in legislation or government policy (Daly and Davis 2021). The National Redress Scheme was initiated by the government in 2018, resulting from the recommendations of the Royal Commission into Institutional Responses to Child Sexual Abuse (Royal Commission 2017c) and focuses on providing redress for sexual abuse only but in the context of both residential and non-residential institutional settings. The government scheme was joined by a range of non-state actors, including several religious organisations. The scheme marks an important conceptual and policy milestone for redress in the context of non-recent abuses as it provides an account of when institutions are primarily or equally responsible for abuse, based on whether the institution had sole, primary, or equal responsibility 'for the abuser having contact with the person'.[4] The scheme also provides for the possibility of eligible victim/survivors requesting a 'direct personal response' from responsible institutions, including:

(1) an apology or a statement of acknowledgement or regret;
(2) an acknowledgement of the impact of the abuse on the person;
(3) an assurance as to the steps the institution has taken, or will take, to prevent abuse occurring again;
(4) an opportunity for the person to meet with a senior official of the institution.[5]

Such an approach provides welcome recognition of the need for redress to function as a form of responsibility-taking by relevant actors rather than as *ex gratia* payments alone, and for redress to contribute to interpersonal and relational repair between victim/survivors and allegedly responsible institutions. However, while still ongoing until 2027, early assessments of survivor experiences are poor, with only a minority of survivors surveyed rating the scheme as good (16%) or very good (11%) and with significant frustrations arising due to the slow pace of establishing and operating the

[3] K Harrison, 'Child sexual abuse inquiry: survivors have waited long enough', *Law Society Gazette*, 20 December 2023.
[4] National Redress Scheme for Institutional Child Sexual Abuse Act 2018, s 15.
[5] ibid, s 54.

scheme and for non-state institutions to opt into the scheme (Cortis and Katz 2022). In 2021, the Australian government approved national redress for the Stolen Generations, which involved forced family separation of Aboriginal and Torres Strait Islander children. This national scheme will supplement existing redress schemes from two Australian states (New South Wales and Victoria). In Australia, reparations are also provided directly by non-state religious actors. In 1996, the Australian Catholic Bishops Conference established 'Towards Healing' to address allegations of sexual, physical, and emotional abuse in the Catholic Church. However, Gleeson (2015, 327, citing Courtin 2013) is critical of the scheme, suggesting it fails to uphold restorative justice principles and 'operates essentially from an "outcome driven approach" whereby participants report feeling "pressure to settle" so that the matter may be closed'.

Beyond the Anglophone world, reparations have been employed to address allegations of non-recent abuses, especially in religious institutions in Austria, Belgium, Germany, the Netherlands, and Switzerland (Aertsen 2021; Patrizi 2021). In the Netherlands, a restorative justice mediation approach was deemed more suitable by survivors than an original judicial-style compensation procedure (Terry 2015, 149). In the context of state-operated schemes in Sweden, Sköld et al (2023, 336) note that such schemes may shift from a focus on acknowledgement of victim/survivor suffering and narrow the state response of compensation only for abuse for which the state is deemed responsible. Across comparative experience, a range of forms of reparation, largely monetary compensation and counselling services, have been employed and resulted in varied victim/survivor experiences. While some aspects of international literature and experience are drawn upon later, comparative experience does not point to any panacea or clear best practice paradigm for reparations in a single jurisdiction.

4. Reparations in the Republic of Ireland

On the island of Ireland, monetary reparations schemes have all been designed and administered by government, with some contributions and some private settlements from religious organisations. There have been some non-monetary reparations, such as counselling, provided directly by both state and religious organisations. Assessing these reparations schemes is challenging in a context of limited publicly available reports on their processes and outcomes for survivors (Daly 2014b, 112) and limited public profile and engagement of victim/survivors. Section 28 of the Residential Institutions Redress Act 2002 in RoI provided a perceived 'gagging order', preventing victim/survivors from speaking publicly about their experiences of it and making research on its operations highly challenging. One journalist noted:

> Nobody really writes about [reparations] because it's very administrative and bureaucratic and boring for journalists in the sense of it's not exciting like an apology is. But in fact, what the State does is say we're really, really sorry and then the dirty bureaucratic work goes into in fact, causing a lot more harm to people by making it very difficult for people to access the justice that we're talking about. (Interview 1)

This quotation speaks to the need for holistic justice approaches to non-recent institutional abuses. The following section provides a brief overview of reparations schemes in RoI, examining both monetary and non-monetary forms of reparation.

Monetary redress

Religious organisations' settlements

No aggregated data is available on the settlement of claims against religious orders and dioceses regarding non-recent abuses on the island of Ireland wherein the diocesan Catholic Church, its religious organisations, and the Church of Ireland operate in both jurisdictions on the island (RoI and NI). This lack of data compares unfavourably to analysis of redress in Australia, which includes aggregated data involving the Catholic Church and its religious organisations (Daly and Davis 2021) or in relation to the Independent Inquiry into Child Sexual Abuse (IICSA) in England and Wales where aggregated information is provided for both the Church of England and Roman Catholic Church (IICSA 2020a, 95; IICSA 2020b, 64). In the absence of comprehensive disclosure from dioceses and religious organisations regarding settlements concerning all forms of non-recent institutional abuses, it remains impossible to effectively assess and compare the financial cost of addressing abuse by the relevant religious organisations.

Residential Institutions Redress Board (RIRB)

The RIRB scheme was the result of victim/survivor campaigning and political and legal pressure and ran concurrently with the Commission to Inquire into Child Abuse (CICA), discussed in Chapter 5. In October 2000, the Irish government agreed to establish a scheme to compensate victim/survivors formerly resident in institutions 'in respect of which State bodies had regulatory or supervisory functions' who had suffered abuse as defined in the Commission to Inquire into Child Abuse Act 2000,[6] and that such redress would be paid on an *ex gratia* basis without establishing any liability on the part of State bodies but subject to the claimant proving their claim of abuse and injury (Towards Redress and Recovery 2002, 3). In June 2001, an expert Compensation Advisory Committee was established to advise on the criteria for making financial compensation and the amount of those awards. Subsequently, the Irish government clarified its motivations in establishing this scheme. First, there was a perceived urgency to address victim/survivors' needs after decades of failure to accept the nature and scale of the abuse. Second, solicitors for victim/survivors had suggested their clients would not cooperate with the concurrent CICA investigation without a redress scheme being established.[7]

In January 2002, the report of the Compensation Advisory Committee recommended monetary reparation assessed across a weighted scale of four areas: the severity of abuse, the extent of the applicant's physical and mental injury, the psycho-social sequelae of the injury, and the loss of opportunity resulting from the abuse and its effects (Towards Redress and Recovery 2002, vii). The report proposed bands of redress to enable awards up to €300,000. In doing so, the report refers to general principles of damages envisaged in civil litigation.[8] However, despite dedicating a chapter to

[6] Section 1 defines 'abuse', in relation to a child, as (a) the wilful, reckless or negligent infliction of physical injury on, or failure to prevent such injury to, the child, (b) the use of the child by a person for sexual arousal or sexual gratification of that person or another person, (c) failure to care for the child which results in serious impairment of the physical or mental health or development of the child or serious adverse effects on his or her behaviour or welfare, or (d) any other act or omission towards the child which results in serious impairment of the physical or mental health or development of the child or serious adverse effects on his or her behaviour or welfare.

[7] Evidence of Michael Woods (former Minister for Education), 24 June 2004 to the CICA.

[8] In *Sinnott v Quinnsworth Ltd* [1984] WJSC-SC 1719, the Irish Supreme Court concluded that in assessing damages for irreparable personal injuries regard should be had to the ordinary living standards and general level of income in the country, and to the things upon which the plaintiff might reasonably be expected to spend money as compensation beyond their medical costs.

documenting existing understanding of the effects of child sex abuse, the Committee report offered little consideration of the need for a redress process that sought to mitigate the risk of re-traumatisation or distress experienced by survivors in the specific context of non-recent institutional abuses.

Following this report, the Residential Institutions Redress Act 2002 was enacted. In the parliamentary debates regarding the scheme, there were proposals to include day schools, Magdalene Laundries, foster care, and hospitals, in addition to the industrial and reformatory schools that formed the focus of the concurrent CICA inquiry. In introducing the legislation in November 2001, the Minister for Education urged against this extension of the scheme, noting that the scheme was 'not . . . a vehicle for dealing with every injustice and abuse committed on children and young people in the past'.[9] Nonetheless, section 4 of the 2002 Act provided that the Minister for Education may add further institutions to the scheme including institutions 'in which children were placed and resident and in respect of which a public body had a regulatory or inspection function'. This power was exercised in 2004 and 2005.[10] The Schedule to the Act ultimately listed 154 institutions that were eligible sites where an applicant could allege that abuse had occurred. The recognition of the State's regulatory or inspection function across a range of institutions provides the key site of State responsibility, especially in circumstances of knowledge or notice of the abuse.

The original forecasted cost of the RIRB was €250m but its eventual total cost was an estimated €1.25bn (Comptroller and Auditor General 2016, 10). Although 15,579 applicants were successful, the known population who attended industrial and reformatory schools was around 37,000 (O'Sullivan 2014, 202). The Schedule to the 2002 Act provided for a wide range of institutions beyond industrial and reformatory schools, operated by a range of State and church actors. As a result, the total potential population that could have applied to the RIRB remains unclear. The average award was €62,250 and 85% of the awards were at or below €100,000 (Comptroller and Auditor General 2016, 10). Enright and Ring (2020, 75) note that although the RIRB scheme was announced as being intended to provide compensation roughly equivalent to civil litigation, 'the average payment was roughly half that made in successful civil cases against religious orders'. With its

[9] Minister for Education and Science, Residential Institutions Redress Bill, 2001: Second Stage, Dáil Éireann debate, Vol 543 No 3, Wednesday 7 November 2001.

[10] See Residential Institutions Redress Act 2002 (Additional Institutions) Order 2004 and Residential Institutions Redress Act 2002 (Additional Institutions) Order 2005.

ex gratia nature, significant expense, poor survivor experiences, and 21% of expenditure going to individuals other than victim/survivors, principally their lawyers and the Board's own expenses, the RIRB model failed to achieve the potential of reparations as a justice measure, provide official recognition of responsibility for survivor harm, or function as a meaningful relational tool.

Magdalene Restorative Justice Scheme

Following the McAleese Report (IDC 2013), discussed in Chapter 5, Mr Justice Quirke was tasked with advising the Irish government on the establishment of an *ex gratia* and non-adversarial scheme regarding women who were admitted to and worked in a Magdalene Laundry (Quirke 2013). A small advisory group informed the process and aided the voluntary recruitment of 40 psychologists, counsellors, and barristers to help with the work. This 'Magdalene Commission' suggested that to be non-adversarial any reparation scheme could not reflect the principles and methods of assessing damages in litigation, unlike the RIRB scheme. Instead, restorative justice and alternative dispute resolution should inform the design of the scheme, rooted in the 'blameless' status of the women affected by Magdalene Laundries (Quirke 2013, 2). One State official noted that 'from the point of view of the State, it was a much more efficient way of distributing money to people who were going to benefit' (Interview 62). Between March and May 2013, the Commission spoke with 337 women who had expressed an interest in the proposed scheme and with senior representatives of the relevant religious organisations. The proposed *ex gratia* scheme was intended to avoid antagonistic roles, invasive and individualised assessment of victim/survivors, be a speedy procedure, and reflect the wishes of the women consulted (Quirke 2013, para 2.01).

In addition to the provision of a specialised card for access to healthcare services, discussed later, the Commission recommended that all women who were admitted to and worked in the Laundries would receive a state contributory pension for the remainder of their lives (Quirke 2013, 8). While some women would have been entitled to receive this pension anyway, for others the intention was that provision of the pension would acknowledge the work done by women in Magdalene Laundries as work in and for the State (Quirke 2013, 8). The Commission report also recommended monetary payment to women based on the traumatic and damaging effects of admission and incarceration within Magdalene Laundries, with a further payment to acknowledge the 'work undertaken' there (Quirke 2013, 9). One lawyer affirmed the approach taken by Quirke:

> Credit should be given to Judge Quirke. One of the principles was that he should try and meet as many survivors as he could either in person or through telephone conversations between survivors and a wonderful team of young women barristers . . . That wasn't a given at the time. (Interview 21)

While the process of establishing the scheme involved meaningful consultation, the implementation and practice of the scheme frustrated its restorative purposes and inhibited the rebuilding of trust with survivors.

Symphysiotomy

In November 2013, the Irish Minister for Health appointed Judge Yvonne Murphy to evaluate the cost of an *ex gratia* scheme regarding victim/survivors of symphysiotomy (Murphy 2014). Judge Murphy's report noted that 154 symphysiotomy-related High Court proceedings had been initiated and that the preference of victim/survivors was for a public apology and payment of €250,000–450,000. Her report suggested that an *ex gratia* scheme would reduce a high burden of proof from elderly survivors but, in turn, would justify a lesser award than in civil litigation of €50,000–150,000 (Murphy 2014, 51–3).

In November 2014, an *ex gratia* scheme was published, adopting Judge Murphy's recommendations regarding payments and was to be administered 'as a matter of urgency' by Judge Maureen Harding Clark (Murphy 2014, 51). The scheme offered only 40 working days for individuals to apply. A lawyer who represented applicants was critical of the short time frame, 'it obviously meant that you were not necessarily taking as great care with the applications as you would have liked to because you just had to get them in' (Interview 34).

In November 2016, the report on this scheme indicated the intention to pursue a 'compassionate and generous' approach (Harding Clark Report 2016, 9). The scheme awarded €29.8m to 399 successful applicants, with 185 unsuccessful applicants, with Judge Harding Clark concluding that 'hearing the testimony of others led many applicants who did not undergo symphysiotomy to acquire false memories and to fill in the blanks' (14). The format of the report, revisiting historical research and medical evidence and calling into question the bone fides of applicants (97) is impossible to reconcile with the claimed 'compassionate and generous' approach.

O'Keeffe v Ireland: Day Schools Scheme

Following the decision of the European Court of Human Rights (ECtHR) in *O'Keeffe v Ireland*,[11] discussed in Chapter 4, the Irish government established a redress scheme to address abuse suffered by survivors in open or day schools. The scheme required applicants to demonstrate that their abuse had occurred after a prior complaint of abuse that was not responded to, which resulted in several applicants being deemed ineligible (O'Neill 2019, 1). Under a revised scheme, which came about as a result of the decision of an independent review of the scheme discussed later, an individual must have issued legal proceedings against the State by 1 July 2021 seeking damages for childhood sexual abuse in a recognised day school, have issued those proceedings relating to abuse occurring before November 1991 in respect of a primary school, or before June 1992 in respect of a post-primary school, and must demonstrate that had the Guidelines for Procedures for Dealing with Allegations or Suspicions of Child Abuse been in place at the time the sexual abuse occurred there would have been a real prospect of altering the outcome or mitigating the harm suffered by them as a result. The scheme offered monetary reparations up to €84,000 per individual and closed in July 2023.[12] At present, less than one-third of the €31m assigned for the scheme has been paid to survivors and over one-quarter of applications to this revised scheme have been rejected.[13] One academic noted:

> They plucked this date out of the sky of the 1st July 2021 . . . [O]f course, they didn't announce this date until three weeks after it had passed, which meant that nobody could adjust their position by instructing a lawyer up to that point. And the whole point was that all along lawyers were telling people well, don't litigate. (Interview 12)

In 2024, the Report of the Scoping Inquiry into Historical Sexual Abuse in Day and Boarding Schools Run by Religious Orders noted that 'Some 128 survivors of sexual abuse have received redress under the revised *ex*

[11] *O'Keeffe v Ireland* [2014] ECHR 96.

[12] Government of Ireland, 'Revised Ex Gratia Scheme remained open until 20 July 2023', https://www.gov.ie/en/service/90a42-revised-ex-gratia-scheme/ (accessed 10 January 2024).

[13] J Casey, 'Less than a third of fund for school sex abuse victims paid out', *The Irish Examiner*, 2 July 2023.

gratia scheme, with the total sum of awards made to date amounting to €10.752 million (Scoping Inquiry 2024, Vol 4, 599). However, despite the substantive overlap between the *O'Keeffe* scheme and the subject matter of the Scoping Inquiry on sexual abuse in day schools, the report failed to recommend redress along the lines of the former scheme, instead recommending merely that government consider a redress scheme for survivors and 'that the Government approach the relevant religious orders about contributing to a redress scheme' (Vol 1, 11–12). The limited recommendation is likely influenced by the scale of relevant and potentially eligible victim/survivors related to sexual abuse in day schools. The Scoping Inquiry Report indicated that based on Central Statistics Office estimates among persons aged 35 years and older, some 15,300 men and 26,000 women are estimated to have experienced sexual violence as a child in a school—a total of approximately 41,000 victim/survivors (Vol 1, 18). Such figures of potentially eligible victims suggest a redress scheme costing billions of euro on the quantum from RIRB or *O'Keeffe* schemes. Nonetheless, the decision of the ECtHR in *O'Keeffe v Ireland* is clear: Ireland is liable for its failure to prevent child sexual abuse in day schools and owes victim/survivors an effective remedy, including redress.

Mother and Baby Institutions Payment Scheme

The Mother and Baby Homes Commission Report proposed redress for women who had spent more than six months in mother and baby institutions before 1974 and for people who were resident as *unaccompanied* children only in a mother and baby institution or county home and who did not qualify for reparation under the RIRB Scheme (CoI MBH 2021, Recommendations, para 19). In addition, the Commission recommended redress for women in county homes, women in Tuam Mother and Baby institution, and women who worked outside the institutions without pay on the basis that these categories engaged in the equivalent of 'commercial work' (CoI MBH 2021, Recommendations, para 31).

The Irish government commissioned both a consultation with survivors on redress and established an Inter-Departmental Group (IDG) to develop a Mother and Baby Institutions Payment Scheme. The OAK consultation (O'Kennedy 2021, 9–14) detailed several survivor priorities: the need for a human rights-based approach to the design of redress; recognition of human rights violations in mother and baby institutions; the need for access to records as part of redress; and the need for staff involved in administering the scheme to have training in restorative justice. Regrettably, the IDG report (DCEDIY 2021, 17) takes survivors' views to mean only the need to act with 'kindness' and to 'do no harm'. The overriding and repeated concern motivating the IDG analysis was the potential cost of any redress scheme (DCEDIY 2021, 5, 7–8, 20, 23, 27, 38, 43). In November 2021, the government approved proposals for redress based on these reports. Under the Mother and Baby Institutions Payment Scheme Act 2023, some 34,000 survivors will be eligible for financial payment at an estimated cost of €800m. However, the Act excludes former child residents who spent less than six months in an institution and fails to provide for the harms suffered as human rights violations; it also excludes harms suffered by those boarded out from homes or the distinct harm of coercive family separation. One survivor notes the significance of forced family separation, 'How could six months be just erased like that and not important. It's just unbelievable' (Interview 65).

An expanded scheme that would provide financial support for all survivors of mother and baby institutions would, on the proposed figures, cost €1.6bn.[14] It remains to be seen whether the scheme will be accepted by survivors and whether a meaningful survivor-led or trauma-informed process will be employed in administering the scheme. It also remains to be seen at the time of writing whether the State will expand the proposed scheme and if any of the relevant religious orders will make a financial contribution to the scheme. In the context of its restrictive eligibility criteria, it is likely that the scheme may be subject to legal and political challenge in the coming years.

Chapter 4 explored the limitations of conventional justice for non-recent harms. Accessing a state redress scheme may be the only option for receiving material and financial recognition of harm for many survivors. Each of these schemes reflects the common trade-off in reparations: an administrative process which purports to be less adversarial or evidentially exacting than litigation and results in lower monetary awards as a result. However, as explored later, the experience of victim/survivors at RIRB, and their exclusion across the other mechanisms considered, means that this claimed benefit is often outweighed by the harmful effects to survivors. Instead, the primary advantage accrues to the state, which can develop predictable and manageable costs of redress (Watts 2020). Where the schemes require survivors to waive their right of access to the courts regarding the

[14] J Bray, 'Redress scheme for all mother and baby home survivors would have cost €1.6bn', *The Irish Times*, 18 November 2021.

same harms, the state avoids the possibility of legal precedents that establish its responsibility for systemic wrongs or mass claims.

Non-monetary redress

In RoI, several non-monetary forms of reparations have been provided for victim/survivors of non-recent institutional abuses. Funded by the Department of Education, the Education Finance Board (2006–13) provided educational grants for former residents of industrial and reformatory schools and their relatives. In addition, on foot of the second contribution by religious organisations to provide redress for industrial and reformatory schools, the Irish State established the Residential Institutions Statutory Fund Act 2012, which established an agency to support the health, housing, and education needs of survivors (Caranua).

As noted previously, memorialisation can also form a key part of the symbolic dimensions of reparation. The Ryan Report recommended a memorial for victim/survivors of residential school abuse (CICA 2009, para 7.02) but despite considerable consultation and planning the proposed memorial was refused planning permission (Comptroller and Auditor General 2016, 36). Since the publication of the Report of the Mother and Baby Homes Commission in 2021, several local authorities have indicated support for local memorialisation and the government commissioned a working group to support these efforts.[15] In addition, the Department of Children also provided funding for a 'Commemorative Grant Scheme to support survivor-centred advocacy organisations in commemorating their experiences in a way of their own choosing'.[16] In March 2022, the Irish government approved high-level proposals for a National Centre for Research and Remembrance to be located on the site of the former Magdalene Laundry on Sean McDermott Street in Dublin 1, which is intended to act as a site of conscience for victim/survivors of industrial and reformatory schools, Magdalene Laundries, mother and baby institutions,

[15] DCEDIY, Working Group on Actions Involving Local Authorities as identified in the Action Plan for Survivors and Former Residents of Mother and Baby and County Home Institutions (2021), https://www.gov.ie/en/publication/cfc83-working-group-on-actions-involving-local-authorities-as-identified-in-the-action-plan-for-survivors-and-former-residents-of-mother-and-baby-and-county-home-institutions/ (accessed 1 June 2024).

[16] DCEDIY, Grant Scheme for Mother and Child Institutions Commemorative Events (2020), https://www.gov.ie/en/publication/5879cb-grant-scheme-for-mother-and-child-institutions-commemorative-events-/ (accessed 1 June 2024).

county homes, and related institutions (National Centre for Research and Remembrance Steering Group 2022, 1).

A further non-monetary form of redress is the provision of psychosocial counselling. The National Counselling Service was established in 2000 in RoI to provide counselling support to victim/survivors of sexual abuse including institutional abuse and, since 2021, extends to former residents of mother and baby institutions. Early reviews of the service by survivors were generally positive (National Counselling Service 2003). Up to 2016, the Irish State had spent €176m on health, housing, educational, and counselling services for victim/survivors of industrial and reformatory schools (Comptroller and Auditor General 2016, 10). In 2002, 18 religious organisations signed an agreement with the Irish State indemnifying them against potential litigation in claims related to institutions listed in the Schedule to the RIRB Act 2002 for a contribution of €128m to redress. As part of this agreement, the religious congregations agreed to continue to provide counselling to the value of €10m provided through Faoiseamh, established in 1996 to provide support and independent counselling for victim/survivors of abuse perpetrated by clergy or religious brothers and sisters or their agents. In 2011, Towards Healing replaced Faoiseamh—both bodies are funded exclusively by the religious congregations and the Irish Conference of Bishops (Comptroller and Auditor General 2016, 36). A 2021 review of Towards Healing described it as 'a very positive presence in the lives of its clients' (Fallon 2021, 2).

The Magdalene Commission recommended Magdalene women should have access to the full range of services currently enjoyed by holders of the Health (Amendment) Act 1996 Card (the 'HAA card') (Quirke 2013, 7). In May 2015, the Redress for Women Resident in Certain Institutions Act was enacted, giving a regular medical card and other support to women committed to Magdalene Laundries, including to women living outside Ireland but not the enhanced HAA card as recommended by Quirke. Magdalene survivors criticised this failure with one survivor stating, 'Don't make promises they're not going to keep to people' (O'Donnell and McGettrick 2020, 20). One academic-advocate in the present study noted that 'if we'd had the HAA medical card . . . that would have been an enormous justice measure' (Interview 7). The role of reparations as a form of healing and rehabilitation depends on access to non-monetary services, which are appropriate to respond to the changing needs of victim/survivors. With few longitudinal studies of counselling services and limited progress on memorialisation, how effective the Irish approach has been to date is not evidenced.

5. Reparations in Northern Ireland

Monetary redress

In its final report in 2017, the Hart Inquiry recommended an apology, a memorial, a statutory commissioner for survivors of institutional childhood abuse, the provision of specialist supports and care for survivors, and financial compensation to be administered by a redress board (HIA 2017, 227–56). One victim/survivor noted the challenging role of Northern Irish politics in delaying redress, noting that politicians could publicly say, 'get the redress up and running, get the apology up and running even though they knew the Executive was going to collapse. But what did they do? They sat on their hands. So for almost three years we were left out in limbo' (Interview 15).

In briefing the government during debates on the legislation governing redress, the late Sir Anthony Hart, the Inquiry chairperson, underlined the need to consider 'the welfare of the public purse'.[17] This stance was criticised by several interviewees including victim/survivors: 'That was a flaw that wasn't challenged by ministers, wasn't challenged by TOE [sic]' (Interview 15).[18] Although there had been engagement and submissions from survivor advocacy groups in advance of these recommendations (Lundy 2016), one victim/survivor advocate noted that 'there was not a sufficiently good alternative process for gathering victims' views about the design of the scheme' (Interview 35).

The Historical Institutional Abuse (Northern Ireland) Act 2019 established the Historical Institutional Abuse (HIA) Redress Board to evaluate applications for redress from those who experienced abuse in residential institutions in NI between 1922 and 1995. The Board has a mandate to operate for five years and has a capacity to prioritise applicants based on age but excludes cases currently pending or dismissed by the courts on their merits. The Board can make awards in bands from £10,000 to £100,000 to victim/survivors, which is less than would be possible for the same harms in civil litigation. While this trade-off is consistent with comparative trends in reparations schemes, one survivor criticised the reduced range of compensation compared to civil cases: 'if you're going to make an acknowledgement

[17] Official Report (Hansard), Committee for the Office of the First Minister and deputy First Minister, Session 2011/12, 4 July 2012. Inquiry into Historical Institutional Abuse Bill: Inquiry Panel Briefing.

[18] TEO is the acronym for The Executive Office, the Northern Irish Civil Service office mandated to oversee the coordination of Executive policies and programmes.

then it has to be tangible where if a survivor today was offered £10,000 they would actually bite your hand to take it not realising they could get more' (Interview 15). Nonetheless, the same survivor affirmed the value of reparations in this scheme as a means of validation: 'when I got the determination letter of offer they found my story incredible. The credibility they gave me, and that, for me, wasn't about the money, that word alone said somebody actually believed me. And that, for me, was a great satisfaction' (Interview 15).

The HIA Redress Board will operate until 2027 and a review of its processes has been conducted by the Northern Ireland Executive office but not published. The final engagement of survivors with the redress process, and their degree of satisfaction and validation, remain to be determined.

Non-monetary redress

In NI, at the time of writing, a permanent physical memorial in the grounds of Stormont is being considered. Proposals for memorialisation in the context of HIA reparations reflect the challenges in providing an appropriate memorial[19] for all survivors and viewpoints:

> There are individual victims and survivors who will not be represented by that memorial who will want nothing to do with it, who will never go to see it. If you're going to put it in Stormont there are very, very few people going to jump on a bus from Derry and go to Stormont to see 'here's our statue', it won't be our statue, it will be their statue so how is it our memorial if they decide? I think we need to get round the interpretation of what it memorialises. Is it about the Inquiry, is it about the search for justice, is it about the pain that happened in the past? (Interview 9)

A victim/survivor advocate in NI noted the potential reluctance of some survivors to engage with the all-island, Catholic Church-funded counselling services:

> No reflection on the quality of those counsellors but I know that some victims did not want to go down that road because it was like, it was

[19] For a critical review of the literature around the politics of memorialisation, see Viejo Rose (2011) and Robins (2014).

> almost felt like going cap in hand to the Church or letting the Church . . . [be] able to say, 'Oh we're providing counsellors for these poor people'. (Interview 35)

A different perspective was offered by a lawyer in NI: 'Towards Healing is what I get the best feedback on and it's the one thing that the Catholic Church have done well . . . But what I would say about it is they also failed to properly advertise it' (Interview 33). Based on existing publicly available data, it remains unclear whether and how the non-monetary forms of redress have met victim/survivor needs or have any different value or impact in NI in comparison to RoI.

6. The Value and Limits of Reparations

In identifying reparations as both a process and outcome, Moffett (2017, 394) notes that reparations can be guided and evaluated by '(a) completeness and comprehensiveness; (b) complexity and coherence; (c) appropriateness and proportionality; (d) acknowledgement; and (e) transformativeness'. These key issues were reflected in interviews with stakeholders, in terms of restrictive interpretation of redress eligibility, problematic delivery of reparations, the limits to acknowledgement in existing *ex gratia* redress schemes, concerns about the distribution of payment for redress between state and church organisations, and the failures of redress as relational repair.

Eligibility for redress

In each redress scheme on the island, some victim/survivors have been excluded. No one scheme can address all prior wrongdoing, and reparations eligibility is an inevitable choice for policymakers. A scheme's completeness and comprehensiveness refer to whether and how it excludes and justifies exclusion of categories of victims or violations (de Greiff 2006). Several individuals judicially reviewed their exclusion from the RIRB or Magdalene schemes with limited success (McPartland 2018).[20] The Magdalene Commission Report recommended that the scheme's administrators 'apply

[20] See *MKL and DC v Minister for Justice and Equality* [2017] IEHC 389 re the Magdalene scheme.

a fair and robust eligibility or qualification process', including enabling access to institutional and other relevant records and the provision of support and assistance to applicants as required. Applicants had only to prove that they had been 'admitted to or worked in a relevant institution'. However, duration of stay was known for only 6,151 of the 14,1607 admissions referred to in the McAleese Report (IDC 2013, ch 8, 168).

After 27 complaints to the Office of the Ombudsman regarding the administration of the Magdalene scheme, the Ombudsman commenced an investigation in 2016, which concluded that the Department of Justice had failed to examine all available evidence when it 'wrongly refused' some women access to the scheme (affecting approximately 106 women who had applied to the scheme), resulting in a situation which was 'manifestly unfair' (Opportunity Lost 2017, 34). The Ombudsman's investigation noted that, 'There was an overreliance on the records of the congregations, and it is not apparent what weight if any was afforded to the testimony of the women and/or their relatives' (Opportunity Lost 2017, 8). One State official interviewed for the current project suggested that 'the religious orders who were giving us the records had no incentive not to be correct' (Interview 62). However, such a perspective does not sufficiently address the limits of documentation acknowledged in the McAleese Report (IDC 2013), discussed earlier.

In addition, the Ombudsman's Report found the Magdalene scheme as applied failed to include all relevant institutions associated with Magdalene Laundries, including those which formed part of St Mary's Refuge in High Park, Drumcondra, Dublin (Opportunity Lost 2017, 24–5). The same State official offered the following perspective:

> [The excluded institutions] in our eyes, were clearly not Magdalene institutions. They may have been on the same campus but, you know, if you use the campus argument, then everybody, all the nuns who were in the convent would be entitled to compensation and anybody in the boarding school would have been entitled to compensation. (Interview 62)

In April 2018, the Irish government announced that the scheme would be broadened to include the women who had been excluded and appointed Senior Counsel Mary O'Toole to examine the approximately 200 cases where an issue had arisen on assessing the length of stay in an institution. A journalist noted the inconsistency in the State's approach where 'we have the State saying on the one hand, "We believe you". And then as we learned from the Magdalene Redress Scheme, the Department of Justice saying, "Well, in fact we don't". I find that that's the way things are done all the time' (Interview 1). Indeed, the potential of the Quirke approach was undermined by the manner in which it was administered by the Department of Justice, evidenced in significant survivor frustration and legal challenges.

The *O'Keeffe* scheme has also been independently evaluated and found to be overly restrictive in its application. In November 2017, Mr Justice O'Neill was appointed by the government as an independent assessor to review cases where applicants to the State's *ex gratia* scheme had their applications declined by the State Claims Agency (SCA). In rejecting the obligation on survivors to make a prior complaint to be eligible, Judge O'Neill notes that the ECtHR decision in *O'Keeffe v Ireland* does not concern 'the responsibilities or failures of individual actors' nor the 'operational failure' of the State. Instead, Judge O'Neill noted:

> The judgment of the ECtHR establishes a liability on the part of the State for a breach of Article 3 based solely on the failure to have in place, at a minimum, effective mechanisms for the detection and reporting by and to a State controlled body, of child sexual abuse in national schools. (O'Neill 2019, para 40)

The attempts to introduce a 'prior complaint' criterion serve the function of moving responsibility from the state for a systemic failure to have effective mechanisms to prevent child abuse, to individual survivors who would only be eligible if they had raised a non-recent complaint.

In NI, one State official noted a gap under the existing HIA redress scheme in capturing effective redress for individuals with multiple forms of institutionalisation or experiences of state care: 'there's a gap when you're dealing with, say if somebody's left the home, gone into foster care, back into the home' (Interview 73). However, one civil servant noted the perception of diverse eligible institutional contexts may create challenges for some victim/survivors: 'the policy was an issue for those in residential homes but it's opened up a lot to youth justice and to prisons, and their view is that well . . . if we're speaking frankly, we're being lumped in with the joyriders and the thugs' (Interview 45).

After successive judicial reviews and independent assessments of the administration of state-operated schemes in RoI, it is fair to conclude that there is a culture of highly conservative interpretation of agreed eligibility criteria and administration of reparations schemes. Such an approach seems at odds with the finite pool of potential applicants and with meaningful recognition of the power imbalance involving applicants engaging with state institutions and has the effect of denying eligible victims a prompt and effective remedy.

The delivery of reparations: adversarialism and legalism

The delivery of reparation offers the most lasting impression for survivors of how seriously they are being treated. The UN Principles provide that states should provide equal, fair, and effective access to justice and access to information, support, and legal advice to enable survivor access and participation in reparations (UN Principles, Principle 11). Moffett (2017, 392–3) emphasises that the process of reparations must also be prompt and timely. While the RIRB scheme involved in-person hearings, the majority of reparations schemes on the island of Ireland involved a paper-based application and bureaucratic administration. The process of delivery of reparations to victim/survivors is the key mechanism by which the state or church as responsible actors can aim to validate survivors and rebuild trust and legitimacy (de Greiff 2010, 22–3). This is an opportunity that in the Irish context has been woefully neglected.

Section 5 of the RIRB Act 2002 obliged the RIRB to act as informally as possible and precludes the RIRB from making findings of fact or fault. Section 10 provided that the RIRB was to operate otherwise than in public and provided that the Board had broad discretion to determine its procedures but enabled the use of oral hearings with an entitlement to legal representation. As a result, the RIRB had an opportunity to provide a victim/survivor-centred and trauma-informed process. However, many survivors described their experiences of the RIRB process as 'adversarial, difficult, traumatic, and negative' (Walshe and O'Connell 2019, 4). The panel administering the RIRB scheme was criticised as being in place too long and becoming 'cold, hardened and indifferent' to survivors (Walshe and O'Connell 2019, 16). Pembroke (2019, 52) notes that 'the redress scheme application procedure itself (writing a detailed statement, and an assessment by a psychologist in order to verify their trauma), resulted in psychological wounds being opened up after years of consignment'. Fox and Crean (2017, 22) emphasise that 'victims report a lack of understanding of their individual circumstances coupled with a failure by the Board to understand

and empathise with their past experiences of abuse and ongoing issues as a result'.

Survivors interviewed for this book were equally critical of the RIRB scheme: 'It was blood money. It was hush money' (Interview 22). The scale system intended by the RIRB was seen as 'horse trading': 'the price attached to the horse was how many deep scars could the Commission see on you, and if you had the deep scars, well then you got your pot of money. If you didn't, then you got very little' (Interview 22). One victim/survivor confirmed that 'It was retraumatising without question . . . I know people who ended up in hospital after it. I had to get a GP for somebody in the building . . . I didn't meet a single person who had a positive experience of that' (Interview 6).

Section 11(8) of the RIRB Act 2002 provided that the RIRB would inform a person against whom an allegation of abuse was made or a person who was responsible for the management of an institution in which it was alleged that abuse had occurred and give them the opportunity to provide evidence and to cross-examine victim/survivors in person or through legal representation. Representatives of female religious organisations interviewed distinguished their organisational response from any response of individual alleged abusers:

> If there were named people in it and they were alive, they got the opportunity to read and if they wanted to challenge it, they were free to, but it was our policy not to challenge, in order to allow, at least to reduce the pain by virtue of recalling all of this as much as we could. (Interview 48)

Another representative of a female religious organisation emphasised that 'We never questioned their application for redress unless, and in about three cases where it was downright untrue and we had evidence to show' (Interview 42). In contrast, a senior member of a male religious organisation stated that 'we were also quite critical of the government in . . . the lack of stringent analysis of the complaints, that they were more inclined to, if someone was there and had a complaint, that they would just give out the money' (Interview 23). The ability of allegedly responsible actors to cross-examine alleged victim/survivors would not be surprising in the context of a criminal or civil trial, which is seeking to establish legal liability. However, it remains remarkable and contradictory that this process of cross-examination was permitted in an *ex gratia* scheme, conducted in private hearings, with confidentiality regarding the outcome, which was not designed to establish findings of fact or liability.

Similar concerning processes arise regarding Caranua in RoI. A governmental consultation with survivors found that while Caranua was well intentioned, 'there was a mismatch between the intention and the way the service was structured' and that it was 'bureaucratic and unwieldy' (Walshe and O'Connell 2019, 17, 4). In the current project, some victim/survivors experienced Caranua as re-traumatising, disempowering, and demeaning:

> Caranua, I have never felt so humiliated. I had to tell American workmen my story because the Irish Government would not pay me the money to pay the workmen.... [T]hey submitted their expenses to me, I submitted them to Caranua, Caranua made the cheque out to the workmen. We were not allowed. (Interview 20)

Advocates in the present study also noted the overly ambitious but under-equipped nature of Caranua: 'The scheme promised a lot and actually couldn't deliver, and when they realised they couldn't deliver they changed the rules in a way that wasn't really helpful or respectful and . . . there was so much discourtesy and rudeness' (Interview 54).

In NI, one interviewee saw value in the inter-disciplinary nature of decision-making panels at the Redress Board in assessing the quantum of damages: 'being able to bring in a lot more around our understanding of trauma, understanding of long-term impact' (Interview 73). However, inadequate legal advice to victim/survivor applicants was identified by one State official as the key limitation of the scheme's operation: 'the amount of solicitors we have to go back to and say, "Look, you need to give your client more help here", because . . . it's clearly screaming out that they should have a psychiatric report and that would maybe move them, the difference between maybe 20,000 and 60,000, a significant difference' (Interview 73). This quote indicates how the use of psychiatric reports by both sides in assessing quantum in *ex gratia* schemes has become normative and a battleground for assessing 'damage', especially when victim/survivors clearly indicate the re-traumatising impact of the retelling of their experiences. Further, for survivors who are thriving, the very idea of having to revisit how 'damaged' they are or have been by their experience is truly against the spirit of responsibility-taking and being accountable. Similar to RIRB, the HIA Redress Board is obliged to provide relevant organisations that operated residential institutions with an opportunity to provide written evidence in response to allegations of abuse in applicants' claims. The same interviewee noted the cooperation of religious organisations with the redress scheme:

> They will reply back by saying, you know, we believe there's no evidence of that, or Brother whoever or Father whoever was not or Sister whoever was not present in the home at the time . . . [T]hat is always very helpful, and sometimes there's also a very basic thing of, actually the name of maybe the nun they've given or the brother they've given isn't accurate but the physical description is exactly as they were . . . [T]hat information against the backdrop of what was determined at the statutory inquiry, the parallel of the two pieces of information is very helpful. (Interview 73)

As a form of law and policy intended to provide repair, recognition, and healing to survivors, the process is as important as the outcome in both monetary and non-monetary reparations schemes. Unfortunately, in RoI, the process has often undermined the reparative goals of successive schemes. As noted, at the time of writing a review of the NI redress scheme has been conducted but not published so it remains to be seen whether its processes suffered the same flaws as some schemes in RoI.

The meaning of reparation and the limits of acknowledgement

In academic literature, reparations are intended to serve as a form of official acknowledgement of responsibility for the commission of wrongdoing or failure to prevent that wrongdoing by the state or non-state actor. As de Greiff (2010, 22) argues, reparations 'demonstrat[e] a sufficiently serious commitment so as to invest resources, and, in well-crafted programs, by giving beneficiaries the sense that the state has taken their interests to heart'. However, every Irish reparation scheme is *ex gratia* and so excludes considerations of legal liability or responsibility for the harms experienced (Winter 2009, 49). The *ex gratia* nature of the Irish schemes has been problematic for some victim/survivors:

> There's no money in the world can take away what happened to me. It is the acknowledgement of what happened to me that they let me down and the way they fought the case and the way they're actually continuing

> to fight it . . . still isn't acknowledging that wrong that was done, and because like, to me, that money and the only way I have of describing it is it's dirty money. (Interview 31)

A lawyer described *ex gratia* reparations as 'an abdication of State responsibility' (Interview 34). The need for an alternative meaning of redress and a relationship of equality between victim/survivors and state and church organisations is integral to a more nuanced account of taking responsibility and accountability for non-recent institutional abuses.

Alternative meanings of redress have been offered in the design of Irish schemes but it is at best questionable whether these interpretations have been effectively communicated in the operation and processes of reparations. The 2001 Irish government-commissioned report 'Towards Redress and Recovery' (2001, 37–8) treated 'redress' and 'compensation' as synonymous but intended compensation as a 'form of solace designed to provide some degree of comfort to the victim for his or her injury and to make some attempt to put right the wrong which he or she has suffered'. Having identified the role of other non-monetary forms of redress, the 2001 report suggested:

> The award of appropriate financial redress can at least provide some tangible recognition of the seriousness of the hurt and injury which has been caused to the victims of institutional child abuse . . . [and] may allow many of those victims to pass the remainder of their years with a degree of physical and mental comfort which would otherwise not be readily attainable. (66)

There is some recognition in the report of 'policy wrongs', that the mere act of institutionalisation is itself a form of abuse but only as an exceptional form of aggravated damages (2001, 76). The report claims that money can provide 'tangible recognition' of the hurt and injury done but, notably, not recognition of responsibility for the harm or a failure to prevent it.

The Magdalene Commission Report envisaged redress as intending to 'contribute to a healing and reconciliation process' and to 'reflect the wish of the Irish community to reduce the hurt and pain suffered by the Magdalene women by providing them with monetary payments and with sufficient health and other state benefits to ensure that the remainder of their lives will be made as comfortable as is reasonably possible' (Quirke 2013, 19). The report acknowledges the limits of reparations: 'such monetary payments cannot and will not fully compensate them for what they have endured. However, the payments are intended to address their current needs and interests and reduce the level of injury pain and hurt which they have suffered' (Quirke 2013, 22).

While the Quirke scheme references several other redress schemes as having been considered in establishing the level of *ex gratia* payments (Quirke 2013, 40–1), no further guidance is offered on how the Commission reached the quantum of its awards. In the absence of any mention of rights or responsibility, McGettrick et al (2021, 135) write regarding the Magdalene scheme that, 'The government's designation of the Scheme as "ex gratia" effectively functioned as a declaration that neither State departments nor religious congregations were to be treated as wrongdoers who might be inclined to treat survivors with a lack of respect.'

Regarding mother and baby institutions, the Inter-Departmental Working Group stated the commitment of the State 'to acknowledging the experiences of mothers and children, as well as the impacts which these experiences continue to have on many individuals' (DCEDIY 2021, 17). Such an approach echoes that taken at the RIRB where recognition of victim/survivor experience, but not recognition of responsibility for or causes of that experience, is prioritised. In identifying quantum of payment based on length of stay, the IDG report notes that 'the amount of time spent in Magdalene Institutions was, on average, longer than time spent in Mother and Baby Institutions and that they operated in a different context in that they were specifically designed for commercial work to be undertaken by the residents' (DCEDIY 2021, 36). The result was a proposed minimum general payment of €12,500 but for a minimum stay of six months in an institution, compared with €10,000 minimum for any length of stay in a Magdalene Laundry (Quirke 2013, 65).

In NI, the stated aim of the HIA Redress Board is 'to deliver the recommendations for redress in the HIA Inquiry Report'.[21] The HIA Inquiry (2017, 228) report recommended that 'the nature and scale of the experiences of children abused whilst in residential institutions in Northern Ireland are appropriately acknowledged'. The report also noted that in some institutions there was a 'harsh environment that affected all the children in that institution at that time' (Hart Inquiry 2017, 238). While recognising that such policy wrongs amounted to abuse, the HIA approach does not

[21] The Historical Institutional Abuse (Northern Ireland) Act 2019, Sch 1, para 4

go so far as to recognise institutionalisation per se as a policy wrong that warrants reparation. One State official noted the limited nature of acknowledgement for survivors if eligible:

> They get a summary really of what they have said and then, what we, as a panel, have felt and then . . . [a letter which] says is under the Act, that I'm entitled to redress . . . it's not saying that because of the harm happened to you that the Department of Health in Northern Ireland acknowledges that you were hurt. No. There's none of that. (Interview 73)

The HIA Report recommended financial awards aligned with those amounts already paid as a result of litigation (Hart Inquiry 2017, 246). Such an approach implicitly affirms reparations as compensation, which suggested 'this was just about money' (Interview 9). There was broad consensus, especially among victim/survivor and advocate interviewees, that a fuller conceptualisation of redress, embracing the responsibility of state and church organisations would be welcome. A retired Irish judge noted that there remains potential for government to pass reparation legislation that acknowledges policy wrongs directly:

> I can't see any reason in principle why government, so far as itself is concerned at least, can't, couldn't even pass a law that would allow some form of redress for things that were lawful at the time but where we would now consider them not to be. It's obviously a policy question for government whether they want to do that. (Interview 40)

A survivor in RoI noted that there remains a gap in the acknowledgement of church responsibility for non-recent abuses in the context of reparations. While acknowledging some efforts to date, the survivor stated that 'it's never fully sincere until you put your hand in your pocket because that's actually what's required in the end' (Interview 65). In contrast, one senior representative of a religious organisation welcomed the role of reparation in providing recognition of prior harm but sought to separate that from church responsibility:

> I would believe we need to have this space, which is a recognition that harm happened, people got a bad hand in life, that they do really need support. But trying to blame an institution or a system, you're blaming a

> culture, and a culture only exists, as you know, in a subliminal way in its own time. (Interview 48)

The *ex gratia* nature of reparation in Ireland is one of the key limitations in reparations making an effective contribution to the State and church institutions taking responsibility for non-recent institutional abuses. Although several alternative conceptions of the intended purpose of reparation have been offered, none of these seem to have effectively avoided the sense of reparation as compensation without acknowledgement nor offered clear justification of quantum in 'length of stay'-style schemes.

Who pays? The cost of appropriate and proportionate redress

Those interviewed for this book expressed a range of views as to who was responsible to pay for redress to victim/survivors of non-recent abuses. Across state officials and civil servants, the chief concern regarding reparations was the need to forecast and contain cost. One senior politician in RoI suggested, 'you are going to need to spend money and it needs to be quantifiable. So that's a big issue and your legacy becomes positive or negative to the extent that you make a difference, and your difference is usually related to how much money you get' (Interview 51). Another senior politician emphasised that for reparations:

> It's not the State that picks up the bill, it's taxpayers . . . [T]hese bills are being paid for by many people who are experiencing the cost of living crisis, the housing crisis . . . I think people are willing to do it though because they do want to see wrongs put right. But . . . there should be limits for that very reason because the people paying the bill are, actually, in no way responsible for what happened. (Interview 64)

Such a concern raises the issue of intergenerational and social responsibility for providing redress. Public support to provide redress for survivors offers the basis to consider the extent of social complicity and responsibility for non-recent abuses, considered further in Part III of the book. However, the limits of financial compensation are also evident in the views of some state and religious actors. Representatives of a female religious organisation stated that 'the money changed everything and I think it was the worst probable thing that could ever have happened because it didn't allow the truth of the story to come out' (Interview 57). One representative of a male religious organisation was also critical of the role of money: 'I am convinced money doesn't solve or heal anything really' (Interview 23).

In the context of non-recent institutional abuses, concerns arise as to whether state or church institutions or both should cover the cost of redress. In RoI, under the 2002 indemnity agreement, discussed earlier, religious organisations made different levels of financial contribution given the range of institutions they had operated and sought to have included in the RIRB schedule. The cost of damages against these organisations arising in court litigation regarding listed institutions was thus covered by the State. The indemnity was invoked 33 times in court litigation against religious orders, with the Irish State covering the cost of awards amounting to €4.4m. Legal and other costs in litigation amounted to €5.7m, which represents 57% of the total overall cost to the State, being approximately €10m. The average award was €133,000 (Comptroller and Auditor General 2016, 11).

It is notable that several religious organisations sought and obtained the inclusion of institutions in the indemnity, which had not been the subject of investigation at the CICA. As a result, those organisations benefited from an indemnity in the absence of any scrutiny of their conduct or responsibility within particular institutional contexts. Information on the awards made by the RIRB regarding each of the 139 scheduled institutions covered by the scheme is not available. The 2016 Comptroller and Auditor General report published the top ten institutions, which were all investigated at CICA, with the highest number of applications received (Comptroller and Auditor General 2016, 28) as detailed in Table 6.1.

On publication of the CICA report, religious organisations made a commitment to provide further voluntary contributions, totalling €352.6m, which funded Caranua, discussed earlier. However, there were significant multi-year delays in obtaining the voluntary contributions from some religious organisations.[22] As a result, across these two contributions, religious organisations have paid a minority of the bill for the state-administered redress schemes to victims of abuse in residential schools in RoI, including the industrial and reformatory schools examined in CICA, with the most recent figures suggesting a payment of a mere 13% of the total bill (Comptroller and Auditor General 2016, 11). Data are not available on

[22] C O'Fatharta, '"Imminent" redress payment delayed', *The Irish Examiner*, 16 August 2019.

Table 6.1 Institutions with the highest number of RIRB applications

Institution	Responsible organisation	Number of applications at RIRB
Artane Industrial School	Christian Brothers	1,946
St Joseph's Industrial School, Letterfrack	Christian Brothers	745
St Joseph's Industrial School, Salthill	Christian Brothers	467
St Joseph's Industrial School, Ferryhouse	Rosminians	1,040
St Patrick's Industrial School, Upton	Rosminians	567
St Vincent's Industrial School, Goldenbridge	Sisters of Mercy	869
St Kyran's Industrial School, Rathdrum		456
St Conleth's Reformatory School, Daingean	Oblates	965
Finglas Child and Adolescent Centre	De La Salle Order	467
St Patrick's Industrial School, Kilkenny	Sisters of Charity	452
Total		**7,974**

what the religious orders have paid out to former pupils and residents via other mechanisms, including mediated settlements or in civil litigation. This gap leads to an unclear picture regarding the distribution of accountability between church and state as pertaining to monetary redress. There also remains the possibility of a survivor seeking reparation from state and church through separate legal or administrative processes, placing a burden on individual survivors to engage with multiple processes, possibly with attendant legal fees, in a context of systemic and institutional wrongdoing.

While government policy suggests a 50% contribution to the cost of redress (Comptroller and Auditor General 2016, 11), several representatives of both male and female religious organisations affirmed that their organisations never agreed to a 50% contribution to the RIRB redress scheme. Other senior representatives of a female religious organisation noted how they calculated their contribution to the redress scheme: 'how we came to the figure was to look at our exposure in terms of litigation . . . that was assessed and we doubled that' (Interview 42). Several members of female religious orders challenged the fairness of financial contributions from their religious organisation in the absence of criminal accountability of individual members. One senior representative of a female religious order stated, 'We have nobody convicted of anything in any institution' (Interview 48). Another representative of a female religious organisation emphasised that 'abuse happened or that people were treated poorly or whatever way you want to say it and no findings were made against anybody except a generalised finding' (Interview 42). Such concerns suggest financial payment for redress is derived from concerns about potential liability rather than a broader sense of responsibility for wrongdoing in the absence of forensic and legal accountability.

In addition, there has been some revisionism regarding the position and reflections of religious orders on their contribution to redress. Representatives of one female religious order, which was not investigated regarding residential institutions but contributed to the indemnity agreement, 'would have questions ourselves [as to] whether that was the wisest thing or not [to contribute to the scheme] at the time' (Interview 58). One male religious congregation, the Oblates, challenged calls for their further contribution to the RIRB and the approach it took to redress, stating that, 'The bill incurred by the Government for the redress fund is not a benchmark of the responsibility of any of the others who were involved, including the religious. It was a bill incurred by a Government and Dáil on their own legal and moral responsibility' (An Oblate of Mary Immaculate 2017, 9). Similarly, in a letter to the Irish Department of Education in 2019, a male religious order, the Rosminians (Institute of Charity) wrote:

> Those who were involved in the Redress Scheme know well that it was purposely designed with a very low burden of proof to facilitate the State. The motivation was as much to do with politics as with justice . . . Future generations will naively take as truth the submissions to the Redress Board and lead to the eternal besmirching of the names of good people. Injustice heaped upon injustice.[23]

(See also O'Rourke 2020, 3.) One senior politician doubted the utility of pursuing further the religious orders for contributions to redress:

[23] C O'Fatharta, 'Religious order did not want "eternal besmirching of names of good people" by keeping abuse records', *Irish Examiner*, 13 June 2019.

> I do think it was always inevitable the State was going to pick up the vast majority of the bill because . . . [I]t's unlikely that in many cases there would have been findings of damages against the religious institutions, either due to statute of limitations or because in each individual case, they'd have to prove that the harm was done. (Interview 64)

Similarly, one State official noted the limited ability to pressure financial contributions from the religious orders in the context of Magdalene Laundries: 'there was no record . . . that the religious institutions that ran the Magdalenes were engaged in systematic abuse, physical or sexual, or that they would be liable in any legal action against them or that the State would be liable in any legal action against them' (Interview 62). At the time of writing, negotiations between the State and the religious organisations involved in mother and baby institutions remain ongoing regarding a potential contribution to redress. In NI, some have been critical of the lack of church contributions to the HIA scheme. As one State appointee reflected, 'victims and survivors have half-jokingly said to me . . . "sure I've paid for my own redress, you know, through my taxes" ' (Interview 14).

To date, several existing schemes involve a waiver of victim/survivors' rights to sue regarding the abuse that is the subject of the redress scheme,[24] effectively precluding any further compensation or vindication of rights through the courts. This measure appears overly crude as the payment of state redress, on an *ex gratia* basis, could be discounted from any damages payment that also recognises the violation of victim/survivor rights. At present, this interoperability only works in favour of the state where those who previously received awards through litigation have that considered in the administration of the redress scheme.[25] Alternative designs of such schemes would offer a more holistic and rights-respecting approach to reparations. While available data on other payments by religious orders to victim/survivors remain incomplete, limited contributions and resistance to further contributions to state schemes creates a public impression of a desire to avoid financial cost and responsibility or to incur financial cost only when litigated or via their own restorative justice processes and redress schemes (see Chapter 8).

[24] See Residential Institutions Redress Board Act 2002, s 24; Mother and Baby Institutions Payment Scheme Act 2023, s, 32(3); and Historical Institutional Abuse (Northern Ireland) Act 2019, s 15(6).

[25] See eg Historical Institutional Abuse (Northern Ireland) Act 2019, ss 3–4.

Reparations as relational repair

In academic literature, one of the goals of reparation is to restore relationships between citizens and between citizens and the state (de Greiff 2010, 22) while noting the inherent limits of administrative redress as a tool of relational and emotional engagement. Winter suggests that redress inevitably operates through 'impersonal bureaucracies' and often involves an unsatisfying process of form-filling and compliance with legalistic regulations (2022, 7). Attempts at direct relational repair involve repair between victim/survivors and contemporary representatives of organisations seeking to embody institutions and 'people who ran the institutions and committed the actual abuses [who] are long past any accountability' (Winter 2022, 7). In the absence of personal encounters between victim/survivors (who wish for it) and responsible institutions, developing recognition and acknowledgement of survivor harm and potentially ongoing needs arising from non-recent abuses can be limited. Offering personal encounters to those survivors interested and taking responsibility for long-term supports, beyond financial compensation, can also strengthen the claim that responsible institutions are taking their claims of wrongdoing and rights violation seriously (see further Chapters 8 and 9) and in so doing dignify the belief of survivors and their experiences of harm.

In our empirical research, interviewees recognised the need for greater empathy from political and religious leaders around redress. One senior Church official in NI recognised that 'we're not actually facilitating healing and reconciliation with a large number of survivors of abuse . . . [M]y experience is that even those who have received, in some cases, a very substantial settlement compensation for abuse, remain upset, angry and in some cases, dismissive of the efforts that the Church has made' (Interview 69). A representative of a female religious organisation noted that their congregation was 'always open to meeting the people who were complaining' (Interview 41), including members of the organisation who were involved in industrial schools or Magdalene Laundries. A senior representative of a male religious organisation suggested the potential for pre-redress dialogue: 'I think the idea of someone coming and making a complaint, meeting the accused, and having some sort of safe place where people can talk about what happened could be very valuable. It . . . hopefully could be healing, both for the accused . . . and the person coming with the complaint' (Interview 23).

Several stakeholders were critical of the role of the legal profession regarding reparations, especially in the RIRB context, where its engagement led to both significant fees for legal professionals and firms and high levels of survivor distress and dissatisfaction. A State official reflected on the experiences of victim/survivors with reparations, 'two things that struck me: one, the thing they hated most was their lawyers and the second thing they hated most was the process for awarding the money' (Interview 62). One victim/survivor noted the exploitative nature of some lawyers (also discussed in Chapter 4): 'The particular solicitor I had offered me £200 for every survivor I could sling his way' (Interview 22). One senior politician noted the disregard of aspects of the legal profession for survivors' interests: 'various legal firms entered the scene. There was one legal firm did say . . . "Forget about your therapy forums. Just get to the redress and get the compensation out there" ' (Interview 68).

One State official contrasted the role of lawyers at RIRB with the non-adversarial nature of the Magdalene scheme: 'there was a very good social relationship with the girls in our office and the women, because we deliberately structured the scheme that they didn't need lawyers' (Interview 62). While not involving significant legal representation, the administration of the Magdalene scheme remained deeply frustrating and exclusionary for several survivors as detailed earlier, suggesting the process and administration of redress schemes also requires considerable in-depth reflection.

Similarly, concern was expressed by religious interviewees regarding how the legal process inhibited a broader attempt at relational repair:

> The element of compensation seemed to appeal more than the actual healing, and so then the problem was the whole legal, you know, people taking civil claims and whereas, we would have met people and, but immediately, they started going down the civil claims. Their solicitors were saying to them, 'Don't deal with the [name of religious order], this is a civil matter'. So in many ways, a lot of the one to one gatherings or meetings on a one to one basis diminished quite considerably by then. (Interview 23)

The role and impact of lawyers on justice responses to non-recent abuses is a cross-cutting issue, affecting other responses discussed in Part II of this book (see especially Chapter 4). A different form of engagement from the legal profession with non-recent abuses is explored in Chapter 9. The limits of current justice responses are reflective of the need to view the state's responsibility for redress in relational terms and accountability in interpersonal as well as broader institutional terms.

7. Conclusion: Towards Transformative Reparations

Claims that victim/survivors should receive reparations 'must rest on some theory of responsibility' (Gray 2010, 1071). To date, the approach taken has largely viewed reparations as questions of charity and political benevolence. In the absence of clearly communicated public narratives around these schemes, there is a real risk that the monetary values and distressing processes of reparations are all that are remembered from this attempt to address the past. Each scheme has been negotiated and practiced, divorced from questions of victim/survivor rights and from recognition of state and church responsibilities to provide reparation.

An alternative, and rights-based, approach to reparations is legally and morally possible and may address some of these concerns more effectively. In two instances, there have been direct consideration of the nature of the Irish State's responsibility for reparation. In drafting the RIRB Act 2002, the language of the State's obligation to regulate and inspect institutions was included. This language re-emerges in the decision in *O'Keeffe v Ireland* and in Judge O'Neill's independent assessment of the operation of the resultant *ex gratia* scheme. However, there has been limited recognition of the State's responsibility as a duty-bearer to provide reparations to its harmed citizens in moral as well as legal terms (see Chapter 4).

These limitations have been compounded by restrictive eligibility and harmful administration of reparation schemes. If there is limited clarity in the intended meaning of reparations, the processes of their delivery form the key site for an allegedly responsible actor to demonstrate the sincerity of their interest in respecting and dignifying victim/survivors. Victim/survivor accounts demonstrate that they are largely unsatisfied with these processes, leading to litigation and independent review, and that they find the experience of seeking redress distressing or re-traumatising. The eligibility criteria of state-administered redress schemes has often led to criticism for being under-inclusive, excluding individuals from institutional contexts relevant to a scheme or excluding forms of harm not recognised by the scheme. While too early to fully evaluate the NI experience of redress as the work of the Redress Board is ongoing, some emergent themes and experiences reflect those in RoI. These include a siloed approach with a focus on the institutions examined in the Hart Inquiry to the exclusion of other forms of institutional abuse, the inadequate legal advice and other supports received by victim/survivors in applying for redress, and limited effective acknowledgement and financial contribution from religious organisations to state-run redress schemes. Greater integration of the knowledge and expertise of addressing trauma and of the effects and contexts of non-recent harms may improve the administration of redress schemes and transform legal representation before such schemes (see Chapter 9).

Most reparations schemes on the island have been designed and financed by state institutions with a limited contribution from religious organisations. There is no comprehensive data on other payments by religious organisations to victim/survivors in confidential settlements, mediation, restorative redress schemes, or civil litigation. While this gap leads to an unclear picture regarding the distribution of accountability between church and state regarding monetary redress, repeated concerns from religious organisations related to their involvement in the RIRB scheme and its indemnity in public arose in the course of the interviews. Nonetheless, the failure to financially contribute to any further state scheme creates an impression of resistance to the responsibility to repair, including to provide financial redress. For their part, religious organisations see the limitations of monetary redress and wish to consider alternative and additional relational forms of engagement and reparation, including restorative dialogue and restorative redress. On their account, the capacity of redress to function as a form of relational repair is inhibited by concerns about legal liability and the role of lawyers, explored further in Chapters 4 and 9.

A better and more legitimate process of reparations for non-recent abuses rests on both a taking of responsibility by state and church institutions and a process that reflects the sincerity of that responsibility in their respectful and dignifying treatment of survivors. Operating from the presumption, expressed in law and policy, that survivors are credible and trustworthy, as opposed to seeking to financially exploit state and church, would offer a clear signal of a new approach. However, reparations may remain an inescapably complex area of policy. One senior politician in RoI noted that policy proposals, including regarding reparations, may represent solutions that 'assume no trade off, assume unlimited financial resources, unlimited skills and personnel and unlimited legislative time' (Interview 64). Instead, Moffett (2023a, 16) suggests reparations as balance, seeing reparations as 'an agonistic space where victims and responsible actors/perpetrators struggle to find the sweet-spot where they can reach a value-based compromise on redress'. The final part of this book explores the potential to achieve greater responsibility and engagement for non-recent abuses in that agonistic space.

7
Apologies

1. Introduction

The overall purpose of this chapter is to critically examine the use and potential of apology as an effective 'justice' response to non-recent institutional abuses, within Ireland, North and South, and internationally. In keeping with the overall rubric of the book, it seeks to: (1) consider the extent to which apologies may function as a tool of responsibility and ultimately accountability; (2) balance the voices and experiences of key stakeholders; and (3) explore the potential for transformative apologies. The chapter is divided into seven main sections. Section 2 provides a critical overview of the literature on apologies as a response to wrongdoing. Sections 3 and 4 comprise comprehensive documentary analysis of key official apologies by church and state within Northern Ireland (NI) and the Republic of Ireland (RoI) and internationally. This includes a brief comparative examination of some of the underlying differences concerning the official recognition of abuses within predominantly Protestant and predominantly Catholic societies as well as within both settler-colonial and post-colonial contexts.

Drawing on interview data and a range of voices, Sections 5–7 consider three principal questions related to the what, how, and why dimensions of the apology-responsibility dyad: what do victims/survivors want or need from official apologies for non-recent institutional abuses; *how*, and in what ways, do church and state actors construct apologies related to the acceptance or repudiation of responsibility; and what are the *motivations* of these constituencies which may serve to either facilitate or impede the fuller acceptance of responsibility in both a moral and legal sense? Section 8 examines the challenges and limitations of public apologies as an effective response to non-recent institutional abuses, including addressing the relational and human dimensions. The concluding section draws out the 'transformational' potential of apologies and the learning for discourses around reframing responsibility.

Transforming Justice Responses to Non-Recent Institutional Abuses. Anne-Marie McAlinden, Marie Keenan, and James Gallen, Oxford University Press. © Oxford University Press 2025.
DOI: 10.1093/9780191967399.003.0007

2. Apologies: Form and Function

There is an expansive interdisciplinary literature on the role and function of apology which spans, *inter alia*, law (eg Vines 2007; Smith 2014), political science (eg Cunningham 1999; Nobles 2008), history (eg Weyeneth 2001; Marrus 2007), sociology (eg Goffman 1971; Tavuchis 1991), anthropology (eg Borneman 1999; Trouillot 2000), social psychology (eg Blatz and Philpot 2010; Wohl et al 2012), and management and communication studies (Hearit 2006; Barth 2010). Core elements of these intersecting literatures are drawn upon in the following sections.

Elements of a meaningful 'apology'

Attempts to define apology are often dominated by the sociological tradition. Goffman (1971, 143) defined apology as 'gestures through which an individual splits himself in two parts, the part that is guilty of an offence and the part that disassociates itself from the delict and affirms a belief in the offended rule'. Alternatively, Tavuchis (1991, 19) delineated apology as 'an acknowledgement and painful embracement of our deeds, coupled with a declaration of regret'. These definitions affirm the importance of acknowledgement of wrongdoing and the unambiguous expression of remorse. More recent academic and policy literature emphasise the centrality of the acceptance of responsibility for wrongdoing as well as the importance of repair (see eg Blatz et al 2009; McEvoy et al 2019). Slocum et al (2011), for example they propose three central components of a 'true' apology: (1) 'affirmation'—requiring perpetrators to accept and explain their wrongful behaviour; (2) 'affect'—conveying remorse and a perpetrator's emotional response to the wrong; and (3) 'action'—including behavioural attempts to repair the harm and avoid repetition. As discussed throughout, it is the balance of these three elements—acknowledgement, emotion, and tangible reparations—which emerges as being pivotal to the perceived sincerity of apologies for non-recent institutional abuses by victim/survivors.

Within the specific domain of non-recent institutional abuses, others have undertaken comprehensive content analysis of apologies utilising a broad set of ten criteria (see eg Gallen 2023a, ch 9, drawing on Blatz et al 2009). However, this list can be distilled further to five essential elements of a meaningful apology: (1) acknowledgement of wrongdoing; (2) acceptance of responsibility; (3) expression of remorse or regret; (4) assurance of non-repetition; and (5) offer of repair/corrective action (Catterall 2018). The critical analysis of apologies draws on these criteria. These core elements, co-developed by one of the authors (McAlinden), became the structuring principles of the first State apology delivered to victim/survivors of non-recent institutional abuses in NI in March 2022. Apology can be distilled further to the essentialist dual backward- and forward-looking aspects—it must simultaneously acknowledge responsibility for past wrongs as well as offer a tangible commitment to future corrective action (usually via tangible reparations or policy reform) (see Alter 1999).

A growing proportion of the literature emphasises the non-verbal, performative aspects of public apologies in terms of their sequencing, choreography, and delivery (see eg Celermajer 2009; Wilson and Bleiker 2013). Such material aspects may be equally if not more significant for victim/survivors in demonstrating the sincerity of the remorse for past abuses than the discursive elements and the actual words themselves. Within 'the age of apology' (Gibney et al 2008), however, the overuse of public apologies by political figures for a wide range of wrongdoing gives rise to a 'normative dilution effect' (Blatz and Philpot 2010; Okimoto et al 2015) or 'apology fatigue'[1] whereby the cultural saturation of apologies weakens their significance and impact. Thus, it becomes important to distinguish apologies from 'non-apologies' (Eisinger 2011). Lazare (2004, 9) outlines the key characteristics of a 'pseudo-apology': (1) vague and inadequate acknowledgement of the offence; (2) failure to express genuine remorse; and (3) failure to offer appropriate reparations, including a commitment to changed behaviour. In the eyes of victim/survivors, therefore, it is possible for church or state leaders to espouse apologetic rhetoric and to 'say sorry' without really apologising. Such 'incomplete' (Swart 2008, 50) or 'safe' (Taft 2000, 1151) apologies may express sympathy or regret without the admission of responsibility and are unlikely to meet the expectations and affective needs of victim/survivors in terms of acknowledgement, reparation, and healing.

There are many illustrative examples of platitudinal statements of regret by church and state within Ireland, North and South, and internationally which purport to apologise without expressing genuine remorse or admitting institutional responsibility for historical or structural failures concerning non-recent institutional abuses. In this respect, for a range of reasons explored later, the underlying motivation of public apologies by

[1] J Downing, 'The nation is close to "apology fatigue" and now mother and baby institution survivors need restitution', *Irish Independent*, 15 January 2021.

church and state representatives may be about the avoidance of responsibility. This may manifest as non-engagement with victim/survivors and a focus on expressing responsibility in solely moral rather than fuller legal or human and relational terms.

Apologies within restorative and transitional justice discourses

The literature on apology within the fields of restorative justice (eg Bolivar et al 2013; Suzuki and Jenkins 2022) and transitional justice (eg Teitel 2006; Cárdenas et al 2015) affirms the 'transformative' potential of apology (Tarusarira 2019) and the cathartic or healing benefits for victims, perpetrators, and wider society as 'gestures of finality and closure' (James and Stanger-Ross 2018, 289) at interpersonal (individual) and intergroup (collective) levels. Yet, as discussed further, for many victim/survivors, apologies represent the beginning rather than the end of a pathway towards just outcomes or personal healing.

Apologies can feature within restorative justice (RJ) processes, whereby the perpetrator may offer an apology to the victim as part of reparation and acknowledgement of wrongdoing within mediated dialogue or conferencing settings (Rossner 2013). Apology can also function as a restorative measure and a means of emotional reparation (Scheff 1998), relieving victims and perpetrators of the emotional burdens of harm or offending (Strang 2001; Wang 2020). While there is divergence in opinion by practitioners on the material role of apology in RJ,[2] for many RJ scholars, 'shame' emerges as the 'master emotion' within restorative processes (Harris et al 2004). As detailed in Chapter 2, 'shame', stemming from families, society, and organised religion, was a pivotal cultural factor underpinning the 'architecture of containment' (Smith 2007) or network of 'coercive confinement' (O'Sullivan and O'Donnell 2012) within RoI with far-reaching intergenerational consequences (see Wills 2024). These historical complexities of shame problematise apologies for non-recent institutional abuses in determining who should apologise, for what, and to whom.

Restorative discourses also recognise that shame can be 'managed' and used in a positive way (Ahmed et al 2001) where the shame and regret

[2] eg in research by Keenan and Zinsstag (2022, 162), 61.3% of respondents indicated that an apology is 'never/rarely' a prerequisite for a successful outcome in sexual violence cases.

expressed through apology can promote reparation (Páez 2010). At the interpersonal level, the cycle of apology and forgiveness can be an important vehicle for managing shame and of redirecting shame from the victim to the perpetrator (Strang 2002). At the collective or intergroup level, public apologies which are given on behalf of institutions (such as church and state), as well as wider society, may have a broader role in national reconciliation and in restoring the dignity of victims (Govier and Verwoerd 2002) as well as societal trust between communities and institutions (de Greiff 2008; Herman 2023). Apologies can provide an effective means of managing 'shame' and 'self-blame' for those affected by abuses—survivors, apologisers, institutions, and wider society—providing truth for victims, accountability of perpetrators, leadership of institutions; and reimagining national or institutional identity (McAlinden 2022a). Key aspects of the potential utility of apology in addressing non-recent institutional abuses are highlighted later.

Apologies have also featured as part of symbolic reparations within transitional justice (TJ) discourses and are usually deployed as part of a broader package of measures encompassing prosecutions, truth recovery, and institutional reform (Teitel 2000). The significance of the 'transitional apology' (Teitel 2006) is said to lie in its wider 'transformative potential' (Gready and Robins 2014, 341). Apologies may function as a means of addressing state and societal accountability and aspects of national identity and values which may have underpinned abusive regimes. That is, apologies can represent a break with previous regimes and a commitment to social, political, or institutional change within settled democracies (Winter 2013; Henry 2015) as well as within paradigmatic post-conflict or post-authoritarian settings. As noted at the outset of the book, Australia (McAlinden and Naylor 2016; Gleeson and Ring 2021), Canada (Llewellyn 2002; Nagy 2013), and RoI (Gallen 2020; McAuliffe 2017a) and NI have all used a mixture of official investigations, redress schemes, and apologies in response to non-recent institutional abuses. As discussed further, however, there are latent challenges with collective public apologies for non-recent institutional abuses in terms of their transformative potential.

Apologies, law, and language

The literature on apologies and law establishes that there are manifold limitations on apologies within legal, including civil and criminal, contexts (see eg Vines 2007; Smith 2014). Apologies are potentially incongruent with legal frameworks as, by acknowledging wrongdoing, apologies also bring possible legal consequences for perpetrators and institutions. In fact, liability risk shapes not only the specific language of apologies but also the timing, sequencing, and context in which they are delivered (Cohen 1999). Furthermore, by focusing on the contested nature of 'blame', legalistic framings of remorse can also displace the moral dimensions of apology and therefore undermine the therapeutic and transformative benefits for victims (Taft 2000, 1136; McAlinden 2022b).

Official apologies by church and state actors for non-recent institutional abuses are subject to 'sanitising' processes and legal oversight by lawyers (McAlinden 2023) with the aim of diluting agency for wrongdoing or disassociating from institutional responsibility. In consequence, the human and relational aspects of saying sorry are thereby removed. Viewed in this context, the ultimate goal of apologies is not healing or closure for survivors but rather to avoid admitting legal responsibility. As a result, official apologies for non-recent institutional abuses may accept moral responsibility but stop short of full acknowledgement of wrongdoing concerning past abuses in legal, including human rights, terms. The choice of language, therefore, becomes pivotal to the construction of official public apologies.

A small body of research analysing the text of apologies by Christian churches for abuses (see eg Bavelas 2004 in the context of Canada; McAlinden 2022a; 2022b in context of Ireland, North and South) has documented a number of linguistic techniques. These include the use of: (1) the passive voice (eg avoiding the 'we' or 'I' pronouns) (Bavelas 2004); (2) oblique or euphemistic language (McAlinden, 2022b) (eg using the words 'pain' or 'hurt' rather than 'abuses' or 'harm' suffered); and (3) 'interpretative denial' (Cohen 2001)—where facts are given an alternative meaning and abuses explained by reference to the cultural context of the time (see McAlinden 2022a). This linguistic framing of abuses has a 'backgrounding effect' (Bavelas 2004, 8) in obscuring or diluting agency and the proximity of the apologiser to the abuses. It thus serves to minimise the extent of wrongdoing as well as personal or institutional responsibility for abuses.

Apology discourses have strong religious connotations with links to 'contrition', 'repentance', 'forgiveness', 'redemption', and 'reconciliation', (see eg Koesten and Rowland 2004; Celermajer 2009). However, religious rhetoric may also be used as a 'distancing tool' to 'sanctify' any wrongdoing and undermine the cause of victim/survivors (see eg Marrus 2008; McAlinden 2023). Moreover, as the theological literature makes clear, true contrition is evidenced 'not [by] a mere apology but a change in behaviour' (Pittelli 2017, 4). This is also congruent with transitional justice discourses and the broader 'transformative' potential of apologies (Tarusarira 2019). However, framing apologies without explicit reference to commitments to broader reparations or non-recurrence also means that responsibility is expressed in only spiritual or pastoral rather than legal terms (see also Gallen 2023a, 244).

3. The International Dimension

Official apologies for non-recent institutional abuses have featured in a range of countries typically as an integral part of the announcement or conclusion of investigatory processes (see Sköld and Swain 2015). This includes, for example, non-Anglophone countries such as Sweden, Finland, Norway, Denmark, Iceland, the Netherlands, Belgium, Spain, France, Chile, Poland, Switzerland, and Malta as well as Anglophone countries such as Australia, New Zealand, Canada, the United States, Scotland, England and Wales, and NI and RoI. Previous comprehensive empirical analyses of public apologies have been undertaken in the context of Australia and Canada (see Daly 2014b, Appendix 4) as well as in the broader international context including the United States, Canada, Australia, the UK, and Ireland (see Ring et al 2022, ch 11; Gallen 2023a, ch 9, Appendix 3). Building on these previous analyses, we undertook our own documentary analysis, broadening the range of countries and including examples of more recent apologies. These are used later to illustrate the thematic analysis.

Although systematic cross-cultural comparison of apologies is difficult due to the lack of empirical scholarship (see generally Renteln 2008), it is nonetheless possible to identify broad transcultural similarities and differences. In this respect, Sköld and Swain (2015, 15) argue that there are discernible 'transnational' features of apology derived in a 'transnational history' of approaches to child welfare in many countries. This they attribute partly to the fact that the ideals and practices of religious and charitable institutions, especially those of Catholic religious orders, spread across the world (see also Swain and Hillel 2010; Yeates 2011). Moreover, commonalities in the occurrence and official recognition of non-recent institutional abuses internationally can also be related to child migration and overseas adoption schemes. Children within the UK and the island of Ireland, for example, were forcibly removed from their families by the Church of England

and the Catholic Church and sent abroad (see eg Lynch 2020a; 2020b) and thereafter many suffered abuses and neglect whilst in and out of institutional care.

In addition, Catholic cultures such as France and Southern Germany were slower to recognise sexual abuses as a moral, legal, and social problem compared to Protestant or secularised cultures such as the United States, England, Canada, Sweden, Norway, the Netherlands, and Northern Germany (Chesnais 1981). Similarly, research by Melossi (2001 412) demonstrates that religion and culture shape approaches to punishment where predominantly Protestant and Catholic cultures are differentiated by punishment rhetoric based on 'strong penal repression' and 'soft authoritarian paternalism' respectively. While this argument may presuppose that Protestant cultures would be more open to formally recognising and condemning abuses, the following analysis demonstrates that this distinction is not always so clear-cut.[3] Nonetheless, as a result of these broader cultural trends, it is possible to discern similar approaches to the formal recognition of non-recent institutional abuses via apology globally and to the construction and delivery of official apologies by states and the Catholic Church in particular.

Australia, with a history of settler colonialism, has had a concentrated history of national apologies for historical abuses relating to 'out-of-home care' of children (see McMillan and Rigney 2018). This has included Kevin Rudd's 2008 national apology for Australia's treatment of 'the Stolen Generations' of aboriginal children, followed by his 2009 apology to 'Forgotten Australians' and former child migrants. In addition, further apologies were given by Julia Gillard in 2013 for forced adoptions and by Scott Morrison in 2018 to victim/survivors of institutional child sexual abuses and their families. There have also been related apologies by state leaders across all eight Australian states and territories. Similarly, Canada, as another settler or post-colonial country, has also had a lengthy history of official state apologies (Nagy 2012), including Stephen Harper's 2008 apology for the Indian Residential Schools system (see Funk-Unrau 2014) and Justin Trudeau's 2014 and 2021 apologies for the abuses of Indigenous children in church-run residential schools.

Further examples of national state apologies for non-recent institutional abuses can be found across Europe including in predominantly Protestant

[3] Within the island of Ireland specifically, abuses in Protestant institutions have been a neglected dimension of academic and policy discourses: see Chapter 1, n 20.

societies such as Sweden (Arvidsson 2020),[4] Finland,[5] Norway (Simonsen and Pettersen 2015),[6] England and Wales,[7] and Scotland (Kendrick et al 2015)[8] and within predominantly Catholic countries such as Switzerland (Baer 2016; Patrizi 2021)[9] and Belgium (Willems 2013).[10] Collectively, these analyses confirm that acknowledging previous wrongdoing is firmly rooted in the willingness of states to not only publicly disavow the ideologies or policies of the past but to simultaneously accept responsibility for the abuses of the past in the present. In some of these nations, this was evidenced, for example, by the adoption of a human rights framework, as in the case of Scotland, or by the setting up of state financial redress schemes, as in Norway.

In other countries, however, survivors have struggled to have their victimhood officially recognised by the state via apologies or statements of regret (see eg Druliolle 2018 in the context of children abducted and adopted within Francoist Spain). While there was a discernible historical reluctance by successive governments in Denmark to engage with discourses on apology and regret surrounding non-recent institutional abuses (see Rytter and Rasmussen 2015; Arvidsson 2020), an official apology to children abused in care homes in Denmark during the post-World War II era was issued in 2019.[11] Arvidsson (2020) contrasts state redress campaigns within Sweden and Denmark, both predominantly Protestant societies. An official apology for abuses in out-of-home care was issued in Sweden in 2011 as a result of the dominance of 'reparations politics' (Arvidsson 2015, 75–9).[12]

[4] See eg state apology by Sveriges Riksdag, former speaker of the Swedish Parliament, for abuses in out-of-home care, 21 November 2021.

[5] See eg state apology by Juha Rehula, former Minister of Family Affairs and Social Services in Finland, to children who suffered abuses in state-run welfare institutions, 23 November 2016.

[6] See eg state apology by Jan Tore Sanner, former government minister, to Tater- and Romani people, 1 June 2015.

[7] See eg state apology by Gordon Brown, former British Prime Minister, to child migrants, 24 February 2010.

[8] See eg state apology by Jack McConnell, former First Minister of Scotland for institutional child abuses, 1 December 2004.

[9] See eg state apology by Alphons Egli, former President of the Swiss Federal Council, for forced removal of Yenish children, June 1986 and by Simonetta Sommaruga, former Swiss Minister for Justice, for policies of removal of children from their families and forced sterilisations, 26 March 2013.

[10] See eg state apology by Charles Michel, then Belgian Prime Minister, for segregation, deportation, and forced adoption of mixed-race children during Belgium's colonial rule, 4 April 2019.

[11] Mette Frederiksen, Danish Prime Minister, 13 August, 2019.

[12] Per Westerberg, former Speaker of the Swedish Parliament, 21 November 2011.

In Denmark, in contrast, the official opposition to apology and redress is attributed to what she refers to as the 'politics of time' (Arvidsson 2020) and the preference for locating abuses within the moral framework of the past. As discussed further later, appeals to historical context—emphasising the need to avoid judging historical abuses against contemporary moral standards—continue to feature within both church and state apologies for non-recent institutional abuses. What is important, however, is that although historical context is important in understanding how practices were considered a legitimate part of care in the past, it cannot be used as a tool to avoid taking responsibility and being held accountable for practices which we now regard as abuses in the present.

Fully addressing the injustices stemming from non-recent institutional abuses entails a resolution of this 'retroactivity dilemma' (Arvidsson 2020, 159) and the need to address the enduring historical structural factors underlying abuses. Perhaps the greatest collective deficit of official public apologies, as Cuthbert and Quartly (2013, 197–8) have argued in the context of Australia, is that 'the politics of apology' tends to render the power-based structural factors underlying the abuses invisible, and especially those injustices related to not only gender but also to race and class. As Gallen (2023a, 228) suggests, such concerns may be even more acute in settler colonial contexts such as Australia or Canada where 'it may be possible to apologise for specific sub-sets of harms, such as forced child migration or institutionalisation, but may remain impossible to apologise for the structure of settler colonialization itself'. However, this argument may be extended to all societies coming to terms with the legacy of past abuses, including within the island of Ireland, which have also tended to adopt a piecemeal and reactive approach to addressing particular forms of non-recent institutional abuses.

As outlined in the previous two chapters, justice and broader 'redress' for abuses, whether in the form of official investigations or monetary redress schemes, have tended to evolve on an ad hoc basis in terms of responding to individual forms of abuses as they come to prominence within the context of media discourses and advocacy campaigns (see eg in the Australian context, Cuthbert and Quartly 2012 and McGettrick et al 2021 in the Irish context). This is also vividly demonstrated by the scattered pattern of apologies for particular abuses within individual states, as illustrated above. In this respect, as Arvidson (2015, 79) argues, citing Winter (2011), redress mechanisms such as apology may be motivated by the need to maintain or restore state legitimacy rather than the actual needs of victims. Therefore, as this book contends and as will be explored further in the final part of the book, addressing not only the abuses themselves but the broader ideological and structural frameworks which underpinned them for decades via apology or other justice responses, in a victim-centred and holistic way, is central to the conceptualisation of a new transformative justice approach to non-recent institutional abuses.

Church apologies for non-recent institutional abuses have also been offered, often in response to state apologies or around the publication of investigatory reports. However, as Gallen (2023a, 242) argues, 'Christian churches have a long and problematic use of apologies for historical abuses'. As outlined in Chapter 2, the complexity of structural features and institutional frameworks around non-recent institutional abuses on the island of Ireland—comprising church and state aspects and societal factors—can blur lines of accountability and obfuscate questions of responsibility. There have been church apologies for various forms of non-recent institutional abuses within individual countries or states issued by the Catholic Church at national, diocesan/archdiocesan, or individual religious order levels,[13] as well as a number of papal apologies relating to a range of countries.

Pope Benedict, for example, has apologised for clerical abuses during visits to Australia[14] and England and Wales,[15] and Pope Francis for abuses suffered and/or the handling of complaints in Ireland (see below), South America, including Bolivia and Chile,[16] Pennsylvania (United States),[17] and Canada.[18] Such apologies fail to meet the core elements of meaningful apologies set out earlier (relating especially to acknowledgement of wrongdoing, acceptance of responsibility, and assurance of non-repetition) and have been criticised on a number of fronts: first, for being directed to multiple audiences, including appeals to God as a higher authority, rather than to victim/survivors directly (Marrus 2008, 265; McAlinden 2023, 12); Second, for denouncing abuses, typically attributed to a few 'bad apples' or

[13] See eg apology by bishops in the Netherlands following the publication of the Deetman Commission Report (2011); A Cowell, 'Dutch Bishops Apologize for Sexual Abuses', *The New York Times*, 16 December 2011.

[14] Pope Benedict, apology during World Youth Day celebrations, Sydney, 19 July 2008.

[15] Pope Benedict, apology to victims of clerical abuses at a mass, London, 18 September 2010.

[16] Pope Francis, apology for abuses against native peoples of South America during visit to Bolivia, 9 July 2015; see M Schmalz, 'Pope Francis' Apology for Abuses in Chile Would Once Have Been Unthinkable', *The Conversation*, 17 April 2018.

[17] Pope Francis, apology in a letter to 'the People of God' following publication of the grand jury report into abuses in Pennsylvania, 20 August 2018.

[18] Pope Francis, apology to Indigenous people for abuses suffered in Catholic-run residential schools, the Vatican, 1 April 2022.

'errant clergy' (Dunne 2004, 492) rather than acknowledging the full extent of institutional knowledge, denial, and even cover-up of allegations of systemic abuses for decades.[19] More recently, during a visit to Belgium, in response to public criticisms from the King and the Prime Minister about the inadequate response of the Catholic Churches to abuses, Pope Benedict apologised for clerical sexual abuse using the language of shame, asking for forgiveness, and promising to do everything possible to make sure such abuses never occur again. However, the apology was criticised by some survivors as 'damage control' which 'will have few meaningful consequences'.[20] Indeed, as discussed further later and in the last part of the book, a central element of an effective apology, and transformative justice, is follow-through on the commitment to non-recurrence including via institutional policy reforms and changed ideologies and practices.

Although the concentration of church apologies for non-recent institutional abuses has occurred within Catholic cultures, there have been myriad national church apologies by other Christian churches including Protestant denominations in England and Wales,[21] Scotland,[22] Australia,[23] and Canada.[24] As noted earlier, the ideals and practices of religious and charitable institutions, especially those of Irish Catholic religious orders, spread across the world, accounting for a 'transnational' approach to child welfare (see Sköld and Swain 2015) and thus institutionalisation. Moreover, the higher concentration of apologies by the Catholic Church is in large part attributable to the plethora of official investigations into non-recent institutional abuses relating to Catholic institutions (eg in NI and RoI) or civil suits (eg in the United States and Australia (see Chapters 4 and 5)) which place the issue firmly in the public domain, prompting institutional responses.

[19] D Batty, 'Pope's letter to Irish Catholics, disappoints abuses survivors', *The Guardian*, 20 March 2010.

[20] EA Allen, 'Pope's Apology to Abuse Victims Rejected by Survivors' Group as "Damage Control"', *Catholic Herald*, 28 September 2024.

[21] See eg the apology by the Church of England for clerical sexual abuse, 1 March 2012; apology by the Archbishop of Canterbury, Justin Welby, following publication of the Anglican Church Investigation Report by the Independent Inquiry into Child Sexual Abuse, 6 October 2020.

[22] See eg apologies by a number of religious institutions within the Church of Scotland during the first public hearing of the Scottish Child Abuses Inquiry, 1 June 2017.

[23] See eg the national apology by the Anglican Church Diocese of Sydney to victims/survivors of institutional child sexual abuses, 22 October 2018.

[24] See eg apology by the United Church of Canada to Indigenous peoples, 15 August 1986.

4. Church and State Apologies in Ireland, North and South

Within RoI, there have been three notable state apologies for non-recent institutional abuses. The first of these was delivered by Bertie Ahern in 1999 on behalf of the Irish State to those abused as children in residential institutions, whilst announcing the setting up of the Commission to Inquire into Child Abuse and the Redress Board.[25] Although this apology was publicly praised and subsequently framed as a pivotal moment in Ahern's leadership, marking a 'transformation in attitudes',[26] Pine (2014, 22–3) notes that the apology was inexorably limited by the fact that it failed to admit for decades the full extent of Ireland's knowledge and inaction surrounding abuses in residential schools. Moreover, given that this apology was limited to victim/survivors who had been in residential institutions, some survivors, including those of black or other minority cultures or those who had attended day schools, felt excluded: 'I remember thinking, that means absolutely nothing to me. It means jack shit to me, and I began to think, why does that heartfelt apology just go over my head, and it was because I was never included' (Interview 22) and 'I wasn't included in that apology at all. That apology meant nothing, as far as I was concerned, to the day pupils' (Interview 31). This speaks not only to the limited impact of official state apologies for particular types of abuse but also, as discussed below, to broader state concerns with public audience.

This was followed by an apology by Enda Kenny to survivors of the Magdalene Laundries in 2013 following publication of the McAleese Report (IDC 2013).[27] Kenny's apology has been praised both within public discourses[28] and in the course of empirical research with stakeholders, including survivors and lawyers, as 'powerful' (Interview V) and 'impactful' (Interview K) (see eg McAlinden 2022a; 2022b). What is less discussed in academic and policy discourses is that Kenny had issued an earlier stinting apology to survivors a few days previously which was heavily criticised as

[25] Bertie Ahern, former Taoiseach (Irish Prime Minister), 11 May 1999.

[26] J Morahan, 'Ahern apology on behalf of State to abuse victims "momentous"', *Irish Examiner*, 22 July 2004; see also Judge Sean Ryan, statement preceding a CICA hearing where Ahern gave testimony, 7 May 2004.

[27] Enda Kenny, former Taoiseach, *Dáil Debates*, 19 February 2013.

[28] M O'Regan, 'Taoiseach makes historic apology to Magdalenes', *The Irish Times*, 19 February 2013.

a 'non-apology' (Eisinger 2011).[29] The second more expansive apology was subsequently issued almost two weeks later. However, in referring to Magdalene Laundries as 'our nation's shadow' and 'a national shame', he effectively 'redirects responsibility to Irish society' (Gallen 2023a, 245), and without reference to the potential influence of large religious organisations (or the State) on society itself. In contrast, the subsequent apology to Magdalene survivors by the President of Ireland, Michael D Higgins, for the 'profound failings' of Church and State and his hosting of survivors, was well received.[30]

A state apology was also issued by Micheál Martin to survivors of mother and baby institutions following publication of the Final Report of the Commission of Investigation into Mother and Baby Homes (2021).[31] Like Kenny, within his apology Martin also contextualises mother and baby institutions and the abuses therein within 'a dark and shameful . . . part of our national history' consigning the problem from the present to the darker chapters of Ireland's past. Both of these state apologies, which are derived in the language and rubric of shame, arguably demonstrate at least some acceptance of moral responsibility and self-shame on the part of the State for non-recent institutional abuses (McAlinden 2022a). However, consistent with broader state actions within RoI and elsewhere, they deliberately stop short of admitting responsibility in a fuller legal sense—principally in terms of the serious breaches of international human rights norms and the state's duties of care to its citizens—as to do otherwise would trigger the need for remedial action (see generally McAlinden 2022b).

As Smith (2020, 145) puts it, this shifting of 'blame' within the apology to either Irish society or past political administrations effectively results in 'a double displacement' of state responsibility for abuses. In addition, as noted in Chapter 5, criticism also emerged in the following weeks and months of the veracity of the Mother and Baby Homes Commission Report, including that it had misrepresented or omitted victim testimonies. As such, as a form of 'testimonial epistemic injustice' (Fricker 2007), such deficits within that report are likely to have impacted negatively on the perceived sincerity of the accompanying official apology and the extent to which it had fully acknowledged wrongdoing and abuses. As discussed later, both of

[29] S Collins, 'Kenny under fire for failure to issue full apology to Magdalene women', *The Irish Times*, 6 February 2013.

[30] '"Ireland failed you": President Higgins apologises to Magdalene Laundries survivors at Áras an Uachtaráin event', *Irish Examiner*, 5 June 2018.

[31] Micheál Martin, Taoiseach, *Dáil Debates*, 13 January 2021.

these examples underline the fact that official apologies for non-recent institutional abuses must be appraised holistically, not solely on their intrinsic merits but within the broader context of other justice responses by church and state.

As noted in Chapter 2, the official recognition of non-recent institutional abuses by church and state in NI, including via apology and 'inquiries', has lagged someway behind RoI. As a settler colonial jurisdiction, this can be attributed at least in part to the history of violent and political conflict in NI. Research has highlighted how 'the conflict' has contributed to a 'silencing' of alternative discourses on violence for decades (McCormick 2017) and impeded nuanced understandings of victimhood and harm related to sexual and gender-based violence (see eg McWilliams 1997; O'Rourke and Swaine 2017). Moreover, it can also be linked to the prevalence of a deeply conservative morality around sex and sexuality (see eg Tonge et al 2014; Ellison 2017).

There have been a number of apologies by state and religious actors, coalescing around the publication of the Hart Inquiry Report in January 2017, many of which acknowledge inadequate care rather than the systemic nature of abuses.[32] The Hart Inquiry recommended that the NI Executive and those responsible for each of the institutions where there were systemic failings should make a public apology as 'a whole hearted and unconditional recognition' that they failed to protect children (HIA Inquiry 2017, ch 4, paras 9–11). On 11 March 2022, some five years after the publication of the Hart Inquiry Report, an official apology was delivered to victim/survivors in NI by five members of the Executive, representing each of the main political parties. As noted, this official apology was based on academic research setting out the five elements of a sincere or meaningful apology (Catterall 2018) and was also constructed in consultation with survivors.

As a result, this State apology was, for the most part, well received.[33] One victim/survivor, reflecting on their experience of sitting in the Assembly Chamber hearing the apology being delivered, appraised the sincerity of the State apology by the visible emotion on the part of the apologiser:

> . . . sitting like ten feet away from the Justice Minister . . . when she was apologising. I could actually watch and hear that paper quivering as

[32] 'Historical Institutional Abuses Inquiry: Reaction', BBC News, 20 January 2017.

[33] 'Northern Ireland: Historical institutional abuses victims told "the state let you down" in long-awaited Stormont apology', Sky News, 11 March 2022.

> she was holding it. . . . [S]he was engaging at the level that we're talking about, something being meaningful and it wasn't just being meaningful to us, it was being meaningful . . . to them as well. And the same with . . . the Health Minister. He was nearly in tears, you know, you could see that and I think that impacted on our people. (Interview 9)

Other victim/survivors or their advocates, however, were of the view that the State apology 'fell short' (Interview 35) or was 'downgraded'.[34] This was attributed to the significant delay of five years after the Hart Inquiry; the fact it was a 'proxy' apology (Interview 35) as it was not delivered by the First or Deputy First Minister in the absence of a functioning Executive; and also to victim/survivors 'having to fight for that . . . we shouldn't have had to force them. They were leaving that on the long finger as well' (Interview 2). This also demonstrates the symbolic importance of so-called 'leader apologies' in the appraisal of sincerity by victim/survivors (Basford 2013).

However, the six accompanying attempts to 'say sorry' by representatives of religious orders or secular institutions, comprising mostly Catholic but also some Protestant institutions (De La Salle Brothers, Sisters of Nazareth, Sisters of St Louis, Sisters of Our Lady of Charity of the Good Shepherd, Barnardo's NI, and Irish Church Missions), were perceived less favourably.[35] They were deemed 'hollow' (Interview 35) due to their lack of emotion and ownership of wrongdoing and the use of qualification or excuses and created a 'sense of uncomfortableness' where some survivors got up and walked out of the assembly chamber as these apologies were being delivered (Interview 9). One victim/survivor attributed the shortcomings of these apologies to the lack of prior consultation with victim/survivor groups on the content of the apologies and framed them as a 'lost opportunity':

> There was no empathy, there was no understanding, there was no real 'we're really sorry' . . . Had we had drafts of the apology as we got with the State . . . we could say 'listen, it's not fit for purpose, it's not hitting the right notes, it's not saying what we want to hear' . . . and then when we heard it . . . I saw so many people in that chamber just crying, and . . .

[34] N Deeny, 'Apology prompts mixed emotions from abuses survivors', *News Letter*, 12 March 2022.

[35] C Leebody and G Hargan, 'Historical abuse victims refuse to accept "qualified" apology from church and institutions', *Belfast Telegraph*, 11 March 2022.

some of the people in the gallery were very, very upset. So, loss of opportunity. Unfortunately, it's gone. (Interview 15)

There are further examples of official church apologies to victims and survivors in NI and RoI, predominantly by the Catholic Church, which have been criticised as lacking sincerity and adequate acknowledgement of wrongdoing which often goes beyond the abuses themselves, as well as those which have been widely praised as genuine and well-meaning.[36]

In the former category, Cardinal Sean Brady, then Archbishop of Armagh and Primate of All-Ireland, apologised for his role in the cover-up of allegations made against Fr Brendan Smyth decades previously, during a mass on St Patrick's Day in 2010.[37] Cardinal Brady's apology has been criticised for its use of the passive voice and euphemistic, distancing language (McAlinden 2022a, 146). In the latter category, this includes an apology given by then Archbishop of Dublin, Diarmuid Martin, during a special 'Liturgy of Lament and Repentance' offered for victim/survivors of clerical sexual abuses where the celebrants also washed and dried the feet of eight survivors.[38] This apology was notable for the fact that it had a pronounced tone of humility and humanity within the expression of remorse, where the vernacular of forgiveness was coupled with the promise of corrective action (McAlinden 2023, 12–13). Indeed, other research on apologies has suggested that the Catholic Church 'has gotten better at saying sorry', although such 'good' apologies are often hidden from public consciousness (Ganiel and Ní Dhónaill 2024; Ní Dhónaill 2024).

However, as acknowledged later, there is a significant performative aspect to apology where the self-presentational and communicative skills, and perceived standing of the apologiser, may impact its delivery and perceived effectiveness. Following the publication of the Final Report of the Commission of Investigation into Mother and Baby Homes in January 2021, some of the leaders of Protestant churches within RoI issued apologies to victim/survivors which are also characterised by the choice of particular language, including reference to historical cultural mores. For

[36] See also church apologies issued on publication of the 'Mother and Baby Homes and Magdalene Laundries in Northern Ireland, 1922–1990' Report in January 2021 (McCormick et al 2021), such as the apology by the Right Rev Dr David Bruce, Head of the Presbyterian Church in Ireland.

[37] Armagh Cathedral, 17 March 2010. See 'Cardinal should quit, say victims of abuses', *Irish Examiner*, 17 March 2010.

[38] St Mary's Pro-Cathedral, Dublin, 20 February 2011.

example, the apologetic statement issued by the Church of Ireland references 'hypocrisy', 'judgement', and 'stigma' as part of the moral framework of the past without explicit accompanying recognition of the wrongness of such abuses and the harm and suffering they caused or continue to cause in the present.[39] Given that churches had a central historical role in shaping social morals (see Chapter 2), this also has the effect of distancing institutions from moral and ideological responsibility for abuses by separating a morally repugnant past from contemporary institutional thinking and practices.

Two of the most notable apologies by the Catholic Church for non-recent institutional abuses pertaining to the island of Ireland are those by Pope Benedict in a pastoral letter to the Catholics of Ireland in 2010[40] and by his successor Pope Francis during a papal visit to Ireland in 2018.[41] Pope Benedict's statement of regret was directed at multiple audiences—including victims and their families; bishops; priests and religious; priests and religious who have abused; children and young people; and the faithful—rather than recognising victim/survivors directly. However, the letter received mixed responses from survivors[42] and has been criticised for the 'failure to mention in any way the role of the Vatican' and the Roman Curia 'in the handling of abuse complaints' (Keenan 2012, 196). While Pope Francis's apology was broadly welcomed by victim/survivors, others were critical of the failure to specify what would be different going forward and what would happen to bishops and religious figures found to have covered up allegations of abuses.[43]

As noted, some of the state apologies were well received by victim/survivors. Previous field research conducted by one of the authors (McAlinden 2022a; 2022b)[44] and media analysis conducted for this book reveal that this can be attributed to at least two factors. The first is that in the context of the Ahern apology in RoI and the State apology in NI, these apologies were constructed, choreographed, and delivered in conjunction with victim/

[39] See press release by the Church of Ireland, 'A Joint Statement from the Archbishop of Armagh and the Archbishop of Dublin', 15 January 2021.

[40] https://www.vatican.va/content/benedict-xvi/en/letters/2010/documents/hf_ben-xvi_let_20100319_church-ireland.html, 19 March 2010.

[41] Apology delivered at a mass in Croke Park during the World Festival of Families, 26 August 2018.

[42] P Newenham, 'Mixed reaction to pastoral letter', *The Irish Times*, 21 March 2010.

[43] D McConnell, 'Apologies from the Pope simply not enough', *Irish Examiner*, 27 August 2018.

[44] See Chapter 1, n 27.

survivors.[45] It is well established that a victim-centric approach, where apologies take account of the needs and experiences of victims, is pivotal to their perceived effectiveness by victimised communities (McEvoy et al 2019, 5). This also accords with a 'hermeneutical' epistemic approach to justice (Fricker 2007), outlined in Chapter 1, where victims' experiences are made central to collective understanding and the formulation of official justice responses. Moreover, by not only consulting victim/survivors but by actively listening, apologisers may gain a deeper understanding of the other and the impact of the abuses on victim/survivors, thereby augmenting the perceived sincerity of the apology. As one senior politician in RoI reflected:

> One thing that I found useful . . . was to meet with people and families, because it's not just about what you say in the Dáil or you say publicly, it's what they get to say to you. . . . And I'm not sure how much of that is done, and . . . that's kind of an important thing . . . I kind of felt, in order to make the apology, in order for it to be sincere . . . it was important for me to hear from them. (Interview 64)

The second is that there is an unequivocal performative aspect to apology as 'performative redress' (Borneman 2005) or 'stage events' (Cels 2015, 355), where the emotional expression of shame or regret by the apologiser is often pivotal to the perceived sincerity of apologies by victimised communities. For example, victim/survivors from McAlinden's (2022a) previous research on apology praised some of the official State apologies in RoI as 'meaningful . . . [and] made with feeling' (Interview V). Similarly, the staging of the apology during the homily at mass said by Pope Francis in Croke Park on 26 August 2018 as part of his visit to Ireland was described as 'very moving . . . it meant a lot' (Interview T). Of those victim/survivors in NI who regarded the State apology or those from some of the religious orders as genuine, this was also attributed to the fact that the apology was delivered with sincerity and feeling: 'it was palpable coming from the heart' (Interview 15). For other victim/survivors, however, the absence of meaningful and tangible follow-through, in terms of the assurances of non-repetition and the offer of tangible repair, meant that such apologies are often downgraded.

In this respect, while some of these apologies by church and state leaders appeared to have been initially well received by victim/survivors, as Gallen

[45] P McGarry, 'Bertie Ahern: State's 1999 apology to abused children was "absolutely necessary"', *The Irish Times*, 11 May 2019.

(2023a, 241) contends, they have been ultimately 'undermined over time by the treatment of survivors' in other contexts. In order words, the capacity of apologies to deliver justice and accountability is potentially eroded by the lack of follow-through in terms, for example, of tangible redress (such as monetary and other forms of redress) or inconsistency of action in terms of acknowledging past harms on the one hand but refusing access to a fuller 'truth' such as survivor records on the other. Furthermore, apologies may also be undermined by what victim/survivors witness happening to other survivors who are treated unfavourably or dismissively by institutional actors. The effectiveness of official apologies in delivering justice and accountability for victim/survivors, therefore, is ultimately to be judged as a holistic process and as part of broader justice responses rather than as a single one-off event.

5. What Victim/Survivors Want from Apologies: Truth and Acknowledgement

The primary aspiration which victim/survivors held in relation to apologies for non-recent institutional abuses was the need for truth and 'victim-centred acknowledgement' (Govier and Verwoerd 2002, 74). In tandem with the broader literature on restorative justice (eg Ahmed et al 2001), apology emerged as a potential means of providing 'truth' or validation for victim/survivors by displacing their feelings of shame and self-blame and restoring their sense of personal power, identity, and human dignity (see also Murphy 2011). Furthermore, consistent with transitional justice discourses, collective public apologies also extend the truth-telling function to wider society by providing a more open account of the past (Weyeneth 2001). Put simply, 'apologies are not simply about justice; they are fundamentally about recognition and the overt removal of blame from victims' (McAlinden 2022a, 146).

Many victim/survivors conceptualised an official apology as a basic need for recognition and open acknowledgement that the abuses had happened and that they were in no way to blame. For example, victim/survivors on both parts of the island underlined the value of a public apology as the 'naming' or 'spelling out' (Govier 1999, 7) of abuses where the apology 'acknowledged them as people who had experienced certain experiences that they shouldn't have experienced, that society had treated them very badly' (Interview 6). This view was also echoed by lawyers across the island of Ireland who represented survivors: 'to make a true apology you have to recognise what was really done' (Interview K) and there needs to be 'absolute honesty about the wrongs . . . it has to be encompassing all elements of the wrong committed' (Interview Q). Other interviewees, including a Church official, explained the significance of an apology in terms of accepting responsibility and the cathartic benefits of this for survivors: 'it was about saying, look, we now accept responsibility for this. You don't have to carry this anymore. This is not about you, it's about us' (Interview J). Furthermore, acknowledgement in this sense is about recognising not only the impact of physical, sexual, emotional abuses, and neglect but also sometimes lifelong and intergenerational traumas impacting, for example, the denial of educational opportunities and the capacity to form healthy interpersonal relationships.

For other victim/survivors on both parts of the island, true acknowledgement of wrongdoing and abuses, and from the state in particular, means an apology which is explicitly framed in human rights terms: 'They denied us what I felt was a human right of an apology which was profound, unequivocal and accepted that they failed in their duty of care, and their obligations to the children' (Interview 15) and 'the Irish Government refused consistently to acknowledge that human rights were violated. We have asked for a public apology to say those words—human rights were violated' (Interview 20). To date, however, as noted, the governments on both parts of the island have failed to apologise for non-recent institutional abuses in terms which acknowledge the state's obligations to its citizens which also brings with it the responsibility for repair.

More broadly, however, the fulcrum of those apologies deemed to lack true acknowledgement is a relational disconnectedness on the part of the apologiser. Several interviewees, including a victim/survivor advocate in RoI, underlined this failing in terms of their experiences of dealing with the Catholic Church, where those apologising 'really do not understand and don't want to understand and are in denial even of the huge impact the experience of abuses has had on the survivor' (Interview I). In this respect, an apology which is perceived as genuine or sincere involves 'a common understanding of the injustice' (see Thompson 2008, 42) and involves constructing a narrative about the past which has been accepted by both victims and perpetrators. A key part of this shared understanding is that true and victim-centred acknowledgement relates to not only the systemic occurrence of institutional abuses but also the historical reluctance of the institutions of church and state to deal with such abuses.

As noted at the outset of the chapter, the literature also establishes that via genuine acknowledgement of responsibility, offending institutions, if not individual perpetrators, may also be held accountable for abuses committed in the past (see eg McAlinden 2022a). As with truth or acknowledgement, accountability, via the full acceptance of responsibility, is often perceived as the 'hallmark' of apology (Minow 1998, 115). In this respect, for some victim/survivors, holding institutions to account means that the acknowledgement of wrongdoing and abuses has to be given in public. For others, however, accountability is more appropriately evidenced at a collective rather than individual level by a public commitment to legal or policy reform. As one academic-advocate expressed it reflecting on the views of survivors:

> They will say, 'I want to see an apology but an apology means nothing without evidence of change'. So, 'I want to be able to see that this organisation is putting in place processes and structures where this can never be repeated'. And they always say exactly the same words at the end of that or close to it, 'Because I don't want anybody else to go through what we've gone through'. (Interview 3)

However, as the next two sections will explore, for a range of reasons, there is often a fundamental disconnect between what victim/survivors want and need and the response of church and state actors within apology discourses where institutional representatives may deploy a range of distancing techniques to avoid acknowledgement or being held accountable for non-recent institutional abuses.

6. Obviating Responsibility

As outlined earlier, previous research has demonstrated some of the core techniques deployed within official apologies to avoid acknowledgement of wrongdoing or accepting responsibility for non-recent institutional abuses. This includes institutional recourse to lawyers and legal oversight of apologies; and the use of specific language including religious vernacular and appeals to historical relativity (see eg McAlinden 2022b). Both of these themes found some support within the empirical research conducted for the present study. A more prominent theme, however, was the refusal of church or state actors to specify further redress.

Avoiding wider redress

Building on this literature, the deliberate avoidance of explicitly naming wider redress mechanisms within apologies is a primary technique of obviating legal responsibility for non-recent institutional abuses shared by church and state. Even the most expansive apologies may acknowledge the violation of moral norms or institutional values but may explicitly lack an awareness of harm to others including the violation of rights and the ensuing responsibility for repair. The literature affirms the importance of tangible as well as symbolic reparations where apologies without subsequent action are regarded as 'empty symbolism' (Zutlevics 2002, 63), 'empty gestures' (Govier and Verwoerd 2002, 146), or 'apology lite' (Wenger 2009). Although some survivors simply wanted acknowledgement, others in a range of contexts, including residential childcare and mother and baby institutions across NI and RoI, deemed perfunctory apologies in the absence of action and follow-through as 'lip service' (Interview N), 'not worth the words spoken, or the paper it's written on . . . worthless' (Interview 36), and 'they're meaningless, because they're not backed up' (Interview 31).

Echoing this, lawyers representing victim/survivors, in reference to some of the key state apologies for non-recent institutional abuses in both NI and RoI, also affirmed the importance of follow-through on tangible redress as well as consistency of action by church or state actors: 'you very publicly apologised at the HIA and you said . . . "This definitely happened and this is wrong." So why aren't you giving my client the apology today and why aren't you admitting liability?' (Interview 33) and 'why did you apologise if you're saying that the scheme's *ex gratia* . . . it doesn't make any sense. It's *ex gratia*, that means you're not liable so if you're not liable what are you apologising for?' (Interview 5). Wider legal forms of redress for victim/survivors include not only monetary redress or access to counselling or other support services but also access to birth and other records held by either the state or religious institutions which remains a primary and ongoing issue for many victim/survivors and their families.

To date, however, official apologies for non-recent institutional abuses have often been used, in the words of a journalist in RoI, as 'a set piece moment' (Interview 1) by the state where they are characterised by a high-profile public statement of regret without subsequent meaningful or effective follow-through. In this sense, as the literature suggests, apologies can also serve as a 'full stop' on the past (Lundy and Rolston 2016, 115) in that once an apology is issued it may actually silence survivors by closing down public discourses on broader redress. As a lawyer representing victim/survivors in RoI explained, 'they want a meaningful apology and not just a, "yeah, we're sorry that happened to you but now, go away and leave us alone", which is very much what a lot of them feel that they got over recent years' (Interview 34). This also speaks to the wider institutional and political utility of official public apologies as 'performative redress' (Borneman 2005).

Therefore, an optimal version of apologies as a vehicle for accountability for non-recent institutional abuses necessitates explicit reference to wider forms of tangible redress within the terms of the apology. This also reflects the notion of 'remedial responsibility' (Thompson 2012, 223; see also Miller 2007) highlighted in Chapter 1, and stems from the legal maxim, *Ubi jus, ibi remedium*—'where there is a right, there is a remedy'. That is, the duty of the state in particular to apologise in a legal sense and to make the offer of repair stems from a breach of its primary obligations to its citizens, including the protection of human rights (see eg O'Rourke 2011; Gallen and Gleeson 2018). While this section has explored *how* church and state may avoid the taking of responsibility for wrongdoing within official apologies for non-recent institutional abuses, the next section explores *why* by addressing institutional motivations.

7. Motivations and Barriers to Responsibility

The literature affirms that official apologies for non-recent institutional abuses are typically offered or elicited in the immediate aftermath of high-profile cases or scandal as part of 'image repair' where institutions seek to engage both individual victims and wider society (Benoit 2015). As noted, apologies offer a potential means of acknowledging individual and collective wrongdoing, validating the suffering of victims, and furthering individual and societal healing by marking a symbolic break from the past. However, questions have also emerged within public discourse concerning the adequacy, sincerity, and intent of official apologies (see eg Cuthbert and Quartly 2013). At the level of praxis, the reality is somewhat of a mixed picture. That is, analysis of the interview narratives confirms the theoretical literature that there are a number of potential barriers to accepting responsibility via apology where the motivations of elite-level actors can be attributed to consequentialist and ideological concerns. However, there were also pragmatic considerations as well as evidence of more altruistic motivations on the part of church or state actors, novel themes which have not featured within previous literature.

Consequentialist concerns: legal and financial liability

Regarding the Catholic Church and non-recent institutional abuses, several scholars have highlighted concerns about 'crisis' or 'reputation management' (Hearit 2006; Barth 2010) and the fear of widespread legal and financial liability (Tyler 1997; Alter 1999). Rather than espousing Christian values, this often leads to 'goal displacement' (Barth 2010, 784) and to 'equivocation' (Bavelas 2004, 8) or 'strategic ambiguity' (Tyler 1997, 51) in institutional communication where apologies are carefully crafted to avoid any admission of legal wrongdoing. This was the primary motivation of church and state actors as discerned by many victim/survivors. One survivor in NI explained that 'if they apologise that's admitting guilt and liability and it was all about money in the end' (Interview 2). Consistent with this view, one senior member of a religious organisation voiced the fact that institutions are mindful of public apologies and the personal and institutional risks they faced in this regard:

> We had to prepare the [members of the Order] for the fact that we were making an apology, and even at that stage, I'd say the majority of the [members of the Order] felt this was just people seeking compensation... Very often people would say, 'Look, it's not the money, it's the apology that's important'. Well, we became slightly cynical about that after a while... when the civil claims came. (Interview 23)

Similarly, for state actors, the concern is not with issuing the public apology per se but with what might follow in the aftermath of the apology. As succinctly framed by one senior politician, 'what follows from that then is state apology. You're into a process then' (Interview 68). Such fears, therefore, may result in religious institutions in particular opting for private interpersonal apologies to particular victim/survivors, delivered orally rather than in writing, in place of collective public apologies. Indeed, although such consequential concerns also have resonance within the context of other justice mechanisms outlined elsewhere in this book (see especially Chapter 4), they are arguably more acute within the construction and delivery of official collective apologies by church and state due to the overtly public nature of the apology. We found in the present study that victim/survivors often want and appreciate *both* public and private apologies: the latter in writing accompanying any monetary redress (see further Chapter 9).

Ideological concerns: audience and 'imagined communities'

A further barrier to the acceptance of responsibility by churches in particular are ideological concerns relating to the broader public audience as well as to how the church views itself. The historical reserve of the Catholic Church to offer fulsome and unequivocal public apologies for non-recent institutional abuses was related by several interviewees to its own internal constituency. In the words of one victim/survivor in NI, there is a discernible motivation to avoid public shame and the suggestion of 'any dirtiness coming from their Church' (Focus Group, Female 1). As highlighted in Chapter 2, there is often a stark contrast 'between an institution's or nation's benevolent self-image as morally pure or progressive' and the legacy of institutional abuses (see also McAlinden 2022a, 153). In the view of some members of religious orders, an apology for non-recent institutional abuses was not appropriate as they believed they had not acted wrongly when viewed within the historical and cultural context of the time. As a result, as a female member of a religious organisation explained, their religious order issued a 'statement of regret' instead:

> It's more a statement of regret probably for what wasn't done rather than an apology because some people were saying you should make an all-out apology, and I didn't feel, at the time, that that was the right thing to do that . . . That taking the [Ryan] Report and everything into consideration, that we'd done the best we could at the time we were in. (Interview 57)

This may be interpreted as the unwillingness of the hierarchical Catholic Church to fully accept responsibility for institutional abuses, resulting in what Dunne (2004, 492) has labelled a 'defeasibility' strategy—that it lacked knowledge or control of the problem. However, as discussed further in the final part of the book, these underlying motivations or concerns of religious orders also point towards the need for a reframing of discourses on accountability and responsibility. This entails moving away from blame-focused interpretations of responsibility in favour of fuller contextualised and forward-looking understandings of what it means to be accountable for non-recent institutional abuses.

In contrast, many of the state apologies for non-recent institutional abuses in RoI evoke the language of 'national shame' and make explicit reference to a radically transformed Ireland in the present and future with a new shared normative identity. Enda Kenny, for example, concludes his 2013 apology to Magdalene survivors as follows:

> Today we live in a very different Ireland with a very different consciousness awareness—an Ireland where we have more compassion, empathy, insight and heart. . . . [W]e are trying to make sure we quarantine such abject behaviour in our past and eradicate it from Ireland's present and Ireland's future.[46]

However, as one senior politician acknowledged, sometimes the motivation of state leaders is also shaped by the public audience and the expectation and demand for public accounting of the past:

> By the time they have that official apology, some of the elites have changed their hearts . . . Maybe not necessarily all of them, but you actually have to do an apology because, again, you won't get away with it anymore in the public and largely, it's due to the incredible work of the survivors and the people who support them . . . [T]here's been a reluctance, but eventually they admit it. Why do they eventually admit it, is because of the ways in which all the other different actors are trying to work towards a different outcome. (Interview 51)

As discussed further in the final part of the book, fuller acknowledgement of the historical–structural contexts of abuses, and the role of church and state therein, entails confronting and reframing their historically entrenched institutional ideologies and identities as 'imagined communities' (Anderson 1983) in the present.

[46] See n 26.

Pragmatic concerns: sincerity, sequencing, and follow-through

Both church and state actors were mindful of a range of pragmatic issues that may impact the timing and delivery as well as the perceived sincerity of official apologies. For example, one senior politician reflected on the issue of sequencing and the optimum timing of an apology—whether to apologise immediately following the publication of an official investigation report or wait to allow time for fuller reflection:

> I know there was criticism in terms of should there have been a gap between the apology. I suppose, we discussed this across government but the sense was that what was revealed was so great that, for the government to be seen to take any sense of time could have been misinterpreted as the government not facing up to the reality of this. (Interview 61)

For some victim/survivors, however, apologies may more appropriately come later, and after 'truth' or monetary redress, once the fuller extent of wrongdoing and abuses by church or state actors has been officially established and acknowledged. One State official in NI reflected on these sometimes conflicting priorities among survivors: 'there are conflicting priorities for some groups in that they, quite understandably, didn't want an apology without having redress sorted, which other groups wanted an apology, you know. "We need our apology now". So trying to find . . . that balance between what different groups and different individuals wanted' (Interview 45). Victim/survivors or their advocates in NI noted in relation to the State apology and the recommendations stemming from the Hart Inquiry that 'the synchronisation of it has been totally wrong' (Interview 15) and 'there was also cart before horse, in that . . . apologies on behalf of the State, notionally, were being given before other crucial things had been actually delivered' (Interview 35). While on one level the timely or reflexive delivery of an official apology may again reflect their performative dimension and the broader concern of elites with societal audience, it also speaks to the need for careful institutional decision-making around the choreography, timing, and sequencing of apologies as part of broader redress processes that often goes unacknowledged.

For some interviewees, including the same senior politician in RoI quoted above, there was also broader recognition that apologies on their own are inadequate to evidence sincerity on the part of the state to address non-recent institutional abuses and that they need to be evaluated holistically: 'a genuine apology at the start, but follow through, I think, is probably one of the best things a government can do in order to show . . . that there is sincerity behind an apology . . . there's a depth behind it (Interview 61).

Altruistic motivations: human and relational approaches

Benign motivations on the part of some church and state actors were evidenced by humility on the part of the apologiser and recognition of the need for an empathetic, human approach focused on the other, along with admittance of a basic level of responsibility for institutional abuses. One senior member of a religious organisation reflected, 'when we came together as a team in 1998, we said we really need to offer an apology . . . it was a rather humbling and sad event really, to recognise that the [members of the Order] had abused children' (Interview 23). Senior politicians on both parts of the island also explained how they were motivated by the need for a relational or interpersonal approach:

> When I first heard about the [case] . . . I went to [place] and wrote, I called it a poem, and said those words in my own apology because I knew it—that was my effort to try to begin to treat them as individuals and that we still have responsibility . . . So it was that approach of empathy . . . other-centredness and doing that and then, them hearing that, that showed them some of their emotion. (Interview 51)

> You only get one chance to do these things and it's important that you do it right . . . when you're trying to . . . offer up the apology that is sincere, that's genuine. It needed to address certain things that we knew that survivors wanted to get, or wanted to hear . . . so I think that was important. (Interview 72)

Several religious sector interviewees across the island, including senior Church officials, acknowledged the complexities of survivor needs and expressed an aspiration to offer what was perceived as a genuine apology by survivors:

> There's a spectrum of victims and survivors. . . . They're not all members of survivor groups. Some of them are quietly going through this journey

> and they do like to see [religious leader] going on the news and saying, 'Look, I am very sorry for what happened', and that might be their only interaction with me is through the screen. . . . The complexity of it is that every victim and every situation is different. So the mechanism of being able to offer an apology, and I've done it and I hope that the people have felt it was genuine, and it was. (Interview 69)

This highlights not only the limitations of apologies as an effective response to non-recent institutional abuses but also the very real challenges for elite-level actors in delivering official public apologies which are perceived as meaningful and sincere by a broad cohort of survivors.

8. The Challenges and Limitations of Meaningful Apologies

The range of challenges concerning the reception of official collective public apologies as symbolic reparation by victimised groups are well established within the literature. This includes the magnitude and systemic nature of the wrongs, the diversity of victim/survivors and their needs (see eg Keenan 2014; Lundy 2016), and the perceived authenticity of 'inter-temporal or historical' (Celermajer 2009, 15) or 'leader apologies' (Basford 2013) typically offered decades later by institutional representatives for wrongdoing and abuses by predecessors. In addition, as noted previously, the enmeshed historical network of 'coercive confinement' of vulnerable and marginalised groups in Ireland (O'Sullivan and O'Donnell 2012), underpinned by the coalition of church, state, family, and community undoubtedly complicates discourses on accountability and obfuscates questions concerning who bears responsibility for issuing an apology and to whom in turn any acceptance or forgiveness might be directed.[47] However, although the literature focuses on the reception of apologies by victimised groups, a broader range of challenges surrounding apologies for non-recent institutional abuses relate to not only survivors but also to those church or state actors tasked with constructing or delivering an apology. This section considers both of these dimensions.

[47] 'Forgiveness' is a multi-dimensional process that involves compassion by victims towards perpetrators but also healing for victims (Allan et al 2006) as well as elements of societal reconciliation (Shapland 2016).

An apology, for many victim/survivors, is regarded as 'a very, very important part of the healing process . . . that allows people to move forward' (Interview 9). Some victim/survivors, however, do not want an apology no matter how well it is constructed, choreographed, or delivered or may not accept it when they receive it. In the words of two victim/survivors in NI, one a survivor of residential care and the other of a mother and baby institution, 'How could I accept any apology? . . . I haven't got the capacity to accept anything that they say that might resemble an apology' (Interview O) and 'I don't want an apology from anybody . . . I wouldn't care if X made an apology to me . . . it wouldn't make any difference to my life whatsoever' (Interview R). Equally, the journey towards closure or healing for many survivors is often not static or linear so that apologies sought and accepted at one point in time might subsequently be rejected as inappropriate or inadequate. A senior Church official explained:

> There have been examples of people saying, 'I don't want court cases, I don't want any compensation. I just want you to hear my story and tell me you're sorry'. And you've done that with maybe mediation and help, and you've reached that moment. Two years later, you hear the person on the news say, 'The Church tried to palm me off with an apology', because they've now come back round on the trauma and the other parts weren't done. (Interview 69)

In this sense, experiences and perceptions of collective public apologies are subjective and highly complex (Allan and Carroll 2017) and any ensuing journey to potential acceptance (or forgiveness if that is desired) by survivors is similarly deeply personal and complex. Therefore, as Bentley (2020) contends, the 'closure' intended by apology cannot always reconcile competing intra-group tensions among victim/survivors who may seek alternative avenues of addressing wrongdoing (such as via redress schemes or civil suits) and thus perceive their justice needs or interests in broader terms beyond apology.

That said, previous empirical research on apologies also demonstrates that victim/survivors appear more likely to perceive official collective apologies as effective or sincere when perpetrators offer apologies that are 'congruent' (Cowden et al 2019)—that is, not only commensurate with their expectations but which meet their affective or emotional needs in terms of demonstrating empathy and remorse (McAlinden 2023, 15). Some writers have questioned whether it is ever possible for leader apologies to offer genuine remorse or regret on behalf of a collective (see eg Trouillot 2000; Thaler 2012). Following this literature, several interviewees, including a female member of a religious organisation and a former Church official, were sceptical of the perceived sincerity and utility of apologies delivered by institutional leaders for historical wrongdoing and abuses which they themselves did not commit: 'one of the big blockages against the acceptance of apologies . . . was that it wasn't the people who did the harm who were making the apologies . . . And no matter who stands up to make an apology for someone else, there's a gap . . . [Y]ou're only a stand-in persona' (Interview 48) and '[it] can just feel like PR speak' (Interview 18). These viewpoints not only echo the broader concerns with public audience as 'gestural' politics (Cunningham 1999, 288), but also the interpersonal and temporal gap between survivors and those apologising.

Indeed, from the point of view of the religious orders, however, aside from content, the performance and delivery of apologies are often difficult given the passage of time. For example, in relation to the church apologies to victim/survivors in NI, following the Hart Inquiry, one senior Church official reflected that 'the congregations agonised over how to do that, how to say it, who should say it. But on the day, it was nearly impossible because it's distant' (Interview 69). In this sense, public apologies which demonstrate emotion and humility and recognise the truth of the other's experience represent an attempt to connect with victim/survivors and their suffering and can overcome some of the challenges of collective apologies outlined earlier. One senior politician stated that apologies which take an 'approach of empathy . . . other-centredness' and which 'showed them some of their emotion' (Interview 51), essentially help reduce the historical distance from abuses committed decades previously and demonstrate both a proximity to previous wrongdoing and abuses and a connection to victim experiences. In this sense, victim/survivors across a range of contexts tended to appraise the sincerity of a collective apology with reference to the degree of emotion conveyed by the apologiser. As noted, in the case of the NI State apology to victim/survivors of abuses in residential care, there was a sense of 'something . . . meaningful and it wasn't just being meaningful to us, it was being meaningful . . . to them as well' (Interview 9).

In brief, therefore, the relational and expressive dimensions of apology—how it is said or delivered—are just as pivotal as the rhetorical or verbal aspects. As one senior member of a religious organisation put it, 'with the apology, more important is . . . not the words, it's the relationship that's established' (Interview P). Put another way, 'while they cannot undo past wrongdoing, apologies are an attempt at humanisation' (McAlinden 2022a, 157). Effective collective public apologies by church or state, therefore, are those which attempt to replicate the human and affective dimensions of private, interpersonal apologies at some level. Acknowledging the human emotions which lie at the heart of many effective apologies for non-recent institutional abuses also points towards new understandings of responsibility and towards enhanced accountability.

9. Conclusion: Towards Transformative Apologies

Apologies offer a potential means of meeting the primary needs of victim/survivors in terms of truth and acknowledgement of non-recent institutional abuses. However, the analysis has also highlighted that apologies are to be evaluated not only in terms of their rhetorical or verbal aspects but also their relational and performative dimensions. Here, the display of emotion on the part of the apologiser and the promise of tangible reparations emerge as key elements of the perceived legitimacy of apologies for survivors. In short, in moving beyond purely moral acknowledgement of abuses, the relational and legal dimensions of apology are important in demonstrating sincerity on the part of institutional actors and bridging what might be deemed an accountability gap for survivors.

At the heart of bridging this gap is recognition of the key limitations of apologies for some survivors as well as the particular institutional and inter-temporal challenges for apologisers in constructing and delivering meaningful apologies. For many survivors, the symbolic value of apologies is maximised not simply by saying sorry but by openness and follow-through on broader reparations. For institutional actors, a range of consequential, ideological, and pragmatic concerns may impede timely and fuller acknowledgement of abuses. Understanding these sometimes competing viewpoints lies at the heart of developing better engagement between survivors and church and state actors and more just and effective responses to non-recent institutional abuses. A senior Church official in NI reflected on this tension, 'I do believe that it's very complicated to hold, let's say a criminal, a civil, a pastoral, a redress [approach] to apology—how do you hold all of those things together, sometimes at the same time' (Interview 69). Similarly, for another Church official in RoI, there is a potential conflict within apologies 'between the pastoral approach and the legal approach' (Interview J) in terms of meeting the affective and pragmatic needs of victims. Moving towards accountability, however, involves the apologiser exposing their vulnerability in not simply emotional but also broader reparative terms (Minow 1998, 114). As one senior politician stated, reflecting on the work of the State Claims Agency which handle potential legal cases against the Irish State:

> I couldn't understand why they wouldn't just, you know, settle cases quicker, why they took this view that an apology was an admission of liability when it isn't. In my view . . . apologising and open disclosure was the best way to avoid being sued actually. (Interview 64)

On the one hand, therefore, accepting these broader considerations under which victim/survivor voices can be heard inevitably involves the church or the state opening themselves up to institutional 'risks' posed by countenancing non-recent wrongdoing and abuses with resulting benefits for these constituencies (see generally, Enright and Ring 2020).

On the other hand, however, this also points towards a broader and more nuanced meaning of responsibility in reparative contexts which implies ownership of wrongdoing in emotional and ideological, rather than simply moral or legal, terms. This suggests a better balance between the backward- and forward-looking elements of discourses on dealing with the legacy of non-recent institutional abuses—eschewing legal discourses on blame attribution for past wrongdoing in favour of an emphasis on reparation or corrective action including via changed institutional thinking and practices in the present and future. It also points to the limitations of narrow legal perspectives alone and a need to critically examine the role of legal culture in this space.

Co-designing official apologies in conjunction with victim/survivors from the outset is undoubtedly important to their ultimate legitimacy and effectiveness. However, there is an emerging additional dimension. Apologies which focus on 'others' rather than 'self', in terms of the needs and feelings of those to whom the apology is directed, are more likely to be considered effective or sincere (see eg Nigro et al 2020; McAlinden 2022b). When the apologiser truly understands what they are apologising for at an intellectual, moral, emotional, or spiritual level and truly appreciates the impact on victims by 'deep listening', then the apology is likely to be given in appreciation of the other and will thus be more likely to be considered sincere.

To be effective, therefore, apologies must be considered in a holistic way and offered in combination with other restorative and transitional justice mechanisms (see eg Teitel 2000), including monetary redress. As one victim/survivor in NI stated, reflecting on the State apology to survivors of residential care, 'it was just another piece in the jigsaw' (Interview 2). In this respect, apologies can function as an important marker and conduit for accountability by signifying a commitment to non-recurrence and enabling broader discourses on the social and structural changes which are necessary to address the contemporary consequences of non-recent institutional abuses. A 'transformative apology', as Tarusarira contends (2019, 206), is one which not only expresses remorse and acknowledges wrongdoing but 'transform[s] the social political . . . cognitive and epistemic subjectivities underpinning wrongdoing'. As explored in the final part of the book, this complex interplay of the socio-cultural, ideological, individual, and institutional aspects of responsibility for wrongdoing and abuses is key to a deeper understanding of accountability and a transformative approach to apology and to justice more broadly.

PART III

TOWARDS TRANSFORMING JUSTICE

8
Restorative, Transitional, and Transformative Justice

1. Introduction

Part II of this book examined existing responses to non-recent institutional abuses. Chapter 4 evaluated the potential and limits of conventional justice responses. Chapters 5, 6, and 7 assessed inquiries, reparation, and apologies created and implemented to address the same abuses. This analysis found a mixed picture of some value added but also significant limitations which led academics and practitioners to search for new ways of conceptualising justice. The multilayered complexity of institutional abuses suggests the need for innovative and integrated responses to address the varied, changing, and complex range of justice needs and interests in ways that are fair and just for all. Part III of this book considers the potential of models of 'innovative justice' for non-recent institutional abuses and wrongdoing, which may work in tandem with conventional justice, be independent of it, or indeed work to modify and transform it. Drawing on Daly's (2011, 9) work, we define innovative justice as 'a mixed model of responses that incorporates formal legal mechanisms, relationally focused justice interventions and civil society practices, that focus on participation rights for all parties, acknowledgement, truth-telling, accountability, reparation and healing'.

This chapter evaluates the contributions of restorative justice (RJ), transitional justice (TJ), and transformative justice towards a new way. Section 2 addresses RJ and its application to non-recent institutional abuses, including existing practices and new empirical data on its use on the island of Ireland. Section 3 considers the application of TJ to non-recent institutional abuses, exploring its effect on existing state practices regarding non-recent institutional abuses and its nascent application on the island of Ireland. Section 4 briefly considers the potential contribution of transformative justice to addressing non-recent institutional abuses. Section 5 considers

Transforming Justice Responses to Non-Recent Institutional Abuses. Anne-Marie McAlinden, Marie Keenan, and James Gallen, Oxford University Press. © Oxford University Press 2025.
DOI: 10.1093/9780191967399.003.0008

the potential relationships between these justice alternatives and Section 6 explores the shared and distinct values of each alternative towards a new justice paradigm considered in Chapter 9.

2. Restorative Justice

There is no agreed definition of RJ, described as a 'compass more than a blueprint' (Zehr 2023, 173), a lens through which to see crime and justice. At a basic level, RJ can be distinguished from criminal justice by the questions it asks. While criminal justice asks what laws were broken, who broke them, and what they deserve (mostly in terms of punishment), RJ asks who has been harmed, what are their needs, and whose obligation is it to respond? Victims of crime are at the heart of RJ (Zehr 2023, 56). Others impacted directly and indirectly (including direct perpetrators and institutional actors) are also part of the field of concern. A theory of relationality, involving the interconnectedness of individuals, communities, and institutions, ground the orientation (Llewellyn 2012). It is a humanising, harm/needs-based concept of justice as distinct from a legalistic/punitive-based one (Llewellyn 2012, 19). Despite the term 'restorative', there is recognition that many of the abuses and wrongs experienced by victim/survivors and others impacted by many abuses are 'unrectifiable' (Zolkos 2016). The aim, therefore, is to find new ways to ease the suffering, by acknowledgement, truth-telling, honesty, and human engagement (van der Kolk 2015; Keenan 2020). As Zehr (2023, 34) puts it, '[a] core element of trauma is disconnection. The road to transcending trauma is through re-connection'.

The most frequently used RJ approaches in response to institutional abuses and wrongdoing are victim/offender mediation/dialogue,[1] restorative conferences, healing circles, restorative inquiries, and restorative redress (Aertsen 2021; Keenan and Zinsstag 2022). The pillars that guide these approaches include voluntary participation; responsibility and accountability; inclusive, collaborative, and non-adversarial engagement; comprehensive and holistic understandings (taking contexts, causes, and circumstances into account); flexibility in process design; prevention of future harm; and reintegration (see eg Braithwaite 2003; Pranis 2007). The

[1] Umbreit suggests that victim-offender dialogue is a more appropriate term for the complex dialogues that take place in RJ meetings in response to serious harms, abuses, and wrongs involving unequal power relations (see Umbreit et al 2003).

moral repair work of RJ in changing the minds and hearts of identified offenders, institutional leaders, communities, and implicated subjects is seen as one of its strengths (see Ward et al 2014; Keenan and Zinsstag 2022).

Restorative justice evolved in 'hybridised forms' (Wood 2016, 1), leading to *process* definitions that focus on restorative interventions (see eg Marshall 1999; UNODC 2020) and *reformist consequentialist* definitions that focus on structural as well as interpersonal transformations (see eg Walgrave 2000; 2021). As discussed in Chapter 1, the definition of RJ adopted for this book is the reformist one in which RJ is seen as a 'movement for a higher quality of social life, governed through a better, more participatory, more inclusive, more responsive and more just democracy, promoting the cohesion of individual self-interests into a project of common self-interest' (Walgrave 2021, 324). While some argue that RJ is best confined to justice after crime (including institutional contexts of wrongdoing) (Walgrave 2023), others suggest its focus should extend beyond criminal matters to justice in the social world more broadly (Rosenblatt and Mazzucato 2023, 344; Rossner and Taylor 2024). The reformist aim is for restorative narrations at the micro level to bubble up and filter down in recursive motion to inform institutional culture at a structural level (Braithwaite and Parker 1999; Braithwaite 2007, 148) and act as a driver for policy and institutional change (Braithwaite 2007, 150).

Outcomes of RJ for victim/survivors can include a renewed sense of control, empowerment, reintegration, healing from trauma, and improved psychological well-being (Pelikan 2010; Bolitho 2015). Studies also evidence an increased perception of security for victim/survivors, greater involvement in justice processes, satisfaction with information, with the exercise of voice, validation, and accountability, and these outcomes achieved in a procedurally responsive and flexible manner (see Koss 2014; Nascimento et al 2023). Outcome studies for known offenders or other stakeholders are fewer but also demonstrate positive results (see eg Keenan and Zinsstag 2022, ch 5; see also empirical data later).

However, tensions, critique, and debates are evident inside and outside the field of RJ. As a transforming movement, RJ scholars suggest that it is not possible to transform abusive systems without transforming the contexts in which they exist (Burford et al 2019; Rossner and Taylor 2024). From this perspective, transforming institutional abuse and wrongdoing involves significant changes to legal practice and culture, criminal justice systems, family lives, and organisational and workplace cultures (see Keenan 2012; Rosenblatt and Mazzucato 2023). It also points to the necessity for accountability by actors in these implicated contexts (see eg Chapter 4, for discussion on legal culture). An important concern also expressed in scholarly work is the risk of co-option and dilution of RJ if used by institutions or governments that do not fully support a restorative ideology (Menkel-Medow 2007). There are related concerns about the true voluntariness of participants in such settings where their choice can be effectively reduced to either participation in RJ or suffering further punitive processes (Acorn 2004).

Some scholars critique RJ for its tendency to focus on the urgent needs of individuals, groups, and communities rather than more long-term structural change which has left the potential of RJ as a theory of justice itself and the structures, systems, and institutions through which justice is pursued, untapped by RJ (see eg Rosenblatt and Mazzucato 2023). Some believe retribution is incompatible with a restorative ideology and find no place for potentially punitive outcomes or agreements in RJ, while others believe punishment, and even detention, if practised in a reparative manner, can be restorative (see Daly 2013 for an overview; see also Brookes 2023). Feminist scholars raise concerns that certain offences, particularly child abuse and gender-based violence, could be privatised or minimised by means of RJ (Daly and Stubbs 2006; Al-Alosi 2021, 3), along with concerns about revictimisation and re-traumatisation of victim/survivors because of the unequal power dynamics between the parties (Stubbs 2002; Moore 2003). These critiques are also addressed in the RJ literature (see Keenan and Zinsstag 2022; Keenan et al 2025). Other critiques of RJ include that it is a 'soft' option, is coercive of victims/survivors, and prevents precedent or rule-generation (Menkel-Meadow 2007). Daly (2022) notes the need for further empirical evidence of the effectiveness of RJ for specific crime types rather than its current focus on more generic outcomes. Recent studies are filling the empirical gap in relation to sexual violence (McGlynn et al 2012; Keenan and Zinsstag 2022, ch 8).

Turning to non-recent institutional abuses specifically, Llewellyn (2002) argues that RJ may be able to address non-recent institutional abuses in ways that legal systems simply cannot because of its systemic emphasis on engagement, accountability/responsibility, and its holistic approaches that seek to address the root causes of problems from multiple perspectives. Park (2016) argues that by drawing on the approaches used in RJ, such as circles and community-based ownership of processes, RJ can help transform official narratives about historical abuse. While the South African Truth and Reconciliation Commission is commonly understood as a paradigmatic transitional justice mechanism (van Zyl 1999), that Commission also self-identified as concerned with restorative justice (TRC 1998, Vol 1, ch 5, paras 80–100). Llewellyn (2007) suggests that *restorative* truth commissions, can provide organic responses to past abuses while promoting the creation of a just future. While previously on the margins rather than within mainstream justice responses to non-recent institutional abuses, the landscape of RJ involvement in this field is now changing.

Restorative *inquiries* have been initiated in several jurisdictions to try to achieve better outcomes for victim/survivors and interested parties (Shilliday et al 2023). Restorative inquiries in Nova Scotia (Province of Nova Scotia 2019), New Zealand (Wailling et al 2019), and Canada (Llewellyn et al 2015; Truth and Reconciliation Commission Canada 2015) are well documented. Several principles identified for restorative inquiries emphasise inclusion, co-design, participation, dialogue, transparency, truth-telling, information-sharing, accountability, and specific care for the needs and interests of victim/survivors,[2] similar to RJ principles outlined earlier. Vegh Weis and Cunneen (2024) examined the intersections of truth commissions, RJ, and Indigenous peoples and concluded that such approaches provide a useful means for creating new narratives on human rights violations. Daly and Stubbs (2006), however, caution that RJ has been imposed on some Indigenous communities and care must be taken that RJ is not used to uphold neo-colonial power dynamics. Restorative *redress* schemes have also been developed in many parts of the globe including in Belgium, Switzerland, and the Netherlands (see Aertsen 2021; Patrizi 2021).

In the Republic of Ireland (RoI) and Northern Ireland (NI), several RJ initiatives have been established by the Catholic Church and some NGOs across the island in response to non-recent abuses. Towards Healing,[3] a counselling and support service for victim/survivors, funded by the Catholic Church, operated a facilitated listening/RJ service for victim/survivors between 2011 and 2019 and facilitated 75 cases and two healing circles. Evaluating the service, Kennedy (2013, 3) noted that victim/survivors felt the meetings gave them 'a platform to seek and achieve some closure, to be listened to, in some cases receive an apology and the opportunity to seek assurance that procedures had been put in place to prevent such abuse occurring now or in the future'. One in Four, a therapy and advocacy service

[2] See M Keenan and I Marder,' Restorative inquiry would put survivors at the centre of response to school abuse', *The Irish Times*, 28 February 2023.

[3] Towards Healing, https://towardshealing.ie/.

in RoI for victims of sexual abuse, offered RJ services between 2012 and 2016. It facilitated 26 cases, most of which appeared to be within a family context.[4] Empirical data on encounters between survivors and Church leaders were noted in the current and other studies (see eg Keenan et al 2016). The scripted model[5] used by One in Four was seen as a limitation. As one Church leader noted, 'Had I been on my own with that man . . . things would have worked better . . . [T]hey kept interrupting with questions and asking this and in the end, I was unable to establish a personal relationship with the other person' (Interview P).

Restorative justice schemes were also established by two religious organisations in RoI in response to non-recent institutional abuses in elite boys' day schools. The first comprised three aspects: (1) facilitated dialogues between survivors and institutional members on issues identified by a survivor-led consultation group (Walshe and O'Connell 2019); (2) a narrative historical record of the abuses perpetrated by one member of the religious organisation (see Joint Past Pupils—Jesuit Steering Group 2024); and (3) a redress scheme based largely on civil mediation principles (see Jesuit Province 2024). The second programme, developed between a group of past pupils and the religious organisation involved restorative conferences between victim/survivors, institutional leaders, and other relevant persons (see Spiritan Education Trust 2022) and at the time of writing a restorative redress scheme is being designed by a collaboration of the victim/survivors and the religious order.[6] Some further RJ initiatives also included non-documented healing circles for the members of the religious orders themselves.[7]

Scholars both give weight to and problematise the resonances and principles shared by RJ and Catholic theology, including repair of harm, transformation, and reconciliation (where applicable) (Gavrielides and Coker 2005; Gleeson and Zanghellini 2020). Some see RJ as suited to accountability-taking by the Church (Noll and Harvey 2008), to healing and rehabilitation of the institutions (Doyle 2014, 177), and to provoking

[4] See One in Four Annual Reports 2012–2016, https://www.oneinfour.ie/annual-reports (accessed 1 June 2024).

[5] For a full understanding of the various approaches and models used in RJ dialogues, see Keenan 2018.

[6] See Blackrock College Union, 'Update on Process to Support Victim/Survivors of Sexual Abuse in Spiritan Schools' (2024), available at https://www.rockunion.ie/news/news-from-past-pupils/416/416-Update-on-Process-to-Support-VictimSurvivors-of-Sexual-Abuse-in-Spiritan-Schools (accessed 10 October 2024).

[7] Marie Keenan was involved in this work.

institutional cultural change (Foley 2019). A genuine commitment on the part of the Church to repair the harm and avoid recurrence is deemed necessary for the success of RJ in those contexts (Knoll 2021). In evaluating a variety of responses to sexual abuse within the Dutch Catholic Church, Ormskerk et al (2024) found that when assessed through the theoretical lens of procedural justice too little space was afforded to the voice of victim/survivors; when assessed through the restorative lens the responses were too individualistic, failing to integrate the systemic aspects of the problem at institutional, societal, and familial levels (see also Aertsen and Schotsmans 2020).

Turning attention to Magdalene Laundries, while academic and media analysis point to critiques of the promise of RJ as part of the Magdalene Commission Report in RoI in 2013,[8] empirical data gathered for this book point to the 'good efforts' of the chairperson in meeting survivors to understand their needs and interests, aided by female barristers who were trained for the work by a victim/survivor. One lawyer noted, 'I think the Magdalene Commission was a good effort . . . at the restorative idea' (Interview 21).

Following the example of the Australian Defence Force (Vernon 2017), the IRG Report (2023) of the Irish Defence Forces recommended a RJ service be established within the Irish Defence Forces to respond to allegations of institutional abuse and wrongdoing and to drive cultural change. At the time of writing, the service had not been established. In NI, restorative justice initiatives have been developed by the Catholic Church in individual dioceses and religious organisations on a case-by-case basis but, in general, restorative justice initiatives in response to non-recent abuses are less developed in NI than in RoI as the examination of these issues lags somewhat behind RoI.

To address a gap in knowledge regarding the extent of RJ being practised by religious organisations and dioceses in response to non-recent abuses across the island of Ireland, a RJ survey was developed for religious organisations and dioceses as part of the current study. As noted in Chapter 1, while the sample responses of 25 cannot be considered representative, taken together with our interview data,[9] they nonetheless illuminate the uses of

[8] M O'Rourke and J Smith, 'Magdalene Survivors are still waiting for Restorative Justice', *The Irish Times*, 6 February 2014.

[9] Quotations from interviews are cited as (Interview X), quotations from the survey are cited as (Respondent X).

RJ by Church personnel, the information gaps, the untapped potential of RJ, the positive outcomes for institutional leaders who participated, the interest in RJ going forward, and recommendations for implementation.

Interview data indicated a range of approaches being practised by some religious organisations and dioceses in this space, including victim/offender dialogues, restorative conferences, healing circles, restorative inquiries, and redress schemes. In contrast, there was also a general lack of awareness of RJ among many interviewees and survey respondents, consistent with findings reported in other studies (see Keenan 2014; Keenan et al 2023). The knowledge gap on restorative and innovative justice existed amongst legal and criminal justice professionals as well as more generally. Yet, the untapped potential of RJ in response to institutional abuses also emerged as a strong theme.

One victim/survivor who saw the potential for RJ in terms of accountability acknowledged a potential barrier to institutional engagement: 'I think the institutions need to be treated carefully and with considerable respect . . . [T]hey're being driven into defensive positions that they may not necessarily want to be in' (Interview 2). Survivors in the Irish Defence Forces were happy that the IRG Report (2023) recommended RJ but believe the Irish Defence Forces are not open to restorative conversations with victim/survivors. Despite this, one survivor wanted an opportunity to 'look the perpetrator in the eye' and ask him 'Why did you do that? Why did you do that to me?' (Interview 66), noting that this would give her closure. Victim/survivors and advocates saw the potential in RJ to get answers to questions: 'that's what survivors ask all the time, why . . . That's what they want to know—why did you do this?' (Interview 4). Church personnel saw RJ as 'a great opportunity for the Church to learn from the humility of these processes' (Respondent 21) and as creating the 'conditions for a "reckoning with the past"' (Respondent 18).

None of the victim/survivors interviewed for the study had been offered or participated in RJ but many Church personnel had done so and highlighted several important positive outcomes for them. This included increased openness leading to greater institutional accountability:

> [W]e . . . never had the experience of talking to so openly about issues like this among ourselves and . . . even though it was very painful because the issues are very painful, it was very refreshing. You can almost sense when people are being authentic and being honest. (Interview 56)

The shift in power dynamics that occurred during RJ meetings was another benefit:

> The agenda was largely created by those who had been abused and the [name of Order] responded to this. Restorative meetings were . . . transformative experiences. One of the big outcomes . . . was moving from central ownership of the problem to ownership by the wider [religious] community. They read testimonies in advance of meetings and realised the need for accountability. Another outcome was that it increased their trust so that they shared more openly with victims about what they knew and recalled. (Respondent 18)

Being 'present' and listening so that 'people feel heard' (Interview 58) meant for Church personnel that 'there was a sense of treating people fairly and being able to formally apologise to them for their experiences' (Respondent 9). Members of religious organisations gained 'a clearer knowledge of the extent of the abuse and its impact' (Respondent 2) and from their perspectives RJ meetings also 'created a transparent and open line of communication'. One member of a religious organisation who met face to face with a victim/survivor reported that 'he was quite challenging to the institution and to me . . . but he was also just at a human level so affirming . . . I had a sense of healing . . . I could feel my defences melt . . . [H]e got back to me afterwards and . . . was so appreciative of our meeting' (Interview 56). A State official in RoI noted that 'the practice around [RJ] is really positive . . . [T]he punitive is always . . . much more headline grabbing . . . kind of black and white in terms of goodies and baddies . . . but in terms of actually sustaining a solution and delivering a feeling of being . . . justified in and recognised and seen, that's a much more powerful option' (Interview 55). As discussed further, these viewpoints collectively highlight the significance of the micro interactional aspects of RJ at a relational or human level as well as the centrality of trust in determining levels of engagement between survivors and institutional actors and the implications of these processes for structural change.

Furthermore, there was interest in a role for RJ going forward as an alternative to 'engaging in adversarial . . . processes' (Respondent 6). This potential of RJ as an alternative to formal law was also recognised by a variety of interviewees. State officials in NI commented that there was 'room to develop that thinking a bit further' (Interviews 46). Criminal justice professionals in NI saw real value in the potential of RJ for victim/survivors as 'there is often not a lot else for them by means of a criminal justice response' (Interview 71) or because of its 'relatively unsatisfactory conclusion' (Interview 60). One lawyer in RoI believed that victim/survivors are 'looking for a safe space in which these conversations can take place. Certainly, in the adversarial system, cross examination . . . is a very unsafe space indeed' (Interview 21). A professional victim/survivor advocate in RoI believes victim/survivors and religious organisations are open to RJ. One lawyer in NI saw potential for involvement of victim/survivors with institutional actors if they were 'willing to engage on a genuine level' (Interview 34). Despite this, the Report of the Scoping Inquiry into Historical Sexual Abuse in Day and Boarding Schools Run by Religious Orders (Scoping Inquiry 2024) refrained from recommending that a RJ service be established for victim/survivors of day and boarding schools in RoI. Instead, it recommended a feasibility study, thus long-fingering the initiative, despite some victim/survivors requesting an RJ service. Seen as a lost opportunity that also was in conflict with government and Department of Justice policy to support the provision of restorative justice at all stages of the criminal justice system, there have been calls for government to reject this recommendation[10] (see also further critiques of the Scoping Inquiry in Chapter 5). Changes in ideological thinking on the part of key professionals and institutional leaders that can develop in restorative encounters is an integral part of broader structural and social change and is central to transforming justice approaches in this space, as highlighted later and considered further in Chapter 9.

The empirical data also points to how RJ could be implemented, including the importance of institutional leadership: 'Fundamentally the attitude and values of the leadership within a diocese is critical in determining the culture and approach' (Respondent 9). Those who had been involved in restorative responses also note the need for enhanced victim supports alongside RJ or that it be 'combined with restitution' (Interview 69) (see further Chapter 9). One State official in RoI agreed: 'there's three . . . separate areas . . . the restorative justice which is acknowledgement that somebody has suffered hurt because of somebody's failings . . . the question of some kind of apology and financial gesture' (Interview 62). One religious

[10] See M Keenan, 'The Government should go beyond the Scoping Inquiry recommendations on restorative justice', *The Journal*, 10 September 2024, https://www.thejournal.ie/readme/restorative-justice-6483049-Sep2024/ (accessed 10 October 2024).

organisation noted what it learned: '1. Important to have a skilful facilitator; 2. Time given needs to be flexible so that the victim has ample time to tell their story and get the feedback they deserve. 3. It would be helpful to have a victim-friendly redress scheme in place before the RJ process begins' (Respondent 2). Others, including a criminal justice professional in RoI, emphasised the need for RJ 'to be done and accommodated within an environment . . . that can support that' (Interview 44), including with adequate resources. Religious organisations pointed to the importance of authenticity in RJ and the need for integrity in facing the challenges of the temporal aspect of abuse including the challenges for all parties, especially survivors, who are meeting someone 'who wasn't there and who's not going to pretend to know what [the survivor] went through' (Interview 48). This challenge is explored further in Chapter 9.

In summary, advocates contend that RJ enables a different type of justice not constrained by legal criminal parameters when the abuse/wrongdoing occurs in an institutional context. While not 'a panacea' (Al-Alosi 2021, 3), RJ offers constructive whole system, human justice responses to the range of justice needs and interests that arise in these complex contexts. Despite the carceral impulse towards more legalistic and punitive responses, Braithwaite (2007, 148) argues that RJ offers greater possibilities than more punitive measures for building institutional and state legitimacy and restoring victims' rights. By combining restorative values with other innovative justice perspectives, as part of the ongoing mutual learning between fields such as TJ (discussed below) (and with those aspects of conventional justice that are valued), new ways of doing justice and being accountable can be conceptualised that centre victim/survivors, include all stakeholders, and go some way towards overcoming the limitations of each single justice conception (ideas we take up further in Chapter 9).

3. Transitional Justice

Transitional justice is defined by the United Nations as:

> the full range of processes and mechanisms associated with a society's attempts to come to terms with a legacy of large-scale past abuses, in order to ensure accountability, serve justice and achieve reconciliation. These may include both judicial and non-judicial mechanisms, with

> differing levels of international involvement (or none at all) and individual prosecutions, reparations, truth-seeking, institutional reform, vetting and dismissals, or a combination thereof. (UNSG 2004, 4)

Transitional justice elements reflect the rights of victim/survivors in international human rights law (Ambos 2009; Gallen 2019a) and as a result should not be seen as optional or discretionary but as reflective of a state's international legal obligations. In addition, each mechanism is designed to make a primary contribution to its specific goal, including truth and accountability reparation but also a secondary contribution to the restoration of trust and the rule of law for those most affected, victim/survivors, and for society as a whole (de Greiff 2010; 2012). Recent TJ policy emphasises mental health and psychosocial supports for victim/survivors to add further goals of rehabilitation and non-recurrence of violence (Hamber 2023).

Transitional justice developed in the late 1980s and early 1990s and focused on how societies addressed large-scale human rights violations, during a period of change from dictatorship to democracy, later expanding to address the transition from armed conflict to peace (Arthur 2009, 355). Transitional justice can be understood as having backward- and forward-looking dimensions, addressing past harms to victim/survivors and seeking to guarantee future non-recurrence of violence (Mihr 2021; Welre and Vormbaum 2022). In addition, it can be framed as a 'top down' exercise of centrally controlled, state-led policy and also as a 'bottom up' exercise in grassroots social movements (Lundy and McGovern 2008; McEvoy and McGregor 2008). As a concept, TJ recognises that widespread or systematic abuses and wrongdoing require a distinctive whole system response rather than one that focuses on isolated criminal offences (Van Zyl et al 2000, 46–7). It can be framed as a distinct application of justice (de Greiff 2010) or as operating on the end of a spectrum that spreads from single offences to widespread abuses (Posner and Vermeule 2004).

As TJ expanded to post-conflict societies and beyond (de Greiff 2020, 254), amid limited effectiveness of its measures and institutions, the field moved into a 'premature mid-life crisis' and scholarship became increasingly reflective and self-critical (Bell 2009). The field has thus been criticised as not addressing root causes of violence, including socio-economic rights issues and causes (Nagy 2008; Gready and Robins 2014), as being of limited effectiveness when subjected to empirical evaluation (Balasco 2013, 211), and as disadvantaging women and girls in its implementation (Kent 2016, 3). Balint et al (2014, 200–1) suggest that the concept of TJ is limited in its ability to address structural harms, especially for non-recent intergenerational injustice. It has also been criticised as being indifferent to context, formulaic, and technocratic (de Greiff 2020, 255).

Amid expansion and self-criticism, the application of TJ to non-recent (institutional) offences in settler democracies has emerged principally in the contexts of Canada (eg Nagy 2013) and Australia (eg Balint et al 2020), while Gallen (2023a) has considered TJ as an evaluative framework in the contexts of non-recent abuses in Ireland, the UK, the United States, Canada, and Australia. A range of justice mechanisms that respond to allegations of non-recent institutional abuses have been assessed as TJ mechanisms or at least as 'mimicking some of the forms of transitional justice' (McAuliffe 2017b, 455), including the Ryan Commission in RoI (McAlinden 2013), the National Inquiry into the Separation of Aboriginal and Torres Strait Islander Children from Their Families (Henry 2015), and the Hart Inquiry in NI (Hamber and Lundy 2020). Some scholars (eg Murphy 2017, 44, 75–8; Balint et al 2014; 2020) suggest that the application of TJ depends, among other factors, on the existence of sufficiently unjust and harmful conduct. In this sense, Winter (2013) notes that TJ has the potential to repair the political legitimacy of the state in addressing such conduct.

Beyond its use of justice mechanisms to address victim/survivor needs, TJ is concerned with social change, conceived of as a transition, with the original understanding of transition referring to the shift from authoritarian rule to democracy (Teitel 2000, 13). However, rather than be exclusively focused on those contexts, TJ can be understood as a harm-centric application of justice to a situation of a seismic breakdown of rules and law-compliance and occurrence of widespread or systemic harms (de Greiff 2010; Henry 2015). Nonetheless, a single paradigm of TJ 'ignores the problem that human rights abuses may continue to take place in circumstances where, in theory at least, the norms of liberal democratic accountability prevail' (Lundy and McGovern 2008, 273).

In RoI, existing scholarship considers the possibility of recent justice mechanisms, such as inquiries, apologies, and redress, considered in Part II, as contributing to a broader social change, thus framing them as making a contribution to TJ. As noted in Chapter 5, inquiries have broader societal aspects including signalling a change in societal values and restoring confidence in justice systems (McAuliffe 2017b) and influencing our understanding of abuse and trauma (Gleeson and Ring 2021). Similarly, Smith (2020, 142, 150) affirms the potential for access to archival evidence as a means of truth-telling about the past that challenges 'the state's readiness to unknow what it knew about institutional abuse'. In this sense as McAlinden (2013, 213) suggests, inquiries in RoI form part of a 'regime change' where officially addressing abuses 'offers a unique opportunity to make a permanent break with the past'. Despite this potential, as Earner-Byrne (2011, 51) has pointed out, there is the absence still of 'any real "national conversation" regarding the ways in which Irish society as a whole facilitated "the system" that ultimately violated the rights of poor families and led to the abuse of so many children'.

In considering the potential usefulness of a TJ framework, Rubio-Marin (2022, 141) argues that Ireland represents an 'unfinished democracy' in need of further transition: 'a state/church/patriarchal regime that treats women as second-class citizens, imposing on them a gendered moral order, including through violent methods, cannot be but an unfinished democracy so that the self-reflective effort to overcome it can indeed be identified as a constitutional moment for the country'. Relatedly, Ní Aoláin (2022, 154) suggests that resort to TJ in societies where the rule of law applies, such as RoI and NI, represents a paradox, given the field's origin and creation in circumstances of gaps in legal and political capacity in authoritarian societies. As a result:

> There is a grave danger that the state may view its remedial work as done by enabling a truth-recovery process and not address the legal lacunae exposed by decades of largely unrewarded legal challenges in the Irish courts by individual victims . . . [T]he legal responsibilities of those institutions and legal processes are not displaced by invoking transitional justice, even if transitional justice tends to occlude those obligations in the short term. (Ní Aoláin 2022, 155)

Thus, while there is cautious interest in the potential of TJ to reframe issues of non-recent abuses as human rights concerns, O'Donnell et al (2022, xvi) express concern that 'the language of transitional justice may be co-opted by the state to justify offering a "specialised", selective, and limited justice model that in fact stymies accountability by denying access to established "democratic" institutions such as the courts, the coroners' system, academic research and cultural and artistic expression and participation'.

Neither governments in RoI nor NI have adopted an explicitly TJ approach to addressing non-recent abuses, with the exception of a former Irish Minister for Children and Youth Affairs (Zappone 2020) who pursued a TJ approach to addressing the needs of mother and baby institution survivors through the establishment of a Collaborative Forum of victim/survivors in 2018. The intended purpose of the Forum was to 'enable survivors to identify, discuss and prioritise the issues of concern to them, and facilitate their active participation in recommending actions and solutions to address those concerns' (Collaborative Forum Report 2022, 5). The Forum report made 44 recommendations across the areas of identity and terminology, healthcare and well-being, and memorialisation and personal narratives.

However, this collaborative approach was fatally undermined by the Irish government's multi-year refusal to publish the Forum's report. Having raised expectations for meaningful survivor engagement, the failure to publish the report significantly damaged trust between survivors and the Irish State, with several survivors resigning from the Forum in protest at the failure to publish.[11] One interviewee was critical of the government but noted the potential for broad collaboration as the basis for an innovative conception of justice:

> We had the Collaborative Forum which was a farce in that the government didn't even publish our report, it took Mr O'Gorman to do that. But when you have a collaboration of human rights lawyers, Irish constitutional lawyers, academics, researchers, survivors and other representatives then I think you begin to . . . maybe work out a road map for what true justice looks like. (Interview 20)

Another survivor stated regarding the Collaborative Forum:

> [T]hat seemed like a really good idea, you know, and all of us who joined really engaged with it . . . it was really very evenly divided. As I said, you had the mothers, you had the adult adopted, you had ex-industrial school, and you had advocates for some very elderly people. So it was a really good mix and everybody, we learned to work really, really well together, and recognising that we all had very different skills which we shared amongst us . . . So it was a real shame that, once again, the government did us down. It really was, because you had some great minds in there, great experiences. (Interview 22)

[11] O Ryan, 'Mother and Baby Homes: Collaborative Forum's report to finally be published—after years of delays', *The Journal*, 11 November 2022.

A further survivor and former of member of the Forum stated:

> [O]ne of our chief recommendations from that Forum and for my part on that Forum, will be realised when the National Commemoration Centre is developed at Sean McDermott St which is the exact place where my mother lived for all those years. So that means an awful lot. (Interview 65)

Despite this chastening and nascent experience of TJ, some participants spoke about the field's potential as a justice alternative. One participant noted the potential for alternative models of inquiry:

> I wonder is there some scope for some sort of truth and reconciliation forum where people can, where things can be spoken about publicly. . . . I do think if there's some way people can be encouraged to speak to their experiences, and I think that's the same of the Church, whether or not they'd be willing to do that I don't know. (Interview 1)

Other participants, including a victim/survivor, recognised that the existing application of TJ-like measures in RoI was problematic: 'the four pillars of transitional justice are haphazardly included in such a mealy-mouthed way that you know, it's not effective at all' (Interview 20). One academic-advocate noted the potential for TJ as a more holistic approach: 'it's a way of proceeding, it is not specific specialised mechanisms alone, you may have additional ones, you may have forums that didn't exist before that, which are temporary, or new kind of permanent ones' (Interview 4). As a field of justice that purports to be victim/survivor-centred, the same interviewee noted the risk that TJ functions as a site of exclusion:

> The thing it should not be . . . fundamentally is a way of excluding people who have already been disenfranchised from all the democratic justice mechanisms that like Irish society understands to operate normally and that it being, you know, a 100-year old democratic state has actually developed . . . [F]or me, one huge issue is that transitional justice should not mean solely specialised responses. It should actually mean you taking to task, like taking our existing institutions and having them respond in transitional justice i.e. human rights-based manner so that they are changed for the future. (Interview 4)

One senior politician, while emphasising the central capacity of TJ to address questions of responsibility and accountability, noted the challenges in adopting a state-led approach to TJ in RoI addressing non-recent institutional abuses coherently:

> [T]here's Tulsa, there's the Adoption Authority, there's the Department of Health, there's the Department of Education, the newly created Department of Children, and this is what I found then—who is the State? The State is all of these bodies, actors and if that is the case, and if you want an appropriate response from the State, then you need all of them to work together and collaborate. (Interview 51)

In NI, there has been significant application of TJ theory and practice in the context of the conflict (Lawther 2018b; Bryson and McEvoy 2023). To date, there has been limited scholarly focus or practice from a TJ perspective regarding non-recent institutional abuses. Lundy's engagement with victim/survivors of non-recent institutional abuse (Lundy 2016; 2017) builds significantly on her earlier 'bottom up' TJ work in the context of the conflict (Lundy and McGovern 2008). Lundy (2022, 16) noted the potential and limits of activist research in NI: 'spaces can be created to enable survivors to mobilize more effectively to challenge power and bring about social change. When challenging powerful institutions, the odds are usually stacked against activists.' Similarly, Hamber and Lundy (2020, 760–4) affirm the possibility of TJ to add value to addressing non-recent institutional abuses but also to replicate some of the limitations and criticisms of that field in a new context. The authors outline five areas of note, with potential and risk, drawing from TJ: prioritisation of victim/survivor needs, drawing on thinking beyond TJ, preventing the instrumentalising of victims, supporting grassroots advocacy and initiatives, and constructing systemic narratives of the past.

In terms of practice, NI arguably holds more feasible potential than RoI as the 'integrated truth investigation' model (Mahon et al 2021; as discussed in Chapter 9) offers a concrete alternative justice practice, contrasted with the use of a more traditional inquiry model in RoI. Transitional justice thus offers a distinctive contribution to non-recent institutional abuses, both theoretically and in practice, rooted in centring victim/survivor justice needs and recognition of their status as rights-holders but this contribution is one that is often hard-fought and imperfect in its application.

4. Transformative Justice

Partly in response to the criticisms of RJ and TJ, transformative justice emerged as a movement with abolitionist roots with some focus to date on addressing race and gender-based violence (Morris 2000; Rojas et al 2011). It is rooted in the political analysis of systems of power. Transformative justice processes always function outside formal justice systems (Kim 2018), unlike RJ and TJ which are practised in both community and state systems and settings. Gready and Robins (2014, 340) define transformative justice as 'transformative change that emphasizes local agency and resources, the prioritization of process rather than preconceived outcomes and the challenging of unequal and intersecting power relationships and structures of exclusion at both the local and the global level'. As Kim (2018, 226) notes, '[r]ejecting the criminal justice system as primarily responsible for the violent oppression of marginalized communities, transformative justice responses to gender violence and other forms of interpersonal or community violence seek resolutions within more intimate systems of community or civil society' (see also Cullors 2019). Transformative justice's emphasis on community or grassroots responses also focuses on community accountability (Kim 2010).

Proponents of the transformative justice paradigm critique RJ for neglecting the social and structural oppression in which wrongdoing occurs and macro-level social and structural change (see Coker 2002, 129; Nocella 2011). However, Harris (2007) notes that, properly understood, RJ and transformative justice both aim at interpersonal *and* social/structural transformation. As others point out, much remains to be done to achieve RJ's fundamental commitment to transformation (see Gal 2020; Llewlyn 2021, 379). Proponents of the transformative justice paradigm also point to legalistic and formalistic existing practices of TJ and suggest either fundamental reform of the goals and methods of TJ or its replacement with a transformative justice framework (Robins and Gready 2014). Despite such critique, the bottom-up approach to and practice of TJ (Lundy and McGovern 2008) reflects much of the concerns and critiques of transformative justice within a TJ paradigm, particularly with regard to incorporating the 'voices from below'.

While transformative justice discourse has prompted consideration of radical reform or replacement of RJ and TJ approaches, it has offered limited consideration of obstacles to such change or consideration of its feasibility in practice (Sharp 2019, 583). It is equally unclear whether and how the abolitionist roots of transformative justice operate in the context of non-recent institutional abuses, particularly child sexual abuse. In delegitimating state-led enterprises, a transformative justice approach may compromise a desire for a multi-stakeholder approach involving victim/survivors and allegedly responsible state and church organisations and representatives. In a context of information asymmetry, with state and church holding significant data and records relevant to victim/survivors, and church and state actors seeking to re-legitimate church and state institutions, future and ongoing state and church involvement with victim/survivors in finding new pathways towards justice appears necessary and inevitable. While transformative justice can inform justice alternatives for non-recent institutional abuses, it requires significant adaptation, reflection, and feasible practices, including within the context of non-recent institutional abuses.

5. Relationship between Different Justice Paradigms

Each justice paradigm offers value within the context of non-recent institutional abuses. Restorative justice's emphasis on interpersonal and structural transformation through a systematic approach to justice that centres victim/survivors and includes all voices offers a non-adversarial, granular approach to filling the responsibility and accountability gaps evident in conventional justice approaches. Transitional justice centres the participation of victim/survivors in a similar holistic approach to justice practices but is distinct in predicating all justice processes on the recognition of victim/survivors as rights-holders and on responsible actors as duty-bearers, including duties to pursue investigation, accountability, and reparation. Both RJ and TJ mechanisms claim to contribute to meeting victim/survivor justice needs and interests, as described in Chapter 3, and both engage with state and legal systems to achieve their aims. Restorative justice aims to transform state and criminal legal systems by filtering outcomes of restorative justice processes upwards (Braithwaite 2007) but mechanisms to do so have not been adequate to date. Transitional justice does not reject adversarial approaches to law to achieve its aims and may engage the resources of the state and defence of rights of all stakeholders offered by legal advocates but as a result may risk creating sites of exclusion and authority in how to address the past (Evans 2018; Gready 2019, 21).

In contrast, transformative justice proposes more radical and systemic reform, designed to address the historical and structural root causes of violence (see Chapter 2) and in so doing problematises and implicates existing social, political, and legal structures, including conventional justice systems. Restorative and transitional justice can thus learn from transformative justice in enhancing their structural transformative endeavours. As a theory, however, transformative justice remains in need of a theory of change (but see Gready and Robins 2020) that can address questions of political feasibility and foreseeable resistance.

A variety of possible relationships exist between these conceptions of justice. The existing influence of RJ on TJ is well documented (Lambourne 2009; Clamp 2016), though there remain calls to more deeply incorporate RJ principles into TJ practices (Braithwaite 2016; Waldorf 2021). In turn, TJ theories and practices may prompt greater consideration in RJ of complex victimhood or of the role of the state in social conflict (Clamp 2019; Lawther 2022). Restorative and transformative justice may be understood as distinctive, or as entirely overlapping, with some suggesting they operate along a spectrum and that RJ practices have transformative dimensions when engaged with broader conflicts, communities, and social structures (Harris 2007, 556; Llewellyn, 2021). Transitional justice and transformative justice have a variety of potential relationships. Transformative justice may seek to reform or replace TJ concepts and practices. However, in the absence of momentum regarding such replacement, it may be best positioned 'at the radical end of a transitional justice continuum' and remains in need of more sustained constructive practices across jurisdictions (McGill 2017, 80).

A hybrid approach to these justice conceptions may be possible. As one participant in the present study noted, a TJ approach should add value to rather than replace existing conceptions and justice practices: 'I really believed that [a] transitional justice/human rights-based approach to gross and systematic human rights violations is supposed to be an enhancement, like an opportunity to enhance existing democratic justice mechanisms as well as adding to them' (Interview 4). The question is not merely whether the three conceptions of justice discussed previously are theoretically or practically distinct but the political and power dynamics involved in the use and misuse of each justice conception. Each mechanism may be used to enhance, restrict, or frustrate the choices of those affected by justice needs, principally victim/survivors. If RJ is used with limited possibility of criminal or civil responsibility, survivors may view it as an attempt by allegedly responsible actors to avoid responsibility and to limit material or financial consequences. Where TJ is used by state actors to provide an exceptional form of justice, designed to keep conventional justice away from victim/survivors, and to avoid addressing calls for broader systemic reforms, it offers a de-legitimatising approach to the distinctive nature of addressing non-recent abuses and harms (O'Rourke 2022; Gallen 2023a). A transformative justice approach risks being rejected by those concerned with the scale of its ambition and radical nature but also by victim/survivors who may not share its desire for a radical change as a justice need.

While each approach bears significant potential to enhance the other, lack of trust or the competitive interests of academics and practitioners risk inhibiting such important collaborative work. This book seeks to identify key elements common to each justice paradigm that can inform a new justice paradigm, that is guided by (1) a new conception of responsibility and accountability, (2) the desire to encourage engagement of all stakeholder perspectives, and (3) new innovative justice practices.

6. Themes for a New Paradigm

Micro/interactional levels of justice

Each conception of justice offers guidance on how to enable effective and meaningful stakeholder engagement. Restorative justice focuses on the needs of victim/survivors, their families, those who have a stake in what happened, and those who have a part in resolution (Zehr 2023, 18–19). It has three well-developed main focuses and practices: an *encounter focus*, bringing those impacted by crime and wrongdoing together in developing a solution; a *reparative focus*, generating where possible non-punitive outcomes that address harm; and a *transformative focus*, promoting values that reimagine the way to respond to crime and wrongdoing, stressing human rights, non-violence, and social justice (see Zernova and Wright 2007; Johnstone and Van Ness 2013). As noted, RJ has been criticised for its failure to realise its transformative aims at a structural level.

A TJ approach is centred on and owned by the people most affected by human rights abuse: victim/survivors and their families (McEvoy and McGregor 2008; Robins 2011, 77). A failure to involve victim/survivors meaningfully damages the legitimacy and effectiveness of any TJ initiative. To date, victim participation in TJ has been criticised as more 'an aspiration rather than a reality' (Hamber and Lundy 2020, 747). Taylor (2014, 24) describes a typology of victim/survivor participation in TJ with a maximalist conception involving full victim/survivor empowerment whereby 'victims would participate at each stage of a TJ mechanism—from conception to design to implementation—as decision-makers, with real decision-making power. Powers are thus conferred on victims, with corresponding obligations on state and/or international implementing authorities to give form to these powers.' Lundy and McGovern (2008, 280) argue that participation can be most successful when it involves 'co-generative dialogue' as a result of the 'transfer of power' in decision-making processes. Beyond extensive forms of consultation or empowerment, transitional, restorative, and transformative justice literatures increasingly speak of 'co-design', explored in Chapter 9.

Structural justice via institutional and social change

Each conception of justice has a maximalist dimension where it seeks to engage justice mechanisms as a means not only of meeting victim/survivor justice needs and interests at a micro/interactional level but also at a structural/social change level. 'Restoration' as a return to some ante state of right relationship is often neither possible nor desirable. Instead, in working for transformation at the structural/social level RJ engages with victim/survivors, implicated subjects, and impacted systems in the bubbling up/filtering down motion described earlier. In practice, this means developing philosophical and procedural changes in the theology and actions of institutions that have been part of the injustice and harm (Braithwaite 2007; Rossner and Taylor 2024). However, as noted, much remains to be done to foster these transformative aims at a structural level.

'Transition' may be a nebulous concept for addressing non-recent harms, where institutions have already closed and the involvement of religious actors in public life has already dramatically diminished on the island of Ireland (Ganiel and Holmes 2024). Gallen (2023a, 103) suggested that TJ processes can change ideas, practices, and structures linked to past abuses and wrongdoing and may require that some claims to power and legitimacy such as a settler colonial state or a proselytising religion be refuted: 'Instead, to effectively respond to violence, coercion and claims to authority over time, the structures need to change to redistribute and re-imagine the nature of the institutions and their use of power.'

For transformative justice, 'transformation' may involve wholesale reform of the legal and criminal justice system but it remains unclear what distinctive priorities emerge from this approach for widespread change in the context of non-recent institutional abuses. Across each justice conception, what constitutes social and structural change in the context of non-recent abuses remains ambiguous but non-recurrence, institutional and organisational reforms that replace inequality, abuse, marginalisation, and oppression with equality, care, inclusion and support, particularly for those oppressed by virtue of class, race, gender, age, poverty, disability, and health would seem to be essential. As a result, how social change is framed, and who is involved in its construction and participates in its achievement, may be emancipatory and inclusive but can also function as a new site of exclusion and assertion of authority. Care needs to be taken to anticipate and avoid such unintended consequences.

Trust-building between victim/survivors, state, religious organisations, and society

Criminal and civil justice processes are recognised for being capable of estranging individuals from one another, re-victimising participants especially victim/survivors as well as doing little to ensure non recurrence or real institutional change (see Zehr 2002; Smith and Freyd 2014). Further, responses that are guided by individualistic, punitive ideologies can create the conditions for individual and institutional secrecy, defensiveness, and concealment rather than acknowledgement, truth-telling, and accountability-taking (see Keenan 2012); some of the primary justice interests of victim/survivors (see Chapter 3). To date, the engagement of victim/survivors with state institutions and bureaucracies and some religious organisations has been confrontational, adversarial, or non-cooperative. One consequence of this pattern of engagement, since early advocacy in the 1990s, is a reduction of trust between all stakeholders. Thus, re-establishing trust is at the heart of a new way (see further Chapter 9).

To trust is to maintain a perception or expectation that another party will act in my interest (Hardin 1999, 25) or at least will not harm me. Relevant to non-recent institutional abuses, civic trust is a qualified conception of trust, focused on horizontal civic trust (between citizens) and vertical civic trust (between citizen and the state) (Offe 1999, 55–63). Equally relevant to the present context is a relational trust between citizens and non-state religious and other organisations. In the absence of civic trust, secrecy may sustain or proliferate and stakeholders may pursue 'aims in secret' (Preston-Roedder 2017, 7), working to prevent others from learning and knowing.

Trust-building is at the heart of RJ (London 2011) and TJ (de Greiff 2009). Violators are seen as 'untrustworthy,' and trust is the lens through which state and institutional actions are assessed. When abuse or wrongdoing breaches trust it needs to be repaired and restored as 'an essential precondition of social cooperation' (London 2011, 9). The practice and principles of RJ are designed with that in mind. Voluntary participation and careful preparation work to ensure the principles are upheld and the values honoured in a safe process for all participants. Skilled practitioners specifically trained for this work are essential (Keenan 2018). For de Greiff (2009), each TJ mechanism, such as a truth commission or reparations, can contribute to the building of civic trust between citizens and between citizens and the state, thereby contributing to the building of legality and the rule of law, where the delivery of justice mechanisms are aligned with their stated and intended purposes. Kitagawa (2023, 3) theorises that TJ could build trust via 'costly signalling through the policy's institutional features, which conveys the credibility' of the state and 'political communication accompanying the policy, which conveys information about the morality of officeholders and thereby shapes perceptions of their trustworthiness, even in the absence of costly action'. This aligns with recent scholarship which emphasises the need for belief in the testimony and statements of victim/survivors (Enright and Ring 2020; O'Donnell 2022), which would have a foreseeable trust-building effect.

Addressing relationality/social bonds

Walker (2006, 23) suggests that when the social bonds are broken by violence, abuse, or wrongdoing, the threat to social life necessitates the need for social as well as individual moral repair. Liberal philosophies of justice (from Kant to Rawls), based on a conception of an individual rational self, recognise 'the surrounding context of values, personal relationships or community influences' and suggest that one cannot engage in rational choice 'without having absorbed the intelligibilities of a community' (McNamee and Gergen 1999, 8). It is here that the communal context of non-recent abuses and understandings of social responsibility come to the fore. As Wills (2024) makes clear, communities and societies are implicated in the wrongs of the past to a greater or lesser extent and the need for honest engagement with silences and secrets (88), remembering and forgetting (8), and distances between 'us' and 'them' (22) cannot be ignored when it comes to responses to non-recent institutional abuses.

Restorative justice offers a framework for moral repair work in such circumstances at macro as well as micro levels through honest dialogue that engages context. The taking of responsibility and accountability is also furthered by means of healing dialogue and rituals (Keenan and Zinsstag 2022, 321). A RJ system that focuses on reintegration also offers the possibility of community engagement and ownership following abuses and wrongdoing. Proponents of innovative justice contend that the respect and dignity central to RJ might help society move beyond blaming and towards a more proactive stance (Keenan 2011; Claffey et al 2013) and function to promote transformative change by addressing social injustice as well as interpersonal harms (Burford et al 2019; Llewellyn 2021). Similarly, TJ has long established concerns with social coexistence and reconciliation (Bloomfield 2003). In the present content, Gallen (2023a, 248) has argued that practices and discourses of reconciliation 'have tended to operate as a form of inappropriate and premature settlement or closure of the grievances of victim/survivors and their descendants'. In contrast, some interviewees in the current study suggest that the project of reconciliation after non-recent institutional abuses has not yet begun. Whatever the case, it becomes evident that legitimate and effective relational repair may necessitate addressing both individual relationships, predicated on dignity and respect, and also broader structural injustices that operate as the context of these relationships (Lu 2017, 212). These twin dimensions are addressed further in Chapter 9 in mapping a new justice paradigm.

7. Conclusion

This chapter examined the intersections and differences in restorative, transitional, and transformative justice. No innovative justice conception has fulfilled its potential fully in any context, let alone in the challenging setting of non-recent institutional abuses, nor can one justice conception alone be adequate to address the nature and scale of abuses and wrongs in non-recent institutional abuse contexts. Further, healing, recovery, and overcoming the past are all part of a journey that no justice mechanism can ever hope to fully recognise. At best, justice can provide spaces for acknowledgement and recognition, respect and reparation, truth to be told, accountability/responsibility to be taken, and for justice processes to feed into and influence social and structural change. Evidence from interviews across all stakeholders, including Church personnel, state actors, criminal justice professionals, and victim/survivors suggests that there is an appetite for new and innovative forms of justice that would offer forums for truth telling and reconciliation, reparation and accountability.

Building on existing knowledge and paradigms, this book develops a new justice response to non-recent institutional abuses and wrongdoing utilising and progressing the thinking and practices that have worked to date in restorative, transitional, and transformative conceptions of justice. Across the literature in each field, the need for a holistic, multidisciplinary, and multidimensional approach to conceptions of justice is recognised (Lambourne 2013; Nickson and Braithwaite 2013). A multi-dimensional approach that draws from restorative, transitional, and transformative justice thus has the potential to enhance justice responses and balance the seemingly competing values of individualism, legalism, relationality, rights, and social change in a manner that is pluralistic, empowering, and responsive to stakeholders' concerns. As Llewellyn (2021, 378) notes, 'What is so clearly and desperately needed in this moment, is a movement, whatever the name, with unity of purpose and commitment to the pursuit of justice.' Pursing a multi-dimensional conception of justice that draws on restorative, transitional, and transformative conceptions offers the means to address non-recent institutional abuses in the deepest, most holistic and potentially most effective manner.

9

Re-Imagining Justice Approaches to Non-Recent Institutional Abuses

1. Introduction

The previous chapter outlined the key values and principles of restorative justice (RJ), transitional justice (TJ), and transformative justice as conceptual antecedents of a new approach to justice. With a shared emphasis on acknowledgement, accountability, reparations, and addressing both individual and collective abuses, the analysis has demonstrated that these paradigms can address the failings of legalistic formulations of justice by recognising the micro/interactional as well as the macro/structural elements of justice, through trust-building between key stakeholders, and institutional and societal change within an overall context of relationality.

However, while infused with potential, these paradigms of justice are not without their limitations. Within a reformist rather than abolitionist agenda, there is scope for the further development of a holistic, pluralistic approach to justice concerning non-recent institutional abuses which seeks to balance legalism and rights, relationality, and ideological and social changes in a way that is empowering and responsive to stakeholder concerns. In taking up this challenge, this chapter focuses on a maximalist version of accountability and responsibility and innovative justice approaches as foundational elements of a reimagined and more responsive justice approach to non-recent institutional abuses, grounded in the primary research.

The chapter is divided into four main sections: Section 2 begins by recapitulating the case for a new justice approach drawing on the learning from Parts I and II of the book, including the structural failings of legal frameworks and the institutional and ideological motivations of church and state actors. Sections 3–5 respectively address the three central questions of the book relating to both the interactional and structural

Transforming Justice Responses to Non-Recent Institutional Abuses. Anne-Marie McAlinden, Marie Keenan, and James Gallen, Oxford University Press. © Oxford University Press 2025.
DOI: 10.1093/9780191967399.003.0009

elements of justice: (1) how can we address the key temporal challenges underlying justice responses which have impeded engagement between victim/survivors and institutional actors; (2) taking account of those challenges, and the limits of adversarial approaches, how may we broaden understandings of accountability and responsibility; and (3) how, in turn, may we develop more innovative, non-adversarial justice approaches, alongside broader institutional and societal changes, based on these richer understandings of responsibility, accountability, and justice? The concluding section highlights the need for accountability moving beyond binaries by engaging, *inter alia*, the perspectives of survivors and institutional stakeholders, the retrospective and prospective aspects of justice, interpersonal and systemic harms, and legalistic and more relational approaches.

2. The Need for a 'New Way'

Part II of the book outlined the structural failings of legalistic and adversarial frameworks which have characterised primary justice responses to non-recent institutional abuses on the island of Ireland, comprising Northern Ireland (NI) and the Republic of Ireland (RoI), and internationally. Prosecutions and civil suits, legal challenges under national or international human rights frameworks brought by victim/survivors (Chapter 4), state-mandated inquiries or commissions of investigations (Chapter 5), state and church approaches to reparations, including monetary redress (Chapter 6), and official public apologies (Chapter 7) are inherently limited in their capacity to deliver truth, justice, and accountability for non-recent institutional abuses. In particular, these various justice mechanisms are ill-equipped to address the historical and systemic complexities of attributing responsibility for wrongdoing and abuses, including 'policy wrongs' (see Chapter 2) at both individual and institutional levels, as well as the complexities of harm, trauma, and loss experienced by individual victim/survivors (see Chapter 3). Further, justice processes as currently constructed also eschew the human and relational aspects of accountability and justice which can impact engagement between survivors and institutional actors. Indeed, many of the barriers to just processes and outcomes for survivors can be related to not only the broader macro/structural level of justice but what might be deemed the micro/interactional level of justice.

The accountability gap: fear and trust

The analysis presented in Parts I and II has established that, at the micro/interactional level of justice, the presence of fear and the absence or breakdown of trust operate as significant barriers to effective and meaningful stakeholder engagement. This has resulted in an accountability gap for survivors between seeking and achieving just outcomes in the aftermath of non-recent institutional abuses. First, the reluctance of church actors to acknowledge wrongdoing or admit responsibility for abuses can be distilled to 'fear' about not only being blamed for abuses but also the potential financial costs of settling civil cases or of contributing to state redress schemes (see Chapters 3, 4, 6, and 7). A female member and a male member of two religious organisations reflected that 'often the letters were coming in here, I was afraid that one would be for myself . . . [Y]ou would be conscious of that. . .it stunted you thinking forward' (Interview 58) and 'as it [redress] grew, a real kind of sense of fear on the part of who's going to have to pay for all of this at the end of the day' (Interview 27). As one lawyer in RoI who had represented religious organisations explained, 'they're afraid of being blamed. I think they feel under attack . . . and they become defensive like anyone else' (Interview 21). Moreover, as a lawyer for survivors in NI suggested, this fear of reputational damage on the part of religious institutions, most commonly evidenced within the context of their engagement with public forms of justice, such as inquiries or apologies (see Chapters 3, 5, and 7), can also spill over into private requests from individual survivors for access to their records: 'obviously, they're afraid that the records would end up in the public domain, so they're [an] extremely closed shop when it comes to discovery request' (Interview 33). Access to records is pivotal to a holistic understanding of justice for survivors and is discussed later.

Similarly, the decision-making of state officials was also consistently expressed within a rubric of fear where, as one lawyer in NI explained, the 'protective approach that we see being taken by the departments—well, how can we limit the State's exposure—is a huge barrier to any real amount of justice' (Interview 34). Benevolent intentions on the part of some state actors can often be superseded by pragmatic concerns with legal or financial liability. One academic noted that 'they're trying to avoid litigation ever arising and not doing things that they might potentially like to do but not doing it for fear of litigation' (Interview 12). Senior politicians on both sides of the border conceded the significant impact of budgetary concerns at the forefront of political decision-making where state actors 'see the fear . . .

more and more compensation' (Interview 68) and are cognisant of 'budget, you know, how we're going to finance it all, but . . . this was something that we had ringfenced' (Interview 72). For some, this concern was also explicitly related to 'the flood gates' argument and the fear of state exposure to a wider range of claims:

> I always felt that . . . once we did cross into Magdalene Laundries, it would then at some point lead to mother and baby homes, just as I think the whole issue of boarding out will become an issue. So, we always have to be aware of that, that one thing leads to another and any time people say it's not a precedent, that's not necessarily true. (Interview 64)

As highlighted throughout the book, such cautious and self-protective institutional posturing has led to closed engagement between victim/survivor groups and church and state actors.

Second, the absence of trust also emerges as the crux of institutional unwillingness to engage with survivors within the course of individual justice mechanisms. In the words of one lawyer, reflecting on the perceived failings of the Magdalene Redress Scheme and highlighting the importance of the relational aspects of justice, 'The listening was so important. Where I think it failed—where I know it failed—was we couldn't succeed in putting the Magdalene survivors in contact with the religious institutions . . . [T]here wasn't enough time to create trust between the parties' (Interview 21). As noted in the previous chapter and within Part II of the book, since the public emergence of non-recent institutional abuses from the early 1990s, the pattern of engagement between victim/survivors and church and state institutions has been shaped by adversarial justice and legalism resulting in a distinct lack of trust between all stakeholders. Indeed, from the perspective of many survivors, their lived experience of seeking justice for non-recent institutional abuses is one of a lack of openness and cooperation on the part of church and state institutions (see Chapter 3). An academic in RoI highlighted the use of defensive tactics and 'the approach of using every technicality there is in the book to fight cases' (Interview 12). As a result, as a professional victims' advocate in RoI explained, for many victim/survivors this has inevitably resulted in 'an incredibly retraumatising, dehumanising system' of justice (Interview 26).

As also noted in the previous chapter, political scientists interpret trust as perceptional, based on the expectation that the other will act in your interest (see eg Hardin 1999, 25). Survivor experiences of justice processes to date, however, indicate that institutional actors have a range of motivations, many of them self-interested rather than altruistic (see eg Chapters 3 and 7). The older sociological literature helpfully suggests that trust is inversely related to the willingness to become vulnerable to the actions of another person or group (see eg Kee and Knox 1970; Gambetta 1988). On one level, as argued in Chapter 7, truly listening to victims and expanding the circumstances under which their voices can be heard requires the state to expose its vulnerability in not only moral but also legal terms, or as Enright and Ring (2020) put it, to open itself up to 'risks'. On the other hand, however, as discussed later, state actors need to balance resources and priorities between past, present, and future policy exigencies. Following Ben-Yehuda (2001, 6–7), the notion of trust is applicable to the varied social contexts surrounding the occurrence of and responses to non-recent institutional abuses, including interpersonal, group, organisational, and even national contexts. According to this view, trust involves a particular type of relationship wherein the participants perceive that a genuine, authentic, and truthful interaction exists based on perceived reliability, faithfulness, and the taking of responsibility (2001, 11–13).

Closing the accountability gap, therefore, entails developing justice processes which address the historical lack of trust between victim/survivor groups and institutional actors. As discussed further later, this means recalibrating the failures of conventional approaches to justice by downplaying an exclusive emphasis on responsibility in purely legalistic and individualistic terms in favour of more human or relational approaches which interpret responsibility and accountability in much broader, comprehensive ways. Moreover, as discussed later, recognising the complexity and sensitivity of language, and in particular the potentially exclusionary nature of legal terminology in this space, are central to the rebuilding of trust between key stakeholders and the reaching of a common understanding of justice.

Addressing barriers to justice: law, legal culture, lawyers, and language

At the macro/structural level of justice, the analysis presented thus far (see eg Chapters 3, 4, and 6) has also highlighted that victim/survivors have faced significant barriers to justice derived from adversarial legal frameworks. This includes, for example, statutes of limitations, data protection legislation, and exclusionary redress schemes as well as overarching factors such as the costs of bringing legal proceedings. Within this broader context, law and legal culture have been utilised by lawyers acting for church and state institutions as a site of disengagement and non-cooperation with survivors, often effecting further traumatisation. As one academic-advocate and a survivor in RoI noted, 'it's extremely adversarial' (Interview 16) and there is an 'absolute lack of humanity within the whole system' (Interview 31). Furthermore, as explored later, formal legal frameworks, particularly in the context of conventional justice proceedings (see Chapter 4), are ill-equipped to address broader issues of institutional change necessary for non-recurrence.

Within the interview narratives of institutional actors, the machinery and tools of law were also recognised as structural barriers to justice where there was a discernible appetite for doing justice differently. One senior politician in RoI stated, 'I definitely think the current process is sort of set up an inquiry, make an apology and have a financial compensation scheme, and I'm not sure that's the best way to do it' (Interview 64). For some interviewees, the way forward was framed as removing money, lawyers, and legal language from justice processes as the key to enhanced institutional openness and engagement. A victim/survivor with experiences of abuses on both sides of the border pinpointed money and 'compensational culture' as a barrier to the taking of institutional responsibility:

> [I]f anyone takes responsibility for anything they feel like it's going to cost them money. That's why I think maybe it would be better to take money out of the whole equation and just, you know, have it be a conversation rather than something that is going to mean people have to sign cheques. (Interview 8)

Similarly, senior politicians in RoI recognised how money and lawyers impede both engagement and the taking of institutional responsibility: 'how do you get these various interests . . . collectively working together as distinct from their lawyers etc., I think would come up with better answers for accepting the responsibility' (Interview 51) and:

> If the State sees it coming now a mile away, the State is reluctant to go to the source of this issue and deal with it maybe in a proactive way, and very often knows it's coming, awaits its arrival, then a kind of a battle ensues and it's all law. (Interview 68)

As noted, some victim/survivors simply want 'recognition and truth' (Interview 65) (see eg Chapters 3 and 5) rather than monetary redress which can never compensate for abuses suffered. For others, however, monetary redress is an important element of official acknowledgement of wrongdoing and abuses so that the overriding principle of survivor choice is paramount.

Nonetheless, by expanding the focus of justice responses beyond legal and financial consequences, such an approach has the potential to lead to enhanced openness and integrity between the parties and fuller acknowledgement of wrongdoing on the part of institutional actors, which emerged as the primary measure of justice for victim/survivors (see especially Chapters 3 and 7). Echoing some of the principles of restorative processes and dialogue outlined in the previous chapter, one lawyer who had represented Church organisations referred to the possibilities of 'the creation of a of safe forum in which there can be . . . integrity, acknowledgement, apology, standing separate to the continued need for criminal processes to take their course' (Interview 18). As this interviewee notes, such an approach 'might seem to require or imply a need to dismantle the whole criminal law structure which clearly must not happen' (Interview 18) and to abandon concepts of civil liability, which as of right some victims may still wish to pursue. The basic principle nonetheless conveys the potential of relational forms of justice to dispense with institutional defensiveness and secrecy and to provide open and unequivocal acknowledgement in moral terms.

A further structural challenge and barrier to engagement between survivors and institutional actors is the role and complexity of language, including legal language. Language is central to 'the production, exercise, and subversion of legal power' as 'an everyday reality' (Conley et al 2019, xiii, 2). Specialist legal language, including 'vagueness' (Marmor 2014, ch 4), can not only have a distancing effect (see eg Chapter 7) but can also make justice 'impenetrable' (Gibbons 1999, 160). This is exacerbated by legal culture and by the significant inequality of arms which exists between church and state institutions and victim/survivors (see Chapters 4, 5, and 6). The absence of shared understanding of terminology among stakeholders may constitute a barrier to more effective collaboration. McGregor et al (2023) note that several terms related to mother and baby institutions, such as various categorisations of 'mother', were deemed problematic by victim/survivors who in turn problematised the victim/survivor designation itself. As a result, the choice of terminology is highly sensitive and demands careful use, especially by those in positions of power, in framing official responses to non-recent institutional abuses.

Before moving to consider a pluralistic and reconfigured framework of responsibility and accountability and how consequently we might develop more innovative forms of justice, it is useful at this juncture to revisit some of the key challenges which have arisen over the course of the book stemming from the non-recent nature of the abuses. Addressing these challenges is fundamental to bridging the accountability gap and lies at the heart of transforming discourses on responsibility, engagement, and justice.

3. Temporal Challenges

One of the cross-cutting themes of the book has been the complexities of the historical context (see Chapter 2) and its impact on justice discourses concerning non-recent institutional abuses. As noted, at a pragmatic level, there are several time-related structural barriers to justice for victim/survivors including the impact of delay on memory and the availability of witnesses or documents and statutes of limitations which may time-bar legal proceedings (see especially Chapter 4). At a normative level, in reframing justice responses, one of the central questions thus becomes how, and in what ways, the past is relevant to the determination of responsibility for non-recent institutional abuses. Against this broader backdrop, several temporal challenges emerge: (1) the relevance of 'the culture of the time' to determining levels of responsibility; (2) the distribution of responsibility across church, state, and societal levels; and (3) delivering justice over time.

The historical context and 'the culture of the time'

Reference to the historical context and culture of the time has been explicitly made by religious organisations within the course of justice responses, such as official apologies (see Chapter 7). Many religious interviewees interpreted non-recent institutional abuses within a narrative of 'the culture of the time' which can have the effect of distancing them from accepting responsibility. Female members of one religious organisation referred to the 'social system of the time' (Interview 57) and that 'this was the way things were done' (Interview 57). A male member of one religious organisation also voiced both a general and personal concern with being called to account for non-recent institutional abuses devoid of their historical context: 'What runs around the place and, to some extent, runs around me, was that we weren't put into a context' (Interview 27). However, as an academic interviewee acknowledged, it becomes important 'to challenge those narratives and versions of the past' (Interview 50) to come to more nuanced understandings of responsibility and accountability.

Here a distinction needs to be made between reflections on the past which try to simply make sense of the past, from statements which are designed not only to be defensive but to justify, excuse, or even deny wrongdoing and abuses and thus deliberately avoid taking responsibility. On the one hand, references to the culture of the time can be interpreted within Cohen's much-quoted framework of denial (2001) where states or large institutions seek to deny their responsibility for mass atrocities or suffering via strategies of deniability or 'not-knowing'. According to this view, institutional appeals to the historical context may be understood as both a form of 'interpretative denial'—where facts (or in this case, abuses) are not denied but given a different meaning—and 'implicatory denial'—where facts (or abuses) are not denied but their broader implications, including the moral, institutional, or political implications, are denied or minimised (Cohen 2001, 7–8). On the other hand, however, as Wills (2024, 137, 177) points out, 'one of the tasks of the historian is to get to a place where the behaviour of people in the past seems comprehensible . . . given the context in which they were living' and 'explaining why people behaved as they did is not the same as justifying their actions, or it shouldn't be'. Viewed in this way, while historical narratives can often be misused by religious within justice discourses as a means of denial or justification, they can also be a means of making sense of their institutional history which included systemic institutional abuses. Thus, when historicity is not used as a defence or deflection of institutional responsibility but as a medium of reflection, it becomes pivotal to disrupting a continuation of the past and to ideological and institutional changes as part of transforming justice.

In this vein, other religious interviewees made clear the distinction between historically accepted practices which persisted at the time of abuses and contemporary acknowledgement that these were manifestly wrong. A female member of one religious organisation commented that 'it was accepted that that was the way to care for children that weren't cared for elsewhere . . . [I]n today's terms it was certainly wrong, but in those times I don't think it was seen as wrong' (Interview 41). Similarly, male members of a religious organisation stated that 'it was the understanding at the time, but they were hopeless decisions . . . with children taken from their families and put in institutions' (Interview 23) and 'it should never have been allowed to happen' (Interview 27). Indeed, consistent with the views of victim/survivors (see eg Chapters 3 and 7), clear and unequivocal acknowledgement of wrongdoing and abuses, including those relating to historical policies in place at the time, and their continuing impact is fundamental to survivor understanding and expectations of justice.

For some of these religious interviewees, the underlying emphasis was on broader structural factors rather than the individual agentic elements of responsibility for non-recent institutional abuses. Some further elaborated, for example, in relation to Magdalene Laundries, that 'we didn't bring any of these girls [in], they were sent to us' (Interview 57) and that 'we'd done the best we could at the time we were in' (Interview 58). However, comparatively, RoI in particular had a marked increase in institutionalisation when elsewhere in the world institutions were closing or in decline (see Chapter 2). The increased use of institutions and persistence of harmful and shaming ideologies, particularly regarding women, can reflect either an avoidable or deliberate form of structural injustice (McKeown 2024, 1) on the part of state and church actors.

In addition, consistent with our dual definition of non-recent institutional abuses presented at the outset of the book, even acknowledging institutionalisation as a 'policy wrong' does not excuse or account for the range of abuses, many of them criminal offences at the time, or violations of international human rights norms, which many victim/survivors experienced after they had become institutionalised. Indeed, individual survivor accounts (see eg Doyle 1989; Fahy 1999; see also Chapters 3 and 5) document not only a litany of institutional abuses but also of cruelty and a lack of care and compassion on the part of many religious figures. Although attributions of wrongdoing lie fairly with some institutional actors, this book has deliberately set out to move beyond the language of censure and blame for non-recent institutional abuses in the interests of a more progressive approach to justice and increased engagement between survivors and institutional actors. This analysis suggests the need for a more nuanced understanding of the historical context within discourses on responsibility and for explicit recognition and acceptance of responsibility for non-recent abuses, including on the part of institutional actors.

As also noted in Chapter 5, for several religious interviewees there was a desire to contextualise their work and make 'the whole history' (Interview 57) of their institutions public, including examples of 'good works'. This is consistent with institutional account-making within the context of inquiries in New Zealand where the state's partial acknowledgement of responsibility for abuses is interspersed with claims as 'protector' and 'saviour' of the vulnerable (Stanley et al 2024, 1). However, such mixed narratives of responsibility are challengeable in several respects. There is a clear risk of false equivalence here in framing abuses as aberrational or exceptional within a context of normative 'policy wrongs' and broader 'good work'. As noted previously, this goes against the grain of accepted survivor testimony and the findings of many official investigations in RoI which established the systemic nature of abuses. Moreover, a dominant narrative of goodness or benevolence on the part of religious organisations also contributed to the sustaining of institutional regimes and to the silencing of victim/survivors for decades. In the words of one survivor, 'some [of it] was about the mystique of these holy men and holy orders . . . And I think people got caught up in all of that just refusing to want to believe' (Interview 9).

For a small minority of religious interviewees, there was a need to separate individual and institutional wrongdoing and to draw a line under public accounting for the past:

> I'm totally convinced that wrongdoing should be called out, established and should be brought to the individual person. I think the culture that allows, if you like, a pattern of behaviour at any given time, that's the culture of the time. Our [contemporary] culture is going to be held to account in the same way, but do you want your children to carry the guilt and to pay out? (Interview 48)

As discussed later, this argument is also relevant to balancing the backward- and forward-looking tensions surrounding reframing justice responses which emerges as a further temporal challenge in addressing non-recent institutional abuses.

Distributing responsibility: church–state–society

As detailed in Chapter 2, a fusion of structural, legal, institutional, and cultural frameworks gave rise to abuses, whereby the symbiotic relationship between church and state on the island of Ireland, particularly in RoI post-partition, and the involvement of families and Irish society legitimised and helped sustain 'the architecture of containment' (Smith 2007).

Furthermore, in relation to the Catholic Church, there are intricate institutional structures and governance mechanisms across religious orders, societies, and dioceses (see Chapters 2 and 6). In consequence, and as highlighted at the outset of the book, there are inevitable difficulties in unpacking this triumvirate of responsibility for non-recent institutional abuses across church–state–society and in determining who bears moral or legal responsibility and for what. This complexity was also pinpointed by several interviewees, including one victim/survivor of illegal adoption who likened the intricate rubric of responsibility surrounding abuses to 'a great big spider's web' (Interview 52). Seeking individualised versions of accountability or responsibility relating to either particular institutions or individual perpetrators thus becomes challenging. While the issues are very much enmeshed, for the purposes of critical analysis, the challenges of unpacking collective responsibility for non-recent institutional abuses, or what Killian (2015, 31) terms 'an architecture of accountability', operate along two planes: the first relates to the distribution of responsibility among church and state actors and the second to the role of society.

As regards the first dimension, several members of religious orders noted the historical blurring of roles, and thus of accountability and responsibility, between church and state. As a male member of one religious organisation explained:

> I think the lines of accountability and the boundaries of responsibility . . . were never clear. So, in some ways, the State would let you at it if they thought you were doing a good job, and didn't interfere . . . [W]e were happy to be left at it and not interfered with by either Church or State. (Interview 27)

Religious interviewees noted the lack of funding and training from the State where 'a group of men, celibate men, untrained for childcare . . . would take on the running of an institution with 700 or 800 children' (Interview 27) and where 'the structures were disastrous' (Interview 23):

> How could you have a proper type of care. As [the religious organisation] said, they were on duty almost 24 hours a day, 7 days a week, and that wasn't healthy . . . [T]here were people put into institutions with very little resources from the State . . . [A]t one stage, [institution] had 800 students in it, and 30 [members of religious organisation] taking care of

> them. . . . So it was a hopeless set up really, and a lack of understanding of what was needed. (Interview 23)

However, whilst these were undoubtedly contributing factors to institutional abuses, once more the emphasis on structural determinants downplays the agency and roles of individual actors and institutions. Moreover, in relation to the Irish State, over successive decades, official institutional inspections, particularly relating to industrial schools and residential care, were deeply flawed. Reports of failings in the standards of care, education, and support were suppressed, inadequate, or ignored and, even when noted, there was little or no follow-up (see Carrigan Report 1931; see further Chapter 2). Put simply, however, assumed official historical knowledge of abuses implies responsibility. As one academic and a victim/survivor in NI put it, 'there was kind of knowledge within the system at all times' (Interview 49) and 'if they knew about it, then they were responsible for everything that happened, particularly since then' (Interview 9).

In relation to the second dimension, the role of society emerges as being deeply complex within the broader debate about the contemporary purchase of historical relativity. In thinking about who was responsible for non-recent institutional abuses, many interviewees, including lawyers and survivors, stated that 'it was the whole of society' (Interview 54) or 'it was in the whole society' (Interview 23). This was generally attributed to 'the continuum of knowing' (Keenan 2013, 101), where societal knowledge and complicity lent cultural support to the processes of institutionalisation. However, while there may have been 'a culture of conformity' (Brangan 2024, 394)—for example, the role of families in committing women and girls to Magdalene Laundries—this obfuscates the often costly personal, social, and even economic implications of such decisions for families who failed to conform to prevailing religious and cultural mores around respectability. In this sense, the keeping of 'secrets' may have functioned as 'a form of care' on the part of individuals and families as 'a way of hiding from scrutiny' (Wills 2024, 174, 136). As one interviewee put it, 'for many families, this was a strategy of survival' (Interview 49). Moreover, as Earner-Byrne (2023) has helpfully noted, just as with the institutions of church and state, the Irish family is not a singular institution and there are both acts of conformity as well as resistance among Irish families in the face of institutional power structures around unmarried mothers. Nonetheless, as discussed further later, the intrinsic value in examining the societal role in non-recent institutional abuses is that it speaks not only to the structural determinants of abuses but also to 'the soul of the nation' and the ideological elements of transforming justice responses to institutional abuses.

There is an acknowledged danger, however, that framing responsibility collectively, including extending this to wider society, may dilute or at the very least obscure questions of institutional responsibility and ownership of the abuses. This viewpoint was shared by several interviewees including an academic-advocate and a lawyer in RoI, 'There was . . . a weaponization of extending responsibility, "we're all responsible therefore nobody is responsible", which is the real danger here' (Interview 11) and 'the Mother and Baby Homes Commission was certainly anxious to just blame it on society but . . . when it's everybody's fault it's nobody's fault' (Interview 5). In this sense, for many interviewees, including survivors, the State is ultimately responsible in a legal sense for non-recent institutional abuses: 'I used to blame the Catholic Church a lot . . . But it's the State because they were responsible' (Interview 29). However, as has been noted (see eg Chapters 5, 6, and 7), the motivation on the part of the state in particular in shifting the blame to Irish society is to avoid the taking of responsibility in legal terms, including via monetary redress. Therefore, 'legal' or 'remedial responsibility' (Thompson 2012, 223; see also Miller 2007) which acknowledges the violation of legal codes, including human rights frameworks, and consequently the responsibility for repair, is fundamental to state accountability for non-recent institutional abuses. It is for this reason, as outlined in Chapter 7 in relation to apologies, that many victim/survivors want to see the State express its acknowledgement of abuses in legal, and explicitly human rights, terms (see eg O'Rourke et al 2018; O'Rourke 2020).

Justice over time

The broader literature on transitional justice (Bentley 2021) and international human rights law (McNeilly 2019) highlights the temporal challenges of doing justice over time. More particularly, the failure to remedy long-standing human rights violations may amount to 'continuing violations' of international human rights law, constituting a new form of violation and creating further liability beyond the temporal limits of the original wrong (Gallen 2019a). Moreover, justice mechanisms, including international law, are potentially limited in their capacity to address historical systemic human rights violations due to an inherent structural focus on individuating responsibility (see also Gallen 2019a). Two particular challenges to delivering justice over time arose from the interview narratives. The first relates to what has been termed 'the intergenerational gap' where contemporary institutional representatives are given responsibility for 'doing justice' on behalf of their predecessors; the second, to the need to balance the backward- and forward-looking aspects of justice.

First, the literature on apologies and restorative justice respectively highlights the difficulties of justice by proxy, often deemed 'inter-temporal' or 'historical' forms of justice (Celermajer 2009, 15). Against this broader context, several religious interviewees, including a female member of a religious organisation, voiced concerns about 'intergenerational culpability' where institutions are asked to account for broad historical wrongdoing where it is not possible to ascribe responsibility to particular individuals: 'I have a big question about intergenerational culpability . . . and the projection of wrong onto people not yet born . . . I'm looking at how is it fair to let the next generation, who had nothing to do with that reality . . . carry that fault of the generation before? (Interview 48). However, as Gallen (2023a, 282–3) has noted, citing the apology by former Archbishop of Canterbury for the Church of England's role in the slave trade,[1] for Christian churches more broadly 'such a severance of the past and present and harm and responsibility is especially pernicious' as they have 'specific spiritual and theological obligations to address the harmful aspects of the past', especially where this continues into the present.

A related issue for the religious organisations emerging within the present study was the issue of contemporary religious leaders being tasked with delivering or participating in justice mechanisms for abuses and harms that predated their involvement in religious life. This can in their view create a double injustice for both members of religious organisations and victim/survivors, contributing to the lack of trust on both sides: 'the vicarious liability kind of picture . . . is a form of injustice' (Interview 48), 'the survivor . . . doesn't trust because there isn't the personal connection, and the other side doesn't trust or . . . understand the depth of what is really being asked . . . I'm not pretending to be the person then who did harm . . . I'm someone at some distance and you're in different time and space with each other' (Interview 48). Indeed, tasking contemporary institutional actors with dispensing justice for historical wrongdoing as 'surrogate offenders' (Gavrielides 2013, 635–6) may be inadequate to meet the needs of some victim/survivors who

[1] S Bates, 'Church apologies for benefitting from slave trade', *The Guardian*, 9 February 2006.

are denied the opportunity of directly confronting those who have abused them. In this vein, the perceived sincerity or adequacy of so-called 'leader apologies' (Basford 2013), given by contemporary church or state leaders for non-recent abuses, have also been questioned (see Chapter 7).

Second, the literature on innovative justice, including transitional justice, highlights the need to include both backward- and forward-looking aspects of delivering justice for non-recent institutional abuses as central to ensuring non-recurrence (see eg Mihr 2021; Werle and Vormsbaum 2022). The legal literature also denotes that responsibility for actions is not fixed at the time the wrongs were committed but extends into the present to the time we are called to account for those wrongs (see eg Gardner 2003). Many State interviewees in RoI articulated the need to balance past and present policy concerns particularly around resource allocation where there 'is the trade-off between the future and the past . . . very often resources are limited . . . so money spent putting right the wrongs of the past can be money that might have been spent dealing with issues of today, like child protection issues' (Interview 64). For others, the priority focus should be on the present and future generations of citizens rather than the past as 'on a moral question . . . you have to solve the problem that's in front of you today first and then you can give attention to resolving the issues of the past' (Interview 55). However, there is a risk that the past/present is presented as a false dichotomy—those advocating for their needs arising from non-recent harms to be addressed remain among a live and present generation of citizens for whom the impacts continue into the present. For some, resource limitations were not simply about money but about human resources as pointed out by the following State official: 'you can't actually get the people and if you could, they won't have the experience and they won't have the skills and it will take a while to get them up to speed, but actually getting them is the real challenge' (Interview 55).

Notwithstanding these temporal and practical challenges, as other scholars have also argued, the state can 'dispense justice and arbitrate on temporality' (Bentley 2021, 598). In this sense, a transformative approach to justice requires imaginative ways of addressing the intergenerational gap and of including both the backward- and forward-looking elements of dealing with the legacy of non-recent institutional abuses as a contemporary justice and policy issue, encompassing both a recognition of wrongdoing as well as ensuring non-recurrence. Indeed, for other interviewees, including one State appointee in RoI, the issues are not mutually exclusive but rather intertwined as 'we cannot properly deal with the contemporary issues until we deal with the past' (Interview 17). As a senior politician in NI succinctly put it, 'it's not an either or in my book. It's absolutely a must do both' (Interview 72). As discussed later, this entails extending beyond a sole focus on the existing legal framing of what justice means with inherent implications of responsibility as blame for past abuses, in favour of including broader understandings of responsibility and accountability which encompass repair and corrective action, including via changed law and policy-making and institutional thinking and practices. For victim/survivors, in seeking balance between past, present, and future, justice becomes not only about adequate redress, as broadly understood, for abuses which may have occurred decades previously but also meeting their contemporary affective and pragmatic needs as survivors.

4. Towards a New Typology of Responsibility and Accountability

One of the central tenets of our argument has been that given the structural or macro-level complexities underlying the emergence of non-recent institutional abuses, both accountability and responsibility need to be understood in much broader terms than a reductionist *moral* or *legal* sense. Within Chapter 1, it was noted that purely retrospective and *legalistic* models of accountability, linked to shaming and attributing blame for past actions, are unhelpful in terms of 'lesson learning' (Shoesmith 2023). Furthermore, legalistic discourses serve to enhance fear on the part of institutions and to promote disengagement and mistrust between survivors and institutional actors. In addition, the narrow framing of abuses in terms of illegality may be dismissive of historical legally permitted policies and contexts and the moral and political dimensions of responsibility for systemic violence (Krebs 2017; Hearty 2021). At the same time, however, purely *relational* models, such as meetings between survivors and institutional actors, may neglect power differentials and be ineffective in securing justice outcomes through law or in challenging institutional *ideologies* or practices.

A balanced and broader understanding of accountability and responsibility within the context of justice discourses on non-recent institutional abuses has the potential to address both the macro (or structural) and micro (or interactional) levels of justice. As noted, although the terms accountability and responsibility are often used interchangeably, following Daly (2017) and Duff (2011), seeking accountability means calling institutional actors to account, while the taking of responsibility is the actions taken once such actors have been called to account or to actively 'own the wrong' (Duff 2011, 279). In brief, if accountability is the beginning (being called to account) and the end (being held accountable) of seeking justice, then responsibility, broadly understood, is the means of achieving that end. Thus, there are both normative and material aspects of responsibility and accountability presented later.

As with accountability, responsibility has also been presented along a continuum as having both backward- and forward-looking elements. This encompasses the past violation of the *rights* of survivors as citizens, their justice *interests* as key stakeholders within contemporary justice processes, and their ongoing *needs* as survivors. Further, our analysis has acknowledged both the individual and collective aspects of wrongdoing and abuses across a range of 'implicated subjects' (Rothberg 2019)—at institutional (including church), state, and societal levels—and particularly the difficulties of distributing responsibility at an individualised level. The structure–agency nexus underlying discourses on responsibilisation for non-recent institutional abuses is reflective of the notions of direct and indirect responsibility for abuses across the factions of church, state, and society. Yet, at the same time, the analysis has also discarded the blanket and uncritical use of the notion of collective responsibility as being unhelpful in obscuring responsibility and displacing ownership of the issues. These complexities underline the need to think more imaginatively about justice and in particular to conceive of more nuanced understandings of collective responsibility, including those which sit outside traditional legal frameworks.

Following Duff (2006, 87), responsibility has been broadly interpreted as being 'answerable', in multiple ways, for non-recent institutional abuses. In this respect, it will be remembered from Chapter 1 that the literature interprets responsibility in primarily moral or legal terms. 'Moral', 'agentic' (Oshana 1997), or 'outcome responsibility' (Miller 2007) accepts responsibility for norm violations in causing the abuses or failing to prevent them (Weiner 1995). 'Legal' or 'remedial responsibility' (Thompson 2012, 223; Miller 2007) acknowledges the breaches of legal rules and the ensuing responsibility for repair. However, conventional legal processes, such as civil suits and criminal prosecutions, are fundamentally focused on the attribution of 'basic responsibility' (Gardner 2003) and attempts to call individuals to account (see Chapter 7). They are usually much more limited in the extent to which they can further 'consequential responsibility' (Gardner

2003) and address the broader structural implications of a determination of responsibility (such as ensuing policy or institutional changes). Further, framing legal responsibility in human rights terms explicitly emphasises the state's responsibility to protect its citizens from abuses and thus its ensuing responsibility for breach of this duty and its obligations to provide an effective remedy (O'Rourke 2011; Gallen 2019a).[2] Such broader considerations are particularly pertinent in the present context given the structural and systemic harms, many of them human rights violations, underpinning non-recent institutional abuses.

Over the course of this book, and as synthesised in this chapter, a confluence of factors has pointed to a broader and deeper understanding of responsibility in justice contexts which implies institutional ownership of wrongdoing and the need for enhanced engagement between survivors and institutions in relational and ideological, rather than simply moral or narrow legal terms. These considerations have included: (1) the historical–structural complexities surrounding non-recent institutional abuses which complicate both the distribution of responsibility for non-recent institutional abuses at both individual and collective levels and the task of doing justice over time; (2) the failings of justice measures to date, including conventional justice processes and official investigations, which interpret responsibility in individual agentic, and often exclusively legal, terms and which further institutional defensiveness and a deflection of institutional and political responsibility; (3) the deeply human and emotional aspects of justice processes for victim/survivors which point towards the need for more relational approaches; and (4) the ideological barriers to accepting responsibility and to engagement with survivors, relating to the motivations of institutional actors, including fear of blame or liability and distrust of survivors. Table 9.1 and the following analysis set out a new maximalist typology of accountability and responsibility in the context of non-recent institutional abuses which incorporates these broader understandings of these core terms.

Within this typology, there are four dimensions of accountability—moral, political/legal, relational, and social/institutional—which map on to corresponding pillars of responsibility—moral, legal, relational, and ideological. The moral and legal aspects of responsibility, as set out earlier, relate respectively to acknowledgement of norm-violation and acknowledgement

[2] See Chapter 6 on *O'Keeffe v Ireland* [2014] ECHR 96.

Table 9.1 A typology of responsibility and accountability

Pillars of accountability	Pillars of responsibility	Distributing accountability—individual, institutional, state, and societal aspects	Retrospective and prospective elements
Moral – calling to account for norm-violation	Moral– acknowledges norm violation	Individual, institutional, state, and societal – addresses accountability of individual actors and 'implicated subjects' of church (or other institutions), state, and society	Retrospective focus – on past wrongdoing
Political/legal – calling to account for policy/legal wrongs	Legal – acknowledges breaches of legal codes, including criminal law, and civil law and human rights norms with the responsibility for remedy/repair	Individual, institutional, and state – addresses accountability of individual actors for criminal or civil wrongs or rights violations and of institutional leaders/state actors for failures in governance or policy wrongs	Retrospective focus – on past breaches of legal codes
Relational – calling to account at a human/relational level	Relational – acknowledges the human, emotional aspects; entails deep listening, a focus on the other	Individual, institutional, state, and societal – addresses accountability to the other at a human level within interpersonal or intergroup contexts	Prospective focus – on healing, improved relationships
Social and institutional – calling to account at an ideological level	Ideological – acknowledges the need for changed thinking and practice	Institutional, state, and societal – addresses institutional, state, and societal accountability	Prospective focus – on non-recurrence, improved policies and practices

of breaches of legal codes, including the state's responsibilities to prevent harm and provide remedy or repair. The relational aspect speaks to the interpersonal or interactional elements of justice and accountability by acknowledging the human, procedural, and emotional aspects of justice concerning non-recent institutional abuses, including the need for deep listening and a focus on the other. The ideological aspect acknowledges the need for changed thinking and practices on the part of institutions and society. These elements have the potential to address both the individual and collective aspects of calling to account as well as the retrospective and prospective dimensions of justice discourses on non-recent institutional abuses. A maximalist reframing of responsibility, in particular via explicit recognition of its extra-legal dimensions, simultaneously furthers a more expansive version of accountability. This thicker, more layered version of accountability speaks to the moral, political/legal, relational, and social/institutional aspects of what it means to be accountable or take responsibility for non-recent institutional abuses.

In accordance with the diversity of victim/survivor needs and expectations of justice (see Chapter 3), not every survivor will want to pursue legal processes or seek accountability in legal terms. By way of example, some survivors may prize retributive justice (see eg Pembroke 2019; 2020) or, as noted, may seek an explicit recognition of human rights violations (see eg O'Rourke et al 2018; O'Rourke 2020). However, others seek a broader range of moral or relational outcomes including, *inter alia*, participation, voice, acknowledgement of moral wrongdoing, or recognition such as via apology (see eg Daly 2014b; Keenan 2014). Others still may seek broader structural or social initiatives tied to institutional and ideological changes and non-recurrence, including improving support services and access to justice or developing oral history projects (Lundy 2020; McGettrick et al 2021) to ensure as far as practicable that systemic abuses will not happen again. The pluralistic understanding of responsibility envisaged within this typology means that, for survivors, sites of accountability, truth, or justice concerning non-recent institutional abuses are no longer necessarily rooted in adversarial justice or confined to a zero-sum game with responsible church and state actors. Moreover, opening up the possibility of more innovative and extra-legal responses to non-recent institutional abuses reflects not only the diverse and composite meaning of 'justice' for survivors but also its fluidity and ongoing nature. Collectively, these elements underline accountability in a fuller sense and emerge as being pivotal to moving institutional and societal responses from 'basic' to 'consequential' responsibility (Gardner 2003), thereby bridging the accountability gap. A final question for this chapter is how might these conceptual values be realised and translated into innovative justice?

5. Towards Innovative Justice

Having demonstrated in the previous section how the findings of the study influenced the development of a new typology of responsibility and accountability for non-recent institutional abuses, this penultimate section explores the pragmatic implications for the development and enhancement of innovative justice in this space. The section examines the implications for transforming legal culture, truth-seeking processes, and reparations, along with the importance of change at the broader institutional and societal level and how these transformations might begin. The themes are influenced not only by the critical reviews of the international literature and the empirical data generated by the study, presented in Parts I and II, but also by the core values of restorative, transitional, and transformative justice (discussed in Chapter 8).

Transforming legal culture

A recurring theme of this book has been the 'traumatising' and 'dehumanising' nature of adversarial legal processes for victim/survivors. The limitations of legalism and legal culture were also recognised by many cohorts of interviewees across the empirical data set. Several interviewees highlighted the need for structural and procedural reforms in the legal approaches that dominate this space, including removing the statute of limitations for non-recent institutional abuses, extending legal aid to survivors, allowing class actions, and the state not pursuing cost orders against survivors who litigate against the state (see Chapter 4). In addition, these structural deficits are reinforced by legal culture that permits and endorses persistent, intrusive, 'distressing' (Interview 26), 'intimidating' (Interview 15) questioning by lawyers within the context of criminal and civil proceedings (see Chapter 4), inquiries or investigatory commissions (see Chapter 5), and redress schemes (see Chapter 6). It has been demonstrated that the manner in which cross-examination is allowed to be conducted, which has become normative in legal culture, goes to the very heart not only of re-traumatisation and secondary victimisation but also undermines the dignity and identity of survivors. The result is that adversarial legal processes and legal culture as currently construed fail to take account of the deeply human and emotional dimensions of justice. Whilst recognising cross-examination as a necessary part of forensic or provable truth-finding, two key innovations that would transform and improve survivor experiences of legal processes include trauma-informed legal practice and the use of non-legal language.

Trauma-informed lawyering

Interviewees on both sides of the border advocated the need for a 'trauma-informed approach' in explicit recognition of 'the fragmented nature of traumatic memory' (Interview 14) and 'the need for 'fundamental reform to avoid some of those re-traumatising components' of legal culture (Interview 26). Some interviewees highlighted pockets of good practice on trauma-based training within criminal justice or legal sectors and emphasised the need for 'trauma informed lawyering' (Interview 17) as standard. As one State appointee in RoI noted, this needs to begin with trauma-informed training in law schools and related professional bodies on 'the psychological impact' on survivors of engaging with 'the legal representative' or legal processes (Interview 17). For many interviewees across all cohorts, including a State official in NI, the need 'to have a human response' (Interview 72) from legal actors whether on the prosecution or the defence side of proceedings was specifically founded on the need to increase survivor engagement: 'some of these things can be too legalistic and then, that's really damaging in terms of building confidence with victims and survivors, and their willingness to engage' (Interview 72).

Non-legal and non-technical policy language

The choice of language, including legal language, within official documents or official communications with victim/survivors also emerges as being fundamental to not only transforming legal culture but to the consequent nature of institutional engagement with victim/survivors. One State official in RoI reflected on the experiences of survivors and the need to reconsider official correspondence with survivors in less legal or bureaucratic and more human terms:

> They [survivors] inevitably get a legal response . . . because that's the way we're set up . . . [G]oing back to language, I'd try and humanise that to the greatest degree possible and try and train people in relation to that . . . [Y]ou have a department full of lawyers, they inevitably default to the law . . . [I]n so many instances, you're kind of asking yourself . . . what's their justice . . . It's not necessarily about law. (Interview 55)

As the same interviewee continued, 'putting the humanity into how you say "No" to people is something that's difficult . . . to do on a systematic level but I think the tone on those things has to come from the top' (Interview 55). At a practical level, therefore, the use of non-legal and victim-centric language is key to transforming legal culture and to a transformative approach to justice that includes building trust and engagement between stakeholders. Indeed, consistent with more relational approaches to justice, a corrective to the dominance of 'legalism' is 'the encouragement of legal humility' (McEvoy 2007, 425–8).

Transforming truth-seeking processes

The detailed analysis of investigatory models in Chapter 5 has established that despite their enormous costs, they may provide limited truth and accountability for victim/survivors and are often utilised or have the unintended consequence, in the words of one lawyer in NI, 'to keep justice away, rather than to progress justice' (Interview 43). In addition, as noted in the previous section, heavily shaped by adversarial justice, they are often deeply traumatising for survivors. As one academic-advocate articulated, 'they revisit the suffering and then they do more damage' (Interview 3). These twin deficits prompt the need to consider reform of existing inquiry structures as well as alternative models which presuppose different modes of truth recovery which have been used elsewhere.

Holistic, modularised approaches

Investigatory models elsewhere, including the Australian Royal Commission (RCIRCSA 2017c) and the Independent Inquiry into Child Sexual Abuse (IICSA 2022b) in England and Wales, have adopted modularised approaches to truth recovery that focus on individual institutions or settings, producing interim research and/or investigatory reports that in turn feed into public hearings and the final report of the investigation (see Shilliday et al 2023; see Chapter 5). The principal benefits of this approach include not only the expediency of the investigation and the reporting of specific abuses or contexts but enhanced knowledge and understanding about non-recent institutional abuses by grounding the investigatory framework within research and mapping the systemic learning across all institutional contexts. While some investigatory processes in RoI and NI endeavoured to examine a range of institutions or settings using a modular approach, the deficit in the application was with regard to the lack of systematic analysis across all modules and follow-through in drawing out the collective learning (see eg CICA 2009; HIA Inquiry 2017).

To date, the compartmentalised investigation of individual forms of abuses within RoI and NI has resulted in what one State appointee in NI termed the 'pixelation' (Interview 14) of our understanding of non-recent institutional abuses, inhibiting a fuller picture from emerging. Victim/survivors in RoI reflected on the failings of this approach as 'band aids' (Interview 20) and well as the benefits of alternative, more holistic frameworks:

> You're never going to solve a problem if you look at them in silos because if you combine it all together, you see the trends, you see the commonality and actually, it's a much quicker fix. . . . [T]he cost and the time will both, actually, be saved in the long run if you invest it now. (Interview 59)

A broader, non-siloed approach to dealing with the legacy of non-recent institutional abuses also has the capacity to increase the political and legal accountability of the state by demonstrating the extent of its historical knowledge about abuses across a range of institutional contexts. As one lawyer in RoI explained:

> The State was perfectly aware of the fact that these weren't self-contained institutions, or at least organs of the State were aware . . . [that] it wasn't always possible to make a clear distinction between who was in an industrial school, who was in a Magdalene Laundry, who was in a Mother and Baby Home . . . from the perspective of the people who were actually administering these institutions, this was an integrated mechanism. (Interview 5)

This approach would challenge the 'unknowingness' (Smith 2020, 143) of the Irish State about the broader patterns of historical and structural issues concerning non-recent institutional abuses, a stance which has been reinforced within a series of narrowly focused investigations with restrictive terms of reference.

Victim-centric approaches: multilayered supports and co-design

In recognition of the deeply human and emotional dimensions of truth-telling, there is a clear need for victim-centric approaches to official truth-telling processes including the provision of more tailored, specialist support services in parallel to inquiries. One State appointee in NI emphasised the importance of multilayered supports and having 'a more structural support system from before, during and after that inquiry' (Interview 14). Suggestions from survivors on both sides of the border included provision of a 24-hour counselling service 'to ensure that there's something there for them at 3 o'clock in the morning when they wake up with a nightmare because of something that they spoke about at the inquiry' (Interview 9). Other survivors emphasised the need for continuity of individuals in support roles, as in the past 'they've chopped and changed . . . you would have built up a wee relationship, that changed. You were going from pillar to post and the trauma of people' (Interview 2).

True 'victim-sensitive' (Wright 2002) or 'victim-centric' (Hamber and Lundy 2020) justice processes, however, entail recognition of victim/survivors not merely via add-on structural supports but via maximalist, bottom-up, integrated reforms which involve survivors in co-design of investigatory processes from the outset. As well as enhancing truth-recovery and improving victim experiences of investigatory processes as 'healing truth', such approaches help inculcate state accountability into justice processes from the outset. However, in practical terms, while survivors should be consulted about what they want from justice processes, there are inevitable limitations to this including pragmatic and budgetary constraints as well as due process concerns for all parties. As noted in Chapter 5, therefore, it becomes important to manage survivor expectations about what is feasible in practice.

Going against the grain of top-down, exclusionary justice responses, many survivors framed victim-centric approaches as commensurate with deep listening and meaningful collaboration: 'sit down and they listen to what a victim actually feels' (Interview 59) and 'you cannot have any kind of transitional, transformative justice without allowing survivors to be full, equal, transparent partners in the process. The process is more important than the outcome' (Interview 22). According to this view, the act of consultation constitutes a form of justice in itself and is key to transforming justice approaches to non-recent institutional abuses. As a lawyer in RoI stated, 'I think consultation is another form of justice as well, being actually able to collaborate on things' (Interview 25). In both NI and RoI, there are state-appointed roles in the form of the Commissioner for Survivors of Institutional Abuse (as part of the recommendations of the Hart Inquiry

(HIA Inquiry 2017))[3] and the Special Advocate for Survivors of Institutional Abuse institutions (following the Mother and Baby Homes Commission (CoI MBH 2021)).[4] The National Counselling Service[5] (following disclosures of abuse in industrial and reformatory schools) provided by the state in RoI offers counselling to victim/survivors of child sexual abuse and non-sexual abuse that occurred in institutional settings. However, while these are important developments, significantly more resources are needed alongside justice mechanisms such as inquiries or redress to provide the tailored hands-on support services that many survivors want.

Alternative models and survivor truth as 'common truth'

Our comparative work on state investigations into non-recent institutional abuses on the island of Ireland, North and South, and internationally, previously explored alternative models of truth recovery (see Shilliday et al 2023). As noted in the previous chapter, restorative inquiries have taken place in Canada (see the Truth and Reconciliation Commission of Canada (TRCC 2015) and the Restorative Inquiry into the Nova Scotia Home for Coloured Children (Province of Nova Scotia 2019)) and New Zealand (Wailling et al 2019). In line with the needs and interests of survivors, the principles of best practice emerge as: establishing truth and getting answers to questions; acknowledgement; procedural justice; follow-through; and non-recurrence (Shilliday et al 2023). What is noteworthy about these models is that the focus is largely relational in facilitating engagement between a range of voices and participants who come together and discuss experiences within a trauma-informed approach.

More recently, in NI, the Truth Recovery Design Panel on mother and baby institutions, Magdalene Laundries, and workhouses recommended, *inter alia*, an 'integrated truth investigation' model comprising a non-statutory Independent Panel whose findings would feed into a statutory public inquiry (Mahon et al 2021). As documented in Chapter 5, within previous commission or inquiry structures in RoI or NI, the testimonies of survivors given outside investigatory strands were treated as 'stories' rather than as evidence and were published as separate reports with limited overall impact on the official findings (see eg Ryan Commission (CICA

[3] Historical Institutional Abuse (Northern Ireland) Act 2019, Pt 2.

[4] See 'Action Plan for Survivors and Former Residents of Mother and Baby and County Home Institutions' (Government of Ireland 2021).

[5] See https://www2.hse.ie/mental-health/services-support/ncs/ (accessed 1 June 2024).

2009, Vol II); Mother and Baby Homes Commission (CoI MBH 2021, Pt 4)). In contrast, the integrated truth investigation model presupposes an additional form of truth recovery that will feed into the final report. With the work of the Independent Panel component ongoing, one academic-advocate explained:

> If you've got 20 or 30 people saying the same thing but saying it happened on a different day they're not bothered about the date, they're bothered about the evidential base of what's being said . . . [I]t's about accumulating a body of knowledge and understanding of what all these experiences have been. . . . [N]one of these people know each other and all of these statements corroborate, in general terms . . . but what they're doing is they're giving you an accumulated truth and that's as close as we can ever get to the real truth. And it becomes the evidential base of the inquiry. (Interview 3)

Indeed, this model not only facilitates the public recording of the testimonies of survivors in their own terms in a supportive environment but also produces a new and richer understanding of truth in cumulative terms.[6]

In this respect, there are multiple dimensions of truth-seeking encompassing, for example, both forensic or 'empiricist positivist' as well as 'constructionist' (Sköld 2016, 492) or narrative truth (see Chapter 5). The prevailing version of truth enshrined within formal investigatory mechanisms is that of 'forensic truth' or 'legal truth' (see TRC 1998: Vol 1, paras 29–45; see also Little 2019) in terms of a provable, authoritative account of abuses, albeit with limitations. As such, by their very nature, most investigatory models are ill-designed to accommodate the broader range of truth presented by victim/survivors including 'personal and narrative truth' and 'healing and restorative truth' (see TRC 1998: Vol 1, paras 29–45) that must be acknowledged. As Herremans and Destrooper (2023, 519) note, a 'thicker' understanding of truth with the potential to 'disrupt' legal/forensic framings is possible. Moreover, consistent with promoting epistemic justice (Fricker 2007), a broader understanding of truth and an approach

[6] While in RoI it has been held that aggregation of evidence cannot occur where there is no corroboration in law (see *Murray v Commission to Inquire into Child Abuse* [2004] IEHC 102), the multiplicity of survivor accounts provides corroboration based on the commonalty of narratives. See also the governing principles of the right to a reasonable defence within the context of inquiry processes: *Re Haughey* [1971] IR 217; see Chapter 5, n 19.

to truth-seeking via alternative models centralises the voices of victim/survivors and explicitly recognises survivors in their capacity as 'knowers' (Pemberton and Mulder 2023).

Transforming reparations

The analysis in Chapter 6 demonstrated that reparations on the island of Ireland, particularly in RoI, can be viewed as issues of charity and benevolence by the state, deliberately diverting from questions of legally mandated human rights and from accepting responsibility for reparations for the wrongs of the past. The capacity of redress to function as a form of relational repair is severely curtailed by concerns about legal and financial liability and the role of lawyers and *ex gratia* schemes in contesting or limiting institutional exposure and fashioning the outcomes and levels of monetary redress. These deficits point towards having a rights-based approach to reparations accompanied by acknowledgement of a failure of responsibility to protect and an ongoing responsibility for repair in not only moral but also legal and relational terms.

Redress as a human right

Regarding repair in a legal sense, extending previous jurisprudence on the obligations of the Irish State to provide reparations (see Chapter 6) means not only recognising redress as a human right, by virtue of the breach of international human rights norms and the state's responsibilities to its citizens (O'Rourke 2011; Gallen 2019a), but also accompanying redress with a clear written acknowledgement of responsibility for institutional wrongdoing. One State appointee in RoI reflected on the necessity of this approach for bridging the accountability gap between calling and actually holding institutions to account:

> Sometimes there is a lack of a link between accepting responsibility and accountability, and I think that that's a big gap in our system . . . I believe real access to justice comes when somebody is held accountable for breach of rights, and I don't think that happens. I think the tendency has been to . . . 'well, that was the practice at the time', but that doesn't make it the right practice at the time. And so . . . I believe that it's hugely important when it comes to attributing responsibility that there is accountability. (Interview 17)

While several scholars have called for a rights-based approach to justice regarding non-recent institutional abuses, including to redress (see eg O'Rourke 2011; Gallen 2019a), human rights discourses are traditionally not without criticism at both a philosophical (see eg Douzinas 2000) and operational level with regards to the dominance of legalistic, politically orientated, top-down approaches (see eg Ignatieff 2001; Kennedy 2002). In transitional justice contexts more broadly, however, the responsibility to address such criticisms can be addressed in human rights-informed practice where 'human rights can provide a practical and normative basis for grass-roots justice work' (McEvoy 2007, 429). In the specific context of non-recent institutional abuses, a human rights-based approach to avoid top-down legalism is also evidenced, for example, through the activism of Justice for Magdalenes (see eg O'Rourke 2011; McGettrick et al 2021) and other survivor advocacy groups.

Avoiding 'putting survivors on proof'

Providing redress as of right would avoid 'put[ting] someone on proof again when they're applying' (Interview 25), as one lawyer in RoI put it. This would signify a distinct move away from the entrenched institutional contestation of responsibility for non-recent abuses towards a rebuttable presumption, expressed in law and policy, that survivors of non-recent institutional abuse are credible and worthy of belief when it comes to the seeking of redress. This also underlines the need for justice mechanisms to feed into each other as highlighted previously in relation to investigations. Several interviewees, including a lawyer, suggested the need for legal advice for survivors as standard as part of this approach to redress: 'To make sure there are proper checks and balances to ensure that claimants are properly represented . . . [T]hat if they're making a decision to accept an award under redress [which] will have the legal effect of preventing them from ever suing the State . . . that, you know, they get proper advice' (Interview 28). This also emphasises the need for continuity in support for survivors including not only throughout official investigations but also redress processes.

Relationality and acknowledgement

Regarding relational repair and the particular benefits for survivors, as one State official in NI stated, 'the intended purpose [of redress] is about acknowledgement but I'm not sure that the people applying for it see it as acknowledgement' (Interview 73). One lawyer in RoI articulated the clear and simple acknowledgement needs of survivors: 'these people aren't really doing this for compensation . . . at least, if they got improvident compensation and the proper acknowledgement of either failings or formal responsibility, in return for signing all their rights away, then that might be a better outcome than what's currently on the table' (Interview 28). Other interviewees, including the same State official in NI, highlighted the need for a holistic understanding of trauma within the framework of redress schemes and of the totality of the abusive experiences of survivors: 'it's that lack of understanding of trauma continuity . . . [W]e can give you redress for this bit but although that's very sad what happened to you there, that's actually nothing to do with us' (Interview 73). This also highlights the need for an all-embracing, rather than an either/or approach to justice regarding non-recent institutional abuses.

Apologies as redress

Apologies which demonstrate an appreciation of what they are apologising for and of the impact of the abuses on individual survivors at an intellectual, moral, emotional, or spiritual level are more likely to be considered sincere. As a State appointee in NI noted, for many victim/survivors, 'their perception of justice and what they want from justice is an individualised response as well' (Interview 14). One survivor in RoI explained, highlighting the importance of a human approach and of institutional actors 'just bringing themselves' to interactions with survivors, that:

> For them to leave their Catholic mitre . . . and just bring themselves. . . . I say to them, listen, you're meeting survivors and you're scared . . . and you're big, grown men. But try to put yourself in our shoes . . . [T]hese children experienced it all their lives in institutions. Terror . . . That's exactly how we felt. We were terrified. . . . It's as simple as that. And that's how you learn to identify with survivors. You experience what they feel. (Interview 6)

This relational approach has the potential to demonstrate sincerity on the part of the apologiser, or the institution they represent, whilst recognising and respecting the dignity of survivors.

Follow-through

In tandem with the broader apologies literature (see eg McAlinden 2022a), the analysis in Chapter 7 has demonstrated that apologies are a means of providing moral acknowledgement to victim/survivors of the veracity of their experiences as well as institutional wrongdoing, which has been identified as a primary justice need for survivors (see also Chapter 3). However, for survivors, the sincerity of this acknowledgement is also appraised not by the simple gesture of remorse but by consistency of action on the part of institutional actors including timely follow-through on reparations such as redress schemes. The fact that apologies represent the beginning rather than the end of justice processes also underscores a holistic understanding of justice responses to non-recent institutional abuses. Access to records is a further integral part of follow-through, not only in demonstrating the sincerity and consistency of justice responses by institutions but also of vindicating the suffering and experiences of survivors.

Access to records

Access to records for victim/survivors emerged as a recurring motif throughout the book and a fundamental barrier to accessing justice across varying contexts. The denial of access to records impedes survivors in pursuing legal cases (see Chapter 4) and undermines the perceived legitimacy of official state apologies if institutions are apologising on one hand but refusing to hand over personal records on the other (see Chapter 7). As one State official in NI noted, this issue goes to the very heart of justice responses and of institutional accountability for non-recent institutional abuses:

> If you really want to talk about acknowledgement and accountability, it's at a surface level . . . [W]hy can you not see that somebody has to continue to still search as to 'Who am I and who do I belong to' and 'Who belongs to me and where are they'. . . I think the sharing of information is still a real block and to me, that does go back to, is that accountability if you're still blocking people getting access to their records. (Interview 73)

Although there are varying institutional practices in recording and sharing archival information, other interviewees made practical suggestions including combining all the records from religious orders on the island into one repository. Affording survivors access to their personal records as a matter of right is fundamental to relational and inclusionary justice processes. Following Smith's (2020) rubric of 'knowing' and 'unknowing', providing unhindered access to records for survivors also admits them as 'knowers' of their own histories.

More broadly, however, uncovering the personal histories of survivors is an important form of truth-recovery with the potential to disrupt opposing or contested institutional narratives around historical context and the nature and extent of institutional wrongdoing and to simultaneously further personal, political institutional, and societal understanding of the past. Moreover, providing independent access to administrative records or archives also enhances accountability via professional or academic scrutiny of official narratives related to historical context and practices (see eg Prunty 2017; Smith 2020).

Institutional and societal changes

As noted in the previous chapter, a maximalist conception of justice envisages justice as a means of not only meeting survivor needs at the micro/interactional level but also at the macro level of structural/social change. In this respect, the final element of a transformative approach to justice which arose from the primary research is the need for institutional and ideological changes as well as broader societal changes. Reflecting the 'bubbling up/filtering down' metaphor (see eg Braithwaite 2007, 148), highlighted in Chapter 8, there is also an important interplay between these elements as the institutions of church and state may act as conduits as well as barometers of broader ideological, structural, or social changes in society. While the themes emerging from the interview narratives related primarily to church and state, many of these themes can be related to other institutions which have been faced with allegations of non-recent institutional abuses. Other themes emerged which relate to the state specifically.

For the Church in particular, this new moral 'imagined community' (Anderson 1983) means embracing a redefined church as part of a 'new way' and both an externally visible and inward-facing commitment to change and non-recurrence. Several religious interviewees highlighted the difficult legacy of institutional abuses and viewed the abuse crises as having 'had a very destructive impact on us' (Interview 48) due to 'being lambasted in the public domain' (Interview 48). Others, however, including a Church official viewed the impact of institutional abuses in more positive, forward-looking terms where 'the Church has to integrate this whole experience into its life and its self-understanding' (Interview 74). For this same interviewee, there was a recognition that while institutional abuses may continue to happen at some level, the core learning for the Church was to be proactive in terms of the changed understanding of how to prevent abuses and wrongdoing as well as the changed nature of its response to allegations of abuse: 'we are going to continue to work to prevent this . . . As long as you've human beings, this will happen. It's what you do to prevent it and what you do when it does happen, how you respond. That's what makes the difference' (Interview 74). This understanding was also shared by some victim/survivors where one reflected rhetorically that 'you can't stop it from outside of itself. It has to stop from within, doesn't it' (Interview 52). The need for introspective learning, particularly with regard to changing the factors that contribute to the institutional abuses, as well as responses in the face of allegations of abuses, also has broader applicability for other non-religious institutions.

Implicit in accepting the need for change in terms of greater openness and transparency in institutional engagement with survivors is a basic recognition that past procedures or previous responses were misplaced, wrong, or inadequate. As one lawyer in RoI commented, 'it is not in the best interest of institutions to batten down the hatches and fight cases. Many lawyers and advisors now see this. I do see a change' (Interview 21). Certainly, in addition to the broad levels of engagement with this study from some church and state actors, including at the most senior levels, the findings indicate an appetite on the part of church and state for a new way and to do justice differently. Recent research, for example examining responses to safeguarding by both the Catholic Church and some Protestant religions on the island of Ireland, demonstrates the learning in terms of greater openness and the centring of safeguarding and protection of the vulnerable (Ni Dhonaill 2024). In this respect, several male members of religious organisations also pinpointed the ongoing learning curve for the Catholic Church since the series of investigatory commissions in RoI from the late 1990s. One senior Church official provided an applied example centred on survivor engagement: 'We have identified the issue and we know we need to do something about it, to engage survivors in the actual processes of those safeguarding policies and procedures' (Interview 69). For this same interviewee, this was also linked to a 'one Church' approach and the need for standardised cross-country approaches to safeguarding practices and procedures.

In terms of the incremental process of organisational cultural change at a fundamental ideological level, 'it's only learning to change, a very closed hierarchical culture in the organisation, and that meant that it was hard to involve in truth telling, to speak openly' (Interview 56) and:

> I think there has been a sea change in aspects of the behaviour of Church personnel generally. But it's another step, in my view, to getting that

> behavioural change to actually . . . transform the culture. Has there been a cultural change? That's another question and issue for me. Some days, I think, yes there has and other days, I think, no, there hasn't. (Interview 27)

For the hierarchal Church, this also speaks to the fundamental challenges of theological change, which this same interviewee acknowledged was 'a long-haul task' (Interview 27). The current synodal model of the Catholic Church emphasises consultation, listening, and learning as part of addressing broader social issues and inequalities (O'Hanlon 2017). As part of a global synodal process across the universal Catholic Church, the report of the Irish diocesan consultation identified child abuse and its concealment by the Church in Ireland as the lens through which broader reform in the universal Church must be viewed (General Secretariat of the Synod 2022). This report reflects the change in thinking which has preoccupied the Irish Catholic Church since the late 1990s. Reflecting some of the relational principles of justice outlined in Chapter 8, one survivor suggested 'if the Church had its own type of collaborative forum where they all got together and said, "Look, we have a collective problem here. We did bad things. We need to help pay for those things", in a truth telling way, in an apologetic way, in a humble way' (Interview 65). In implementing 'Towards Peace' in 2013, a spiritual support service for victim/survivors, the Irish Catholic Church also recognised the need for a fundamentally different approach to non-recent institutional abuses which is reflective of both the relational and ideological elements of responsibility: 'Something has to die within the Church as it is now, so that something new can be born. Lying to survivors, manipulating them and sacrificing them to the supposed greater good of the Church must cease. In its place must come humility and recognition of survivors as people' (Towards Peace 2022, 7). Such changes are also fundamental to re-establishing societal trust in institutions.

Similar to institutional or ideological reflection on the part of the Church, one State official in NI highlighted the need for institutional learning as a key part of closing the gap on true accountability: 'accountability has to be more than just "we gave you the money". . . . There's a gap between giving redress and what you are learning so it doesn't happen again' (Interview 73). However, as a victim/survivor in RoI noted, the significance of state reforms has much broader societal and institutional significance in terms of cultural messaging:

> Let's change the environment in which the Church operates. That's what we should be doing. . . . [T]hat was pretty much Children First on a statutory basis, Garda vetting, the constitutional referendum which was part of the process but it involved a lot of other things as well . . . [I]t was culturally relevant because it was about children's rights, so it wasn't about the detail of Garda vetting and the constitution, it was about the cultural statement but also children first on a statutory basis. (Interview 13)

This also signifies the central role of the state in agenda-setting around responses to non-recent institutional abuses, and particularly prevention, and to spearheading societal and cultural change.

As noted in Chapter 3, victim/survivor experiences of engaging with the state or its agents highlight state departments 'fighting over which of them was responsible' for particular classes of survivors (Interview 6) to the extent of 'who was going to pay for the water' (Interview 6) or where 'if a letter lands on their desk, they don't want to deal with it . . . They put it into somebody else's in-tray' (Interview 31) For state interviewees, central to a transformed approach is the need to increase existing cross-departmental cooperation and move away from a 'legally siloed' (Interview 62) approach to dealing with non-recent institutional abuses. More broadly, as acknowledged earlier, the nature of institutional and state engagement with survivors needs to change to a more respectful, open, less adversarial and more trauma-informed approach in recognition of the importance of justice processes as well as outcomes and of the need to try to engage more survivors in justice processes.

A transformative approach to justice also necessitates moral repair, in not only an individual or institutional sense but also at a societal or cultural level (Walker 2006, 23). Thus, the need for broader societal reflection at a national level also emerges as a key element of addressing not just interpersonal harms but also broader social injustice and what it means to take social responsibility for non-recent institutional abuses. Central to this approach in forward-looking terms are societal attitudes to the vulnerable and marginalised and how society responds to survivors and those coming forward with allegations of abuse.

Attitudinal changes, and in particular how society relates to vulnerable and marginalised groups, are important ideological elements of transforming justice responses to institutional abuses. As one female member of a religious organisation articulated:

> We need to look at the soul of the nation . . . that's the level of discussion or discourse that would be welcome . . . to isolate it to Magdalene Laundries, mother and baby homes . . . or at least the industrial schools and their development in all of that is, they're a symptom of what was in place, and of just dysfunction really as a society. (Interview 42)

Victim/survivors also voiced the need to look below the surface and 'the trimmings of a civil society' (Interview 22) and where 'all these institutions were the economic engine of small villages in Ireland' (Interview 22). These are central, yet sometimes unacknowledged, societal or cultural elements of reflecting on justice responses to non-recent institutional abuses.

On one level, institutional abuses of the scale witnessed in Ireland are unlikely to ever happen again due to a range of factors including not only greater social consciousness of abuses but also the diminished cultural deference to the Catholic Church (Scally 2021) within 'post-Catholic Ireland' (Martin 2013; Ganiel 2016), constitutional reforms and changed social welfare policies (Dukelow and Considine 2017), and more participatory and accountable forms of governance (MacCarthaigh 2005). On the other hand, however, societal attitudes remain important in challenging bystanding and affording credibility to survivors for different forms of abuses, including those which have recently, or which may not yet have, come into the open. One criminal justice system professional highlighted the necessary aspects of societal change in relation to cases coming before the courts: 'if you're looking at prospects of conviction, a change in societal attitudes and understanding of the dynamics of child sexual abuse [and] the understanding of judges and juries about the nature of this type of offending' (Interview 70).

6. Conclusion: Moving Beyond Binaries

This chapter has reflected on the need for new, holistic justice approaches to addressing non-recent institutional abuses drawing on the structural, legal, and ideological barriers to truth, justice, and accountability. Despite the myriad difficulties of distributing responsibility for shared historical wrongdoing, including systemic 'policy wrongs', it has argued that 'doing justice over time' is possible via institutional and societal recognition of the legacy of the past as part of the present and future. This can occur chiefly via fundamental acknowledgement of wrongdoing in moral terms as well as a clear commitment to political, legal, social, or institutional change. Presenting a new holistic typology of accountability and responsibility—which incorporates the moral, legal, relational, and ideological components of coming to terms with the past—helps unpack some of this complexity and engage the individual and collective aspects of accountability for non-recent institutional abuses. The resulting notion of 'balanced accountability' moves beyond binaries or false equivalences by seeking to simultaneously engage the moral, legal, political, interpersonal, social, and institutional implications of what it means to be accountable or take responsibility for non-recent institutional abuses.

Moving beyond binaries also necessitates a whole system or maximalist approach to justice which explicitly recognises the interconnected parts of justice systems in addressing non-recent institutional abuses. By way of example, this includes recognition in laws and government policy of the fact that the scope of inquiries, dictated by their terms of reference, has consequential impacts on eligibility for redress schemes or that frustrating survivor access to records, especially in the absence of adequate legal resources, also reduces the capacity of survivors to access other aspects of justice, such as civil claims or redress, particularly when they are put 'on proof.' In the words of one survivor, 'words and deeds all add up to a kind of jigsaw puzzle' (Interview 65).

In addition to individual structural or legal reforms, interviewees pinpointed broader structural changes which need to be considered as part of such an integrated approach to justice. One State appointee and a journalist in RoI highlighted the need to balance legalism with rights-based and relational approaches as 'the legal system itself . . . when it comes to obtaining real justice is flawed, and I think that we need to reimagine a legal system that prioritises the rights of victims' (Interview 17) and:

> There's something wrong in a legal system where someone who was in, in this lady's example, in a Magdalene Laundry, was pregnant, lost her child and then many years later through her other children tried to take a case, was told she was statute barred, was told she . . . should have had access to the information earlier. When you think the woman was in institutional care as a child, she was sexually assaulted, fell pregnant, has no education and yet she's supposed to be able to access all of this documentation which she wasn't even entitled to get in the first place and then has the judge tell her 'well, it's too late'. If you're talking about injustice, that's injustice in my mind. (Interview 1)

More broadly, therefore, these findings and arguments emphasise the indivisible nature of justice for non-recent institutional abuses on a number of levels: in simultaneously holding together the perspectives of victim/survivors and institutional actors; in presenting the backward- and forward-looking dimensions of justice; and in considering the interconnected nature of justice responses. This means recognising justice and injustice at both an individual (micro) and structural (macro) level and, in so doing, seeking to develop new and innovative pathways towards justice, responsibility, and accountability.

10
Conclusion

1. Introduction

This book has critically examined justice responses to non-recent institutional abuses across the island of Ireland, North and South, within an international context, drawing on insights from interdisciplinary literature (eg law, political science, history, sociology, criminology, and social policy) and extensive primary research conducted for this study. By comparatively examining the dominant forms of justice responses to non-recent institutional abuses, including prosecutions and civil suits, inquiries, redress, and apologies, it has highlighted the value as well as the significant limitations of these established approaches in delivering justice for victim/survivors. It has also situated these justice frameworks against the complexities of the legal, historical, cultural, institutional, and political realities of addressing non-recent institutional abuses.

In advancing a new way of doing justice relationally, one of our aims is to bridge the accountability gap between seeking and achieving justice, which has characterised official justice mechanisms to date. In engaging the voices of victim/survivors and also of church and state actors in a unique project of inquiry, the analysis has made a significant scholarly contribution on a number of fronts. It has provided: (1) richer understandings of responsibility and accountability beyond the established moral or legal elements to also include relational and ideological dimensions; (2) the beginnings of proposals for innovative justice approaches related to changes in legal culture, reparations, truth-seeking processes, and institutional and societal accountability with potential to improve the lived experiences of justice processes for survivors; and, as a result, (3) possible avenues for increased engagement between victim/survivors, institutional actors, and communities with the potential for better outcomes for all. This final chapter offers some brief reflections on the implications of our analysis in terms of how we understand justice in this space; the relevance of the island of Ireland

Transforming Justice Responses to Non-Recent Institutional Abuses. Anne-Marie McAlinden, Marie Keenan, and James Gallen, Oxford University Press. © Oxford University Press 2025.
DOI: 10.1093/9780191967399.003.0010

as a case study, situated internationally; and the pragmatic or policy challenges of this reimagined approach to justice.

2. Justice and Non-Recent Institutional Abuses

In drawing on some of the core values of restorative justice, transitional justice, and transformative justice—and in balancing legalism and rights perspectives with relationality, and ideological and social changes—our analysis has not presented a new conception of justice but rather an approach to doing justice aimed at delivering increased engagement between survivors, institutional actors, and their societies and communities. Within this context, some broader principles have emerged.

First, the analysis has highlighted the significance of the affective and relational aspects of seeking justice or accountability for non-recent institutional abuses. Different models of justice, including procedural, restorative, transitional, and transformative justice, presuppose different emphases and values (see Chapters 1 and 8), not least in relation to the understanding of 'harms', the role of formal justice, levels of participation afforded to victim/survivors, or the degree to which they might effect change or promote accountability at individual–institutional–state–societal levels. What they each have in common, however, is explicit recognition of the deeply human or emotional elements of seeking justice, particularly for victim/survivors. The dominance of adversarialism within not only conventional justice processes (see Chapter 4) but also within the context of other primary justice responses such as inquiries or official investigations (see Chapter 5), redress (see Chapter 6), or apologies (see Chapter 7) eschews these human and emotional aspects. Thus, formal legal, policy, or institutional frameworks underpinning justice responses need to be tempered by the relational elements of justice. In taking responsibility or being held accountable for non-recent institutional abuses, there is a need for institutions, or the lawyers representing them, to foreground these human dimensions of the problem and the impacts on survivors of the harms done. In addition, in drawing upon the shared values of innovative justice approaches, the analysis has demonstrated the underutilised potential of restorative and transitional justice as transformative responses to non-recent institutional abuses which, despite isolated examples or practices, have yet to be fully realised.

Second, within a maximalist and 'mixed model' of innovative justice (Daly 2011, 9), in blending legalistic and relational approaches and drawing on broader civil society and institutional practices, justice itself emerges as being composite and indivisible in several important respects:

(1) *the co-dependence of the micro/interactional and macro/structural aspects of justice*—there is need for changed thinking and practices at both the micro level of human interaction between survivors, perpetrators, and institutional actors as well as at broader macro/structural institutional and societal levels. This would potentially increase engagement with and by survivors by not only formally recognising their experiences but also enabling their experiences to influence future legal, social, and policy developments to avoid recurrence.

(2) *the interconnected nature of justice mechanisms*—the interoperability of different forms of justice usually works to the benefit of institutions (eg accessing *ex gratia* redress schemes can close off civil suits and immunity from prosecution may be afforded via participation in investigations) but to the detriment of survivors (eg preventing access to records reduces survivor capacity to access other forms of justice such as civil proceedings or redress). Fuller recognition of how different forms of justice might relate to each other would address this imbalance and improve justice outcomes for survivors.

(3) *balancing the perspectives of victim/survivors and institutional actors*—although it is axiomatic that justice should be 'victim-centric' (Hamber and Lundy 2020), at the level of praxis this must be balanced with concerns related to due process for allegedly responsible actors, the relational and temporal aspects of institutional actors' participation, the challenges and practicalities of including survivors in the design of inquiries and redress processes, as well as the financial implications of seeking to balance past, present, and future policy objectives. The significance of an integrated approach to justice which includes all stakeholder voices, however, is that it avoids a crude false equivalence between victim/survivors and other actors as well as the exceptionality of justice responses to non-recent institutional abuses (such as official investigations and redress schemes, which have typically avoided approaches based on victim/survivor rights, see O'Rourke 2022; Gallen 2023a).

Third, despite the significant critiques of legal frameworks which can be used to close off access to justice and which have limited capacity to effect longer term change, within a broader reformist agenda law itself also emerges as one potential tool for change among others, notwithstanding the temporal limitations of doing justice over time. In this respect, the previous chapter set out a range of proposed changes to the legal, structural, or cultural foundations of adversarial justice processes in order to improve justice processes and outcomes for survivors. These related to transforming: (1) legal culture—via trauma-informed lawyering including review of how cross-examination is conducted for victim/survivors and the use of non-legal or non-technical policy language; (2) truth-seeking processes—via the adoption of holistic, modularised approaches to investigation, with multilayered practical supports for survivors, co-design of processes, as well as more ambitious proposals which would potentially change the nature and scope of the fact-finding function and broaden understanding of what constitutes 'truth' in such settings; (3) redress—by recognising redress as a human right, accompanied by acknowledgement, and avoiding the need to 'put survivors on proof' a second time; and (4) apologies which are followed through with tangible actions including providing survivors with access to their personal records. As acknowledged later, however, much will depend on political will and the openness of institutions and institutional actors (including the church, other institutions, the state, and legal profession) to cultural transformation in both normative and pragmatic terms.

3. The Island of Ireland as a Case Study

Over the course of this book we have examined justice responses to non-recent institutional abuses not only in Northern Ireland (NI) and the Republic of Ireland (RoI) but in other jurisdictions, including both Anglophone (eg England and Wales, Canada, and Australia) and non-Anglophone countries (eg Denmark, Sweden, Norway, Belgium, and the Netherlands) via conventional and innovative justice processes, such as civil suits and criminal prosecutions; official investigations, restorative inquiries, and truth and reconciliation commissions; reparations including redress schemes and apologies; and restorative and transitional justice mechanisms of redress. As Ring et al's (2022, 307) comparative analysis of England and Wales, Ireland, and Australia concluded, 'it is clear that no one country has delivered full accountability and recognition to . . . survivors'. As noted, however, some innovative practices and structures have emerged, for example in relation to truth-seeking processes in the case of the Australian Royal Commission (RCIRCSA 2017c), the Restorative Inquiry into the Nova Scotia Home for Coloured Children (Province of Nova Scotia 2019), and the Independent Inquiry into Child Sexual Abuse (IICSA 2022b) in England and Wales. The island of Ireland has much in common with other jurisdictions in terms, for example, of complex multi-actor histories and experiences of abuses against marginalised groups and the use of similar conventional justice mechanisms (such as inquiries) as part of the state's response to allegations of non-recent institutional abuses. What makes Ireland unique, however, and distinct from other countries, is not only the enmeshed historical church–state relationship but the duration of institutionalisation and institutional abuses comparatively, particularly in RoI, when in most other jurisdictions the use of institutions as a policy response to perceived social problems had ceased or declined (see Chapter 2). However, one senior politician, situating the island of Ireland internationally, noted the potential transformational benefits for society in the public accounting for the legacy of abuses: 'I think the perception of the island of Ireland, us as a nation, I think have very much become a much more advanced and progressive society because of these stories being told' (Interview 72).

As a counter to the existing literature on institutional abuses which tends to focus on the Catholic Church in various jurisdictions, our analysis sought to examine the experiences of both predominantly Catholic and predominantly Protestant societies. While this was sustained through a critical analysis of the international literature and an examination of justice responses relating to both Catholic and Protestant religious organisations nationally and internationally, despite several approaches by the research team to some Protestant religious organisations, they did not want to engage with the research. Consistent with the small body of scholarship on abuses within Protestant societies on the island of Ireland (see Meehan 2010a, 2010b; Burke 2020; see Chapter 1), one of our interviewees noted an apparent North–South divide across denominational lines where broader cultural and religious factors may stymie official and public discourses about abuses within Protestant-run institutions: 'because of the liberal trajectory of Irish society, they feel that it is brave to talk critically about the Roman Catholic Church. Conversely, they are sensitive talking about other churches because it might seem to be sectarian' (Interview 39).

Certainly in NI, broader societal and official recognition of sexual violence has lagged someway behind RoI. This has been attributed to range of factors, including the historical, socio-political focus on the conflict

(McWilliams 1997) and, related to this, the lack of a functioning Executive for successive and sustained periods over recent decades. Despite the fact that NI was historically a predominantly Protestant society,[1] the non-recent institutional abuses which have come to the fore, including within the context of residential children care (HIA Inquiry 2017) and more recently mother and baby institutions, Magdalene Laundries, and workhouses (Mahon et al 2021), have stemmed predominantly, but not exclusively, from Catholic-run institutions (see further Chapter 5), evidencing perhaps the point made above regarding what is yet unknown regarding Protestant-run institutions and practices. This is an acknowledged limitation in the literature and of this research and perhaps an issue for future study. Furthermore, along with other investigative gaps noted in Chapter 2, such as investigations into foster care/boarding out in NI or RoI or investigation into clerical abuse in NI, the extent of cross-border non-recent abuses, such as illegal adoptions, have not been investigated to date.

In terms of addressing cross-border issues, following partition in 1921, the North and South of Ireland developed different institutional, political, legal, and constitutional structures, albeit retaining some shared legal frameworks (see Chapter 2). Although there has been much less academic and policy focus on non-recent institutional abuses in NI until relatively recently, survivors and their advocates in the present study reported broadly similar experiences of justice processes as survivors in RoI, including those relating principally to the impact of legal culture, investigatory processes and apologies, and lack of engagement by some institutional actors (see Chapters 3, 4, 5, and 7). An enduring and central issue for survivors on both sides of the border, which goes to the heart of their experiences of justice, as discussed in Chapter 9, is access to records. Several interviewees in NI, including a State official and a senior politician, noted the need to build on existing North–South cooperation to enhance the sharing of records for those survivors who were moved or adopted across the border: 'some kind of cross-border protocol that makes that access to records journey a bit easier . . . [I]t doesn't require us to change legislation . . . it's just about authorities working well together on both sides of the border so that it seems like a seamless process for an individual' (Interview 46) and 'there's natural political mechanisms in which we should be cooperating on this . . . [T]he North/South Ministerial Council is . . . an obvious vehicle in which

[1] See Chapter 1, n 20.

we should be progressing these things' (Interview 72). While such cooperation and exchanges of information may have become more challenging on the island of Ireland post-Brexit, more broadly, there are remaining pragmatic and policy challenges common to all jurisdictions, nationally and internationally, which may impede progress on innovating justice responses to non-recent institutional abuses which require addressing.

4. Pragmatic and Policy Challenges

As a final polemic, the pragmatic and policy challenges which underpin the advancement of new or reimagined justice responses to non-recent institutional abuses relate to both individual and systemic levels: first, it is important to acknowledge the limits of justice for individual survivors, given the magnitude of the losses and harms they have suffered (see Chapter 3). Indeed, a latent danger of any justice approach is that it could assume mastery in addressing wrongdoing—that with enough time, money, or political will, justice approaches have the capacity to address all the impacts of the wrongs or harms. Despite the commonality in survivor experiences and their shared primary aspirations of justice (which for many starts with acknowledgement of abuses and wrongdoing), justice-seeking and the meaning of true accountability is deeply personal and individualised. In some cases, no form or amount of justice can ever adequately address the wrongdoing and abuses suffered. As one State official in NI acknowledged in relation to survivors of residential care: 'it's impossible to give someone their childhood back' (Interview 45). Healing, where possible, often involves a highly subjective, personal, and potentially spiritual journey.

Second, there are broader system challenges around accessing and delivering justice. Chief among these are institutionalised bureaucratic responses to victim/survivors across some legal, church, and state institutions and the siloed or compartmentalised approach taken by the state within and across state departments to taking responsibility for investigating or addressing particular abuses devoid of their holistic historical context. As one State appointee in RoI stated, 'I think the balance has tipped too far in favour of bureaucracy and against access to justice' (Interview 17). Thus, reimagining or transforming justice responses, and effecting consequent institutional change in response to non-recent abuses, will depend ultimately on the state and political will as well as religious and other institutions embracing the need for a new way.

Finally, the ongoing and recurring nature of allegations of non-recent institutional abuses in many contexts, across not only the island of Ireland but also the globe, underlines that this is a pivotal moment to look backwards as well as forwards and consider new approaches to justice for non-recent institutional abuses. This means learning from rather than replicating the mistakes of the past and committing to meaningfully and holistically addressing the past and doing justice differently, drawing on the conceptual and empirical body of literature and research findings to which this study contributes.

Our contribution is to emphasise the need for respectful engagement and inclusion, for a healthy scepticism of legalism and reform of legal practice, and for the development of innovative justice approaches that centre the victim/survivor at the heart of justice responses. If pursued within the context of collaborative and transparent governance, the suggestions made for hybrid conventional–innovative justice responses in this study have the potential to increase levels of engagement by individual victim/survivors; to bridge the accountability gap for victim/survivors in their pursuit of justice and ultimately improve justice processes and outcomes for them; to promote deeper engagement by institutional and state actors, including church and state; and to offer possible avenues for improved engagement between victim/survivors, institutional actors, and their societies and local communities with the potential for better outcomes for all.

Appendix 1

Appendix 1 Table of interviews

Interview no	Named/ Anonymous	Designation	Interview date	North/ South/Both
1	Conall Ó Fátharta	Journalist	08/11/22	S
2	Margaret McGuckin	Victim/ Survivor-Advocate	25/11/22	N
3	Phil Scraton	Academic-Advocate	25/11/22	N
4	Maeve O'Rourke	Academic-Advocate	07/12/22	Both
5	Anonymous	Lawyer	13/12/22	S
6	Anonymous	Victim/ Survivor-Advocate	19/01/23	S
7	Katherine O'Donnell	Academic-Advocate	24/01/23	S
8	Anonymous	Victim/ Survivor-Advocate	25/01/23	Both
9	Jon McCourt	Victim/ Survivor-Advocate	26/01/23	N
10	Anonymous	Criminal Justice Professional	31/01/23	S
11	James Smith	Academic-Advocate	03/02/23	S
12	Anonymous	Academic	09/02/23	S
13	Anonymous	Victim/ Survivor-Advocate	16/02/23	S
14	Anonymous	State Appointee	20/02/23	N
15	Gerry McCann	Victim/ Survivor-Advocate	22/02/23	N
16	Anonymous	Academic-Advocate	27/02/23	S
17	Anonymous	State Appointee	28/02/23	S

(*continued*)

Appendix 1 Continued

Interview no	Named/ Anonymous	Designation	Interview date	North/ South/Both
18	Anonymous	Lawyer	01/03/23	S
19	Anonymous	Church Official	08/03/23	S
20	Mary Harney	Victim/ Survivor-Advocate	14/03/23	S
21	Anonymous	Lawyer	21/03/23	S
22	Rosemary Adaser	Victim/ Survivor-Advocate	21/03/23	Both
23	Anonymous	Senior Member of Religious Organisation (male)	22/03/23	S
24	Anonymous	Lawyer	22/03/23	S
25	Anonymous	Lawyer	23/03/23	S
26	Anonymous	Professional Victim/ Survivor-Advocate	28/03/23	S
27	Anonymous	Member of Religious Organisation (male)	03/04/23	S
28	Alan Keating	Lawyer	05/04/23	S
29	Elizabeth Coppin	Victim/ Survivor-Advocate	06/04/23	S
30	Catriona Crowe	Former State Official	14/04/23	S
31	Louise O'Keeffe	Victim/ Survivor-Advocate	17/04/23	S
32	Anonymous	Member of Religious Organisation (male)	17/04/23	S
33	Anonymous	Lawyer	18/04/23	N
34	Wendy Lyon	Lawyer	20/04/23	S
35	Patrick Corrigan	Professional Victim/ Survivor-Advocate	20/04/23	N
36	Anonymous	Professional Victim/ Survivor-Advocate	09/05/23	S
37	Anonymous	Criminal Justice Professional	10/05/23	S
38	Anonymous	Lawyer	16/05/23	S

Appendix 1 Continued

Interview no	Named/ Anonymous	Designation	Interview date	North/ South/Both
39	Niall Meehan	Academic	18/05/23	Both
40	Anonymous	Judge	22/05/23	S
41	Anonymous	Member of Religious Organisation (female)	23/05/23	S
42	Anonymous	Member of Religious Organisation (female)	23/05/23	S
43	Anonymous	Lawyer	26/05/23	N
44	Anonymous	Criminal Justice Professional	31/05/23	S
45	Anonymous	State Official	01/06/23	N
46	Eilis McDaniel	State Official	07/06/23	N
47	Astrid Hamilton	State Official	07/06/23	N
48	Anonymous	Member of Religious Organisation (female)	08/06/23	S
49	Anonymous	Academic	13/06/23	S
50	Patricia Lundy	Academic	15/06/23	N
51	Katherine Zappone	Senior Politician	26/06/23	S
52	Tressa Reeves	Victim/ Survivor-Advocate	05/07/23	S
53	Patsy McGarry	Journalist	11/07/23	S
54	Fionna Fox	Lawyer	13/07/23	S
55	Anonymous	State Official	17/07/23	S
56	Anonymous	Member of Religious Organisation (male)	17/07/23	S
57	Anonymous	Member of Religious Organisation (female)	18/07/23	S
58	Anonymous	Member of Religious Organisation (female)	18/07/23	S

(*continued*)

Appendix 1 Continued

Interview no	Named/ Anonymous	Designation	Interview date	North/ South/Both
59	Diane Byrne	Victim/ Survivor-Advocate	21/07/23	S
60	Anonymous	Criminal Justice Professional	25/07/23	N
61	Anonymous	Senior Politician	26/07/23	S
62	Anonymous	State Official	01/08/23	S
63	Paul Harrison	State Official	01/08/23	S
64	Anonymous	Senior Politician	02/08/23	S
65	Samantha Long	Victim/ Survivor-Advocate	10/08/23	S
66	Yvonne O'Rourke	Victim/ Survivor-Advocate	15/08/23	S
67	Anonymous	Criminal Justice Professional	08/09/23	S
68	Anonymous	Senior Politician	13/09/23	S
69	Anonymous	Senior Church Official	13/10/23	N
70	Anonymous	Criminal Justice Professional	17/10/23	S
71	Anonymous	Criminal Justice Professional	02/11/23	N
72	Michelle O'Neill	Senior Politician	06/12/23	N
73	Anonymous	State Official	10/01/24	N
74	Anonymous	Church Official	23/01/24	S

Bibliography

Acorn, AE. 2004. *Compulsory Compassion: A Critique of Restorative Justice.* UBC Press.

Adriaenssens, P. 2014. 'Mediation and Truth Telling: The Lessons We Have Learned'. Paper presented at the 'Sexual Abuse in the Church and Other Institutional Settings' Conference. Onati, 11 April.

Aersten, I. 2014. 'Sexual Abuse in the Roman Catholic Church in Belgium: A Study of the Phenomenon and Response Mechanisms'. Paper presented at the 'Sexual Abuse in the Church and Other Institutional Settings' Conference. Onati, 11 April.

Aertsen, I. 2021. 'Sexual Abuse in Religious Institutions: Response Models Compared'. In J Tamarit Sumalla (ed). *Abusos sexuales en la Iglesia Católica: Análisis del problema y de la respuesta jurídica e institucional.* Aranzadi.

Aertsen, I. 2024. 'Towards a Multiple Layers Approach of Innovative Justice to Historical Institutional Abuse'. Paper presented at the 'Transforming Justice Responses to Non-Recent Institutional Abuses Conference', Dublin, 5 September.

Aertsen, I, and M Schotsmans. 2020. 'Institutioneel misbruik en geweld uit het verleden:een vergelijking van twee herstelgerichte responsmodellen in België'. *Tijdschrift voor Herstelrecht* 20(3): 9–36.

Aguiar, W, and R Halseth. 2015. *Aboriginal Peoples and Historic Trauma: The Processes of Intergenerational Transmission.* National Collaborating Centre for Aboriginal Health.

Ahmed, E, N Harris, J Braithwaite, and V Braithwaite (eds). 2001. *Shame Management Through Reintegration.* Cambridge University Press.

Akenson, D. 1973. *Education and Enmity: The Control of Schooling in Northern Ireland 1921–50.* Routledge.

Al-Alosi, H. 2021. 'Righting Unrightable Wrongs: Exploring the Potential of Restorative Justice in Dealing with Historical Institutional Child Sexual Abuse'. *University of Tasmania Law Review* 40(1): 1–32.

Aldridge, J. 2018. '"This is Not Just About History . . ." Addressing the Disconnect in Historic (Non-Recent) Child Abuse Investigations'. *Child Abuse Review* 27(1): 24–9.

Allan, A, MM Allan, D Kaminer, and DJ Stein. 2006. 'Exploration of the Association Between Apology and Forgiveness Amongst Victims Of Human Rights Violations'. *Behavioral Sciences & the Law* 24(1): 87–102.

Allan, A, and R Carroll. 2017. 'Apologies in a Legal Setting: Insights from Research into Injured Parties' Experiences of Apologies after an Adverse Event'. *Psychiatry, Psychology and Law* 24(1): 10–32.

Alter, S. 1999. *Apologizing for Serious Wrongdoing: Social, Psychological and Legal Considerations, Final Report for the Law Commission of Canada*. Law Commission of Canada.

Álvarez Berastegi, A. 2017. 'Transitional Justice in Settled Democracies: Northern Ireland and the Basque Country in Comparative Perspective'. *Critical Studies on Terrorism* 10(3): 542–61.

Ambos, K. 2009. 'The Legal Framework of Transitional Justice'. In K Ambos, J Large, and M Wierda (eds). *Building a Future on Peace and Justice: Studies on Transitional Justice, Conflict Resolution and Development*. Springer.

An Oblate of Mary Immaculate. 2017. *The Moral Challenge Posed to Religious About the Cost of Redress*. The Oblates.

Anderson, B. 1983. *Imagined Communities: Reflections on the Origin and Spread of Nationalism*. Verso Books.

Andresen, S. 2021. 'Sexual Violence Against Children and Transitional Justice: Bearing Witness and Preserving Testimony about Injustice in Childhood'. *International Journal on Child Maltreatment: Research, Policy and Practice* 4(2): 193–207.

Arnold, B. 2009. *The Irish Gulag: How the State Betrayed its Innocent Children*. Gill & Macmillan.

Arthur, P. 2009. 'How Transitions Reshaped Human Rights: A Conceptual History of Transitional Justice'. *Human Rights Quarterly* 31(2): 321–67.

Arvidsson, M. 2015. 'Contextualizing Reparations Politics'. In J Sköld and S Swain (eds). *Apologies and the Legacy of Abuse of Children in 'Care': International Perspectives*. Palgrave Macmillan.

Arvidsson, M. 2020. 'Retroactive Responsibility: A Comparison of Argumentation on State redress for Historical Institutional Child Abuse in Sweden and Denmark'. *Scandinavian Journal of History* 45(2): 159–77.

Attrash-Najjar, A, Jacobson, MA, and Katz, C. 2024. '"I Lived but I Wasn't Alive": Examining Responses of Formal Systems to Child Sexual Abuse as Described in Survivors' Testimonies to the Israeli Independent Public Inquiry'. *Children and Youth Services Review* 163: 107818.

Aukerman, MJ. 2002. 'Extraordinary Evil, Ordinary Crime: A Framework for Understanding Transitional Justice'. *Harvard Human Rights Journal* 15: 39–98.

Baer, UM. 2016. 'Switzerland's Apology for Compulsory Government-Welfare Measures: A Social Justice Turn?' *Social Justice* 43(3): 68–90.

Baker, LA, and SJ Herman. 2020. 'Layers of Lawyers: Parsing the Complexities of Claimant Representation in Mass Tort MDLs'. *Lewis & Clark Law Review* 24(2): 469–96.

Balasco, LM. 2013. 'The Transitions of Transitional Justice: Mapping the Waves From Promise to Practice'. *Journal of Human Rights* 12(2): 198–216.

Balboni, JM, and DM Bishop. 2010. 'Transformative Justice: Survivor Perspectives on Clergy Sexual Abuse Litigation'. *Contemporary Justice Review* 13(2): 133–54.

Balint, J. 2016. 'The "Mau Mau" Legal Hearings and Recognizing the Crimes of the British Colonial State: A Limited Constitutive Moment'. *Critical Analysis of Law* 3(2): 261–85.

Balint, J, J Evans, and N McMillan. 2014. 'Rethinking Transitional Justice, Redressing Indigenous Harm: A New Conceptual Approach'. *International Journal of Transitional Justice* 8(2): 194–216.

Balint, J, J Evans, N McMillan, and M McMillan. 2020. *Keeping Hold of Justice: Encounters Between Law and Colonialism*. University of Michigan Press.

Bamford, N, and P Leyland (eds). 2013. *Accountability in the Contemporary Constitution*. Oxford University Press.

Barnes, J. 1989. *Irish Industrial Schools, 1868–1908: Origins and Development*. Irish Academic Press.

Barr, C. 2018. The Re-Energising of Catholicism, 1790–1880. In T Bartlett and J Kelly (eds). *The Cambridge History of Ireland*. Cambridge University Press.

Barth, T. 2010. 'Crisis Management in the Catholic Church: Lessons for Public Administrators'. *Public Administration Review* 70(5): 780–91.

Basford, TE. 2013. 'Leader Apologies: How Content and Delivery Influence Sincerity Appraisals'. *International Journal of Business and Social Science* 4(5): 9–26.

Bavelas, J. 2004. 'An Analysis of Formal Apologies by Canadian Churches to First Nations'. Occasional Paper No 1, Centre for Studies in Religion and Society, University of Victoria.

Bell, C. 2009. 'Transitional Justice, Interdisciplinarity and the State of the "Field" or "Non-Field"'. *International Journal of Transitional Justice* 3(1): 5–27.

Ben-Yehuda, N. 2001. *Betrayal and Treason: Violations of Trust and Loyalty*. Westview.

Benoit, WL. 2015. *Accounts, Excuses, and Apologies: Image Repair Theory and Research* (2nd ed). SUNY Press.

Bentley, T. 2020. 'Settler State Apologies and the Elusiveness of Forgiveness: The Purification Ritual That Does Not Purify'. *Contemporary Political Theory* 19(3): 381–403.

Bentley, T. 2021. 'A Line under the Past: Performative Temporal Segregation in Transitional Justice'. *Journal of Human Rights* 20(5): 598–613.

Birnie E, and D Hitchens. 1999. *Northern Ireland Economy: Performance, Prospects and Policy*. Routledge.

Blackhawk, M. 2019. 'Federal Indian Law as Paradigm within Public Law'. *Harvard Law Review* 132(7): 1787–877.

Blakemore, T, JL Herbert, F Arney, and S Parkinson. 2017. 'The Impacts of Institutional Child Sexual Abuse: A Rapid Review of the Evidence'. *Child Abuse and Neglect* 74: 35–48.

Blatz, CW and C Philpot. 2010. 'On the Outcomes of Intergroup Apologies: A Review'. *Social and Personality Psychology Compass* 4(11): 995–1007.

Blatz, CW, K Schumann, and M Ross. 2009. 'Government Apologies for Historical Injustices'. *Political Psychology* 30(2): 219–41.

Bloomfield D. 2003. 'Reconciliation: An Introduction'. In D Bloomfield, T Barnes, and L Huyse (eds). *Reconciliation after Violent Conflict: A Handbook*. IDEA.

Bolitho, J. 2015. 'Putting Justice Needs First: A Case Study of Best Practice in Restorative Justice'. *Restorative Justice* 3(2): 256–81.

Bolivar, D, I Aertsen, and I Vanfraechem. 2013. 'The Ritual of Apology and Restorative Justice: Exploring the Victim's Perspective'. In D Cuypers, D Janssen, J Haers, and B Segaert (eds). *Public Apology Between Ritual and Regret*. Brill.

Borneman, J. 1999. 'Can Public Apologies Contribute to Place? An Argument for Retribution'. *Anthropology of East Europe Review* 17(1): 7–20.

Borneman, J. 2005. 'Public Apologies as Performative Redress'. *SAIS Review of International Affairs* 25(2): 53–66.

Boven, M. 2007. 'Analysing and Assessing Accountability: A Conceptual Framework'. *European Law Journal* 13(4): 447–68.

Braithwaite, J. 2003. 'Principles of Restorative Justice'. In A von Hirsch, JV Roberts, AE Bottoms, K Roach, and M Schiff (eds). *Restorative Justice and Criminal Justice: Competing or Reconcilable Paradigms?* Hart Publishing.

Braithwaite, J. 2007. 'Building Legitimacy through Restorative Justice'. In A Braga, J Fagan, T Meares, R Sampson, R Tyler, and C Winship (eds). *Legitimacy and Criminal Justice: International Perspectives*. Russell Sage Foundation.

Braithwaite, J. 2011. 'The Essence of Responsive Regulation'. *University of British Colombia Law Review* 44(3): 475–520.

Braithwaite, J. 2016. 'Learning to Scale Up Restorative Justice'. In K Clamp (ed). *Restorative Justice in Transitional Settings*. Routledge.

Braithwaite, J, and Parker C. 1999. 'Restorative Justice is Republican Justice'. In L Walgrave and G Bazemore (eds). *Restoring Juvenile Justice: An Exploration of the Restorative Justice Paradigm for Reforming Juvenile Justice*. Criminal Justice Press.

Brangan, L. 2024. 'States of Denial: Magdalene Laundries in Twentieth-Century Ireland'. *Punishment & Society* 26(2): 394–413.

Breathnach, C. 2022. 'Gender Medicine and the State in Ireland 1852–1922'. In J Alwail, C Breathnach, and SA Buckley. *Gender and History*. Routledge.

Breathnach, C, and E O'Halpin. 2022. 'Sexual Assault and Fatal Violence Against Women during the Irish War of Independence, 1919–1921: Kate Maher's Murder in Context'. *Medical Humanities* 48(1): 94–103.

Brennan, C. 2015. 'Trials and Contestations: Ireland's Ryan Commission'. In J Sköld and S Swain (eds). *Apologies and the Legacy of Abuse of Children in 'Care'*. Palgrave Macmillan.

Brennan, D. 2015. *Irish Insanity, 1800–2000*. Routledge.

Brennan, P. 2004a. 'The Catholic School and Secularization in Ireland'. *Études irlandaises, Hors-Série* 29(1): 85–94.

Brennan, P. 2004b. 'The Family in Ireland'. *Études irlandaises, Hors-Série* 29(1): 95–102.

Brock, R, and Parker, R. 2008. *Saving Paradise: How Christianity Traded Love of This World for Crucifixion and Empire*. Beacon Press.

Bromley, M. 1997. 'Writing Terrorism Out of the Story: Sunday Life and "War Weariness" in Northern Ireland'. In A O'Day (ed). *Political Violence in Northern Ireland: Conflict and Conflict Resolution*. Praeger.

Brookes, D. 2023 *Restorative Justice and Criminal Justice: The Case for Parallelism*. Eleven.

Brownlow, G. 2020. 'Industrial Policy in Northern Ireland: Past, Present and Future'. *The Economic and Social Review* 51(3): 407–24.

Bryson, A, and K McEvoy. 2023. 'Human Rights Activism and Transitional Justice Advocacy in Northern Ireland'. *International Journal of Transitional Justice* 17(3): 453–69.

Buckley, HD, and CD O'Nolan. 2013. *An Examination of Recommendations from Inquiries into Events in Families and Their Interactions with State Services, and Their Impact on Policy and Practice*. Government Publications.

Bunting, L. 2008. 'Sexual Offences Against Children: An Exploration of Attrition in the Northern Ireland Criminal Justice System'. *Child Abuse & Neglect* 32 (Dec): 1109–18.

Burford, G, J Braithwaite, and V Braithwaite (eds). 2019. *Restorative and Responsive Human Services*. Taylor and Francis.

Burke, M. 2020. '"Disremembrance": Joyce and Irish Protestant Institutions'. *Éire-Ireland* 55(1): 201–22.

Byrne, P. 2018. *The Preacher and the Prelate: The Achill Mission Colony and the Battle for Souls in Famine Ireland*. Irish Academic Press.

Byrne, S. 2021. 'Keeping Company with the Enemy: Gender and Sexual Violence Against Women during the Irish War of Independence and Civil War, 1919–1923'. *Women's History Review* 30(1): 108–25.

Byrnes, TA. 2020. 'Catholic Bishops and Sexual Abuse: Power, Constraint, and Institutional Context'. *Journal of Church and State* 62(1): 5–25.

Candea, DM. 2018. 'Shame-Proneness, Guilt-Proneness and Anxiety Symptoms: A Meta-Analysis'. *Journal of Anxiety Disorders* 58: 78–106.

Cane, P. 2014. 'Tort Law and Public Functions'. In John Oberdiek (ed). *The Philosophical Foundations of the Law of Torts*. Oxford University Press.

Caranua. 2021. *Caranua Evaluation Report Executive Summary*. Available at: https://caranua.ie/wp-content/uploads/2021/03/Caranua-Evaluation-Report-Executive-Summary.pdf

Cárdenas, M, D Páez, B Rimé, and M Arnoso. 2015. 'How Transitional Justice Processes and Official Apologies Influence Reconciliation: The case of the Chilean "Truth and Reconciliation" and "Political Imprisonment and Torture" Commissions'. *Journal of Community & Applied Social Psychology* 25(6): 515–30.

Carr, A, E Flanagan, B Dooley, M Fitzpatrick, R Flanagan Howard, M Shevlin, K Tierney, M White, M Daly, and J Egan. 2009. 'Profiles of Irish Survivors of Institutional Abuse with Different Adult Attachment Styles'. *Attachment and Human Development* 11(2): 183–201.

Carr, A, F Nearchou, H Duff, DN Mhaoileoin, K Cullen, A O'Dowd, and L Battigelli. 2019. 'Survivors of Institutional Abuse in Long-term Child Care in Scotland'. *Child Abuse & Neglect* 93 (Jul): 38–54.

Carrigan Committee. 1931. *Report of the Committee on the Criminal Law Amendment Acts (1880-85), and Juvenile Prostitution* (the Carrigan Report). The Stationery Office.

Catino, M. 2013. *Organizational Myopia: Problems of Rationality and Foresight in Organizations*. Cambridge University Press.

Catterall, E. 2018. *Apologies and Institutional Child Abuse*. Queen's University Belfast, September.

Cavallaro, JL, and J O'Connell. 2020. 'When Prosecution is Not Enough: How the International Criminal Court can Prevent Atrocity and Advance Accountability by Emulating Regional Human Rights Institutions'. *Yale Journal of International Law* 45(1): 1–68.

Cavanagh, E. 2013. 'Kingdom or Colony? English or British?: Early Modern Ireland and the Colonialism Question'. *Journal of Colonialism and Colonial History* 14(2), https://dx.doi.org/10.1353/cch.2013.0031.

Celermajer, D. 2009. *The Sins of the Nation and the Ritual of Apologies*. Cambridge University Press.

Celermajer, D. 2014. 'From Mea Culpa to Nostra Culpa: A Reparative Apology from the Catholic Church?'. In M Mihai and M Thaler (eds). *On the Use and Abuses of Political Apologies*. Palgrave Macmillan.

Cels, S. 2015. 'Interpreting Political Apologies: The Neglected Role of Performance'. *Political Psychology* 36(3): 351–60.

Charles-Edward, T. 2000. *Early Christian Ireland*. Cambridge University Press.

Chesnais, JC. 1981. *History of Violence in the West*. Paris: University of Paris.

Christie, N. 1986. 'The Ideal Victim'. In EA Fattah (ed). *From Crime Policy to Victim Policy: Reorienting the Justice System*. Palgrave Macmillan.

Claffey, P, J Egan, and M Keenan (eds). 2013. *Broken Faith: Why Hope Matters*. Peter Lang.

Clamp, K. 2016. 'Restorative Justice as a Contested Response to Conflict and the Challenge of the Transitional Context: An Introduction'. In K Clamp (ed). *Restorative Justice in Transitional Settings*. Routledge.

Clamp, K. 2019. 'Transforming Restorative Justice for Transitional Settings'. In M Natarajan (ed). *International and Transnational Crime and Justice* (2nd ed). Cambridge University Press.

Clamp, K, and J Doak. 2012. 'More than Words: Restorative Justice Concepts in Transitional Justice Settings'. *International Criminal Law Review* 12(3): 339–60.

Clancy, M. 1990. 'Aspects of Women's Contribution to the Oireachtas Debate in the Irish Free State, 1922–37'. In M Luddy and C Murphy (eds). *Women Surviving: Studies in Irish Women's History in the 19th and 20th Centuries*. Poolbeg.

Clarke, G. 2014. *Everyday Violence in the Irish Civil War*. Cambridge University Press.

Clough, M. 2017. *Shame, the Church and the Regulation of Female Sexuality*. Routledge.

Coen, M, K O'Donnell, and M O'Rourke (eds). 2023. *A Dublin Magdalene Laundry: Donnybrook and Church–State Power in Ireland*. Bloomsbury Publishing.

Cohen, JR. 1999. 'Advising Clients to Apologize'. *Southern California Law Review* 72(5): 1009–70.

Cohen, S. 1995. 'State Crimes of Previous Regimes: Knowledge, Accountability, and the Policing of the Past'. *Law & Social Inquiry* 20(1): 7–50.

Cohen, S. 2001. *States of Denial: Knowing About Atrocities and Suffering*. Polity Press.

Coker, DK. 2002. 'Transformative Justice: Anti-Subordination Processes in Cases of Domestic Violence Restorative Justice and Family Violence'. In H Strang and J Braithwaite (eds). *Restorative Justice and Family Violence*. Cambridge University Press.

Colton, M, M Vanstone, and C Walby. 2002. 'Victimization, Care and Justice: Reflections on the Experiences of Victims/Survivors Involved in Large-Scale Historical Investigations of Child Sexual Abuse in Residential Institutions'. *British Journal of Social Work* 32(5): 541–51.

Commissie Samson. 2012. *Omringd door zorg, toch niet veilig. Seksueel misbruik van door de overheid ut huis geplaatste kinderen, 1945 tot heden. Rapport Commissie-Samson*. Boom.

Commission of Inquiry into Mental Illness. 1966. *Commission of Inquiry into Mental Illness: 1966 Report*. The Stationery Office.

Commission of Inquiry into the Reformatory and Industrial School System. 1936. *Report of the Commission of Inquiry into the Reformatory and Industrial School System 1934–36* (the Cussen Report). The Stationery Office.

Commission of Investigation (CoI). 2009. *Report into the Catholic Archdiocese of Dublin* (Chair: Judge Yvonne Murphy). Department of Justice and Law Reform.

Commission of Investigation (CoI). 2011. *Report into the Catholic Archdiocese of Cloyne* (Chair: Judge Yvonne Murphy). Department of Justice and Law Reform.

Commission of Investigation into Mother and Baby Homes (CoI MBH). 2021. *Final Report* (Chair: Judge Yvonne Murphy). Department of Children, Equality, Disability, Integration and Youth.

Commission on the Relief of the Sick and Destitute Poor. 1927. *Report of the Commission on the Relief of the Sick and Destitute Poor*. The Stationery Office.

Commission to Inquire Into Child Abuse (CICA). 2009. *Report of the Commission to Inquire into Child Abuse* (Chair: Judge Séan Ryan), Available at: http://www.childabusecommission.ie/.

Compensation Advisory Committee. 2002. *Towards Redress and Recovery: Report for the Minister for Education and Science*. Department of Education and Science.

Comptroller and Auditor General. 2016. *Special Report: Cost of Child Abuse and Redress* (Report No 96). Office of the Comptriller and Auditor General.

Conley, JM, WM O'Barr, and RC Riner. 2019. *Just Words: Law, Language, and Power*. University of Chicago Press.

Connell, R. 1995. *Masculinities*. Polity Press.

Connolly, L. 2021. 'Sexual Violence in the Irish Civil War: A Forgotten War Crime?' *Women's History Review* 30(1): 126–43.

Connolly, SJ. 2004. 'The Moving Statute and the Turtle Dove: Approaches to the History of the Irish Religion'. *Irish Economic and Social History* 31(1): 1–22.

Connolly, SJ. 2017 'Settler Colonialism in Ireland from the English Conquest to the Nineteenth Century'. In E Cavanagh and L Veracini (eds). *The Routledge Handbook of the History of Settler Colonialism*. Routledge.

Convery, U. 2014. 'Locked in the past: An Historical Analysis of the Legal Framework of Custody for Children in Northern Ireland'. *European Journal of Criminology* 11(2): 251–69.

Corless, C. 2021. *Belonging: One Woman's Search for Truth and Justice for the Tuam Babies*. Hachette Books.

Corrigan, P, and P Lundy. 2021. *Learning the Lessons Seminar Series, Co-designing the Inquiry/Investigation into Mother and Baby and Magdalene Laundry Institutions on Northern Ireland*, Amnesty International and Ulster University, June. Available at: https://www.amnesty.org.uk/files/2021-06/Learning%20the%20lessons%20report.pdf.

Cortis, N, and I Katz. 2022. 'Waiting for Redress: Child Sexual Abuse Survivors' Experiences of Australia's National Redress Scheme'. *Child Abuse & Neglect* 129 (Jul): 1–10.

Costello, K. 2021. '"Inoperative But Insulting:" Residues of the Penal Laws, 1829–1920'. In K Costello and N Howlin (eds). *Law and Religion in Ireland, 1700–1970*. Springer International Publishing.

Coughlin, JJ. 2002. 'The Clergy Sexual Abuse Crisis and the Spirit of Canon Law'. *Boston College Law Review* 44(4): 977–98.

Cowden, RG, EL Jr Worthington, C Jakins, and S Joynt. 2019. 'Do Congruent Apologies Facilitate Forgiveness?' *South African Journal of Psychology* 49(3): 403–16.

Crenshaw, K. 1991. 'Mapping the Margins: Intersectionality, Identity Politics, and Violence Against Women of Colour'. *Stanford Law Review* 43(6): 1241–300.

Crossman, V. 2009a. *Politics, Pauperism and Power in Late Nineteenth-century Ireland*. Manchester University Press.

Crossman, V. 2009b. 'Cribbed, Contained and Confined? The Care of Children under the Irish Poor Law 1850–1920'. *Eire-Ireland* 44(1&2): 37–61.

Crossman, V. 2013. *Poverty and the Poor Law in Ireland 1850–1914*. Liverpool University Press.

Crowe, C. 2008. 'The Ferns Report: Vindicating the Abused Child'. *Eire-Ireland* 43(1): 50–73.

Cullors, P. 2019. 'Abolition and Reparations: Histories of Resistance, Transformative Justice, and Accountability'. *Harvard Law Review* 132(6): 1684–729.

Cunningham, M. 1999. 'Saying Sorry: The Politics of Apology'. *The Political Quarterly* 70(3): 285–93.

Cuthbert, D, and M Quartly. 2012. '"Forced Adoption" in the Australian Story of National Regret and Apology'. *Australian Journal of Politics & History* 58(1): 82–96.

Cuthbert, D, and M Quartly. 2013. 'Forced Child Removal and the Politics of National Apologies in Australia'. *American Indian Quarterly* 37(1–2): 178–202.

Daly, K. 2011. 'Conventional and Innovative Justice Responses to Sexual Violence'. *ACSSA Issues* 12: 1–36.

Daly, K. 2013. 'The Punishment Debate in Restorative Justice'. In R Sparks and J Simon (eds). *The Sage Handbook of Punishment and Society*. Sage Publications.

Daly, K. 2014a. 'Reconceptualisatizing Sexual Victimization and Justice'. In I Vanfraechem, A Pembertron, and F Ndahinda (eds). *Justice for Victims: Perspectives on Rights, Transition and Reconciliation*. Routledge.

Daly, K. 2014b. *Redressing Institutional Abuse of Children*. Palgrave Macmillan.

Daly, K. 2015. 'Sexual Violence and Justice: How and Why Context Matters'. In A Powell, N Henry, and A Flynn (eds). *Rape Justice: Beyond the Criminal Law*. Palgrave Macmillan.

Daly, K. 2017. 'Sexual Violence and Victims' Justice Interests'. In E Zinsstag and M Keenan (eds). *Restorative Responses to Sexual Violence: Legal, Social and Therapeutic Dimensions*. Routledge.

Daly, K. 2018. 'Inequalities of Redress: Australia's National Redress Scheme for Institutional Abuse of Children'. *Journal of Australian Studies* 42(2): 204–16.

Daly, K. 2022. *Remaking Justice after Sexual Violence*. Eleven.

Daly, K, and J Davis. 2019. 'Unravelling Redress for Institutional Abuse of Children in Australia'. *University of New South Wales Law Journal* 42(4): 1254–93.

Daly, K, and J Davis. 2021. 'Civil Justice and Redress Scheme Outcomes for Child Sexual Abuse by the Catholic Church'. *Current Issues in Criminal Justice* 33(4): 438–65.

Daly, K, and J Davis. 2024. Historical Policy Wrongs (ms in preparation).

Daly, K, and J Stubbs. 2006. 'Feminist Engagement with Restorative Justice'. *Theoretical Criminology* 10(1): 1362–4806.

Daly, M. 2006. 'Marriage, Fertility and Women's Lives in Twentieth-Century Ireland (c. 1900–c. 1970)'. *Women's History Review* 15(4): 571–85.

Daly, M. 2007. 'The Irish Free State/Éire/Republic of Ireland/Ireland: "A Country by Any Other Name"?' *Journal of British Studies* 46(1): 72–90.

Deetman, W, N Draijer, P Kalbfleisch, H Merckelbach, M Monteiro, and G De Vries. 2011. *Seksueel misbruik van minderjarigen in de Rooms-Katholieke Kerk* (Chair: WJ Deetman) Balans.

de Greiff P. 2006. 'Justice and Reparations'. In P de Greiff (ed). *The Handbook of Reparations*. Oxford University Press.

de Greiff, P. 2008. 'The Role of Apologies in National Reconciliation Processes: On Making Trustworthy Institutions Trusted'. In M Gibney, R Howard-Hassmann, JM Coicaud, and N Steiner (eds). *The Age of Apology: Facing up to the Past*. University of Pennsylvania Press.

de Greiff, P. 2009. 'Articulating the Links Between Transitional Justice and Development: Justice and Social Integration'. In P de Greiff and R Duthie (eds). *Transitional Justice and Development: Making Connections*. SSRC.

de Greiff, P. 2010. 'A Normative Conception of Transitional Justice'. *Politorbis* 50(3): 17–30.

de Greiff, P. 2012. 'Theorising Transitional Justice'. In M Williams, R Nagy, and J Elster (eds). *Transitional Justice: Nomos LI*. New York University Press.

de Greiff, P. 2020. 'The Future of the Past: Reflections on the Present State and Prospects of Transitional Justice'. *International Journal of Transitional Justice* 14(2): 251–9.

Dekker, JJ, and H Grieten. 2015. Sexual Abuse in Dutch Child Protection, 1945–2010. In JJ Sköld and S Swain (eds). *Apologies and the Legacy of Abuse of Children in 'Care': International Perspectives*. Palgrave Macmillan.

Delacorn A. 2011. 'Royal Commissions in Victoria 1854–2009'. Research Paper, Parliamentary Library, Victoria, July.

Denney, A, K Kerley, and N Gross. 2018. 'Child Sexual Abuse in Protestant Christian Congregations: A Descriptive Analysis of Offense and Offender Characteristics'. *Religions* 9(1): 27–40.

Department of Children, Equality, Disability, Integration and Youth (DCEDIY). 2021. *Report of the Interdepartmental Group (IDG) on the Development of the Mother and Baby Institutions Payment Scheme*. The Stationery Office.

Department of Children, Equality, Disability, Integration and Youth. 2022. *First Report of the Collaborative Forum of Former Residents of Mother and Baby Homes*. The Stationery Office.

Department of Education. 2023. *Scoping Inquiry into Historical Sexual Abuse in Schools run by Religious Orders*. Available at: https://www.gov.ie/en/publication/42b7e-education-scoping-inquiry/.

Department of Health. 1951. *White Paper on the Reconstruction of County Homes and Improved Care of the Aged and Other Classes at Present in County Homes*. The Stationery Office.

Didi, A, K Soldatic, C Frohmader, and L Dowse. 2016. 'Violence Against Women with Disabilities: Is Australia Meeting its Human Rights Obligations?' *Australian Journal of Human Rights* 22(1): 159–77.

Doak, J, and L Taylor. 2013. 'Hearing the Voices of Victims and Offenders: The Role of Emotions in Criminal Sentencing'. *Northern Ireland Legal Quarterly* 64(1): 25–46.

Dolezal, L. 2015. *The Body and Shame: Phenomenology, Feminism, and the Socially Shaped Body*. Lexington Books.

Dooley, T. 2004. 'Land and Politics in Independent Ireland, 1923–48: The Case for Reappraisal'. *Irish Historical Studies* 34(134): 175–97.

Dorsett, R. 2013. 'The Effect of the Troubles on GDP in Northern Ireland'. *European Journal of Political Economy* 29: 119–33.

Douglas, M. 1986. *How Institutions Think*. Syracuse University Press.

Douzinas, C. 2000. *The End of Human Rights*. Hart Publishing.

Downes, J. 2017. '"It's Not the Abuse That Kills You, It's the Silence": The Silencing of Sexual Violence Activism in Social Justice Movements in the UK Left'. *Justice, Power and Resistance* 1(2): 35–58.

Doyle, M. 2014. 'Circles of Trust: Using Restorative Justice to Repair Organizations Marred by Sex Abuse'. *Pepperdine Dispute Resolution Law Journal* 14(2): 175.

Doyle, P. 1989. *The God Squad*. Corgi.

Doyle, TP. 2004. 'Canon Law and the Clergy Sexual Abuse Crisis: The Failure from Above'. In TG Plante (ed). *Sin Against the Innocents: Sexual Abuse by Priests and the Role of the Catholic Church*. Praeger Publishers/Greenwood Publishing Group.

Dressing, H, D Dölling, D Hermann, A Kruse, E Schmitt, B Bannenberg, K Whittaker, A Hoell, E Voss, and HJ Salize. 2021. 'Child Sexual Abuse by Catholic Priests, Deacons, and Male Members of Religious Orders in the Authority of the German Bishops' Conference 1946–2014'. *Sexual Abuse* 33(3): 274–94.

Druliolle, V. 2018. 'The Struggle for Recognition of the Stolen Children and the Politics of Victimhood in Spain'. In V Druliolle and R Brett (eds). *The Politics of Victimhood in Post-Conflict Societies: Comparative and International Perspectives*. Palgrave Macmillan.

Duff, A. 2004. 'Who is Responsible, for What, to Whom?' *Ohio State Journal of Criminal Law* 2(1): 441–61.

Duff, A. 2006. 'Answering for Crime'. *Proceedings of the Aristotelian Society* 106(1): 87–113.

Duff, A. 2011. 'Responsibility, Restoration and Retribution'. In M Tonry (ed). *Retributivism has a Past: Has it a Future?* Oxford University Press.

Dukelow, F and M Considine. 2017. *Irish Social Policy: A Critical Introduction*. Policy Press.

Dunne, EA. 2004. 'Clerical Child Sex Abuse: The Response of the Roman Catholic Church'. *Journal of Community & Applied Social Psychology* 14(6): 490–4.

Earner-Byrne, L. 2003. 'The Boat to England: An Analysis of the Official Reactions to the Emigration of Single Expectant Irishwomen to Britain, 1922–1972'. *Irish Economic and Social History* 30(1): 52–70.

Earner-Byrne, L. 2011. 'Child Sexual Abuse, History, and the Pursuit of Blame in Modern Ireland'. In K Holmes and S Ward (eds). *Exhuming Passions: The Pressure of the Past in Ireland and Australia*. Irish Academic Press.

Earner-Byrne, L. 2018. 'The Family in Ireland, 1880–2015'. In T Bartlett (ed). *The Cambridge History of Ireland*. Cambridge University Press.

Earner-Byrne, L. 2023. 'The Irish Family: Blame, Agency and the "Unmarried Mother Problem", 1980s–2021'. *Contemporary European History* 32(2): 270–86.

Edelman, M. 2015. 'An Unexpected Path: Bankruptcy, Justice and Intersecting Identities in the Catholic Sexual Abuse Scandals'. *Australian Feminist Law Journal* 41(2): 271–88.

Eisinger, RM. 2011. 'The Political Non-Apology'. *Society* 48(2): 136–41.

Ellison, G. 2017. 'Criminalizing the Payment for Sex in Northern Ireland: Sketching the Contours of a Moral Panic'. *British Journal of Criminology* 57(1): 194–214.

Enright, M, and A O'Donoghue. 2021. *Mother and Baby Homes Commission of Investigation Report Draft Alternative Executive Summary*. TU Dublin.

Enright, M, and S Ring. 2020. 'State Legal Responses to Historical Institutional Abuse: Shame, Sovereignty, and Epistemic Injustice'. *Éire-Ireland* 55(1): 68–99.

Erez, E, and T Meroz-Aharoni. 2011. 'Primary and Secondary Victims and Victimization during Protracted Conflict'. In R Letschert, R Haveman, AM de Brouwer, and A Pemberton (eds). *Victimological Approaches to International Crimes: Africa*. Intersentia.

Ericsson, K. 2015. 'Victim Capital and the Language of Money: The Norwegian Process of Inquiries and Apologies'. *The Journal of the History of Childhood and Youth* 8(1): 123–37.

Evans, C. 2012. *The Right to Reparation in International Law for Victims of Armed Conflict*. Cambridge University Press.

Evans, M. 2018. *Transformative Justice: Remedying Human Rights Violations beyond Transition. Routledge.*

Ewick, P (ed). 2006. *Consciousness and Ideology*. Routledge.

Fahy, B. 1999. *Freedom of Angels*. The O'Brien Press.

Fahy, E. 1942. 'Reformatory Schools in Ireland'. *Hermathena* 60: 54–73.

Fallon, F. 2021. *Evaluation of the Counselling and Support Services of Towards Healing*. Towards Healing.

Farren, S. 1992. 'A Lost Opportunity: Education and Community in Northern Ireland 1947–1960'. *History of Education* 21(1): 71–82.

Farrow, TCW, and LA Jacobs. 2020. *The Justice Crisis: The Cost and Value of Accessing Law*. UBC Press.

Fereday, J, and E Muir-Cochrane. 2006. 'Demonstrating Rigor Using Thematic Analysis: A Hybrid Approach of Inductive and Deductive Coding and Theme Development'. *International Journal of Qualitative Methods* 5(1): 80–92.

Ferriter, D. 2009. *Occasions of Sin: Sex and Society in Modern Ireland*. Profile Books.

Figueroa, R, and D Tombs. 2020. 'Recognising Jesus as a Victim of Sexual Abuse: Responses from Sodalicio Survivors in Peru'. *Religion and Gender* 10(1): 57–75.

Finnane, M. 1996. 'Law and the Social Uses of the Asylum in Nineteenth-Century Ireland'. In J Carriere and D Tomlinson (eds). *Asylum in the Community*. Routledge.

Finnane, M. 2001. 'The Carrigan Committee of 1930–31 and the "Moral Condition of the Saorstát"'. *Irish Historical Studies* 32(128): 519–36.

Fischer, C. 2016. 'Gender, Nation, and the Politics of Shame: Magdalen Laundries and the Institutionalization of Feminine Transgression in Modern Ireland'. *Signs: Journal of Women in Culture and Society* 41(4): 821–43.

Fischer, C. 2017. 'Revealing Ireland's "Proper" Heart: Apology, Shame, Nation'. *Hypatia* 32(4): 751–67.

Fitzgerald, J, and S Kenny. 2020. "Till Debt Do Us Part": Financial Implications of the Divorce of the Irish Free State from the United Kingdom, 1922–1926'. *European Review of Economic History* 24(4): 818–42.

Fitzpatrick, M, A Carr, B Dooley, R Flanagan-Howard, E Flanagan, K Tierney, M White, M Daly, M Shevlin, and J Egan. 2010. 'Profiles of Adult Survivors of Severe Sexual, Physical and Emotional Institutional Abuse in Ireland'. *Child Abuse Review* 19(6): 387–404.

Flanagan-Howard, R, A Carr, M Shevlin, B Dooley, M Fitzpatrick, E Flanagan, K Tierney, M White, M Daly, and J Egan. 2009. 'Development and Initial Validation of the Institutional Child Abuse Processes and Coping Inventory Among a Sample of Irish Adult Survivors of Institutional Abuse'. *Child Abuse and Neglect* 33(9): 586–97.

Fletcher, LE, and HM Weinstein. 2017. 'Transitional Justice and the "Plight" of Victimhood'. In C Lawther, L Moffett, and D Jacobs (eds). *Research Handbook on Transitional Justice*. Edward Elgar Publishing.

Flinders, M. 2023. 'Loss of Balance? Exploring the "Dark Side" of Accountability'. In M Flinders and C Monaghan (eds). *Questions of Accountability: Prerogatives, Power and Politics*. Hart Publishing.

Flinders, M, and C Monaghan. 2023. 'Accountability Matters'. In M Flinders and C Monaghan (eds). *Questions of Accountability: Prerogatives, Power and Politics*. Hart Publishing.

Flynn, M. 1983. *Nothing to Say*. Lilliput Press.

Foley, T. 2015. 'Institutional Responses to Child Sexual Abuse: How a Moral Conversation with its Lawyers Might Contribute to Cultural Change in a Faith-Based Institution'. *Legal Ethics* 18(2): 164–81.

Foley, T. 2019. 'Changing Institutional Culture in the Wake of Clerical Abuse—The Essentials of Restorative and Legal Regulation'. *Contemporary Justice Review* 22(2): 171–87.

Fox, F, and A Crean. 2017. *Ryan Report Follow Up: Submission to the United Nations Committee Against Torture 2012 Session 61*. Reclaiming Self.

Fricker, M. 2007. *Epistemic Injustice: Power and the Ethics of Knowing*. Oxford University Press.

Funk-Unrau, N. 2014. 'The Canadian Apology to Indigenous Residential School Survivors: A Case Study of Renegotiation of Social Relations'. In M Mihai and M Thaler (eds). *On the Uses and Abuses of Political Apologies*. Palgrave Macmillan.

Gal, T. 2020. 'Restorative Justice Myopia'. *The International Journal of Restorative Justice* 3(3): 341–55.

Gallen, J. 2018. 'Historical Abuse and the Statute of Limitations'. *Statute Law Review* 39(2): 103–17.

Gallen, J. 2019a. 'The European Court of Human Rights, Transitional Justice and Historical Abuse in Consolidated Democracies'. *Human Rights Law Review* 19(4): 675–704.

Gallen, J. 2019b. 'Redressing Gendered Mistreatment: Magdalene Laundries, Symphysiotomy and Mother and Baby Homes'. In L Black and P Dunne (eds). *Law and Gender in Modern Ireland: Critique and Reform*. Hart Publishing.

Gallen, J. 2020. 'Transitional Justice and Ireland's Legacy of Historical Abuse'. *Éire-Ireland* 55(1): 35–67.

Gallen, J. 2023a. *Transitional Justice and the Historical Abuses of Church and State.* Cambridge University Press.

Gallen, J. 2023b. 'Transitional Justice and Non-Paradigmatic Transitions'. In C Lawther and L Moffett (eds). *Research Handbook on Transitional Justice* (2nd ed). Edward Elgar Publishing.

Gallen, J, and K Gleeson. 2018. 'Unpaid Wages: The Experiences of Irish Magdalene Laundries and Indigenous Australians'. *International Journal of Law in Context* 14(1): 43–60.

Gallen, J, and L Moffett. 2022. 'The Palliative Role of Reparations in Reconciling Societies with the Past: Redressing Victims or Consolidating the State?' *Journal of Intervention and Statebuilding* 16(4): 498–518.

Gambetta, D. 1988. 'Can We Trust in Trust?'. In D Gambetta (ed). *Trust: Making and Breaking Co-operative Relations*. Basil Blackwell.

Ganiel, G. 2008. *Evangelicalism and Conflict in Northern Ireland.* Palgrave Macmillan.

Ganiel, G. 2016. *Transforming Post-Catholic Ireland: Religious Practice in Late Modernity*. Oxford University Press.

Ganiel, G, and AR Holmes (eds). 2024. *The Oxford Handbook of Religion in Modern Ireland.* Oxford University Press.

Ganiel, G, and C Ní Dhónaill. 2024. 'The Catholic Church has Gotten Better at Saying Sorry—But is Anyone Listening?' *QPOL*, 25 March.

Gardner, J. 2003. 'The Mark of Responsibility'. *Oxford Journal of Legal Studies* 23(2): 157–71.

Garrett, PM. 2000. 'The Abnormal Flight: The Migration and Repatriation of Irish Unmarried Mothers'. *Social History* 25(3): 330–43.

Garrett, PM. 2013. 'A "Catastrophic, Inept, Self-Serving" Church? Re-Examining Three Reports on Child Abuse in the Republic of Ireland'. *Journal of Progressive Human Services* 24(1): 43–65.

Garrett, PM. 2016. '"Unmarried Mothers" in the Republic of Ireland'. *Journal of Social Work* 16(6): 708–25.

Gavrielides, T. 2013. 'Clergy Child Sexual Abuse and the Restorative Justice Dialogue'. *Journal of Church and State* 55(4): 617–39.

Gavrielides, T, and D Coker. 2005. 'Restoring Faith: Resolving the Roman Catholic Church's Sexual Scandals through Restorative Justice (Working Paper I)'. *Contemporary Justice Review* 8(4): 345–65.

Geary, LM. 2018. 'From Voluntary Hospitals to Voluntary Health Insurance: A History of Irish Healthcare from the Early-Eighteenth to the Mid-Twentieth Century'. In the *Irish Healthcare System: An Historical and Comparative Review*'. Health Insurance Authority.

Ghavami, N, D Katsiaficas, and LO Rogers. 2016. 'Intersectional Approach in Developmental Science: The Role of Race, Gender, Sexual Orientation and Immigrant Status'. In S Horn, M Ruck, and L Liden (eds). *Advances in Child Development and Behaviour Vol 50*. Academic Press.

Gibbons, J. 1999. 'Language and the Law'. *Annual Review of Applied Linguistics* 19: 156–73.

Gibney, M, R Howard-Hassmann, JM Coicaud, and N Steiner (eds). 2008. *The Age of Apology: Facing up to the Past.* University of Pennsylvania Press.

Gilligan, P. 2012. 'Clerical Abuse and Laicisation: Rhetoric and Reality in the Catholic Church in England and Wales'. *Child Abuse Review* 21(6): 427–39.

Glaser, B, and AL Strauss. 2017. *The Discovery of Grounded Theory: Strategies for Qualitative Research.* Routledge.

Gleeson, K. 2015. 'The Money Problem: Reparation and Restorative Justice in the Catholic Church's Towards Healing Program'. *Current Issues in Criminal Justice* 26(3): 317–32.

Gleeson, K, and S Ring. 2021. 'Confronting the Past and Changing the Future? Public Inquiries into Institutional Child Abuse, Ireland and Australia'. *Griffith Law Review* 29(1): 109–33.

Gleeson, K, and A Zanghellini. 2020. 'Graceful Remedies: Understanding Grace in the Catholic Church's Treatment of Clerical Child Sexual Abuse'. In K Gleeson and T Willem Jones (eds). *Interdisciplinary Feminist Perspectives on Crimes of Clerical Child Sexual Abuse.* Routledge.

Godhavn Inquiry. 2011. *En undersøgelse af klager over overgreb og medicinske forsøg på Drenge- og Skolehjemmet Godhavn samt 18 andre børnehjem i perioden 1945–1976* (Chair: Marie Rytter). Syddansk Universitetsforlag.

Goffman, E. 1961. *Asylums.* Doubleday.

Goffman, E. 1971. *Relations in Public: Microstudies of the Public Order.* Basic Books.

Goldberg, JCP, and BC Zipursky. 2014. 'Tort Law and Responsibility'. In J Oberdiek (ed). *The Philosophical Foundations of the Law of Torts.* Oxford University Press.

Golder, B. 2015. *Foucault and the Politics of Rights.* Stanford University Press.

Golding F. 2018. 'Sexual Abuse as the Core Transgression of Childhood Innocence: Unintended Consequences for Care Leavers'. *Journal of Australian Studies* 42(2): 191–203.

Goode, H, H McGee, and C O'Boyle. 2003. *Time to Listen: Confronting Child Sexual Abuse by Catholic Clergy in Ireland.* The Liffey Press.

Goriely, T. 1994. 'Debating the Quality of Legal Services: Differing Models of the Good Lawyer'. *International Journal of the Legal Profession* 1(2): 159–71.

Government of Ireland. 2021. *Action Plan for Survivors and Former Residents of Mother and Baby and County Home Institutions.* Available at: https://www.gov.ie/pdf/?file=https://assets.gov.ie/204579/0b00bbf2-4319-4298-827e-6b0b01bf09ae.pdf.

Government of Northern Ireland. 1950. *Report on the Administration of Home Office Services, 1948–49.* His Majesty's Stationery Office.

Govier, T. 1999. 'What is Acknowledgement and Why is it Important?' *OSSA Conference Archive.* Available at: http://scholar.uwindsor.ca/ossaarchive/OSSA3/keynotes/1.

Govier, T. 2006. *Taking Wrongs Seriously: Acknowledgement, Reconciliation and the Politics of Sustainable Peace.* Humanity Books.

Govier, T, and W Verwoerd. 2002. 'The Promise and Pitfalls of Apology'. *Journal of Social Philosophy* 3(1): 67–82.

Gray, D. 2010. 'A No-Excuse Approach to Transitional Justice: Reparations as Tools of Extraordinary Justice'. *Washington University Law Review* 87(5): 1043–103.

Gready P. 2019. 'Introduction'. In P Gready and S Robins (eds). *From Transitional to Transformative Justice*. Cambridge University Press.

Gready, P, and S Robins. 2014. 'From Transitional to Transformative Justice: A New Agenda for Practice'. *International Journal of Transitional Justice* 8(3): 339–61.

Gready, P, and S Robins. 2020. 'Transitional Justice and Theories of Change: Towards Evaluation as Understanding'. *International Journal of Transitional Justice* 14(2): 280–99.

Greif, A. 2006. *Institutions and the Path to the Modern Economy*. Cambridge University Press.

Greer, C. 2001. 'Risky Business'. *Criminal Justice Matters* 43(1): 28–9.

Greer, C. 2003. 'Sex Crime and the Media: Press Representations in Northern Ireland'. In P Mason (ed). *Criminal Visions: Media Representations of Crime and Justice*. Willan Publishing.

Grenfell Tower Inquiry. 2024. Grenfell Tower Inquiry: Phase 2 Report. *Report of the Public Inquiry into the Fire at Grenfell Tower on 14 June 2017*. HC 19-I.

Grimes, DL. 2006. 'Practice What You Preach: How Restorative Justice Could Solve the Judicial Problems in Clergy Sexual Abuse Cases'. *Washington & Lee Law Review* 63(4): 1693–742.

Grimes, L. 2023. "We Did What Needed to be Done': Cherish, the First Support Group for Unmarried Mothers in Ireland'. *Women's History Review* 32(1): 21–35.

Guerzoni, MA. 2021. *Child Protection in the Church: An Anglican Case Study*. Routledge.

Guidepost Solutions. 2022. *Report of the Independent Investigation: The Southern Baptist Convention Executive Committee's Response to Sexual Abuse Allegations and an Audit of Procedures and Actions of the Credentials Committee*. Guidepost Solutions.

Hamber, B. 2000. 'Repairing the Irreparable: Dealing with the Double-Binds of Making Reparations for the Crimes of the Past'. *Ethnicity and Health* 5(3–4): 215–27.

Hamber, B. 2023. *Transitional Justice, Mental Health and Psychosocial Support: Renewing the United Nations Approach to Transitional Justice*. OHCHR. Available at: https://www.ohchr.org/sites/default/files/documents/issues/transitionaljustice/sg-guidance-note/SG-GuidanceNote-TJ-Mental-Health-digital.pdf.

Hamber, B, and P Lundy. 2020. 'Lessons from Transitional Justice? Toward a New Framing of a Victim-Centered Approach in the Case of Historical Institutional Abuse'. *Victims & Offenders* 15(6): 744–70.

Hamber, B, and R Wilson. 2002. 'Symbolic Closure through Memory, Reparation and Revenge in Post-Conflict Societies'. *Journal of Human Rights* 1(1): 35–53.

Hamilton, C. 2019. 'Criminal Justice Culture(s) in Ireland: Quo Vadis?' *Irish Probation Journal* 16 (Oct): 6–21.

Hamilton, C. 2023. 'Crime, Justice and Criminology in the Republic of Ireland'. *European Journal of Criminology* 20(5): 1597–620.

Hardin, R. 1999. 'Do We Want Trust in Government?' In M Warren (ed). *Democracy and Trust*. Cambridge University Press.

Harding Clark, M. 2016. *The Surgical Symphysiotomy Ex Gratia Payment Scheme Report* (Harding Clark Report). The Stationery Office.

Harlow, C. 2013. 'What Price Inquiries?' UK Constitutional Law Association Blog, 28 February. Available at: https://ukconstitutionallaw.org/2013/02/28/carol-harlow-what-price-inquiries/.

Harris, MK. 2007. 'Transformative Justice: The Transformation of Restorative Justice'. In D Sullivan and L Tift (eds). *The Handbook of Restorative Justice: A Global Perspective*. Routledge.

Harris, N, L Walgrave, and J Braithwaite. 2004. 'Emotional Dynamics in Restorative Conferences'. *Theoretical Criminology* 8(2): 191–210.

Hatton, TJ, and JG Williamson. 1993. 'After the Famine: Emigration from Ireland, 1850–1913'. *The Journal of Economic History* 53(3): 575–600.

Haydon, D, and S McAlister. 2015. 'Young People, Crime and Justice in Northern Ireland'. In AM McAlinden and C Dwyer (eds). *Criminal Justice in Transition: The Northern Ireland Context*. Bloomsbury.

Healy, C. 2011. 'American and Irish Perspectives on Collaborative Practice'. *Irish Journal of Family Law* 14(4): 98–108.

Hearit, KM. 2006. *Management by Apology: Corporate Responses to Allegations of Wrongdoing*. Lawrence Erlbaum Associates.

Hearty, K. 2021. 'Truth Beyond the "Trigger Puller": Moral Accountability, Transitional (in) Justice and the Limitations of Legal Truth'. *International Journal of Transitional Justice* 15(3): 658–77.

Henry, N. 2015. 'From Reconciliation to Transitional Justice: The Contours of Redress Politics in Established Democracies'. *International Journal of Transitional Justice* 9(2): 199–218.

Herman, JL. 2005. 'Justice from the Victim's Perspective'. *Violence Against Women* 11(5): 571–602.

Herman, JL. 2015. *Trauma and Recovery: The Aftermath of Violence—From Domestic Abuse to Political Terror*. Basic Books.

Herman, JL. 2023. *Truth and Repair: How Trauma Survivors Envision Justice*. Hachette UK.

Herremans, B, and T Destrooper. 2023. 'Moving Beyond Formal Truth Practices and Forensic Truth in the Syrian Conflict: How Informal Truth Practices Contribute to Thicker Understandings of Truth'. *Social & Legal Studies* 32(4): 519–39.

Hindley, N, and L Lord. 2021. 'The Development of Guidance for Responding to Disclosure of Non-Recent Child Sexual Abuse within a Large Provider of Health Services for Adults and Children'. *Child Abuse Review* 30(1): 71–83.

Hirsch, M. 2008. 'The Generation of Postmemory'. *Poetics Today* 29(1): 103–28.

Historical Institutional Abuse (HIA) Inquiry. 2017. *Report of the Inquiry into Historical Institutional Abuse*. The Inquiry into Historical Institutional Abuse 1922 to 1995 and The Executive Office (Chair: Sir Anthony Hart).

Hogan, C. 2019. *Republic of Shame: Stories from Ireland's Institutions from Fallen Women*. Penguin Ireland.

Holder, R. 2018. *Just Interests: Victims, Citizens and the Potential for Justice*. Edward Elgar Publishing.

Holme, I. 2018. 'Spiritual Eugenics as Part of the Irish Carceral Archipelago'. *Journal of Historical Sociology* 31(2): 154–64.

Holohan, C. 2011. *In Plain Sight: Responding to the Ferns, Ryan, Murphy and Cloyne Reports.* Amnesty International.

Howe, G. 1999. 'The Management of Public Inquiries'. *The Political Quarterly* 70(3): 294–304.

Howe, S. 2006. 'Historiography'. In K Kenny (ed). *Ireland and the British Empire.* Oxford University Press.

Howe, S. 2017. 'Northern Ireland and Settler Colonialism to the Good Friday Agreement 1998'. In E Cavanagh and L Veracini (eds). *The Routledge Handbook of the History of Settler Colonialism.* Routledge.

Hudson, B. 2002. 'Restorative Justice and Gendered Violence: Diversion or Effective Justice?' *British Journal of Criminology* 42(3): 616–34.

Huefner, JC, JL Ringle, MB Chmelka, and SD Ingram. 2007. 'Breaking the Cycle of Intergenerational Abuse: The Long-Term Impact of a Residential Care Program'. *Child Abuse & Neglect* 31 (Feb): 187–99.

Hughes, WH. 1985. *Report of the Committee of Inquiry into Children's Homes and Hostels.* The Stationery Office.

Humphreys, M. 2011. *Empty Cradles.* Corgi.

Huyse, L. 2003. 'Victims'. In D Bloomfield, T Barnes, and L Huyse (eds). *Reconciliation After Violent Conflict: A Handbook.* Institute for Democracy and Electoral Assistance.

Ignatieff, M. 2001. *Human Rights as Politics and Idolatry.* Princeton University Press.

Independent Inquiry into Child Sexual Abuse (IICSA). 2019. *Accountability and Reparations Investigation Report.*

Independent Inquiry into Child Sexual Abuse (IICSA). 2020a. *The Roman Catholic Church Safeguarding in the Roman Catholic Church in England and Wales.*

Independent Inquiry into Child Sexual Abuse (IICSA). 2020b. *The Anglican Church Safeguarding in the Church of England and the Church in Wales.*

Independent Inquiry into Child Sexual Abuse (IICSA). 2021. *Child Protection in Religious Organisations and Settings*, Investigation Report, September. Session 2021/22, HC 705.

Independent Inquiry into Child Sexual Abuse (IICSA). 2022a. *The Residential Schools Investigation, Investigation Report*, March. HC 1131.

Independent Inquiry into Child Sexual Abuse (IICSA). 2022b. *Report of the Independent Inquiry into Child Sexual Abuse*, October. HC 720.

Independent Review Group into the Defence Forces (IRG). 2023. *Final Report to the Minister for Defence.* The Stationary Office.

Inglis, T. 1998. *Moral Monopoly: The Rise and Fall of the Catholic Church in Modern Ireland.* University College Dublin Press.

Inglis T. 2005. 'Origins and Legacies of Irish Prudery: Sexuality and Social Control in Modern Ireland'. *Éire-Ireland* 40(3–4): 9–37.

Inquiry into Certain Planning Matters and Payments, 1997–2013. 2012. *The Final Report of the Tribunal of Inquiry into Certain Planning Matters and Payments* (Chair: Judge Alan Mahon). Minister for the Environment and Local Government.

Inquiry into Complaints Concerning Some Gardaí of the Donegal Division, 2002–2008 (Chair: Judge Frederick Morris). Available at: http://www.morristribunal.ie.

Inquiry into Exports of Defence Equipment and Dual-Use Goods to Iraq and Related Prosecutions, 1993–1996. 1995. *Report of the Inquiry into Exports of Defence Equipement and Dual-Use Goods to Iraq and Related Prosecution* (Chair: Sir Richard Scott). House of Commons Paper No 115, Session 1995–96.

Inquiry into Payments to Politicians and Related Matters, 1997–2011. 2011. *Report of the Tribunal of Inquiry into Payments to Politicians and Related Matters* (Chair: Justice Micheal Moriarty). Tribunal Office.

Inter-Departmental Committee (IDC). 2013. *Report of the Inter-Departmental Committee to Establish Facts of State Involvement with the Magdalen Laundries* (Chair: Senator Martin McAleese). Department of Justice.

Irish Catholic Bishops' Advisory Committee on Child Sexual Abuse by Priests and Religious. 1996. *Child Sexual Abuse: A Framework for a Church Response.* Veritas Publications.

Isaacs, T, and R Vernon (eds). 2011. *Accountability for Collective Wrongdoing.* Cambridge University Press.

James, M, and J Stanger-Ross. 2018. 'Impermanent Apologies: On the Dynamics of Timing and Public Knowledge in Political Apology'. *Human Rights Review* 19(3): 289–311.

Jankowitz, SE. 2018. *The Order of Victimhood: Violence, Hierarchy and Building Peace in Northern Ireland.* Palgrave Macmillan.

Jaspers, K. 2000. *The Question of German Guilt*, translated by EB Ashton. Fordham University Press.

Jeffery, R. 2011. 'When Is an Apology Not an Apology? Contrition Chic and Japan's (Un)apologetic Politics'. *Australian Journal of International Affairs* 65(5): 607–17.

Jesuit Province. 2024. 'Jesuit redress scheme for victims of child sexual abuse'. Jesuit Province. Available at: https://jesuit.ie/wp-content/uploads/2024/02/Redress-Scheme-for-Victims-of-Sexual-Abuse-8-February-2024.pdf.

Johnstone, G, and DV Ness. 2013. *Handbook of Restorative Justice.* Routledge.

Joint Past Pupils—Jesuit Steering Group. 2024. 'Fr Joseph Marmion SJ: His abuse, the harm caused, and Jesuit accountability: A narrative record'. Jesuit Province. Available at: https://jesuit.ie/wp-content/uploads/2024/02/Fr-Joseph-Marmion-SJ-A-narrative-record.pdf.

Jones, B, and J Bernath (eds). 2017. *Resistance and Transitional Justice.* Routledge

Jones, TW. 2019. 'Sin, Silence and States of Denial: Canon Law and the "Discovery" of Child Sexual Abuse'. In K Gleeson and TW Jones (eds). *Interdisciplinary Feminist Perspectives on Crimes of Clerical Sexual Abuse.* Routledge.

Joshi, Y. 2021. 'Racial Transition'. *Washington University Law Review* 98(4): 1181–256.

Jülich, S. 2006. 'Views of Justice Among Survivors of Historical Child Sexual Abuse: Implications for Restorative Justice in New Zealand'. *Theoretical Criminology* 10(1): 125–38.

Jülich, S, and F Landon. 2017. 'Achieving Justice Outcomes: Participants of Project Restore's Restorative Process'. In E Zinsstag and M Keenan (eds). *Restorative Responses to Sexual Violence: Legal, Social and Therapeutic Dimensions.* Routledge.

Justice for Magdalenes Research, Magdalene Oral History Project. 2022. Available at: http://jfmresearch.com/home/oralhistoryproject/about-the-magdalene-oral-history-project/.

Keating, A. 2004–6. 'Church, State, and Sexual Crime Against Children in Ireland after 1922'. *Radharc* 5 –7: 155–80.

Kee, HW, and RE Knox. 1970. 'Conceptual and Methodological Considerations in the Study of Trust'. *Journal of Conflict Resolution* 14(3): 357–66.

Keenan, M. 2011. 'Them and Us: The Clerical Child Sexual Offender'. In E McDonagh and V McNamara (eds). *An Irish Reader in Moral Theology, Vol II, Sex, Marriage and the Family*. Dublin: Columba Press.

Keenan, M. 2012. *Child Sexual Abuse and the Catholic Church: Gender, Power, and Organizational Culture*. Oxford University Press.

Keenan, M. 2013. 'Child Sexual Abuse and the Catholic Church: A Multi-Layered Perspective'. In P Claffey, J Egan, and M Keenan (eds). *Broken Faith: Why Hope Matters*. Peter Lang.

Keenan, M. 2014. *Sexual Trauma and Abuse: Restorative and Transformative Possibilities?* University College Dublin, School of Applied Social Science.

Keenan, M. 2015. 'Hindsight, Foresight and Historical Judgement: Child Sexual Abuse and the Catholic Church'. In Y Daly, D Healy, C Hamilton, and M Butler. *The Routledge Handbook of Irish Criminology*. Routledge

Keenan, M. 2017. 'Criminal Justice, Restorative Justice, Sexual Violence and the Rule of Law'. In E Zinsstag and M Keenan (eds). *Restorative Responses to Sexual Violence: Legal, Social and Therapeutic Dimensions*. Routledge.

Keenan, M. 2018. 'Training for Restorative Justice Practice in Sexual Violence Cases'. *The International Journal of Restorative Justice* 1(2): 291–302.

Keenan, M. 2020. 'Why Restorative Justice after Sexual Crime?' Presentation at the Conference 'Whose Justice is Restorative Justice'. Talinn, Estonia, 26 November.

Keenan, M, V Bonini, D Martin, A Haarländer, and A Halonen. 2025. 'Domestic Violence and Restorative Justice: Responding to Feminist Concerns'. *The International Journal of Restorative Justice* (in press).

Keenan, M, D Healy, G McLoughlin Burke, and K Keenan. 2023. *Delays in the Processing of Sexual Crime in Ireland: Stakeholder Experiences*. Department of Justice, Equality and Law Reform.

Keenan, M, and O Lyons. 2023. 'Adult Disclosures of Non-Recent Child Sexual Abuse: Is There a Role For Restorative Justice?' *European Social Work Research* 1(3): 295–311.

Keenan, M, and E Zinsstag. 2014. 'Restorative Justice and Sexual Offenses: Can "Changing Lenses" Be Appropriate in This Case Too?' *Monatsschrift for Criminology* 97(1): 93–106.

Keenan, M, and E Zinsstag. 2022. *Sexual Violence and Restorative Justice: Addressing the Justice Gap*. Oxford University Press.

Keenan, M, E Zinsstag, and C O'Nolan. 2016. 'Sexual Violence and Restorative Practices in Belgium, Ireland and Norway: A Thematic Analysis of Country Variations'. *Restorative Justice: An International Journal* 4(1): 86–114.

Kelly, G, and J Coulter. 1997. 'The Children (Northern Ireland) Order 1995 a New Era for Fostering and Adoption Services?' *Adoption & Fostering* 21(3): 5–13.

Kendrick, A, M Hawthorn, S Karim, and J Shaw. 2015. 'Scotland: Historic Abuse in Care and Human Rights'. In J Sköld and S Swain (eds). *Apologies and the Legacy of Abuse of Children in 'Care': International Perspectives*. Palgrave Macmillan.

Kennedy, D. 2002. 'The International Human Rights Movement: Part of the Problem?' *Harvard Human Rights Journal* 15: 101–25.

Kennedy, E. 1970. *Reformatory and Industrial Schools System Report* (the Kennedy Report). The Stationery Office.

Kennedy, F. 2000. 'The Suppression of the Carrigan Report: A Historical Perspective on Child Abuse'. *Studies: An Irish Quarterly Review* 89(356): 354–6.

Kennedy, F. 2001. *Cottage to Crèche: Family Change in Ireland*. Institute of Public Administration.

Kennedy, P. 2013. *Evaluation of Towards Healing Facilitated Listening Meetings*. Commissioned by Towards Healing.

Kenny, K. 2006. *Ireland and the British Empire*. Oxford University Press.

Kenny, K, and NÓ Dochartaigh. 2021. 'Power and Politics in Public Inquiries: Bloody Sunday 1972'. *Journal of Political Power* 14(3): 383–408.

Kent, L. 2016. 'Transitional Justice in Law, History and Anthropology'. *Australian Feminist Law Journal* 42(1): 1–11.

Killean, R, E Dowds, and AM McAlinden (eds). 2021. *Sexual Violence on Trial: Local and Comparative Perspectives*. Routledge.

Killian, S. 2015. '"For Lack of Accountability": The Logic of the Price in Ireland's Magdalen Laundries'. *Accounting, Organizations and Society* 43: 17–32.

Kim, M. 2018. 'From Carceral Feminism to Transformative Justice: Women-of-Color Feminism and Alternatives to Incarceration'. *Journal of Ethnic & Cultural Diversity in Social Work* 27(3): 219–33.

Kim, ME. 2010. 'Alternative Interventions to Intimate Violence: Defining Political and Pragmatic Challenges'. In J Ptacek (ed). *Restorative Justice and Violence Against Women*. Oxford University Press.

King, J. 2013. 'The Instrumental Value of Legal Accountability'. In N Bamford and P Leyland (eds). *Accountability and the Constitution*. Oxford University Press.

Kitagawa, R. 2023. 'From Political Violence to Political Trust? How Transitional Justice Affects Citizen Views of Government'. *International Studies Quarterly* 67(1): 1–13.

Knoll, M. 2021. 'Silence in Organizations—What We Need to Know, What We Know, and What We Don't Know'. In S Starystach and K Holy (eds). *The Silence of Organizations: How Organizations Cover up Wrongdoings*. heiBOOKS.

Koesten, J, and RC Rowland. 2004. 'The Rhetoric of Atonement'. *Communication Studies* 55(1): 68–87.

Kollar, R. 2004. 'Magdalenes and Nuns: Convent Laundries in Late Victorian England'. *Anglican and Episcopal History* 73(3): 309–34.

Koss, MP. 2014. 'The RESTORE Program of Restorative Justice for Sex Crimes: Vision, Process, and Outcomes'. *Journal of Interpersonal Violence* 29(9): 1623–60.

Krebs, S. 2017. 'The Legalization of Truth in International Fact-Finding'. *Chicago Journal of International Law* 18(1:) 163–83.

Krommendijk, J. 2015. 'The Domestic Effectiveness of International Human Rights Monitoring in Established Democracies. The Case of the UN Human Rights Treaty Bodies'. *The Review of International Organizations* 10(4): 489–512.

Lambourne, W. 2009. 'Transitional Justice and Peacebuilding after Mass Violence'. *International Journal of Transitional Justice* 3(1): 28–48.

Lambourne, W. 2013. 'Transformative Justice, Reconciliation and Peacebuilding'. In S Buckley-Zistel, T Koloma Beck, C Braun, and F Mieth (eds). *Transitional Justice Theories*. Routledge.

Langeland, W, AW Hoogendoorn, D Mager, JH Smit, and N Draijer. 2015. 'Childhood Sexual Abuse by Representatives of the Roman Catholic Church: A Prevalence Estimate Among the Dutch Population'. *Child Abuse & Neglect* 46 (Aug): 67–77.

Lanthier, S, J Du Mont, and R Mason. 2018. 'Responding to Delayed Disclosure of Sexual Assault in Health Settings: A Systematic Review'. *Trauma, Violence, & Abuse* 19(3): 251–65.

Larkin, E. 1972. 'The Devotional Revolution In Ireland, 1850–75'. *American Historical Review* 77(3): 625–52.

Larkin, E. 1976. *The Historical Dimensions of Irish Catholicism*. Catholic University of America Press.

Law Commission of Canada. 2000. *Restoring Dignity: Responding to Child Abuse in Canadian Institutions*. Minister of Public Works and Government Services.

Law Reform Commission (LRC). 2005. *Report on Public Inquiries including Tribunals of Inquiry*. LRC 73-2005.

Lawther, C. 2018a. '"The Cast of the Past": Truth Commissions and the Making and Marginalization of Identity'. *Ethnopolitics* 17(2): 113–29.

Lawther, C. 2018b. *Truth, Denial and Transition: Northern Ireland and the Contested Past*. Routledge.

Lawther, C. 2021a. 'Haunting and Transitional Justice: On Lives, Landscapes and Unresolved Pasts'. *International Review of Victimology* 27(1): 3–22.

Lawther, C. 2021b. '"Let Me Tell You": Transitional Justice, Victimhood and Dealing with a Contested Past'. *Social and Legal Studies* 30(6): 890–912.

Lawther, C. 2022. 'Heroes and Hierarchies: The Celebration and Censure of Victimhood in Transitional Justice'. *The International Journal of Human Rights* 26(3): 518–40.

Lazare, A. 2004. *On Apology*. Oxford University Press.

Lind, EA, and TR Tyler. 1988. *The Social Psychology of Procedural Justice*. Springer.

Lindsay, A. 2002. *Report of the Tribunal of Inquiry into the Infection with HIV and Hepatitis C of Persons with Haemophilia and Related Matters*. Department of Health.

Little, BJ. 2019. 'Violence, Silence and the Four Truths: Towards Healing in US-American Historical Memory'. *International Journal of Heritage Studies* 25(7): 631–40.

Llewellyn, J. 2002. 'Dealing with the Legacy of Native Residential School Abuse in Canada: Litigation, ADR, and Restorative Justice'. *University of Toronto Law Journal* 52(3): 253–300.

Llewellyn, J. 2006. 'Restorative Justice in Transitions and Beyond: The Justice Potential of Truth Telling Mechanisms for Post-Peace Accord Societies'. In TA Borer (ed). *Telling the Truths: Truth Telling and Peace Building in Post-Conflict Societies*. Notre Dame University Press.

Llewellyn, J. 2007. 'Truth Commissions and Restorative Justice'. In G Johnstone and DW van Ness (eds). *Handbook of Restorative Justice*. Willan.

Llewellyn, J. 2012. 'Restorative Justice: Thinking Relationally About Justice'. In J Downie and JJ Llewellyn (eds). *Being Relational: Reflections on Relational Theory and Health Law and Policy*. UBC Press.
Llewellyn, J. 2021. 'Transforming Restorative Justice'. *The International Journal of Restorative Justice* 4(3): 374–95.
Llewellyn, J, J MacIsaac, and M MacKay. 2015. *Report from the Restorative Justice Process at the Dalhousie University Faculty of Dentistry.*
London, R. 2011. *Crime. Punishment and Restorative Justice: A Framework for Restoring Trust.* Wipf and Stock.
Lu, C. 2017. *Justice and Reconciliation in World Politics*. Cambridge University Press.
Lucey, DS. 2021. 'Irish Partition and Poor Law Reform in Interwar Northern Ireland'. *European Review of History: Revue européenne d'histoire* 28(5–6): 793–813.
Luddy, M. 1995. *Women and Philanthropy in Nineteenth Century Ireland*. Cambridge University Press.
Luddy, M. 2007. *Prostitution and Irish Society, 1800–1940*. Cambridge University Press.
Luddy, M. 2011. 'Unmarried Mothers in Ireland, 1880–1973'. *Women's History Review* 20(1): 109–206.
Luhmann, S. 2009. 'Gender and the Generations of Difficult Knowledge: Recent Responses to Familial Legacies of Nazi Perpetration'. *Women in German Yearbook* 25: 174–98.
Lundy, P. 2016. *Historical Institutional Abuse: What Survivors Want from Redress.* Report Commissioned by the Panel of Experts on Redress. Ulster University.
Lundy, P. 2017. *Panel of Experts on Redress, April 2017, Response to Historical Institutional Abuse Inquiry Redress Recommendations: The Panel of Experts on Redress Position Paper and Recommendations.* Ulster University.
Lundy, P. 2020. '"I Just Want Justice": The Impact of Historical Institutional Child-Abuse Inquiries from the Survivor's Perspective'. *Éire-Ireland* 55(1-2): 252–78.
Lundy, P. 2022. 'Pathways to Justice: Historical Institutional Child Abuse and the Role of Activist Research'. *Journal of Human Rights Practice* 14(2): 535–50.
Lundy, P, and K Mahoney. 2018. 'Representing Survivors: A Critical Analysis of Recommendations to Resolve Northern Ireland's Historical Child Abuse Claims'. *The Annual Review of Interdisciplinary Justice Research* 7: 258–91.
Lundy, P, and M McGovern. 2008. 'Whose Justice? Rethinking Transitional Justice from the Bottom Up'. *Journal of Law and Society* 35(2): 265–92.
Lundy, P, and B Rolston. 2016. 'Redress for Past Harms? Official Apologies in Northern Ireland'. *The International Journal of Human Rights* 20(1): 104–22.
Lynch, G. 2020a. 'The Church of England Advisory Council of Empire Settlement and Post-War Child Migration to Australia'. *Journal of Ecclesiastical History* 71(4): 798–826.
Lynch, G. 2020b. 'Catholic Child Migration Schemes from the United Kingdom to Australia: Systemic Failures and Religious Legitimation'. *Journal of Religious History* 44(3): 273–94.
Lytton, T. 2008. *Holding Bishops Accountable: How Lawsuits Helped the Catholic Church Confront Clergy Sexual Abuse.* Harvard University Press.

MacCarthaigh, M. 2005. *Accountability in Irish Parliamentary Politics*. Institute of Public Administration.

MacGinty, R, and J Darby. 2002. *Guns and Government: The Management of the Northern Ireland Peace Process*. Palgrave Macmillan.

Madden, A. 2004. *Altar Boy: A Story of Life After Abuse*. Penguin Ireland.

Maguire, M. 2007. 'The Carrigan Committee and Child Sexual Abuse in Twentieth-Century Ireland'. *New Hibernia Review* 11(2): 79–100.

Maguire, M. 2010. *Precarious Childhood in Post-Independence Ireland*. Manchester University Press.

Maguire, MJ. 2001. 'The Changing Face of Catholic Ireland: Conservatism and Liberalism in the Ann Lovett and Kerry Babies Scandals'. *Feminist Studies* 27(2): 335–58.

Maher, J, C Spivakovsky, J McCulloch, J McGowan, K Beavis, M Lea, J Cadwallader, and T Sands. 2018. *Women, Disability and Violence: Barriers to Accessing Justice. Final Report*. ANROWS, Horizons: Issue 02.

Mahon, D, M O'Rourke, and P Scraton. 2021. *Mother and Baby Institutions, Magdalene Laundries and Workhouses in Northern Ireland—Truth Acknowledgement and Accountability*. Truth Recovery Design Panel, Report for the Northern Ireland Executive.

Mahood, L. 2013. *The Magdalenes: Prostitution in the Nineteenth Century*. Routledge.

Malinen, A, Markkola, P, and Hytönen, KM 2020. 'Conducting Commissioned Research: The Finnish Inquiry into the Failures of Child Welfare, 1937–1983'. *Scandinavian Journal of History* 45(2): 202–20.

Marks, S. 2011. 'Human Rights and Root Causes'. *The Modern Law Review* 74(1): 57–78.

Marmor, A. 2014. *The Language of Law*. Oxford University Press.

Marotta, G. 2021. 'Child Sexual Abuse by Members of the Catholic Church in Italy and France: A Literature Review of the Last Two Decades'. *Journal of Child Sexual Abuse* 30(8): 911–31.

Marrus, MR. 2007. 'Official Apologies and the Quest for Historical Justice'. *Journal of Human Rights* 6(1): 75–105.

Marrus, MR. 2008. 'Papal Apologies of Pope John Paul II'. In M Gibney, R Howard-Hassmann, JM Coicaud, and N Steiner (eds). *The Age of Apology: Facing up to the Past*. University of Pennsylvania Press.

Marshall, T. 1999. *Restorative Justice: An Overview*. Home Office.

Martin, D. 2013. 'A Post-Catholic Ireland?: Renewing the Irish Church From Within'. *America: The National Catholic Review*. 20 March.

Maslen, H, and C Paine. 2019. 'When Should the Police Investigate Cases of Non-Recent Child Sexual Abuse?' *Criminal Justice Ethics* 38(2): 65–102.

McAlinden, AM. 2007. *The Shaming of Sexual Offenders: Risk, Retribution and Reintegration*. Bloomsbury Publishing.

McAlinden, AM. 2012. *'Grooming' and the Sexual Abuse of Children: Institutional, Internet, and Familial Dimensions*. Oxford University Press.

McAlinden, AM. 2013. 'An Inconvenient Truth: Barriers to Truth Recovery in the Aftermath of Institutional Child Abuse in Ireland'. *Legal Studies* 33(2): 189–214.

McAlinden, AM. 2015. 'Public and Official Responses to Sexual and Violent Crime in Northern Ireland'. In AM McAlinden and C Dwyer (eds). *Criminal Justice in Transition: The Northern Ireland Context*. Bloomsbury.

McAlinden, AM. 2022a. 'Apologies as "Shame Management": The Politics of Remorse in the Aftermath of Historical Institutional Abuse'. *Legal Studies* 42(1): 137–58.

McAlinden, AM. 2022b. 'From "Shame" to Guilt: Negotiating Moral and Legal Responsibility within Apologies for Historical Institutional Abuse'. *Journal of Law and Society* 49(3): 470–94.

McAlinden, AM. 2023. 'Acts of Contrition: Forgiveness and Effective Intergroup Apologies for Historical Institutional Abuse'. *International Review of Victimology* 30(2): 358–78.

McAlinden, AM, and B Naylor. 2016. 'Reframing Public Inquiries as Procedural Justice for Victims of Institutional Child Abuse: Towards a Hybrid Model of Justice'. *Sydney Law Review* 38(3): 277–309.

McAuliffe, P. 2017a. 'Comprehending Ireland's Post-Catholic Redress Practice as a Form of Transitional Justice'. *Oxford Journal of Law and Religion* 6(3): 451–73.

McAuliffe, P. 2017b. *Transformative Transitional Justice and the Malleability of Post-Conflict States*. Edward Elgar Publishing.

McCafferty, N. 2004. *Nell*. Penguin.

McCarthy, P. 2013. 'The Murphy Report Revisited'. *Studies: An Irish Quarterly Review* 102(408): 388–95.

McCarthy, RL. 2010. *Origins of the Magdalene Laundries: An Analytical History*. McFarland.

McColgan, M. 1989. 'Chapter 6: Northern Ireland as a Case Study of the Development of Treatment Foster Care'. *Child & Youth Services* 12(1–2): 75–90.

McCormick, FE. 2017. 'Fear, Silence, and Telling: Catholic Identity in Northern Ireland'. *Anthropology and Humanism* 42(1): 50–71.

McCormick, L. 2009. *Regulating Sexuality: Women in Twentieth-Century Northern Ireland*. Manchester University Press.

McCormick, L, and NL Bennett. 2023. 'Relentless, Aggressive, and Pervasive: Exploring Gender Minimization and Sexual Abuse Experienced by Women Ex-Military Veterans'. *Psychological Trauma: Theory, Research, Practice, and Policy* 15(2): 237–46.

McCormick, L, S O'Connell with O Dee and J Privilege. 2021. *Mother and Baby Homes and Magdalene Laundries in Northern Ireland 1922–1990*. Department of Health. Available at: https://www.health-ni.gov.uk/publication-research-report-mbhml.

McDonagh, J. 2013. 'The Representative Sample in the Murphy Report'. *Studies: An Irish Quarterly Review* 102(408): 456–67.

McElvaney, R. 2015. 'Disclosure of Child Sexual Abuse: Delays, Non-Disclosure and Partial Disclosure. What the Research Tells Us and Implications for Practice'. *Child Abuse Review* 24(3): 159–69.

McEntee, P. 2007. *Report of the Commission of Investigation into the Dublin and Monahan Bombings 1974—Final Report*. Department of the Taoiseach.

McEvoy, K. 2006. *Making Peace with the Past: Options for Truth Recovery in Northern Ireland*. Healing Through Remembering.

McEvoy, K. 2007. 'Beyond Legalism: Towards a Thicker Understanding of Transitional Justice'. *Journal of Law and Society* 34(4): 411–40.

McEvoy, K. 2011. 'What Did the Lawyers Do During the "War"? Neutrality, Conflict and the Culture of Quietism'. *The Modern Law Review* 74(3): 350–84.

McEvoy, K, A Bryson, and C Placzek. 2019. *Apologies in Transitional Justice*, invited report for UN Special Rapporteur on Transitional Justice, presented to UN Assembly 74th Session, October.

McEvoy, K, and L Mallinder. 2012. 'Amnesties in Transition: Punishment, Restoration and the Governance of Mercy'. *Journal of Law and Society* 39(3): 410–40.

McEvoy, K, and K McConnachie. 2012. 'Victimology in Transitional Justice: Victimhood, Innocence and Hierarchy'. *European Journal of Criminology* 9(5): 527–38.

McEvoy, K, and L McGregor. 2008. 'Transitional Justice from Below: An Agenda for Research, Policy and Praxis'. In K McEvoy and L McGregor (eds). *Transitional Justice from Below: Grassroots Activism and the Struggle for Change*. Hart Publishing.

McGettrick, C. 2020. '"Illegitimate" Knowledge: Transitional Justice and Adopted People'. *Éire-Ireland* 55(1): 181–200.

McGettrick, C, K O'Donnell, M O'Rourke, JM Smith, and M Steed. 2021. *Ireland and the Magdalene Laundries: A Campaign for Justice*. Bloomsbury Publishing.

McGill, D. 2017. 'Different Violence, Different Justice? Taking Structural Violence Seriously in Post-Conflict and Transitional Justice Processes'. *State Crime Journal* 6(1): 79–101.

McGlynn, C, J Downes, and N Westmarland. 2017. 'Seeking Justice for Survivors of Sexual Violence'. In E Zinsstag and M Keenan (eds). *Restorative Responses to Sexual Violence: Legal, Social and Therapeutic Dimensions*. Routledge.

McGlynn, C, and N Westmarland. 2019. 'Kaleidoscopic Justice: Sexual Violence and Victim-Survivors' Perceptions of Justice'. *Social & Legal Studies* 28(2): 179–201.

McGlynn, C, N Westmarland, and N Godden. 2012. '"I Just Wanted Him to Hear Me": Sexual Violence and the Possibilities of Restorative Justice'. *Journal of Law and Society* 39(2): 213–40.

McGregor, C, C Devaney, and SA Buckley, SA. 2023. *Language, Terminology and Representation Relating to Ireland's Institutions Historically Known as 'Mother and Baby Homes' 'County Homes' and related Institutions*. UNESCO Child and Family Research Centre, University of Galway.

McGuckin, M. 2023. *I Did This For You: One Woman's Journey to Become A Voice for the Voiceless in the Northern Ireland Residential Care System*. Amazon Publishing.

McKeown, M. 2024. *With Power Comes Responsibility: The Politics of Structural Injustice*. Bloomsbury.

McMillan, M, and S Rigney. 2018. 'Race, Reconciliation, and Justice in Australia: From Denial to Acknowledgment'. *Ethnic and Racial Studies* 41(4): 759–77.

McNamee S, and K Gergen. 1999. *Relational Responsibility: Resources for Sustainable Dialogue*. Sage.

McNeilly, K. 2019. 'Are Rights Out of Time? International Human Rights Law, Temporality, and Radical Social Change'. *Social & Legal Studies* 28(6): 817–38.

McPartland, A. 2018. 'The Prism of Statutory Interpretation: The Statutory Compensation Scheme for Institutional Abuse in JGH v Residential Institutions Review Committee (2017) IESC 69'. *Hibernian Law Journal* 17: 108–25.

McPhillips, K. 2018. '"Soul Murder": Investigating Spiritual Trauma at the Royal Commission'. *Journal of Australian Studies* 42(2): 231–42.

McShane, M, and F Williams. 1992. 'Radical Victimology: A Critique of the Concept of Victim in Traditional Victimology'. *Crime and Delinquency* 38(2): 258–71.

McWilliams, M. 1997. 'Violence Against Women and Political Conflict: The Northern Ireland Experience'. *Critical Criminology* 8(1): 78–92.

Mears, D. 2010. *American Criminal Justice Policy: An Evaluation Approach to Increasing Accountability and Effectiveness.* Cambridge University Press.

Meehan, N. 2010a. 'Church and State Bear Responsibility for the Bethany Home'. *History Ireland* 18(5): 10–11.

Meehan, N. 2010b. Protestants . . . Were Left as Orphans'. *Church & State* 102(4): 28–35.

Meehan, N. 2019. 'Child abuse and its concealment did occur within Protestant institutions', *The Irish News*, 7 June.

Melossi, D. 2001. 'The Cultural Embeddedness of Social Control: Reflections on the Comparison of Italian and North-American Cultures Concerning Punishment'. *Theoretical Criminology* 5(4): 403–24.

Menkel-Medow, C. 2007. 'Restorative Justice: What Is It and Does It Work?' *Annual Review of Law and Social Science* 3(10): 161–87.

Menzies, K. 2019. 'Understanding the Australian Aboriginal Experience of Collective, Historical and Intergenerational Trauma'. *International Social Work* 62(6): 1522–34.

Mid Staffordshire NHS. 2013. *Report of the Mid Staffordshire NHS Foundation Trust Public Inquiry*. House of Commons Paper No 898-I, Session 2012–13.

Mihr, A. 2021. 'An Introduction to Transitional Justice'. In O Simić (ed). *An Introduction to Transitional Justice* (2nd ed). Routledge.

Miller, D. 2007. *National Responsibility and Global Justice.* Oxford University Press.

Minow, M. 1998. *Between Vengeance and Forgiveness: Facing History After Genocide and Mass Violence.* Beacon Press.

Moffett, L. 2017. 'Transitional Justice and Reparations: Remedying the Past?'. In D Jacobs, C Lawther, and L Moffett (eds). *Research Handbook on Transitional Justice*. Edward Elgar Publishing.

Moffett, L. 2023a. 'Reparations as Balance'. *Journal of Social Philosophy* 1–19.

Moffett, L. 2023b. *Reparations and War: Finding Balance in Repairing the Past.* Oxford University Press.

Mohr, T. 2021. 'Religion and the Constitution of the Irish Free State'. In K Costello and N Howlin (eds). *Law and Religion in Ireland, 1700–1970*. Springer International Publishing.

Molavi, M. 2022. 'Encountering Class Actions in Swedish Law and Society'. *Mass Claims: An International Journal with a European Focus* 2(2): 19–39.

Molloy, C, and I O'Donnell. 2022. 'The Kerry Babies, Criminology, and Reinhart Koselleck'. *Criminology & Criminal Justice*. Available at: https://doi.org/10.1177/17488958221126674.

Montano, JP. 2011. *The Roots of English Colonialism in Ireland*. Cambridge University Press.

Moore, A, M Keenan, R Moss, and A Scotland. 2021. *Survivors Voices National Consultation: A Consultation With Survivors of Domestic Abuse and Sexual Violence to Establish Awareness, Opinion, and Demand Related to the Ongoing Development of a National Restorative Justice Policy and Practice Framework for Scotland*. Available at: https://research-portal.uws.ac.uk/en/publications/surviv ors-voices-national-consultation-a-consultation-with-surviv.

Moore, C. 2003. 'Women and Domestic Violence: The Public/Private Dichotomy in International Law'. *International Journal of Human Rights* 7(4): 93–128.

Moore, L, and U Convery. 2008. 'Barred from Change: The Incarceration of Children and Young People in Northern Ireland'. *Current Issues in Criminal Justice* 20(1): 79–94.

Morris, R. 2000. *Stories of Transformative Justice*. Canadian Scholar's Press.

Mullaney, M. 2022. 'Child Sexual Abuse Crisis in the Irish Church 1996–2021: Guidelines and Canonical Response'. *The Person and the Challenges: The Journal of Theology, Education, Canon Law and Social Studies Inspired by Pope John Paul II* 12(1): 23–51.

Murphy, C. 2015. 'Transitional Justice, Retributive Justice and Accountability for Wrongdoing'. In C Corradetti, N Eisikovits, and J Rotondi (eds). *Theorizing Transitional Justice*. Routledge.

Murphy, C. 2017. *The Conceptual Foundations of Transitional Justice*. Cambridge University Press.

Murphy, FD, H Buckley, and L Joyce. 2005. *The Ferns Report, presented by the Ferns Inquiry to the Minister for Health and Children*. Government Publications.

Murphy, M. 2011. 'Apology, Recognition, and Reconciliation'. *Human Rights Review* 12(1): 47–69.

Murphy, P, and Intelligence and Security Committee. 2006. *Report into the London terrorist attacks on 7 July* 2005. Command Paper 6785. HMSO.

Murphy, RH. 1998. *Report of the Independent Inquiry into Matters Relating to Child Sexual Abuse in Swimming*. Government Publications.

Murphy, Y. 2014. *Independent Review of Issues Related to Symphysiotomy*. Department of Health.

Nagy, R. 2008. 'Transitional Justice as Global Project: Critical Reflections'. *Third World Quarterly* 29(2): 275–89.

Nagy, R. 2012. 'Truth, Reconciliation and Settler Denial: Specifying the Canada–South Africa Analogy'. *Human Rights Review* 13(3): 349–67.

Nagy, R, and RK Sehdev. 2012. 'Introduction: Residential Schools and Decolonization'. *Journal of Law & Society/La Revue Canadienne Droit et Société* 27(1): 67–73.

Nagy, RL. 2013. 'The Scope and Bounds of Transitional Justice and the Canadian Truth and Reconciliation Commission'. *International Journal of Transitional Justice* 7(1): 52–73.

Nascimento, A, J Andrade, and A de Castro Rodrigues. 2023. 'The Psychological Impact of Restorative Justice Practices on Victims of Crimes—A Systematic Review'. *Trauma, Violence and Abuse* 24(3): 1929–47.

Nash, C. 1993. 'Remapping and Renaming: New Cartographies of Identity, Gender and Landscape in Ireland'. *Feminist Review* 44(1): 39–57.

National Board for Safeguarding Children. 2008. *Safeguarding Children: Standards and Guidance Document for the Catholic Church in Ireland*. Available at: https://www.safeguarding.ie/images/Article_Images/Standards-and-Guidance8.pdf.

National Board for Safeguarding Children. 2016. *Safeguarding Children: Policy and Guidance Document for the Catholic Church in Ireland*. Available at: https://www.safeguarding.ie/policy-guidance/view-all-the-guidance.

National Centre for Research and Remembrance Steering Group. 2022. *Response to the National Centre Consultation Report*. Available at: https://www.gov.ie/pdf/?file=https://assets.gov.ie/204579/0b00bbf2-4319-4298-827e-6b0b01bf09ae.pdf.

National Counselling Service. 2003. *The SENCS Report. Survivors' Experiences of the National Counselling Service; For Adults Who Experienced Childhood Abuse*. National Counselling Service. Available at: http://hdl.handle.net/10147/42899.

National Inquiry into Missing and Murdered Indigenous Women and Girls (NIMMIWG). 2019. *Reclaiming Power and Place: the Final Report of the National Inquiry into Missing and Murdered Indigenous Women and Girls*. Available at: https://www.mmiwg-ffada.ca/final-report/.

National Treasury Management Agency (NTMA). 2005. *Report and Accounts for the year ended 31 December 2005*. National Treasury Management Agency.

National University of Ireland Galway (NUI Galway). 2022. Tuam Oral History Project. Available at: https://www.nuigalway.ie/tuam-oral-history/.

Nelken, D. 2004. 'Comparing Legal Cultures'. In A Sarat (ed). *The Blackwell Companion to Law and Society*. Blackwell.

Ní Aoláin, F. 2022. 'The Inner and Outer Limits of Gendered Transitional Justice'. In K O'Donnell, M O'Rourke, and J Smith. *Redress: Ireland's Institutions and Transitional Justice*. University College Dublin Press.

Ni Dhonaill, C. 2024. *Staying Safe During the Covid-19 Pandemic: Religious Organisations and the Safeguarding of Young People on the Island of Ireland*. *Queen's University Belfast*.

Nickson R, and J Braithwaite. 2013. Deeper, Broader, Longer Transitional Justice'. *European Journal of Criminology* 11(4): 445–63.

Nigro, G, E Ross, T Binns, and C Kurtz. 2020. 'Apologies in the #MeToo Moment'. *Psychology of Popular Media* 9(4): 403–11.

Nobles, M. 2008. *The Politics of Official Apologies*. Cambridge University Press.

Nocella, AJ. 2011. 'An Overview of the History and Theory of Transformative Justice'. *Peace & Conflict Review* 6(1): 1–10.

Noll, DE, and L Harvey. 2008. 'Restorative Mediation: The Application of Restorative Justice Practice and Philosophy to Clergy Sexual Abuse Cases'. *Journal of Child Sexual Abuse* 17(3–4): 377–96.

NOU. 2004. *Barnehjem og spesialskoler under lupen. Nasjonal kartlegging av omsorgssvikt og overgrep i barnevernsinstitusjoner 1945–1980*. Statens forvaltningstjenest.

North Western Health Board. 1998. *The Report of the Inquiry into the West of Ireland Farmer Case*. North Western Health Board.

Nuti A. 2019. *Injustice and the Reproduction of History: Structural Inequalities, Gender and Redress*. Cambridge University Press.

O'Callaghan, M, and L Lundy. 2013. 'Northern Ireland'. In L Gearon (ed). *Education in the United Kingdom*. David Fulton Publishers.

O'Donnell, K. 2022. 'Commission to Inquire into Ireland's Mother & Baby Homes: An Epistemology of Ignorance'. In P Giladi and N McMillan (eds). *Epistemic Injustice and the Philosophy of Recognition*. Routledge.

O'Donnell, K, and C McGettrick. 2020. *Dublin Honours Magdalenes Listening Exercise Report Vol 1: Report on Key Findings*. Justice for Magdalenes Research.

O'Donnell, K, M O'Rourke, and J Smith. 2020. 'Editors' Introduction: Toward Transitional Justice in Ireland? Addressing Legacies of Harm'. *Éire-Ireland* 55(1–2): 9–16.

O'Donnell, K, M O'Rourke, and J Smith. 2022. *Redress: Ireland's Institutions and Transitional Justice*. University College Dublin Press.

Offe, C. 1999. 'How Can We Trust Our Fellow Citizens?' In ME Warren (ed). *Democracy and Trust*. Cambridge University Press.

Office of Director of Public Prosecutions (DPP). 2019. *Guidelines for Prosecutors* (5th ed).

Office of the Ombudsman. 2017. *Opportunity Lost: An investigation by the Ombudsman into the Administration of the Magdalen Restorative Justice Scheme*. Office of the Ombudsman.

O'Gorman, C. 2010. *Beyond Belief*. Hodder and Stoughton.

Ó Gráda, C. 2006. *Ireland's Great Famine: Interdisciplinary Perspectives*. Dublin Press.

Ó Gráda, C, and K Hjortshøj O'Rourke. 2021. 'The Irish Economy During the Century after Partition'. CAGE Working Paper No 552. March.

O'Halpin, E, and D Ó Corráin. 2020. *The Dead of the Irish Revolution*. Yale University Press.

O'Hanlon, G. 2017. 'The Catholic Church in Ireland Today'. *Studies: An Irish Quarterly Review* 106(421): 9–20.

Ohlmeyer, J. 2016. 'Conquest, Civilization, Colonization: Ireland, 1540–1660'. In R Bourke and I McBride (eds). *The Princeton History of Modern Ireland*. Princeton University Press.

O'Kennedy, ML. 2021. *Report of the Findings of the Consultation with Survivors of Mother and Baby Homes and County Homes*. Oak Foundation.

Okimoto, TG, M Wenzel, and MJ Hornsey. 2015. 'Apologies Demanded yet Devalued: Normative Dilution in the Age of Apology'. *Journal of Experimental Social Psychology* 60: 133–6.

O'Mahony, C. 2021. *Proposals for a State Response to Illegal Birth Registrations in Ireland. Special Rapporteur on Child Protection*. Department of Children, Equality, Disability, Integration and Youth.

O'Mahony, D, and J Doak. 2017. *Reimagining Restorative Justice: Agency and Accountability in the Criminal Process*. Bloomsbury Publishing.

O'Mahoney, J, L Bowman Grieve, and A Torne. 2019. 'Ireland's Magdalene Laundries and the Psychological Architecture of Surveillance'. In S Flynn and

A Mackay (eds). *Surveillance, Architecture and Control: Discourses on Spatial Culture*. Palgrave Macmillan.

O'Neill, I. 2019. *Determination of the Independent Assessor to the Ex Gratia Scheme instituted on foot of the Judgment of the European Court of Human Rights (ECtHR) in respect of O'Keeffe v Ireland*. Department of Education.

O'Reilly, A. 2018. *My Name is Bridget: The Untold Story of Bridget Dolan and the Tuam Mother and Baby Home*. Gill Books.

O'Reilly, JT, and MSP Chalmers. 2014. *The Clergy Sex Abuse Crisis and the Legal Responses*. Oxford University Press.

Ormskerk, N, M Kunst, and N Immler. 2024. 'Historical Abuse in Dutch Catholic Institutions: An Ex-Ante Evaluation of Institutional and Non-Institutional Response Procedures'. *The International Journal of Restorative Justice* , Issue 3 (Online first 2024), doi 10.5553/TIJRJ.000199.

O'Rourke, C, and A Swaine. 2017. 'Gender, Violence and Reparations in Northern Ireland: A Story Yet to be Told'. *The International Journal of Human Rights* 21(9): 1302–19.

O'Rourke, M. 2011. 'Ireland's Magdalene Laundries and the State's Duty to Protect'. *Hibernian Law Journal* 10: 200–37.

O'Rourke, M. 2019. 'Prolonged Impunity as a Continuing Situation of Torture or Ill-Treatment? Applying a Dignity Lens to So-called "Historical" Cases'. *Netherlands International Law Review* 66(1): 101–41.

O'Rourke, M. 2020. *Submission to the Scottish Parliament's Education and Skills Committee, on the Redress for Survivors (Historical Child Abuse in Care) (Scotland) Bill, Policy Contribution*. Irish Centre for Human Rights, National University of Ireland Galway.

O'Rourke, M. 2021a. 'The Manipulation of "Vulnerability:" State Responses to So-Called "Historical" Abuses in Ireland'. *Human Rights Quarterly* 43(3): 435–59.

O'Rourke, M. 2021b. *A Human Rights Framework: Background Research for the Truth Recovery Design Process*. National University of Galway. Available at: https://secureservercdn.net/160.153.138.71/w2w.113.myftpupload.com/wp-content/uploads/2021/10/ORourke-Background-Research-Report-27.9.21.pdf.

O'Rourke, M. 2022. 'Ireland's "Historical" Abuse Inquiries and the Secrecy of Records and Archives. In L Black, L Branagan, and D Healy (eds). *Histories of Punishment and Social Control in Ireland: Perspectives from a Periphery*. Emerald Publishing.

O'Rourke, M, C McGettrick, R Baker, and R Hill. 2018. *CLANN: Ireland's Unmarried Mothers and their Children: Gathering the Data: Principal Submission to the Commission of Investigation into Mother and Baby Homes*. Justice for Magdalenes Research, Adoption Rights Alliance, Hogan Lovells.

Oshana, MAL. 1997. 'Ascriptions of Responsibility'. *American Philosophical Quarterly* 34(1): 71–83.

O'Sullivan, E. 2014. 'The Ryan Report: Reformatory and Industrial Schools and Twentieth-Century Ireland'. In R Meade and F Dukelow (eds). *Defining Events: Power, Resistance and Identity in Twenty-First-Century Ireland*. Manchester University Press.

O'Sullivan, E, and I O'Donnell (eds). 2012. *Coercive Confinement in Ireland: Patients, Prisoners and Penitents*. Manchester University Press.

Páez, D. 2010. 'Official or Political Apologies and Improvement of Intergroup Relations: A Neo-Durkheimian Approach to Official Apologies as Rituals'. *Revista de Psicología Social* 25(1): 101–15.
Palmer, C. 2016. *An Affair with My Mother*. Penguin.
Park, A. 2016. 'Remembering the Children: Decolonizing community-based Restorative Justice for Indian Residential Schools'. *Contemporary Justice Review* 19(4): 424–44.
Parkinson, PN, RK Oates, and AA Jayakody. 2012. 'Child Sexual Abuse in the Anglican Church of Australia'. *Journal of Child Sexual Abuse* 21(5): 553–70.
Parsons, J, and T Bergin. 2010. 'The Impact of Criminal Justice Involvement on Victims' Mental Health'. *Journal of Traumatic Stress* 23(2): 182–8.
Patrizi, E. 2021. 'Redressing Forced Removals of Yenish Children in Switzerland in the 20th Century: An Analysis Through Transitional Justice Lens'. *Childhood* 28(4): 540–54.
Pelikan, C. 2010. 'On the Efficacy of Victim-Offender-Mediation in Cases of Partnership Violence in Austria, Or: Men Don't Get Better, But Women Get Stronger: Is It Still True?' *European Journal on Criminal Policy and Research* 16(1): 49–67.
Pemberton, A, and E Mulder. 2023. 'Bringing Injustice Back In: Secondary Victimization as Epistemic Injustice'. *Criminology & Criminal Justice*. Available at: https://doi.org/10.1177/17488958231181345.
Pembroke, S. 2017. 'Exploring the Post-Release Experience of Former Irish Industrial School "Inmates"'. *Irish Studies Review* 25(4): 454–71.
Pembroke, S. 2019. 'Historical Institutional Child Abuse in Ireland: Survivor Perspectives on Taking Part in the Commission to Inquire into Child Abuse (CICA) and the Redress Scheme'. *Contemporary Justice Review* 22(1): 43–59.
Pembroke, S. 2020. 'Acts of Survival and Resistance in Industrial and Reformatory Schools in Ireland in the Twentieth Century'. In F McCann (ed). *The Carceral Network in Ireland: History, Agency and Resistance*. Springer Nature, Palgrave Macmillan.
Pilgrim, D. 2011. 'The Child Abuse Crisis in the Catholic Church: International, National and Personal Policy Aspects'. *Policy and Politics* 39(3): 309–24.
Pine, E. 2014. *Politics of Irish Memory: Performing Remembrance in Contemporary Irish Culture*. Palgrave Macmillan.
Pinkerton, J. 1998. *Making Research Work: Research, Policy and Practice in Child Care*. Wiley-Blackwell.
Pittelli, R Sr. 2017. *Forgiveness: Not Necessarily What You Think*. CreateSpace Independent Publishing Platform.
Popkin, M, and N Roht-Arriaza. 1995. 'Truth as Justice: Investigatory Commissions in Latin America'. *Law & Social Inquiry* 20(1): 79–116.
Posner, EA, and A Vermeule. 2004. 'Transitional Justice as Ordinary Justice'. *Harvard Law Review* 117(3): 761–825.
Pranis, K. 2007. 'Restorative Values'. In G Johnstone and D Van Ness (eds). *The Handbook of Restorative Justice*. Routledge.
Preston-Roedder, R. 2017. 'Civic Trust'. *Philosophers' Imprint* 17(4): 1–23.
Privilege, J, and G Jones. 2015. 'Crisis and Scandal: Government, Local Government and Health Reform in Northern Ireland, 1939–44'. *Irish Economic and Social History* 42(1): 33–52.

Prior, P. 1993. 'Mental Health Policy in Northern Ireland'. *Social Policy & Administration* 27(4): 323–34.

Province of Nova Scotia. 2019. *Journey to Light: A Different Way Forward: Final Report of the Restorative Inquiry—Nova Scotia Home for Coloured Children.* Crown copyright.

Prunty, J. 2017. *Our Lady of Charity in Ireland: 1853–1973.* Columba Press.

Purdue O. 2017. 'Surviving the Industrial City: the Female Poor and the Workhouse in Late Nineteenth-Century Belfast'. *Urban History* 44(1): 69–90.

Quinn, JR. 2017. 'The Development of Transitional Justice'. In C Lawther, L Moffett, and D Jacobs (eds). *Research Handbook on Transitional Justice.* Edward Elgar Publishing.

Quinney R. 1972. 'Who is the Victim?' *Criminology* 10(3): 314–23.

Rafferty, O. 2021. 'The Legal and Constitutional Organization of the Catholic Church in Nineteenth-Century Ireland'. In K Costello and N Howlin (eds). *Law and Religion in Ireland 1700–1970.* Routledge.

Raftery, M, and E O'Sullivan. 2001. *Suffer the Little Children: The Inside Story of Ireland's Industrial Schools.* Continuum.

Rashid, F, and I Barron. 2019. 'Why the Focus of Clerical Child Sexual Abuse has Largely Remained on the Catholic Church Amongst Other Non-Catholic Christian Denominations and Religions'. *Journal of Child Sexual Abuse* 28(5): 564–85.

Reaves, JR, and D Tombs. 2019. '#MeToo Jesus: Naming Jesus as a Victim of Sexual Abuse'. *International Journal of Public Theology* 13(4): 387–412.

Redmond, P, 2018. *The Adoption Machine: The Dark History of Ireland's Mother & Baby Homes and the Inside Story of How 'Tuam 800' Became a Global Scandal.* Merrion Press.

Renteln, AD. 2008. 'Apologies: A Cross-Cultural Analysis'. In M Gibney, R Howard-Hassmann, JM Coicaud, and N Steiner (eds). *The Age of Apology: Facing up to the Past.* University of Pennsylvania Press.

Reynolds, M. 2019. *A Shadow Cast Long: Independent Review Report into Correct Birth Registrations.* Department of Children and Youth Affairs.

Ring, S. 2009. 'Beyond the Reach of Justice? Complainant Delay in Historic Child Sexual Abuse Cases and the Right to a Fair Trial'. *Judicial Studies Institute Journal* 2: 162–204.

Ring, S. 2017. 'The Victim of Historical Child Sexual Abuse in the Irish Courts 1999–2006'. *Social and Legal Studies* 26(5): 558–62.

Ring, S. 2018. 'Our Most Precious Possessional Of All: The Survivor of Non-Recent Childhood Sexual Abuse as the Ideal Victim?' In M Duggan (ed). *Revisiting the 'Ideal Victim': Developments in Critical Criminology.* Policy Press.

Ring, S, K Gleeson, and K Stevenson. 2022. *Child Sexual Abuse Reported by Adult Survivors: Legal Responses in England and Wales, Ireland and Australia.* Routledge.

Robins, S. 2011. 'Towards Victim-Centred Transitional Justice: Understanding the Needs of Families of the Disappeared in Postconflict Nepal'. *International Journal of Transitional Justice* 5(1): 75–98.

Robins, S. 2014. 'Constructing Meaning From Disappearance: Local Memorialisation of the Missing in Nepal'. *International Journal of Conflict and Violence* 8(1): 104–18.

Roche, D. 2003. *Accountability in Restorative Justice*. Oxford University Press.

Rock, E. 2023. 'Questions of Measurement: Striking an Accountability Balance'. In M Flinders and C Monaghan (eds). *Questions of Accountability: Prerogatives, Power and Politics*. Hart Publishing.

Rogan, M. 2022. 'Examining the Role of Legal Culture as a Protective Factor Against High Rates of Pre-Trial Detention: The Case of Ireland'. *European Journal on Criminal Policy and Research* 28(3): 425–33.

Roht-Arriaza, N. 2004. 'Reparations Decisions and Dilemmas'. *Hastings International and Comparative Law Review* 27(2): 157–220.

Rojas Durazo, AC, A Bierria, and M Kim. 2011. 'Community Accountability: Emerging Movements to Transform Violence'. *Social Justice: A Journal of Crime, Conflict and World Order* 34(3): 1–11.

Rolston, B. 1991. 'News Fit to Print: Belfast's Daily Newspapers'. In B Rolston (ed). *The Media and Northern Ireland: Covering the Troubles*. Macmillan.

Rolston, B. 1993. 'The Training Ground: Ireland, Conquest and Decolonisation'. *Race and Class* 34(4): 13–24.

Rolston, B, and F Ni Aolain. 2018. 'Colonialism, Redress and Transitional Justice: Ireland and Beyond'. *State Crime Journal* 7(2): 329–48.

Rolston, B, and P Scraton. 2005. 'In the Full Glare of English Politics: Ireland, Inquiries and the British State'. *British Journal of Criminology* 45(4): 547–64.

Rosenblatt, R, and C Mazzucato. 2023. 'On the 'Restorative Idea': Setting Boundaries, Innovating and Exploring the Unknown'. *The International Journal of Restorative Justice* 6(3): 339–52.

Ross, D. 2002. *Ireland: History of a Nation*. Geddes & Grosset.

Rossner, M. 2013. *Just Emotions: Rituals Of Restorative Justice*. Oxford University Press.

Rossner, M, and H Taylor. 2024. 'The Transformative Potential of Restorative Justice: What the Mainstream Can Learn from the Margins'. *Annual Review of Criminology* 7: 357–81.

Rothberg, M. 2019. *The Implicated Subject*. Stanford University Press.

Royal Commission into Institutional Responses to Child Sexual Abuse (RCIRCSA). 2015. *Redress and Civil Litigation Report*.

Royal Commission into Institutional Responses to Child Sexual Abuse (RCIRCSA). 2017a. *Proportion of Priests and Non-ordained Religious Subject to a Claim of Child Sexual Abuse 1950–2010*.

Royal Commission into Institutional Responses to Child Sexual Abuse (RCIRCSA). 2017b. *Criminal Justice Report Executive Summary and Parts I–II*.

Royal Commission into Institutional Responses to Child Sexual Abuse (RCIRCSA). 2017c. *Final Report*. Available at: https://www.childabuseroyalcommission.gov.au/final-report.

Royal Commission of Inquiry. 2024. *Abuse in Care—Whanaketia—Through Pain and Trauma, from Darkness to Light*. Available at: https://www.abuseincare.org.nz/reports/whanaketia/.

Rubio Marín, R. 2022. 'Reparations for Historic Institutional Gender Violence in Ireland: Learning from Transitional Justice'. In K O'Donnell, M O'Rourke, and J Smith (eds). *Redress: Ireland's Institutions and Transitional Justice*. University College Dublin Press.

Rytter, M, and JK Rasmussen. 2015. 'Denmark: The Godhavn Inquiry'. In J Sköld and S Swain (eds). *Apologies and the Legacy of Abuse of Children in 'Care': International Perspectives*. Palgrave Macmillan UK.

Saville, M, W Hoyt, and J Toohey. 2010. *Report of the Bloody Sunday Inquiry*. House of Commons Paper No 29. Session 2010–11.

Scally, D. 2021. *The Best Catholics in the World: The Irish, the Church and the End of a Special Relationship*. Penguin.

Schabas, W. 2013. 'Criminology, Accountability and International Justice'. In M. Bosworth and C. Hoyle (eds). *What is Criminology*. Oxford University Press.

Scheff, TJ. 1998. 'Community Conferences: Shame and Anger in Therapeutic Jurisprudence'. *Revista Juridica* (UPR) 67: 97–104.

Schwab, G. 2010. *Haunting Legacies: Violent Histories and Transgenerational Trauma*. Columbia University Press.

Scoping Inquiry (2024), *Report of the Scoping Inquiry into Historical Sexual Abuse in Day and Boarding Schools Run by Religious Orders* (Chair: Mary O'Toole SC). Available at https://www.gov.ie/en/publication/42b7e-education-scoping-inquiry/.

Scott, C. 2000. 'Accountability in the Regulatory State'. *Journal of Law and Society* 27(1): 38–60.

Sedley, S. 1989. 'Public Inquiries: A Cure or a Disease'. *Modern Law Review* 52(4): 469–79.

Shapland, J. 2016. 'Forgiveness and Restorative Justice: Is It Necessary? Is It Helpful?' *Oxford Journal of Law and Religion* 5(1): 94–112.

Sharp, DN. 2019. 'What Would Satisfy Us? Taking Stock of Critical Approaches to Transitional Justice'. *International Journal of Transitional Justice* 13(3): 570–89.

Sheridan, G, and A Carr. 2020. 'Survivors' Lived Experiences of Posttraumatic Growth After Institutional Childhood Abuse: An Interpretative Phenomenological Analysis'. *Child Abuse and Neglect* 103: 1–13.

Shilliday, P. 2022. *Remembering What They Can Never Forget: Memorialisation of Historical Institutional Abuse in Ireland*. Thesis submitted for the Degree of Doctor of Philosophy. Queen's University Belfast.

Shilliday, P, AM McAlinden, J Gallen, and M Keenan. 2023. *Non-recent Institutional Abuses and Inquiries: Truth, Acknowledgement, Accountability and Procedural Justice*. University College Dublin, Queen's University Belfast and Dublin City University.

Shoesmith, S. 2023. 'Positive Accountability: From Naming, Shaming and Blaming to Lesson Learning'. In M Flinders and C Monaghan (eds). *Questions of Accountability: Prerogatives, Power and Politics*. Hart Publishing.

Shuman, D, and A McCall Smith. 2000. *Justice and the Prosecution of Old Crimes: Balancing Legal, Psychological, and Moral Concerns*. American Psychological Association Print.

Silbey, S. 1998. 'Ideology, Power and Justice'. In B Garth and A Sarat (eds). *Justice and Power in Sociolegal Studies*. Northwestern University Press.

Silverio, SA, S Bewley, E Montgomery, C Roberts, Y Richens, F Maxted, J Sandall, and J Montgomery. 2021. 'Disclosure of Non-Recent (Historic) Childhood Sexual Abuse: What Should Researchers Do?' *Journal of Medical Ethics* 47(12): 779–83.

Simmons, BA. 2009. *Mobilizing Human Rights: International Law in Domestic Politics*. Cambridge University Press.

Simonsen, E, and KS Pettersen. 2015. 'The Politics of Apology: The Norwegian Case'. In J Sköld and S Swain (eds). *Apologies and the Legacy of Abuse of Children in 'Care': International Perspectives.* Palgrave Macmillan UK.

Simpson, J. 1983. 'Economic Development: Cause or Effect in the Northern Ireland Conflict'. In J Darby (ed). *Northern Ireland: The Background to the Conflict.* Syracuse University Press.

Sköld, J. 2013. 'Historical Abuse—A Contemporary Issue: Compiling Inquiries into Abuse and Neglect of Children in Out-of-Home Care Worldwide'. *Journal of Scandinavian Studies in Criminology and Crime Prevention* 14(sup1): 5–23.

Sköld, J. 2016. 'The Truth About Abuse? A Comparative Approach to Inquiry Narratives on Historical Institutional Child Abuse'. *History of Education* 45(4): 492–509.

Sköld, J. 2023. 'On the Challenge of Historicizing Violence: Conflicts in State Redress for Historical Abuse of Children in Out-of-Home Care'. *Totalitarianism and Democracy* 20(1): 75–92.

Sköld, J, B Sandin, and J Schiratzki. 2023. 'Redressing or Excusing the Past? The Evaluation of Sexual Child Abuse in the Swedish Redress Scheme for Historical Abuse in Out-of-Home Care'. In J Annola, H Lindberg, and P Markkola (eds). *Lived Institutions as History of Experience.* Palgrave MacMillan.

Sköld, J, and S Swain. (eds). 2015. *Apologies and the Legacy of Abuse of Children in 'Care': International Perspectives.* Palgrave Macmillan.

Slocum, D, A Allan, and MM Allan. 2011. 'An Emerging Theory of Apology'. *Australian Journal of Psychology* 63(2): 83–92.

Smith, C, and A Duff. 2020. 'Access to Justice for Victims of Historic Institutional Abuse'. *Éire-Ireland* 55(1): 100–19.

Smith, CP, and JJ Freyd. 2014. 'Institutional Betrayal'. *American Psychologist* 69(6): 575–87.

Smith, JM. 2004. 'The Politics of Sexual Knowledge: The Origins of Ireland's Containment Culture and the Carrigan Report (1931)'. *Journal of the History of Sexuality* 13(2): 208–33.

Smith, JM. 2007. *Ireland's Magdalen Laundries and the Nation's Architecture of Containment.* University of Notre Dame Press.

Smith, JM. 2020. 'Knowing and Unknowing Tuam: State Practice, the Archive, and Transitional Justice'. *Éire-Ireland* 55(1): 142–80.

Smith, N. 2014. *Justice through Apologies: Remorse, Reform, and Punishment.* Cambridge University Press.

Smyth, A. 1995. 'States of Change: Reflections on Ireland in Several Uncertain Parts'. *Feminist Review* 50: 24–43.

Smyth, J. 1995. 'Manning the Ramparts: Ireland and the Agenda of the Roman Catholic Church'. *History of European Ideas* 20(4–6): 681–7.

South African Truth and Reconciliation Commission (TRC). 1998. *Truth and Reconciliation Commission of South Africa Report* Vol. 1. Available at: https://www.justice.gov.za/trc/report/finalreport/volume%201.pdf.

South Eastern Health Board. 1993. *Kilkenny Incest Investigation. Report presented to Mr Brendan Howlin T.D. Minister for Health by South Eastern Health Board*. The Stationery Office.

Spalek, B. 2005. *Crime Victims: Theory, Policy and Practice*. Palgrave Macmillan.

Spiritan Education Trust. 2022. *Group of Past Pupils of Blackrock College and Spiritan Congregation agree to establishment of Independent Restorative Justice Programme*. Available at: https://www.spiritaneducation.ie/wp-content/uploads/2022/11/Statement-Restorative-Justice-Programme-16Nov22.pdf.

Spröber, N, T Schneider, M Rassenhofer, A Seitz, H Liebhardt, L König, and JM Fegert. 2014. 'Child Sexual Abuse in Religiously Affiliated and Secular Institutions: A Retrospective Descriptive Analysis of Data Provided by Victims in a Government-sponsored Reappraisal Program in Germany'. *BMC Public Health* 14(1): 1–12.

Stanley, E. 2015. 'Responding to State Institutional Violence'. *British Journal of Criminology* 55(6): 1149–67.

Stanley, E, Z Gibson, and I Craddock. 2024. 'Performing Ignorance of State Violence in Aotearoa New Zealand'. *Journal of Criminology*. Available at: https://doi.org/10.1177/26338076241252184.

Stanton, K. 2022. *Reconciling Truths: Reimagining Public Inquiries in Canada*. University of British Columbia Press.

Staub, E. 2006. 'Reconciliation after Genocide, Mass Killing, or Intractable Conflict: Understanding the Roots of Violence, Psychological Recovery, and Steps toward a General Theory'. *Political Psychology* 27(6): 867–94.

Strang, H. 2001. 'Justice for Victims of Young Offenders: The Centrality of Emotional Harm and Restoration'. In A Morris and G Maxwell (eds). *Restorative Justice for Juveniles: Conferencing, Mediation and Circles*. Hart Publishing.

Strang, H. 2002. *Repair or Revenge: Victims and Restorative Justice*. Clarendon Press.

Strang, H, and L Sherman. 2003. 'Repairing the Harm: Victims and Restorative Justice'. *UTAH Law Review* 15(1): 15–42.

Strassmann, BI, and AL Clarke. 1998. 'Ecological Constraints on Marriage in Rural Ireland'. *Evolution and Human Behavior* 19(1): 33–55.

Stubbs, J. 2002. 'Domestic Violence and Women's Safety: Feminist Challenges to Restorative Justice'. In H Strang and J Braithwaite (eds). *Restorative Justice and Family Violence*. Cambridge University Press.

Stubbs, J. 2007. 'Beyond Apology? Domestic Violence and Critical Questions for Restorative Justice'. *Criminology & Criminal Justice* 7(2): 169–87.

Sunga, S. 2002. 'The Meaning of Compensation in Institutional Abuse Programs'. *Journal of Law and Social Policy* 17: 39–62.

Surenthiraraj, E. 2022. 'Intergenerational Justice'. In G Elcheroth and N de Mel (eds). *In the Shadow of Transitional Justice: Cross-National Perspectives on the Transformative Potential of Remembrance*. Routledge.

Suzuki, M, and T Jenkins. 2022. 'Apology–Forgiveness Cycle in Restorative Justice, But How?' *International Review of Victimology* 29(2): 259–76.

Swain, S. 2014. *History of Australian Inquiries Reviewing Institutions Providing Care for Children*. Available at: https://www.childabuseroyalcommission.gov.au/research.

Swain, S, and M Hillel. 2010. *Child, Nation, Race and Empire.* Manchester University Press.

Swaine, A. 2023. 'Resurfacing Gender: A Typology of Conflict-Related Violence Against Women for the Northern Ireland Troubles'. *Violence Against Women* 29(6–7): 1391–418.

Swart, M. 2008. 'Sorry Seems to be the Hardest Word: Apology as a Form of Symbolic Reparation'. *South African Journal on Human Rights* 24(1): 50–70.

Taft, L. 2000. 'Apology Subverted: The Commodification of Apology'. *The Yale Law Journal* 109(1999): 1135–60.

Tarusarira, J. 2019. 'The Anatomy of Apology and Forgiveness: Towards Transformative Apology and Forgiveness'. *International Journal of Transitional Justice* 13(2): 206–24.

Tavuchis, N. 1991. *Mea Culpa: A Sociology of Apology and Reconciliation.* Stanford University Press.

Taylor, D. 2014. 'Victim Participation in Transitional Justice Mechanisms: Real Power or Empty Ritual?' *Impunity Watch.*

Teitel, RG. 2000. *Transitional Justice.* Oxford University Press.

Teitel, RG. 2006. 'The Transitional Apology'. In E Barkan and A Karn (eds). *Taking Wrongs Seriously: Apologies and Reconciliation.* Stanford University Press.

Terry, KJ. 2015. 'Child Sexual Abuse within the Catholic Church: A Review of Global Perspectives'. *International Journal of Comparative and Applied Criminal Justice* 39(2): 139–54.

Thaler, M. 2012. 'Just Pretending: Political Apologies for Historical Injustice and Vice's Tribute to Virtue'. *Critical Review of International Social and Political Philosophy* 15(3): 259–78.

The General Secretariat of the Synod. 2022. *Synthesis of the Consultation in Ireland for the Diocesan Stage of the Universal Synod 2021–2023.* Available at: https://synod.ie/wp-content/uploads/2022/08/National-Synthesis-17-50-Fri-12th-August-.pdf.

The Irish Bishops' Conference. 2005. *The Conference of Religious Ireland, The Irish Missionary Union, Our Children, Our Church: Child Protection and Procedures for the Catholic Church in Ireland.* Veritas Publications.

The Magdalen Commission Report. 2013. *Report of Mr Justice John Quirke On the establishment of an ex gratia Scheme and related matters for the benefit of those women who were admitted to and worked in the Magdalen Laundries.* Government Publications.

The Victoria Climbié Inquiry. 1996. *Report of an Inquiry by Lord Laming.* Command Paper 5730. HMSO.

Thompson, J. 2002. *Taking Responsibility for the Past: Reparation and Historical Injustice.* Polity.

Thompson, J. 2008. 'Apology, Justice, and Respect: A Critical Defense of Political Apology'. In M Gibney, R Howard-Hassmann, JM Coicaud, and N Steiner (eds). *The Age of Apology: Facing up to the Past.* University of Pennsylvania Press.

Thompson, J. 2012. 'Is Political Apology a Sorry Affair?' *Social & Legal Studies* 21(2): 215–25.

Tonge, J. 2005. *Northern Ireland.* Polity Press.

Tonge, J, M Braniff, T Hennessey, JW McAuley, and S Whiting. 2014. *The Democratic Unionist Party: From Protest to Power.* Oxford University Press.

Torpey, J. 2003. 'Introduction: Politics and the Past'. In J Torpey (ed). *Politics and the Past.* Rowman & Littlefield.

Towards Peace. 2022. *Annual Report 2021.*

Tribunal of Inquiry into the Kerry Babies Case (Ireland). 1985. *Report of the Tribunal of Inquiry into 'The Kerry Babies Case'.* Department of Justice.

Trouillot, MR. 2000. 'Abortive Rituals: Historical Apologies in the Global Era'. *Interventions: International Journal of Postcolonial Studies* 2(2): 171–86.

Truth and Reconciliation Commission of Canada (TRCC). 2015. *Canada's Residential Schools: The Final Report of the Truth and Reconciliation Commission of Canada.* Available at: https://publications.gc.ca/site/eng/9.807830/publication.html.

Tyler, L. 1997. 'Liability Means Never Being Able to Say You're Sorry: Corporate Guilt, Legal Constraints, and Defensiveness in Corporate Communication'. *Management Communication Quarterly* 11(1): 51–73.

Tyler, TR. 1988. 'What is Procedural Justice?: Criteria Used by Citizens to Assess the Fairness of Legal Procedures'. *Law & Society Review* 22(1): 103–36.

Umbreit, M, B Vos, R Coates, and K Brown. 2003. *Facing Violence: The Path of Restorative Justice and Dialogue.* Criminal Justice Press.

United Nations. 1985. *Declaration of Basic Principles of Justice for Victims of Crime and Abuse of Power*, GA Res 40/34, UN GAOR, 40th sess, 96th plen mtg, UN Doc A/RES/40/34 (29 November) annex Art 6(b).

United Nations Committee against Torture (UNCAT). 2011. *Consideration of reports submitted by States parties under article 19 of the Convention* (17 June).

United Nations Committee against Torture (UNCAT). 2014. *Concluding observations on the initial report of the Holy See.* CAT/C/VAT/CO/1.

United Nations Committee against Torture (UNCAT). 2017. *Concluding observations on the second periodic reports of Ireland.* CAT/C/IRL/CO/2.

United Nations Committee against Torture (UNCAT). 2019. *Concluding observations on the 6th periodic report of the United Kingdom of Great Britain and Northern Ireland.* CAT/C/GBR/CO/6.

United Nations Committee against Torture (UNCAT). 2023. *Decision adopted by the Committee under article 22 of the Convention, concerning communication No. 879/2018.* CAT/C/73/D/879/2018.

United Nations Committee on the Elimination of Discrimination against Women (UN CEDAW). 2017. *Concluding observations on the combined sixth and seventh periodic reports of Ireland.* CAT/C/IRL/CO/2.

United Nations General Assembly. 2006. *Basic Principles and Guidelines on the Right to a Remedy and Reparation for Victims of Gross Violations of International Human Rights Law and Serious Violations of International Humanitarian Law.* A/RES/60/147.

United Nations Office of the High Commissioner for Human Rights (OHCHR). 2008. *Rule-of-law tools for post-conflict States: Reparations programmes.* HR/PUB/08/1.

United Nations Office on Drugs and Crime (UNODC). 2020. *Handbook on Restorative Justice Programmes* (2nd ed).

United Nations Security Council. 2004. *Report of the Secretary-General on the Rule of Law and Transitional Justice in Conflict and Post-Conflict Societies* (S/2004/616) (3 August).

Urquhart, D. 2012. 'Gender, Family and Sexuality, 1800–2000'. In L Kennedy and P Ollerenshaw (eds). *Ulster since, 1600*. Oxford University Press.

Valiulis, MG. 2011. 'The Politics of Gender in the Irish Free State, 1922–1937'. *Women's History Review* 20(4): 569–78.

van der Kolk, BA. 2015. *The Body Keeps the Score. Mind, Brain and Body in the Transformation of Trauma*. Penguin.

Van Zyl, P. 1999. 'Dilemmas of Transitional Justice: The Case of South Africa's Truth and Reconciliation Commission'. *Journal of International Affairs* 52(2): 647–67.

van Zyl, P, C Villa-Vicencio, and W Verwoerd. 2000. 'Justice without Punishment: Guaranteeing Human Rights in Transitional Societies'. In C Villa-Vicencio and W Verwoerd (eds). *Looking Back, Reaching Forward: Reflections on the Truth and Reconciliation Commission of South Africa*. University of Cape Town Press.

Vaughan, D. 1999. 'The Dark Side of Organizations: Mistake, Misconduct, and Disaster'. *Annual Review of Sociology* 25(1): 271–305.

Vegh Weis, V, and C Cunneen. 2024. "Can Indigenous Truth Commissions Overcome the Legacies and Contemporary Effects of Colonialism? *International Journal of Restorative Justice* 7(1): 43–64.

Vernon, A. 2017. 'The Ethics of Appropriate Justice Approaches: Lessons from a Restorative Response to Institutional Abuse'. *Law in Context: A Socio-Legal Journal* 35(1): 139–59.

Viejo-Rose, D. 2011. 'Memorial Functions: Intent, Impact and the Right to Remember'. *Memory Studies* 4(4): 465–80.

Vines, P. 2007. 'The Power of Apology: Mercy, Forgiveness or Corrective Justice in the Civil Liability Arena'. *Public Space: The Journal of Law & Social Justice* 1(1): 1–51.

Voss, T. 2015. 'Institutions'. In J Wright (ed). *International Encyclopaedia of the Social & Behavioral Sciences* (2nd ed). Elsevier.

Wade, A. 1997. 'Small Acts of Living: Everyday Resistance to Violence and Other Forms of Oppression'. *Journal of Contemporary Family Therapy* 19(1): 23–39.

Wade, W, C Forsyth, and J Ghosh. 2022. *Administrative Law*. 12th ed. Oxford University Press.

Wailling, J, CD Marshall, and J Wilkinson. 2019. *Hearing and Responding to the Stories of Survivors of Surgical Mesh in New Zealand*. University of Wellington.

Waldorf, L. 2021. *Local Transitional Justice* (2nd ed). Routledge.

Waldron, J. 1992. 'Superseding Historical Injustice'. *Ethics* 103(1): 4–28.

Walgrave, L. 2000. 'How Pure Can a Maximalist Approach to Restorative Justice Remain? Or Can A Purist Model of Restorative Justice Become Maximalist?' *Contemporary Justice* Review 1(3): 415–32.

Walgrave, L. 2021. *Being Consequential about Restorative Justice*. Eleven.

Walgrave, L. 2023. Concerns about the Meaning of Restorative Justice. Reflections of a Veteran. *The International Journal of Restorative Justice* 6(3): 353–69.

Walgrave, L, T Ward, and E Zinsstag. 2021. 'When Restorative Justice Meets the Good Lives Model: Contributing to a Criminology of Trust'. *European Journal of Criminology* 18(3): 444–60.

Walker, MU. 2006. *Moral Repair: Reconstructing Moral Relations After Wrongdoing*. Cambridge University Press.

Walker, MU. 2010. 'Truth Telling as Reparations'. *Metaphilosophy* 41(4): 525–45.

Walker, MU. 2013. 'The Expressive Burden of Reparations: Putting Meaning in Money, Words and Things'. In A Maclachan and A Speight (eds). *Justice, Responsibility and Reconciliation in the Wake of Conflict*. Springer.

Walklate, S. 2011. 'Reframing Criminal Victimization: Finding a Place for Vulnerability and Resilience'. *Theoretical Criminology* 15(2): 179–94.

Walsh, J. 2012. 'Ministers, Bishops and the Changing Balance of Power in Irish Education 1950–70'. *Irish Historical Studies* 38(149): 108–27.

Walsh, O. 2022. 'Gender and Insanity in Ireland, 1800–1923'. In J Alwail, C Breathnach, and SA Buckley (eds). *Gender and History*. Routledge.

Walsh, T. 2016. 'The National System of Education, 1831–2000'. In B Walsh (ed). *Essays in the History of Irish Education*. Palgrave Macmillan.

Walshe, B, and C O'Connell. 2019. *Consultations with Survivors of Institutional Abuse on Themes and Issues to Be Addressed by a Survivor Led Consultation Group*. Department of Education.

Wang, Y. 2020. 'Lingering Guilt and Shame: Emotional Burdens Upon Those Who Intended but Failed to Apologize'. *The Journal of Social Psychology* 160(5): 675–87.

Ward, T, K Fox, and M Garber. 2014. 'Restorative Justice, Offender Rehabilitation and Desistance'. *Restorative Justice: An International Journal* 2(1): 24–42.

Watts, K. 2020. 'Managing Mass Damages Liability via Law and Tort Alternatives'. *Journal of European Tort Law* 11(1): 57–85.

Weiner, B. 1995. *Judgments of Responsibility: A Foundation for a Theory of Social Conduct*. Guildford Press.

Wemmers, JA, and AM de Brouwer. 2011. 'Globalization and Victims' Rights at the International Criminal Court'. In R Letschert and J Van Dijk (eds). *The New Faces of Victimhood: Studies in Global Justice*. Springer.

Wenger, KD. 2009. 'Apology Lite: Truths, Doubts, and Reconciliations in the Senate's Guarded Apology for Slavery'. *Connecticut Law Review CONNtemplations* 42(1): 1–11.

Werle, G, and M Vormbaum. 2022. *Transitional Justice: The Legal Framework*. Springer Nature.

Weyeneth, R. 2001. 'The Power of Apology and the Process of Historical Reconciliation'. *The Public Historian* 23(3): 9–38.

Whitaker, TK. 1983. *Interests*. Institute of Public Administration.

White, M. 2004. 'Working With People Who Are Suffering the Consequences of Multiple Trauma: A Narrative Perspective'. *International Journal of Narrative Therapy and Community Work* 1: 45–76.

Whyte, JH. 1974. 'Ireland: Politics Without Social Bases'. In R Rose (ed). *Electoral Behaviour: A Comparative Handbook*. The Free Press.

Willems, W. 2013. 'From Apology to Excuse: Abuse Cases Within the Catholic Church as Public and Scientific Objects of Research'. In D Cuypers, D Jansenn, J Haers, and B Segaert (eds). *Public Apology Between Ritual and Regret*. Brill.

Wills, C. 2024. *Missing Persons, Or My Grandmother's Secrets*. Allen Lane.

Wilson, EK, and R Bleiker. 2013. 'Performing Political Apologies'. In E Resende and D Budryte (eds). *Memory and Trauma in International Relations*. Routledge.

Winter, S. 2009. 'Australia's Ex Gratia Redress'. *Australian Indigenous Law Review* 13(1): 49–61.

Winter, S. 2011. 'Legitimacy, Citizenship and State Redress'. *Citizenship Studies* 15(6–7): 799–814.

Winter, S. 2013. 'Towards a Unified Theory of Transitional Justice'. *International Journal of Transitional Justice* 7(2): 224–44.

Winter, S. 2018. 'Two Models of Monetary Redress: A Structural Analysis'. *Victims and Offenders* 13(3): 293–311.

Winter, S. 2022. *Monetary Redress for Abuse in State Care*. Cambridge University Press.

Wise, S. 2024. *The Undesirables: The Law that Locked Away a Generation*. Oneworld Publications.

Wohl MJ, MJ Hornsey, and SH Bennett. 2012. 'Why Group Apologies Succeed and Fail: Intergroup Forgiveness and the Role of Primary and Secondary Emotions'. *Journal of Personality and Social Psychology* 102(2): 306–22.

Wolfe S. 2014. *The Politics of Reparations and Apologies*. Springer.

Wood, W. 2016 'Editor's Introduction: The Future of Restorative Justice?' *Victims & Offenders* 11(1): 1–8.

Wraith, RE, and GB Lamb. 1971. *Public Inquiries as an Instrument of Government*. Allen and Unwin.

Wright, K. 2017. 'Remaking Collective Knowledge: An Analysis of the Complex and Multiple Effects of Inquiries into Historical Institutional Child Abuse'. *Child Abuse & Neglect* 74 (Dec): 10–22.

Wright, K, S Swain, and J Sköld. 2020. *The Age of Inquiry: A Global Mapping of Institutional Abuse Inquiries* (2nd ed). La Trobe University.

Wright, M. 2002. 'The Court as Last Resort'. *British Journal of Criminology* 42(3): 654–67.

Yeates, N. 2011. 'The Irish Catholic Female Religious and the Transnationalisation of Care: An Historical Perspective'. *Irish Journal of Sociology* 19(2): 77–93.

Zappone K. 2020. 'Love's Pursuit: An Approach to Transitional Justice in Ireland'. *Éire-Ireland* 55(1): 315–32.

Zehr, H. 1990. *Changing Lenses: A New Focus for Crime and Justice*. Herald Press.

Zehr, H. 2002. *The Little Book of Restorative Justice*. Good Books.

Zehr, H. 2023 *Restorative Justice—Insights and Stories from My Journey*. Walnut Street Books

Zernova, M, and M Wright. 2007. 'Alternative Visions of Restorative Justice'. In G Johnstone and D Van Ness (eds). *Handbook of Restorative Justice*. Willan Publishing.

Zinsstag, E, and M Keenan (eds). 2017. *Restorative Responses to Sexual Violence: Legal, Social and Therapeutic Dimensions*. Routledge.

Zolkos, M. 2016. '"The Return of Things as They Were": New Humanitarianism, Restitutive Desire and the Politics of Unrectifiable Loss'. *Contemporary Political Theory* 16(3): 321–41.

Zollner, H, V Lecaros, and AL Suárez. 2024. 'Addressing the Catholic Church Abuse Crisis: Responses, Reforms, and Challenges'. In V Lecaros and AL Suárez (eds). *Abuse in the Latin American Church*. Routledge.

Zutlevics, TL. 2002. 'Reconciliation, Responsibility, and Apology'. *Public Affairs Quarterly* 16(1): 63–75.

Index

For the benefit of digital users, indexed terms that span two pages (e.g., 52–53) may, on occasion, appear on only one of those pages.